Babs Kirby is an astrologer and psychotherapist. A Vice President of the Faculty of Astrological Studies and director of its two year course, *Counselling within Astrology*, Babs taught for the Faculty for many years. She has lectured extensively both nationally and internationally.

Babs is a founder member and fellow of the Association of Professional Astrologers International and, in 2001, was appointed to the Advisory Board of the National Council for Geocosmic Research, one of the main astrological organisations within the United States. She is currently a trustee of The Urania Trust, an astrological educational charity in the UK, which provides funding for a variety of astrological endeavours. She is also a member of the Sophia Committee, whose remit is to establish astrology on the curriculum in universities.

Babs writes a regular astrology column for the weekly magazine *TV Choice*.

She lives and practises in London.

For further information visit www.babskirby.com

Also by Babs Kirby

Experiential Astrology - Symbolic Journeys using Guided Imagery, The Crossing Press, California, 1997.

Love and Sexuality, An Exploration of Venus and Mars, with Janey Stubbs, Element Books, 1992.

Interpreting Solar and Lunar Returns, a Psychological Approach, with Janey Stubbs, Capall Bann, Chieveley, 2001.

'Symbols, Guided Imagery and Client-Centered Astrology' in the anthology *Creative Astrology - Experiential Understanding of the Horoscope*, ed. Prudence Jones, Capall Bann, Chieveley, 2002.

21st Century Star Signs

BABS KIRBY

arrow books

Published by Arrow Books in 2006

1 3 5 7 9 10 8 6 4 2

First published in the United Kingdom in 2006 by Arrow

Arrow Books Limited
The Random House Group Limited
20 Vauxhall Bridge Road, London, SW1V 2SA

Random House Australia (Pty) Limited
20 Alfred Street, Milsons Point, Sydney
New South Wales 2061, Australia

Random House New Zealand Limited
18 Poland Road, Glenfield
Auckland 10, New Zealand

Random House South Africa (Pty) Limited
Isle of Houghton, Corner of Boundary Road & Carse O'Gowrie,
Houghton 2198, South Africa

The Random House Group Limited Reg. No. 954009

www.randomhouse.co.uk

A CIP catalogue record for this book
is available from the British Library

Papers used by Random House UK are
natural, recyclable products made from wood grown in
sustainable forests. The manufacturing processes conform to
the environmental regulations of the country of origin

ISBN 9780099456995 (from Jan 2007)
ISBN 0 09 9456990

Typeset by Palimpsest Book Production Limited,
Polmont, Stirlingshire
Printed and bound in Great Britain by
Cox & Wyman Limited, Reading, Berks

With love to Reuben

Acknowledgements

I'd like to thank Hannah Black my editor at Century for making this book possible, Doreen Montgomery at Rupert Crew Ltd who has helped enormously with the whole project and Sandra Levy whose involvement, input and support has been invaluable.

Contents

Introduction   1

Chapter 1
Aries: March 21st to April 19th   9
Introducing Aries   9
Negative Aries   19
The Aries Man   28
The Aries Woman   35
The Aries Child   43

Chapter 2
Taurus: April 20th to May 20th   49
Introducing Taurus   49
Negative Taurus   59
The Taurus Man   66
The Taurus Woman   72
The Taurus Child   79

Chapter 3
Gemini: May 21st to June 20th   87
Introducing Gemini   87
Negative Gemini   96
The Gemini Man   104
The Gemini Woman   112
The Gemini Child   119

Chapter 4
Cancer: June 21st to July 22nd   127
Introducing Cancer   127
Negative Cancer   137
The Cancer Man   145
The Cancer Woman   151
The Cancer Child   158

Chapter 5
Leo: July 23rd to August 22nd   165
Introducing Leo   165
Negative Leo   173
The Leo Man   180
The Leo Woman   187
The Leo Child   193

Chapter 6
Virgo: August 23rd to September 22nd   200
Introducing Virgo   200
Negative Virgo   209
The Virgo Man   217
The Virgo Woman   224
The Virgo Child   230

Chapter 7
Libra: September 23rd to October 22nd   238
Introducing Libra   238
Negative Libra   247
The Libra Man   256
The Libra Woman   262
The Libra Child   270

Chapter 8
Scorpio: October 23rd to November 21st   278
Introducing Scorpio   278
Negative Scorpio   288
The Scorpio Man   296
The Scorpio Woman   303
The Scorpio Child   311

Chapter 9
Sagittarius: November 22nd to December 20th 320
Introducing Sagittarius   320
Negative Sagittarius   329
The Sagittarius Man   337
The Sagittarius Woman   345
The Sagittarius Child   352

Chapter 10
Capricorn: December 21st to January 19th   359
Introducing Capricorn   359
Negative Capricorn   369
The Capricorn Man   377
The Capricorn Woman   386
The Capricorn Child   393

Chapter 11
Aquarius: January 20th to February 18th   400
Introducing Aquarius   400
Negative Aquarius   412
The Aquarius Man   418
The Aquarius Woman   424
The Aquarius Child   434

Chapter 12
Pisces: February 19th to March 20th   442
Introducing Pisces   442
Negative Pisces   454
The Pisces Man   463
The Pisces Woman   471
The Pisces Child   478

Appendix/Astrological Organisations   485

Introduction

21st Century Star Signs offers a new look at the twelve signs of the zodiac. These signs have ancient origins and in this book they are brought bang up-to-date and made relevant to life today. More than any other system of divination, astrology has stood the test of time and still provides a most convincing method by which we can gain a deeper understanding of our loved ones and ourselves.

The star in the title is, of course, the sun, the most important astrological influence on our lives. Since the popularisation of sun sign columns by newspapers and magazines, most people know that their sign is determined by their date of birth. Each sign of the zodiac is actually defined by the sun's presence in a thirty-degree sector of the sky and so, because of leap years, the exact date on which a sign begins and ends can vary each year.

At the start of each chapter, an approximate date is given for the sun entering and leaving the sign. For those who are born close to the day in which the sun enters a sign, please do read both signs to decide which one relates to you or consult an astrologer who can tell you exactly when the sun moved from one sign to the next in the year you were born.

Of course, since Copernicus, we all know that the sun doesn't actually move, the earth does, nevertheless that's how we experience it here on earth and it doesn't affect how we interpret the signs. In fact, in the West, astrologers no longer use the actual constellations – the backdrop of stars that the zodiacal signs are named after. The sidereal zodiac is based on the starry filament in the sky and is used by astrologers in India and the East.

The tropical zodiac is used by astrologers in the West and takes the spring equinox as its starting point, which occurs around March 21st when the sun crosses the equator and there is equal day and night. Both tropical and sidereal zodiacs contain the same signs but they start and finish on different dates and are measured using different criteria.

There are effectively two zodiacs and two thousand years ago they coincided but gradually they have separated; this is known as the precession of the equinoxes. Confusing though this is, it's one of the reasons Eastern and Western astrology is so different. Critics of astrology often assume that astrologers are not cognisant of this and use it in an attempt to discredit astrologers. On the contrary, astrologers are fully conversant with this fact.

The sun spends about thirty days in each sign and imparts a specific influence over those who are born in these periods, colouring their attitude and approach to life. The jury is still out on how exactly this occurs, with differing theories that are not going to be addressed here.

My particular orientation, like many Western astrologers, is to see the zodiacal signs as archetypal images. I prefer a symbolic attitude to astrology, rather than a deterministic or fatalistic one, and am satisfied that astrology shows our innate potential and can help us find direction and meaning in our lives. As well as being an astrologer, with over twenty years' experience, I also practice as an integrative psychotherapist and so my focus is as much on the inner landscape of the twelve signs as their outer characteristics.

Introduction

Our biggest difficulties in life come from aspects of ourselves that we deny or reject – traits that we can't accept about ourselves. Whatever is buried and unconscious has the power to create havoc in our lives. We all have our blind spots and these are discussed with compassion in the following chapters in the hope that we can become more self-accepting and self-aware and, as a result, contented.

Astrology offers a powerful tool with which to understand others, too. It's relatively easy to find out other people's sun signs – all you need is their birthday. Reading about them in the pages that follow will give valuable insights into what makes them behave as they do – where they are coming from. The realisation that what seems to you to be an impossible attitude is actually perfectly valid for that sign, highlights the fact that there is never only one way of being, there are many. Knowledge of the different signs can help to create more understanding and tolerance between people.

There are numerous self-help books offering spiritual and psychological guidance these days, but a perceptive delineation of a sun sign cannot be underestimated, as it gives an instant sense of being recognised and understood.

Now for a brief explanation of some basic tenets in astrology. The signs are categorised by three qualities and four elements. Each sign has a unique combination. The qualities are cardinal, fixed and mutable and describe different modes of operation. The elements are fire, earth, air and water and these describe different ways of being.

The **cardinal signs** are Aries, Cancer, Libra and Capricorn and what they have in common is that, in their different ways, they all like to initiate. Those born under a cardinal sign are trail-blazers, good at starting projects and getting things off the ground. They like to shake things up, believing innovation is always a good thing. These are strongly-motivated, dynamic and enthusiastic individuals who excel at instigating changes.

Taurus, Leo, Scorpio and Aquarius make up the **fixed signs** and, as the name implies, they resist change. Those born under the fixed signs excel where dogged persistence is required, such as seeing projects and tasks through to the end, and bring stability and consolidation. These are reliable, steadfast, loyal and persistent individuals, who are good at maintaining the status quo. Never ones to give up or let go easily, they conserve and preserve whatever they have.

Those born under the **mutable signs**, Gemini, Virgo, Sagittarius and Pisces are adaptable and flexible individuals. With mental agility and physical dexterity, they can adjust easily to changes in circumstances. They have a knack of fitting in to whatever environment they find themselves in and can, metaphorically at least, bend in the wind.

One of my teachers used the following story to illustrate these qualities. Imagine arriving at a crossroads in the middle of nowhere with no signposts. The cardinal individual will charge off down one of the roads, in the belief that all roads lead to the final destination, no matter what. The fixed individual will stay put until someone comes along who can give directions. The mutable individual will go a short way down one road, then come back and try the next and so on, exploring what is down each road.

Besides the three qualities, the signs are made up of the four elements, fire, earth, air and water. The qualities contain one sign from each of the elements, so, for example, there is one cardinal fire sign, Aries, one fixed fire sign, Leo and one mutable fire sign, Sagittarius. When an understanding of a quality and an element are brought together, this immediately gives a lot of information about a particular sign. So let's look at the elements.

The **fire signs** consist of Aries, Leo and Sagittarius and those born under the fire signs radiate warmth and are spontaneous, lively and spirited. Cheerful, optimistic, wholehearted and generous, they rely on their intuition and are visionary, future-orientated individuals.

Taurus, Virgo and Capricorn make up the **earth signs** and produce practical, sensual, grounded and realistic people who trust what's tangible and factual. Those born under an earth sign rely on their five senses, touch, taste, smell, sight and hearing. Typically down-to-earth and matter-of-fact, these are no-nonsense individuals.

Those born under the **air signs**, Gemini, Libra and Aquarius, are sociable, gregarious individuals, who like to talk, exchange ideas and connect with others. With a detached, objective and logical approach, they are idealistic and interested in abstract thought. Their orientation brings perspective and tolerance to bear on all matters.

Cancer, Scorpio and Pisces make up the **water signs** and those born under these signs are soulful individuals, in touch with their feelings and inner world. Empathic, compassionate, imaginative, impressionable and sensitive, they pick up on the subtle undercurrents in situations.

When interpreting a birth chart, the sun's sign is just one factor among many that an astrologer considers. There is also the moon's sign and the signs of the planets, Mercury, Venus, Mars, Jupiter, Saturn, Uranus, Neptune and Pluto. Besides this, there is the rising sign (the sign on the horizon at the moment of birth) and the midheaven (the sign culminating directly overhead at birth) both of which are important in a full consideration of a horoscope. All twelve signs rise and culminate in any given twenty-four-hour period so in order to ascertain this, a time of birth is needed. This sets the orientation of the whole chart, giving an astrologer much more information than the sun's sign alone.

For those who recognise a description of themselves in signs other than their sun's this may well be because this is their rising sign or moon sign or is a sign emphasised by being occupied by several planets. None of us is just one sign; we are each a mixture of several, so having a birth chart, with all its unique complexities, read by an astrologer is a profound and revealing experience.

Despite these other astrological influences the sun is at the centre of our solar system – everything revolves around it and is dependent upon it, and likewise it is of central and unique significance to us all. The importance of the sun's sign can not be over-emphasised and the astrological portraits that follow will be instantly recognisable as well as illuminating.

Each chapter contains five sections. The first provides a description of the main characteristics of those born under the sign, their behaviour, attitudes and what makes them tick. This general introduction discusses the sign's approach to work, money, leisure, and employer/employee dynamics, looking at the sign's strengths and weaknesses.

The second section looks specifically at the negative attributes of the sign, explaining their underlying psychological causes and offering constructive advice to those who struggle with these difficult traits. Those who are involved with someone born under the sign will find this section invaluable, as it reveals just what the problems are and offers suggestions on how to deal with them.

The following two sections deal respectively with men and women, discussing how the sign is expressed more specifically depending on the sex of the individual and how each behaves as a friend, lover and partner. Relationship dynamics are described in a non-gender specific way, to include those in heterosexual and homosexual relationships. Commitment and commitment phobia, responsibility and freedom, loyalty and infidelity, independence and dependency issues, security and autonomy, cooperation, closeness and abandonment issues are all evaluated. The different needs and relationship patterns of the signs are outlined, along with some typical scenarios.

The final section, on the child, is aimed at helping parents to better understand their child. Some may also want to dip into this section to see what they were like and needed as a child. The various stages of child development are mentioned, with reference to how each sun sign negotiates these transitions.

For those who would like to go on to have their birth chart set up or to study astrology, relevant organisations are listed in the appendix.

1

Aries

The Ram

March 21st to April 19th

A cardinal fire sign, ruled by Mars

Introducing Aries

It is easy to recognise an Aries by their warmth and sincerity.
These are individuals who make steady eye contact and
come across as genuine, unpretentious and forthright. Along
with this is a certain innocence and naivety that allows them
to get away with casual, throwaway and, at times, insensitive comments that others would not dare utter.

The ram represents Aries and those born under this sign
have many ram-like traits, not least the tendency to use their
horns – in a metaphorical way. They respond well to those
who stand up to them and meet them head-on if necessary
and can't abide shilly-shallying. They have no time for game
playing; this is a no-nonsense type, who is frank and honest
but may be a bit too outspoken for those who expect more
diplomacy. It's not that they are deliberately rude; in fact
they are refreshing, spontaneous and disarming.

As one of the fire signs (the others are Leo and Sagittarius)
Aries are intuitive and future-orientated, with an abundance
of optimism and faith in what lies around the corner. Others
may see them as lucky, whereas it is their ability to see the

opportunity inherent in any given situation that creates their good fortune. They trust and rely on their hunches, which may seem a dangerous and frightening way to live to those who don't or can't, but is an infallible resource to the fire signs. And if they do come a cropper, they have the capacity to pick themselves up, dust themselves down and start all over again, much to the consternation of those who would be destroyed by far less.

Aries is the first sign in the zodiac, beginning at the spring equinox in the western hemisphere, around March 21st, and their character reflects this. They like to be first and have a fiercely competitive nature that may or may not be obvious, but should never be underestimated. The desire to win runs through everything they do, as every victory, however small and insignificant, is for them a confirmation of their power to succeed. While winning is important to them, so is the way their victory is obtained and they are at all times scrupulously honest and fair. Any other kind of triumph would be hollow and meaningless to them. Besides, they are truthful because it's more effort not to be – lies and deceit make life far too complicated for an Aries.

Brave, courageous and gallant, Aries is ruled by the planet Mars, the god of war in the early Greek pantheon, and there is something warrior-like about these individuals. They have fighting spirit and there's nothing they like better than a cause; they are especially good at championing the underdog. They rally to defend those whom they deem overlooked or neglected by the rest of society. These are individuals who can mount a convincing campaign and inspire others to support it. It suits them temperamentally – they can exercise their leadership qualities and fight the good fight. This they do on behalf of others far more effectively than for themselves and there's no doubt that when they jump on a bandwagon it can become a channel for their own unresolved issues. This is not necessarily a sign with a strong political conscience, although there are plenty of successful politicians born under Aries; it is more that human injustice galvanises them into action.

There has been an impressive line-up of successful Aries politicians in Britain in recent times. These include John Major and Neil Kinnock, who were in office at the same time, as leader of the government and opposition respectively, and William Hague and Iain Duncan Smith, the next two leaders of the Conservative Party. There is nothing about Aries to suggest they'll have conservative views as such but they are pioneers and natural leaders.

Proving their bravery is an occupational pastime for an Aries and consists of tackling all the things in life that scare and daunt them. As they go through life they overcome their fears by becoming proficient at all sorts of odd things. Some of the tasks they set themselves may have no obvious merit – they may not be career moves, for instance – but, to them, they are significant. Others may not realise how important their achievements are to them, as they don't necessarily make a fuss about their accomplishments; they simply pitch themselves in headfirst. This may be quite literal, as one Aries, who was petrified of diving, mastered it over the course of one summer.

Typically, Aries bang their heads on the glass ceiling above them and take on a particular job, role, responsibility or activity that stretches them. It is how they grow and flourish, as they need to continually test their mettle. They instinctively rise to a challenge; it brings out the best in them and they perform well in a crisis and when under pressure.

This does not mean that an Aries individual is fearless; they deal with their fears, whether these are conscious or not, by conquering them. It may be these fears lie dormant in the unconscious, which has the effect of driving them to prove themselves through acts of daring. This can become a compulsive activity; in which case, if they want to stop, they must become conscious of these inner fears. With awareness and maturity, they become more selective about the risks they are prepared to take and can choose what activities and ventures are worth going out on a limb for.

The young and less discriminating Aries tend to rush headlong into activities with no consideration for the consequences. The saying 'Fools rush in where angels fear to tread' must have been written about an immature Arien. This foolhardiness can lead them to overextend themselves. Knowing their own limits is an alien concept to them; what they want is to surpass their previous achievements, in all areas of life. They are ambitious simply because they are driven by their conquering spirit.

The Aries writer, Erica Jong, was catapulted to fame by her book, *Fear of Flying*, which became cult reading in the Sixties. Although the book is not about flying the title implies a challenge, which is classic Aries. Maya Angelou, author of a series of autobiographical books, is another writer who has demonstrated her pioneering Aries characteristics through the life she has lead, breaking ground in all kinds of ways for a black woman from America's deep south. She typifies this sign's ability to overcome tremendous odds and become a role model and inspiration for others.

The impetuous Aries nature can be a bonus for others, as they don't hesitate to offer help when it's needed and won't weigh up the personal costs. This is a generous individual, mainly because he or she acts first and thinks later and responds in an impulsive and wholehearted way. Yet this is a sign that has a reputation for selfishness. This has come about because they know what they want and communicate it clearly and forcibly.

So, for instance, when an Aries rings for a favour, they are more than likely to skip the usual polite introductions and courtesies and launch straight in with their request. They are no good at clever manoeuvres or manipulation. Other, more indirect individuals may be affronted by their lack of guile. Not only that, but their brisk manner cuts to the truth, so that those who are less candid can feel exposed. Perhaps the label of selfishness has emerged as an insult from those who cannot cope with their transparency. Self-centred is a more accurate description, with both its negative and positive connotations.

On the positive side, by placing themselves at the centre the Aries individual emanates integrity and certainty. This is one of the few signs that does not necessarily need others to like them – an Aries does not seek others' approval. This independence of action inspires the confidence of others. Aries appear sure of themselves, which doesn't mean that they actually are, deep inside, but it's more than convincing from the outside. In fact they are as likely as anyone to have a fragile ego or low self-esteem and those who are impressed often fail to see this vulnerability.

Aries are in essence simple souls, with their raw and primitive drives only too apparent to others. What they lack in sophistication, they make up for in sheer energy; this is the human dynamo of the zodiac. Their problem can be in knowing when to stop; they thrive on activity and don't listen to the messages of their body. Some might argue this is displacement activity, that they are running from more complicated feelings.

In fact, as an intuitive type, the world of sensation is fraught with difficulty for Ariens and their relationship to their body exemplifies this. The need to feed it, rest it, take it to the gym or partake in some kind of exercise does not impress them. It's not that they are slothful. For them, the gym is boring, and the 'high' afterwards is soon forgotten, so there is no motivation for going again. The best way to keep them interested in working out is if there's some kind of competition involved; competing with a friend, or even with goals they have set for themselves. Unlike the earth signs, they don't find pleasure in physical activity for its own sake.

Neither do Ariens pay much attention to food and are one of the worst signs for eating on the hoof, in snatched and hurried ways. Gourmet food is wasted on them; food is a necessity and a requirement, not a pleasure. They eventually do learn to respect the needs of their body, but this comes after much abuse and self-neglect. Fortunately, they have a strong constitution and their body puts up with a lot. One young client, who I counselled on this very problem, assured me he had no interest in taking care of his physical needs – his interest was to astral travel, to leave his body behind entirely. He was extreme, but this desire to be rid of the body and its needs lies just below the surface for many an Arien.

Aries generally have a strong vitality that affords them good health; this is just as well considering how impossible they are when ill. When under the weather their first impulse is to ignore their symptoms and soldier on regardless. This may not be as heroic as it first seems. It's because they can't bear to surrender to their physical needs and prefer to deny them. If their illness does reach a point where they become incapacitated they make the world's worst patients. Melodramatic and convinced they are at death's door; they can be demanding and ungrateful. Keep in mind that this is because they are terrified by the feelings of helplessness that go with being laid up. The mental difficulties associated with their loss of autonomy and independence tip them over the edge.

Part of Aries' problem when ill is that they stop functioning rationally. They are so full of fear that the state they are in will last forever, that they lose all perspective. They are desperate to get better immediately. An Aries with a serious condition is suffering doubly; first from the illness itself and secondly from their reaction to being confined.

Much of this can be attributed to the highly developed 'flight or fight' mechanism found in Aries. They are strongly attuned to primitive survival instincts, upon which human life depended in ancient times. Even though this is usually no longer the case it doesn't stop it kicking in forcibly for

14

Aries when they feel in danger. It remains a powerful unconscious drive. When psychologically under threat they can behave in a primitive way, and be overly aggressive and ruthless. Their desire to win at all costs is also linked to this basic survival strategy.

The problems Aries have with the physical realm also intrude on their capacity to handle practical matters. They are notoriously bad at managing their personal paperwork. Filling in forms can be something that fills them with fear and loathing, which they deal with by ignoring. Paying bills (apart from the direct debit facility, which must have been invented for the fire signs) is a haphazard affair. They either pay them immediately, or forget them entirely. Chores such as getting the car serviced and putting air in the tyres are all met with huge resistance.

One Arien has had two car engines seize up because she failed to put oil in the engine. Another who 'forgot' to put in the antifreeze found the radiator frozen and his car a write-off. They often rely on others to help them in these areas and are vulnerable and surprisingly helpless when it comes to most practicalities. Those who do manage the pragmatic and mundane aspects of life have either learned how to do this from experience and do so in a rather mechanical way or they have other features in their horoscope, like planets in earth signs, that give them this facility.

Ariens are notoriously impatient, frequently in a hurry and consequently irritable. They lack patience with themselves as well as with others and because of their high expectations, experience a fair degree of frustration. This, too, is a characteristic that improves with maturity. Until then, they are not likely to keep quiet about their discontent and will voice their annoyance, much to the consternation of more sensitive signs. Fortunately, outbursts of anger pass quickly and are soon forgotten. Temperamentally they resemble blustery weather, when the climate changes are rapid and showers – even hailstones – pass quickly and give way to bright sunshine. They never nurse grievances or hold grudges; if they've been displeased others know about it immediately. They are open and explicit and expect that others can cope with what they have to say and may underestimate the upset and offence they unwittingly cause.

What Aries have in abundance is energy and they enjoy most competitive sports provided they are reasonably good at them (there has to be the possibility of winning). They can be team players too, although in football, for instance, they do better playing forward rather than in defence. They like to have a proactive role. They may participate in some of the more dangerous sports, like car racing, parachuting, skydiving and bungee jumping. The sense of freedom and the adrenaline rush is the motivation. Remember that they feel compelled to conquer their fears and prove that they are courageous.

Aries drive at breakneck speed, with little consideration for their passengers, let alone other road users. They are always in a hurry and bring all their competitive thrust to being behind the wheel. Circumstances permitting, they'll choose a sports car every time and those with small children may even have them cramped up in the small seats in the back. Giving up their two-seater for family life is a major milestone in the life of an Aries and some manage to maintain two vehicles rather than make the sacrifice.

When it comes to domestic chores, Aries individuals fall into two distinct categories: either they are super-quick and efficient or they are totally oblivious to what needs doing. Some may alternate between both. Whichever mode they operate in it is likely to be uncomfortable for those they share domestic space with. Typically, when cooking, they want others to stay out of the kitchen, so that they can get on unimpeded with the job in hand. They don't want anyone under their feet or blocking the route from the cooker to the work surface, which they zip between in their inimitable speedy fashion. If help is offered, they sit their assistant down, somewhere out of their way, and expect them to get on with the job allocated to them. Aries is in charge; their helper is the skivvy. Cooperation and equality are not their strong points.

The other mode, of being unaware of what needs to be done, comes out of Aries' difficulty with practical matters. Because it's an arena they are less than proficient in, they can kid themselves that it's unimportant and beneath them: not a good attitude to have if they want to experience domestic harmony. Check them out before moving in.

The Arien desire to be in control applies in the home and at work. As an employee, they need to be given a fair amount of autonomy and responsibility to carry out their job. They do not do well with someone constantly looking over their shoulder and scrutinising what they are up to. A flexitime working arrangement suits them best. They can't abide being unduly restrained by externally imposed time constraints or petty rules; they have to see the sense of work regulations or their hackles rise and they become uncooperative at best and out and out defiant at worst. Neither do they accept fools gladly – that would be hypocritical – so it's essential that they have genuine respect for those above them and vice versa.

If given enough of a free rein, Aries is a diligent and enthusiastic employee. When working in a team, it's important that the areas of responsibility are clearly defined and that credit can be given where due. They are generous but object to doing more than their fair share if their efforts are not properly acknowledged. They gravitate toward positions of leadership and, because of their own enthusiasm, are good at motivating others.

As the boss, Aries comes into his or her own; they are good at initiating and are dynamic and inspirational. These are naturally bossy individuals and when given the authority to call the shots they rise to the occasion. They make hard taskmasters, not least because this is the standard they set for themselves and they don't see why others should be exempt. Provided employees give one hundred per cent then the Arien employer is satisfied. While they may come across as rather demanding, fierce and uncompromising, they are never petty or mean-spirited. And they get results, big time.

Aries are champions against injustice and, as an employer, this includes in the workplace. They are honourable and principled individuals, who are fair and just, if a little intimidating at times. Perhaps the worst sin is to lie to an Aries boss, so never attempt a false sick day. They would far rather an employee asked them straight for a day off, than be given an excuse which would insult their intelligence. What's more, they are very likely to grant a direct request, as they admire honesty.

One of the biggest assets an Aries employer has is their intuition. Many of their business decisions are based on this, including their choice of whom they employ. They can't easily explain or justify why they act in a particular way – that's one of the difficulties of the intuitive process, it does not bear rational scrutiny. And it means the boss may have a way of knowing more about their employees than they'd wish.

Aries are best suited to careers where initiative, enthusiasm and autonomy are welcome, such as business, politics, the arts, sales and marketing. Aries are good in a crisis, so thrive in any of the emergency services, including medicine, where their speedy reactions compensate for their lack of patience. They have a heroic urge to help those in distress, so any kind of rescue work, especially if it involves an element of danger like at sea or in difficult terrain, can suit them.

Whatever their work or position in life, Aries brings a directness, clarity and simplicity. These are people who always make life seem less complicated. Their take on the world cuts through to the bare bones of a situation, they see through the gloss and the trimmings. They have an innate aptitude to deconstruct. This is their gift.

Negative Aries

Many of Aries' positive characteristics can become negative. They only have to express more extreme or distorted everyday traits for them to be deemed difficult and problematic. Most Aries will at times fall into this and become a very bad example of their sign; when under pressure or dreadfully upset for instance, they can be impatient and aggressive. Some Aries predominantly manifest the more negative pole of the spectrum of possibilities that are available to them. These are likely to be the more damaged individuals. Not that this is an excuse, but it can help when dealing with an objectionable individual to understand why they behave like this. So, this is a look at the negative expressions of those born under this sign, with speculations as to how they got that way.

Aries are optimistic by nature, so some may wonder how this can become negative. Well, if it's so out of touch with reality that the individual is living in cloud cuckoo land, it becomes negative. For some their capacity for initiative dwindles into a search for the next lucky break, which they expect to find just around the corner. They believe that the hard luck they are experiencing is not their fault and will change magically without them having to do anything. They refuse to take responsibility for their situation, blaming it on outside forces and equally they expect something or someone to change their life for them. They've never heard of the saying that 'We create our own good luck.' Such an individual may waste away their life by failing to recognise and seize the opportunities that do present themselves. Rather than be proactive, which is typical of this sign, they become passive and wait for someone else to rescue them.

As an intuitive type, most Aries have keen hunches that

they can rely on. However that is no substitute for hard work. Some may live too much in their head, or the future, but fail to pay attention to their body and the here and now. Neglecting their body to some extent is normal for an Aries but if this is sustained over long periods then various more serious problems arise. They are prone to skipping meals and eating hurriedly, so digestion problems like irritable bowel syndrome and the highs and lows of snacking on sugary foods are common, with worst-case scenarios developing into full-blown eating disorders like anorexia. Anorexia is a complex problem but the deeper underlying issues can be triggered by a chaotic eating pattern.

Aries may dislike their bodies and certainly are not comfortable with bodily functions, which they feel are messy. They are squeamish and some of their self-neglect is based on a denial that these are normal natural aspects of being human. They would rather they weren't. They may well feel encumbered by their physical needs with a tendency to ignore them.

None of this is helpful, to put it mildly, in Aries' relationships. Their difficulty with the physical realm can be problematic in sexual relationships. They are not naturally sensual (that is the domain of the earth signs) and do not automatically enjoy stroking and caressing for its own sake. Intimate contact with someone else's body may only be a means to an end, to sexual gratification. Bodies can literally disgust them. Such an individual is not an attractive proposition and those sexually involved with an Aries may well feel undermined, failing to realise that it's not their problem. Nevertheless these are the issues that have to be addressed for the duration of the relationship. Sex can be a form of athletics for Aries, where they can enjoy the performance but not necessarily the process. This is a negative caricature and with an average Aries, while there may be glimpses of these extremes, it won't be their main mode of operation.

Aries

Hugh Hefner, of Bunny Girl notoriety, is an Aries with a lifestyle that illustrates some of these issues with the physical realm. While some men might envy him, others might think that he props up a rather fragile ego by surrounding himself with numerous scantily-clad women. Putting aside questions of exploitation, Hefner seems to think that the more women the better, which has to be a measure of his competitiveness rather than an ability to relate meaningfully.

Another Aries trait that can turn nasty is their lack of patience. They are extremely quick mentally, often getting the point and grasping a situation way ahead of anyone else and are exasperated by slower individuals. Their impatience can make them poor teachers as they pace themselves with the brightest students and leave the slower ones trailing. An Aries mum attempting to help her daughter with her maths homework traumatised the child with her ferocious criticisms – if the daughter failed to understand she was assumed stupid. In fact she was far from stupid, just not as quick as her mother expected her to be. Aries grasp things intuitively and their unpleasantness is partly a cover up because they can't explain their method in a logical way. And they find it hard not to display their annoyance.

Arien impatience can also be directed at physically slower individuals. They hate being kept waiting. So, on a family outing, they can become irritable if others are not ready when they are, failing to recognise that it's in their nature always to be ready first. They tend to walk briskly and anyone who moves at a more leisurely speed can irritate them. Even with young children and the elderly, who are bound to step out at a slower pace, there is zero tolerance and the walk can become fraught because of their frustration.

The Aries individual has a quick temper at the best of times and at worst an Aries can become an absolute tyrant and erupt with rage. This kind of individual has learned that they can frighten others and thereby control them. Such an individual may feel deep inside a lack of power and so they assert themselves in this over-the-top way. This is typical of the bully, who is a coward on the inside. Such an individual will almost certainly have been bullied themselves as a child, either by peers or by a parent. Of course this doesn't make their behaviour as adults excusable but their view of life may have polarised into either be bullied or bully and they've chosen the latter. For this ugly dynamic to change they must develop awareness that there are other options in life.

At the less extreme end of the spectrum is the brusque manner and everyday scratchiness of some Ariens, which can be particularly hurtful and upsetting for loved ones. In a domestic situation they can bristle with irritability, showering anyone in their vicinity indiscriminately with their bad temper and intolerance. Expect a low comfort zone if you live with one of these individuals – even the way they move about the house can jangle. Often they have no awareness of how they are being, it may well be that they are feeling stressed and don't realise it, yet scatter-gun their irritability everywhere.

For those feeling brave enough, it can help to point the above out. The risk is that Aries gets even angrier and explodes, but for those who can cope with this, it's worth trying – at least Aries may then go on and get to the underlying problem. If this is a tactic that has failed, because they stay in denial, then there is no advantage in objecting to their behaviour. Those who live with them then need to develop a thick skin, not take their petulance personally and learn to stay out of their way. Not that easy!

Aries have a reputation for being selfish and self-centred and they often don't see beyond their own needs and think the world revolves around them. These are self-absorbed individuals who are fascinated by themselves and expect

22

everyone else will be too. Yet it means that often others are never considered. Aries can't step into someone else's shoes and look at things from their perspective because they are so rooted in their own point of view. They fight their corner with tremendous zeal because they are so convinced they are right. While some put up with their 'Me, me, me' approach mainly because of their special brand of child-like innocence, those living with this kind of individual have to be able to hold their own, as if they regularly concede there's a danger they'll store up resentment.

This is a dynamic that can creep up on those who live with a rather dominant Aries. Gradually the balance of power in the relationship tilts in the Arien's favour, which they accept and take for granted, while their mate feels more and more useless and ineffectual. Mr or Ms Aries makes all the important decisions without any real discussion, presenting them as a fait accompli. Something has to give. Either the partner feels so undermined and inadequate that they shrink into a rather cowed version of themselves or they say 'enough is enough' and make a stand, possibly by taking such drastic action as walking out. It's not easy to get an Aries to understand and often a behavioural response is the only way to get the message across.

However, when a loved one is in trouble, Aries will always step in and fight on their behalf. In these incidences a partner may well appreciate and certainly benefit from their warrior spirit. Aries always and without hesitation protects its own.

A further domestic problem may concern the chores and Aries' difficulty with practical matters. As we've seen, some conquer this by becoming super fast and efficient, while others deny there is an issue and are simply not tuned into what needs to be done. This divide may break down along gender lines, with women gaining mastery in the domestic domain and men feigning an absurd superiority by being hopeless in that department. They may see it as unimportant and fail to understand what all the fuss is about – an arrogant attitude and again, not an attractive proposition as a live-in partner. Such a man will need house-training if he's to pull his weight and learn to do housework, put the rubbish out, do shopping, and so on. Of course, the gender divide may not work out this way – the problem is that Aries is not practically minded and may not see this as a problem, imagining that it's someone else's privilege to look after them. Check this out and think it through *before* you move in together.

Typically Aries are active individuals; they are doers and enjoy being busy. This can, however, become extreme, where they use activity to distance others and avoid intimacy. Some can never sit still and even when ostensibly watching television they'll be attending to some other task. They won't readily stop what they are doing for a conversation either and can expect others to follow them around as they 'keep busy' with whatever they are doing. Annoying, yes. Selfish, yes. But also often a displacement tactic to avoid the uncomfortable feelings they have around closeness and inactivity. Activity satisfies their need to constantly feel they are achieving something, even if it's only chores. So when an Aries *is* domestically minded, their attitude may still be uncomfortable for those they live with.

The fiercely competitive streak of Ariens we saw earlier can easily become a negative trait. Their need to win at any cost can turn a friendly game of scrabble into a war zone, with others cowering and ultimately refusing to play. Ariens always play hard and furious, there's no other way for them, so if that's not your style be warned before any kind of game commences. Their competitiveness is not only confined to recreational activities, it is present in all areas of their life and can have a pathological edge to it. They may display a desire to be the best at everything, always trying to top what's gone before, whether in conversation or achievements. This kind of one-upmanship is embarrassing to witness. It's a type of dominant stud syndrome, found in both men and women, visible in the hierarchical structures in many of the animal groups. This behaviour manifests at times when Aries' primitive instincts get the better of them. They act as if their very survival depends on them occupying the top-dog position. Clearly this arouses rivalry and hostility in others, which they may view as undeserved. An Aries may be alert to how others compete with them and blind to how they incite this. These are unsophisticated individuals with their insecurities all too visible for everyone to see.

This naivety has its pluses but the problem is that Ariens miss subtle exchanges which just go over their heads and so their social skills can be impaired. A lot is written now about emotional intelligence – a type of social intelligence that involves the ability to monitor one's own and others' emotions, to discriminate among them, and to use the information to guide one's thinking and actions – and how important this is in getting on in the workplace. Those who are promoted are not necessarily the most intelligent but those with high scores in emotional intelligence – and this could well be a weak spot for Aries.

It can also be a problem in other social situations, where Aries miss certain cues that others who are more empathic pick up on. Something said to them in an ironic or sarcastic way may not penetrate and the subtle undertones are missed. The comment is heard too literally and the intonation is lost on them. At times they can find this quite bewildering, especially when they realise later what was being intimated and that they just didn't get it at the time. It can also leave them feeling rather stupid. Meanwhile, Aries can feel frustrated that others aren't more like them and wish that they'd spell things out in a straightforward way.

Whatever the gender of the individual, Aries is a masculine sign with all the strengths and weaknesses associated with macho behaviour. They may not be that comfortable listening to others' problems but they are good at taking action and finding solutions. They are great at expressing their unique individuality, making a powerful impact on others, but fail spectacularly in what we might call the touchy-feely domain.

This clearly creates problems in their closest relationships. Loved ones have to learn to be clear with their Aries partner and not expect them to mind-read because although they have a strongly developed intuition, they arrive at this information via a different route, gleaning it from their highly-attuned antennae rather than tuning in on a feeling level. This can confuse others into believing they are empathic, when in fact they aren't. It's a rather abstract, impersonal knowledge that they have.

For this reason, many Aries of either sex prefer friendships with men, where communication tends to be less convoluted and more overt. They know where they stand and feel far more comfortable when they don't have to contend with what they see as dangerous undercurrents, which they struggle to register let alone interpret. They are happiest when they can ignore 'all that crap' and just deal with what's presented at face value.

Aries' innate leadership qualities can also be a problem, both for them and others, as they have a tendency to take up this position irrespective of their qualifications for the role. They instinctively move in and take command in a most convincing and impressive way, sometimes when they don't actually know what they are doing. So while Aries' brisk, purposeful step conveys the message that they know where they are going in truth they may not have the foggiest idea of where they are headed. They charge off and others understandably assume they are being lead in the right direction, it's only when they are all spectacularly lost

that anyone realises what has happened and the recrimin-
ations start.

It's not part of Aries' nature to ask others for help or
assistance, either. So, if they do get lost, they tend to push
on regardless, hoping sooner or later to recognise a familiar landmark. You'll notice this especially when they're
driving; they can cover vast distances in the wrong direction before they'll even consider looking at a map. They
rely on their intuition, which while normally right, is not
infallible and when it's wrong and is linked to their instinct
for flight, they can be a disaster on a small scale.

On a larger scale, Aries can find themselves promoted
to positions that they are ill equipped for. They place themselves under unbearable stress as they struggle to come up
with the goods. They assume that they should be able to
carry out a task and others expect it of them because they
display such confident leadership qualities.

Aries' enthusiasm for causes can create problems, too.
They may get carried away and decide to launch a rescue
bid in a situation where it's better to leave well alone or
where no help is being asked for. They muscle in on a
situation and fail to recognise how *they* benefit by acknowledging the ego boost they get when playing the hero. Even
though their intentions are honourable, it's tricky for the
recipient to get them to back off – they don't take no for
an answer.

Typically Aries have a large and fragile ego, so it doesn't
take much for the scales to tip and for this to become a
negative trait. They can be overbearing, arrogant, appear
totally sure of themselves and consequently completely
impossible to deal with. This is, despite appearances, a
defensive ploy because they are constantly trying to shore
themselves up. They are actually as unsure of themselves
as the average adolescent, and in many ways stuck at that
level of development and sophistication. All they can do
to fight off their fears is to put on a good show – and they

become very impressive at this, so much so that they convince themselves they're no longer that insecure youngster trying to make it in the world of grown-ups.

The Aries Man

The Aries man is dashing and charming. He has a dynamism that is extremely attractive and in some ways life seems effortless to him. What might daunt others he takes in his stride; very little fazes or seems too much for this man. He oozes competence and others readily trust him to deliver what he promises. Which he does. His air of natural authority takes him a long way in life. He is quite impressive!

This Mars-ruled man has all the qualities of a warrior; his task in life is to optimise these characteristics, usually in a society that isn't actually at war. He has to find culturally acceptable outlets for his fighting spirit. Sport and the business world are good options. In these arenas, his desire to dominate and beat his opponents is considered fair game.

Determined and headstrong, the Aries man has a single mindedness about the way he approaches situations. He is born to lead. This is the position he naturally gravitates to in social situations and which is somehow conferred upon him by his peers. He is at his best when initiating and others instinctively look to him to show them the way. This he does whether or not he has any idea of what he's doing – he simply rises to the expectation. He can talk a lot of nonsense – spouting off on topics that he actually knows very little about in a most convincing way. Some will be taken in while others will twig that his spiel is thin on facts, but nevertheless be intrigued by how adept he is at holding forth.

Despite his capacity for rhetoric, Mr Aries is not a man given to deep thought – he prefers action and dashes in where others might pause to think. He is gallant and loves being the hero. He opposes injustice, sticks up for those he cares about and can be counted on in times of difficulty. This is definitely not a fair-weather friend. Whether or not he's actively involved in politics, he has a political conscience. He has a moral position and knows what he thinks is right or wrong and lives according to it. Honest and straightforward, he won't condone deceit and is not that good at subtlety or strategy.

One of the downsides to the Aries man is that, because he expects everything to go smoothly, when it doesn't he can have quite a short fuse and may have a reputation for temper tantrums. He reacts, making a fuss where others would be more tolerant and accepting. He has a low frustration threshold and, just like the ram that rules his sign, he has a propensity to charge at obstacles, which can be pretty scary to witness, let alone be on the end of. Those who have this aspect of their personality under control clearly do better and have a more harmonious personal life, while those who still react like two-year olds are actually, as adults, extremely intimidating and don't do their career prospects any good, either.

The Aries actor, Russell Crowe, doesn't seem to have done his career much harm by his displays of temper but then he's in a career where all publicity is considered good publicity. It adds to his edgy image. Some of his outbursts seem to indicate that he finds it difficult being in the media spotlight, so perhaps the loss of anonymity and autonomy can be hard for this independent and headstrong sign.

Even though the Aries man has natural leadership qualities, he won't necessarily make a good boss. He may not have the patience or the diplomacy to manage others and it could be a great strain for him to develop these skills. He is at his best when acting as an inspiration and blazing a trail that others can follow.

Conquest plays a large part in the Aries psyche. For the Aries male, this can mean he is motivated by the idea of a victory in romantic situations and once he has seduced and won his prize his interest wanes. He is then on to his next conquest. This is undoubtedly one of the less attractive sides to his character and at worst he can resemble Don Juan, with notches on the bedpost to mark his successes. The chase is all-important and such a man thrives on the buzz of excitement; he could be addicted to this and lack the emotional maturity to develop a deeper and sustained relationship. He may nevertheless stay with a lover who never truly surrenders to him and remain in hot pursuit – something of a neurotic coupling. This is not a scenario to admire, even if it does have the outer appearance of stability. For those who are about to get involved with an Aries fellow, do check out his track record and see how well he's managing this dynamic. If his record is bad he's probably a heartbreaker.

Another role an Aries man can take on is that of the rescuer. He champions the underdog and will crusade for a good cause and can find himself in the guise of the archetypal knight on a white charger who dashes in and sweeps away his damsel in distress, which does everything for his ego and sense of potency. It means he can fall for the hard luck story and tends to be with those who lean on him and accept his authority at face value. He remains the powerful dominant one in his relationships – in fact he isn't big on any notion of equality. He may believe in it in theory, but in practice he likes to be in charge. For those who like to be with a masterful partner, this is your man.

The more emotionally mature Aries man who has either moved beyond these destructive patterns or never been possessed by them and is able to make a commitment is a loyal and supportive mate. He's spontaneous and generous and gives fully of himself. There's nothing enigmatic about him. Plus he's morally courageous, which comes from his ability to face his fears. Part of his charm is that he is so self-revealing. This can reassure others and help them open up too – he makes it seem so safe and easy.

Not only does the Aries man believe in himself, he also resolutely believes in his loved ones and that kind of on-going encouragement goes a long way. Through imbibing his high opinion of them a partner's self-esteem and confidence blossoms. This is a cheerful man to live with; his optimistic and enthusiastic take on life means he has a lot to offer – he always looks on the bright side of things and inspires hope in others. He's not moody, doesn't bear grudges, isn't at all fazed by another's bad temper and bounces back from adversity with admirable speed. While his ability to make a rapid recovery can be annoying to a loved one, who wonders if he's learned his lesson yet, it does also serve as an example in positive thinking.

As a father, the Aries man is equally generous in his encouragement of his child. He helps them believe that they can achieve their goals and follow their dreams. He's less likely than most parents to try to mould his child in any particular way; he is interested in discovering who they are. Neither does he impose on them his own unfulfilled aspirations or dreams – he's more than likely to have lived his life fully, doing whatever he needed as and when he needed to, the positive side of the selfish label that so often gets thrown at him.

While his child is young and unquestioningly admires Dad, trusting his authority, seeing him as the leader, the Aries man thrives. What he may be less able to cope with is the rebellious stage of adolescence. Having an angry teenager stomping around the house is no one's idea of fun, but the Aries father may come down on them very hard if his temper is triggered, which will only increase the tension. However, provided he doesn't over-react in this way with his older children, he makes for a very involved father. He won't squash their adventurous spirit; he doesn't see danger around every corner and trusts his offspring to be sensible and able to take care of themselves. He knows how important autonomy and freedom are and won't unduly restrict them – he makes for a liberal parent in this respect.

Partly because the Aries man has a low tolerance for frustration, he is susceptible to stress. Competitive sport is the perfect antidote. He needs the physical challenge as his body stores tension without an appropriate release, plus sport can be a vehicle in which he can channel some of his aggression in a healthy way. A game of squash, where he can pound the opposition, is just what he needs after spending a day in the office trying to stay polite. He has his primitive instincts fairly close to the surface, with his triumph and pleasure in victory all too apparent, and finding socially acceptable outlets is essential if he's not to implode. This is someone who likes to win more than most and always plays a hard game.

Not all Aries men find physical activity to their liking and for some mental competition, like chess, also serves as a release. He won't be the subtlest of players but he will play a razor-sharp game. His competitive edge drives him to succeed in all he undertakes in life and often brings him success. Losing simply doesn't suit him. His natural position is first and he strives to occupy that place.

Mr Aries is well placed in careers that require a ruthless streak. Unlike some, he is able to make snap decisions and stand by them. He has little time for regrets, does not rake over the past and his focus remains on what lies ahead. He hates to waste time, which is how he's likely to see being introspective. This does not necessarily mean he lacks awareness, he just doesn't get it through navel gazing. He gains his awareness of himself, others and situations through his intuition. Others may find he has hunches that they can't trust, but for the Aries man this proves to be his most reliable source of information. It can mean that he appears to make quantum leaps and can't readily explain the process by which he arrives at his decisions, but that shouldn't cast doubt on their validity.

The Aries man gravitates to a career where courage and quick decisions are vital: a surgeon, test pilot, ambulance driver, fireman or racing driver are all good examples. All rely on having nerves of steel. When he applies himself and utilises his verbal skills, he can become a fantastic sales-man, too, beating all previous sales records. He loves the competition. His unerring sixth sense gives him a talent for any business that relies on being in tune with the zeitgeist. His gift is in being able to anticipate what lies ahead. He does well in the media and arts, provided he has someone else to attend to all the administration.

What the Aries man is not good at is what he sees as boring, everyday tasks; in fact he can be positively arrogant and superior in this respect and can make mistakes because of his lack of attention to detail. Others frequently pick up the pieces, not only in work but in his private life too and this doesn't do him any favours in the long run. His failure to recognise his own shortcomings is infuriating for those who have to deal with the essential run-of-the-mill work.

The Aries man does get better at this with practice and over time. However, for those who work alongside him and especially those who share a domestic set-up with him, do step aside sometimes; leave him to flounder and allow him to gain that all-important experience. He has a clever way of flattering those who are effectively his dogsbodies, so it's essential for his own development that loved ones don't succumb to it.

Elton John, Eric Clapton and David Frost are three Aries men that illustrate typical yet different Arian traits. A documentary on Elton John captured his infamous temper tantrums and his low threshold for frustration. His impulsive generosity and extravagant lifestyle are equally well documented; who else would spend £15,000 on flowers in one year?

In interviews Eric Clapton is surprisingly frank and without guile. He comes across as honest and straightforward and the songs he writes are frequently about intensely personal matters. The way he reveals himself has a naivety and an innocence that undoubtedly wins him popularity.

David Frost, the television journalist, is renowned for his hard-hitting interview style, in which he takes on politicians and insists on getting answers for the viewers. His quick retorts, fierce to-the-point questioning and clarity of mind are typical of this sign. No one is able to fob him off as he simply cuts through to the heart of the matter.

All three have reached the top of their chosen professions and broken new ground in various ways but all three display the same Arien ambition and determination. Other famous Aries include Charlie Chaplin and Spike Milligan, both comedy geniuses, who were way ahead of their time and remain important influences in comedy to this day. Milligan pushed back the frontiers of radio shows while Chaplin took slapstick to a new level in the early silent films.

Finally, Marlon Brando is another Aries who made a huge impact as a 'method actor' in his heyday and put this kind of acting on the map, leading the way for some of the finest actors of today. He, too, broke the mould and increased the expectations of what an actor could convey regarding the psychological truth and behavioural honesty of the character he was portraying. (Interestingly, the film that propelled Brando to stardom, *A Streetcar Named Desire*, was written by another Aries, Tennessee Williams.)

Perhaps more than anything Aries men lead the way in whatever arena they choose to enter. Not all are famous but many are shining examples of what overcoming their limitations is all about.

If only, when the Aries man gets to the top of whichever mountain he happens to be climbing, he could be persuaded to pause for a moment. Instead, he's already spotted the next mountain peak in the distance and so rather than drink in the pleasure of his success, he feels the necessity to press ever onwards, as if his present achievement counts for nothing. Those who love him would do well to remind him how far he's come.

The Aries man's faults are clear to see – there's no dispute – he's not a perfect human being. But then who is? For those thinking of getting involved with an Aries man, at least you know from the start what you are getting, with no nasty surprises six months down the line. What you see is what you get. Enjoy!

The Aries Woman

Ms Aries and, yes, this woman is far more likely to be Ms than a Miss or Mrs, is a feminist by nature, whatever her actual politics. This is a fiercely independent woman, in both her actions and thinking. She carries her own bags, thank you, and opens her own doors, has opinions and speaks her mind. In fact, she can seem quite formidable, particularly to those who expect a woman to be rather more docile and compliant.

Mars-ruled Aries is probably the most assertive sign of the zodiac and, as such, is not easy for women in cultures where female passivity is valued. Madonna, although she's not an Aries (she's a Leo), nevertheless spoke for all empowered women when she said she'd got a masculine brain. While this perhaps assumes women can't be assertive without adopting a masculine attitude, it does describe Ms Aries. Qualities that are found positive and attractive in men are devalued in women; where a man is self-assured and confident, a woman is deemed bossy and domineering with its implicit criticism.

The Aries woman often discovers early in life that her competitive and combative spirit does not go down well with others and may curb her natural feisty nature, finding ways to express herself that don't threaten the way gender is perceived in society. Clearly she has a better chance of being true to her innate nature in a more egalitarian society but, even within this, the attitude of those who are in her immediate vicinity will influence the extent to which she can realise herself.

Instead of being the ram that the sign is associated with, some Aries women adopt sheep-like characteristics, in an attempt to be liked. It's not that she's particularly concerned to obtain others' approval, because she's not, but persistent and consistent devaluing of some of the core qualities she possesses is bound to take its toll. But in doing this she loses out all round. By adopting a 'false self' she becomes alienated from what will bring her fulfilment and satisfaction. It is important that she finds an avenue of expression for her strong and dynamic personality and in many ways this can be seen as her life task and challenge.

If the Aries woman masquerades as a follower when, in actuality, she's born to be a leader, she'll be extremely critical of those who take on this dominant role. On one level she knows this is where she belongs but lacks the courage or the confidence to take this position. It would be better for her to take on any position of leadership, even a relatively lowly one, as she can then begin to flex her muscles. And many do. Typically the Aries woman is found assuming this role, even when it's not hers by right. With as much natural authority as her male counterpart, she has usually been socialised into developing better relating skills, so can go far.

The Aries woman makes her mind up very quickly. In fact she does everything at speed. When decisions have to be made she knows instantly what she wants. It is as if there's an invisible lightning conductor to her brain that she trusts implicitly. So there's no arguing the toss with her or trying to persuade her. She knows what she wants and more often than not, she wants it now. Patience is not her strong point and she really doesn't understand why others take so long over things. It baffles and confounds her.

This is not your typical damsel in distress. But although the Aries woman may not appear to need rescuing, she still has her vulnerable side and harbours romantic dreams. When in love she is a hopeless idealist. She falls for gallant gestures and heroic demonstrations of love and passion. She admires courage, a quality she possesses in abundance and will look for someone who doesn't give up easily.

As an intuitive type, the Aries woman has an innate talent for tuning into the hidden potential in others. She spots the creative spark in others and is inspired and excited by it. When her deeper feelings are engaged, her imagination works overtime and she can get carried away. At times a relationship may exist more in her mind than in reality, as she has the ability to breathe life into seemingly insignificant interactions. She is capable of weaving a fantasy around her lover, creating a make-believe shared future life. When this occurs, she adjusts to the reality of her situation slowly and painfully. Although she has this tendency to 'fast forward', she can nevertheless withstand a lot of difficulties in a relationship – her loved one doesn't have to be perfect. This is someone who has grit and determination and is not easily put off.

For those who intend to woo the Aries woman, it's essential that they can hold their own with her – to feel pleasantly challenged and stimulated rather than intimidated by her forthrightness. She may find she attracts puppy-dog types, who like to sit adoringly at her feet, gaze up with admiring eyes and follow her around. While this may briefly flatter her ego, if she hooks up long-term with this type she will become frustrated and unhappy. She needs someone who sees through her somewhat gruff self-sufficiency to her naivety and innocence. To develop she must wait to meet her match – someone equally strong – a worthy opponent with whom she can spar without a major upset ensuing. With such a mate an exciting, dynamic partnership can develop.

More than anything, the Aries woman thrives in a partnership that has scope, where there is a sense of adventure and unknown territory to explore. If life settles into too much of a routine and she finds her circumstances boring and monotonous, she feels trapped and could well break free. Even on a day-to-day basis, she doesn't necessarily want to account for exactly where she is every moment of the day or to know where her partner is, either. It's not that she's up to no good, she just needs freedom of movement.

Suspicion and unfounded jealousy annoy her deeply and in such an emotional climate the Aries woman may well fulfil her partner's worst fears. She won't stay in an unhappy situation, she's not a victim or a martyr and will voice her unhappiness and take action. However, if she were involved elsewhere, then her partner would be the first to know. Remember, she's always honest and straightforward. She refuses to be controlled or manipulated, expects to be trusted implicitly and once emotionally committed, is capable of deep and abiding loyalty. In fact she is among the least likely to have a secret affair.

Clearly then, the Aries female is not a 'yes' woman. She can be brash and abrasive, defiant and strong willed. This is an extremely competent woman, who thrives on challenge and is resolute; she can cope with just about anything life throws at her. This does not mean she finds life easy, it's more that her character doesn't allow her to whinge or back down. She's cheerful and optimistic and approaches problems in a positive and upbeat way.

This often results in the Aries woman taking on far more than most would consider feasible. Despite becoming overloaded, she soldiers on regardless. She refuses to accept her limitations and is spurred on by her competitive zeal to overcome exhaustion and depletion and to deliver whatever she has undertaken – even if it was an impossible undertaking in the first place. Anything less and she feels a failure.

A partner has to be tolerant of this. On no account criticise the Aries woman when she's taken on too much and is in the midst of all this. To say 'I told you so' when she's at her wits' end is very high risk indeed. When stressed she's extremely inflammatory. Her life is never going to be humdrum or run of the mill and it's essential that those who are intimately involved with her feel undaunted by the merry-go-round of her everyday existence.

Despite her self-sufficiency, what the Aries woman can't abide is if, in a quarrel with others, her partner doesn't support her. She always and without fail champions those she loves. So for her, it's simple; she expects her friends and partner to back her up, regardless of anything else. To side against her is an absolute betrayal. What's more, she's at her least logical, reasonable and rational in these matters.

When the Aries woman is at war, or even just having a minor quarrel, she wants those who love her to step into her shoes and offer empathic understanding, not detached or objective feedback on the situation. In time she gains perspective but, if her partner attempts to offer an alternative view before she's ready to listen, the situation will become heated and escalate. What's more, she'll feel emotionally abandoned. The upset could drag on for ages, undermining trust and closeness. The key is to back her up wholeheartedly in the moment and stay quiet until she reaches the point when she's ready to be reflective.

In a live-together scenario, the Aries woman may appear to call the shots but this isn't necessarily the reality, she may just be more vocal and state her opinions rather loudly. Victoria Beckham is a good example of a modern Aries woman. While the media portray her as bossy and controlling, she protests that she does not wear the trousers in her marriage to David Beckham. What is clear is that she attracts criticism for being a strong woman, with a mind of her own.

Victoria Beckham also demonstrates nicely that because she has 'masculine' qualities, this doesn't necessarily equate with a masculine appearance. She has the high, well-defined cheek-bones and good bone structure typical of Aries. These Mars-ruled women are just as feminine, alluring and attractive as other signs, although they may choose not to exploit their assets in coquettish ways. Playing mind games is not their style. The only games they know are competitive, which they play to win.

Whether or not the Aries woman gets married, opts for a committed relationship or stays single, her calling remains the same – being true to herself. All of these choices are available to her. She can cope with being single better than most, but that does not mean that this is what she wants. She can manage more than one relationship at a time too although, again, this would be without any duplicity. All concerned would know the score, as she is emotionally honest.

The Aries woman is as likely as the next to want children. She may not be the classic maternal type but if that's her desire she'll pursue it with passion. If no suitable partner were available, she could opt to be a single parent. A lesbian Aries woman might use her situation in a political way, too, as she is happy to act as an example to others. Whatever her sexual orientation, she wouldn't allow the lack of a mate to stop her.

That said, the Aries woman would prefer to have a child in a committed relationship, not least because she holds idealistic notions regarding a shared future with a lover. Plus, the reality of having a child on her own threatens to hem her in and restrict her too much. Despite her tendency to take on and manage an awful lot, her independent spirit means she finds the constant demands of a small child taxing, so being able to pass the baby to someone else equally involved is an important consideration.

As a mother, the Aries woman is excellent at giving her children scope to be true to themselves, the one thing that she herself has needed the most. She's a no-nonsense sort of mother, good at organising her children's activities, always prepared to have their friends over, never daunted by a hectic schedule. Patience is not her strong point and she tends to be in a hurry, whether in fact there is a real rush or not. Because she enjoys competitive games, her children learn to play hard and to win at an early age, something that can turn them into winners later in life.

The Aries woman is ambitious for her children and wants them to do their best and is there alongside them, ready with praise, encouraging them in all they attempt, which is all the reward they need. As her children grow older, she is one of those mothers least likely to suffer from 'empty nest syndrome', as she is busy with her own life. She may or may not take time out of her work to raise children, but she's not likely to stay out of the workplace for long. She needs the stimulation and satisfaction of a career as well.

In her work, the Aries woman is likely to be successful and well regarded. She gets on with the job, is efficient and hardworking and doesn't moan. What more could a boss want? She prefers a job where she is left to her own initiative as being told what to do frustrates her. For these reasons she's often in senior positions, having shown that she works well unsupervised.

Careers that best suit the Aries woman are those that utilise her innate characteristics; leadership, initiative, competitiveness, honesty, intuition and courage. Sales, if it's a service or product that she believes in, business and commerce and anything to do with the arts are all possibilities. Not to mention areas like the emergency services where strength and speed of reaction are vital.

Often, the Aries woman is her own boss, which is

probably her best option. More than anything, this motivates her and gives her the freedom and autonomy to create the kind of working pattern that suits her. It allows her to exercise her freewill and demonstrates how good she is at organising herself. She especially shines in a creative endeavour, where there are no prescribed rules as to how things are done.

Famous Aries women include Diana Ross, Aretha Franklin, Chaka Khan and Billie Holiday, all singers who have been leaders in their particular genres and have made a major contribution in their field, influencing those who followed. Diana Ross, originally a member of the Supremes, went on to build a solo career for herself, which is actually more typical of this sign. In interviews, the other original members of the Supremes still harbour bitterness about the break and her success as a solo artist, which is an indication that some strong rivalry existed – something Aries often inadvertently stir up by their blatant ambition. Diana Ross typifies Aries in all kinds of ways, not least in establishing herself, in her own right, against the odds.

Betty Ford, who established the famous rehabilitation clinic in America, is also an Aries. She has pioneered this kind of work and recognised that those with a celebrity lifestyle needed complete space and anonymity in order to deal with their addictions, which her clinics provide. She decided to set up the clinics because of her own problems, exacerbated by being thrust into the limelight herself during her husband's term as US president. Typical of Aries, she built upon her own experiences to mount a cause that has gone on to help many others, not all of them rich and famous by any means.

For those who are thinking of getting involved with an Aries woman, you will be expected to be behind her work efforts, not feel threatened by her success and offer a shoulder to cry on when it occasionally all becomes too much. This is one exciting woman to be involved with, for those who are up to the challenge.

The Aries Child

The Aries child has an independent spirit and early on in life insists on doing things their way. More than most children, they resent being told what to do or when to do it, so the more autonomy parents can give a young Aries the better. They value being entrusted with the responsibility of running their own affairs – obviously in age-appropriate ways – and are then more cooperative in the areas that they cannot be left to manage by themselves.

The Aries child is a warrior in the making and has to be carefully socialised if he or she is to adapt to society. It is apparent that this child has a strong will from the word go. 'No' may well be their first word. The trick for the parents is to help their child develop into a socially integrated adult, who can cope with frustration and consider others' feelings, without crushing their spirit.

Many parents are overly alarmed by their Aries child's wilfulness, imagining later anti-social behaviour if they don't curb it early in life. These parents try to mould their offspring into being obedient and adaptable, which won't work and, even worse, the child's spirit could be permanently damaged. By all means coax and encourage good behaviour, but don't meet might with might as these youngsters are far more fragile than they may appear. Their spirit can easily be crushed. Life is hard enough; they'll need all their feistiness to survive.

Aries who have been repressed in early life can find that as adults they are like a cat without claws with no means of defence or escape from dangerous situations. Parents who can tolerate their child's unruly volition and encourage healthy self-assertion lay the foundations for success later in life.

Notwithstanding the above, this child is naturally bossy and will, if given half a chance, boss the whole household. Clear limits must be set to avoid them ever having too much power since this would not be good for them, let alone the rest of the family. This is an ongoing dynamic that has to be renegotiated at the various ages and stages of growing up. However it is always appropriate to allow a young Aries a bit more freedom than you'd offer a more timid child.

The Aries child is a natural leader, who likes to be in charge of games from an early age and readily tells other children what to do. They are high spirited, boisterous and easily bored – they need a lot of stimulation and enjoy fast-moving activities. Whatever the gender, this child thrives on demanding physical activity and challenge.

Aries children need to test their courage and prove that they are brave time and time again. Each time they are successful they grow in stature and self-esteem. The more scope they have to direct their energy in healthy and acceptable pursuits the less likely they are to get up to mischief. If you're the parent of an Aries who is behaving destructively, then try to find them some alternative avenues for their self-expression. Any physical activity which involves an element of danger, such as rock climbing (most cities have artificial walls for youngsters to practice on) is a good option.

For those Aries children that end up committing petty crimes, there is potentially long-term damage to their self-esteem. This is far worse for them than the punishment meted out for the crime; they will keenly feel the lack of an outlet in life where they are valued and rewarded. And finding an appropriate vehicle for their energetic self-expression can be quite a challenge for parents, too. Trying to suppress this child's energy at best won't work and at worst stunts them. Any of the martial arts, which will enhance self-confidence and self-esteem and also teach discipline and control, are worth considering.

Aries

The Aries girl has lots in common with her male counterpart. She may well be a tomboy and needs much the same in the way of physical challenges. She is unlikely to be interested in dolls, other than Action Man (and 'how come there's no Action Woman?' she'll quiz). If she has a brother she may gravitate to his construction toys and may like to play with fake guns and enjoy adventurous games like cops and robbers.

This doesn't mean that the Aries girl won't grow up to be every bit as feminine as the next girl. She's just as likely to be interested in make-up and clothes – especially if she's been allowed to express the boisterous side of her nature while young and encouraged to develop her leadership qualities. She then develops confidence in her physical abilities and strength, which stand her in good stead throughout her life.

Take young Ariens to the adventure playground, let them climb trees (don't watch), give them a bicycle and football. Let them set their own limits in all their activities early in life. If they are prevented from doing this by over-anxious parents this can become a pattern they're stuck with, in that they rely on others to define their limits forever more. And, as it's not a very rewarding role, try not to assume it in the first place. If they want to attempt something that you consider beyond them, let them find this out for themselves if at all possible, and take care to give them a graceful way out. Never humiliate them by saying, 'I told you so'. Don't set up a challenge for them, they already challenge themselves enough. They need to regularly prove to themselves how brave they are, by doing something that frightens them.

An Aries child without a garden in which to play and let off steam can be a nightmare. This is an outdoor child. If they live in a flat then the playgrounds and public parks are a godsend and help parents to stay sane.

Besides being physically active children, young Aries are

mentally quick and extremely competitive. They like to win and work hard at school if there is the possibility of coming top or being best at an activity. If the situation looks hopeless, then this child refuses to compete. For this reason, if the school operates streams, they do better when near the top of a stream and thrive better in this position in a B stream than in the middle of an A stream, for instance. They have more incentive to work if there is the possibility of coming top of the class.

The Aries youngster can be drawn to the sciences, especially maths and physics, where their ability for abstract thought allows them to make the kind of inspired leaps that underpin these subjects. They are intuitive rather than rational or logical, so can't easily explain the process by which they arrive at a given answer, but that doesn't mean it is any the less valid. They have a quick grasp of the whole, may well have an acute visual perception and can become easily bored or impatient if others are slow, including their teachers. If under-stimulated these children can go off into a daydream or be disruptive. Either way, they are not learning. If they are under-achieving don't assume they have an intelligence deficiency; they could well be bored and inattentive because they are especially bright.

Aries children have a rich imagination and can enter into a world of make-believe very easily. They have potential in the arts, especially drama, art and music, so if they show an interest in any of these topics this should be encouraged. However, don't try to tie them down; allow their interests to wax and wane and trust that they will find their way. While it's important that parents have hopes for their future, remember it is theirs and not yours. This is a child who could develop in many different ways and it's essential that they are allowed to experiment and test out their options.

Despite how robust these children sound, they actually need heaps of encouragement. They thrive best when their indomitable spirit is directed in a subtle and gentle way as they take criticism to heart and are easily crushed. Their confidence consists largely of bravado, which has to be consolidated over the course of their life by actual achievements. These are innocent, earnest, sincere children and, for them to develop a secure base within themselves, make sure, if you're their parent, that you don't put them down. Others surely will and they need to know you are always behind them, no matter what. They are a lot more fragile than they appear and without constant support they can flounder and lose their finest quality, their courageous, adventurous spirit.

It is a part of the Aries psyche to expect loyalty from those who love them, to be backed up one hundred per cent and to see anything less as a betrayal. Parents should make sure that they never favour their child's friend in a dispute. If they come home from school with a tale of woe, they need parents to be unflinchingly on their side. This is an area where they are particularly vulnerable.

If there are siblings, then parents may find their squabbles tricky to deal with, as any disputes have to be dealt with fairly and impartially, rather than with the emotional well-being of just their Aries offspring in mind. However, as long as no favouritism is shown and as long as the Aries child feels that their grievance is being listened to and taken seriously, then they can accept the outcome.

If Aries is the oldest child, they can boss younger siblings around to an intolerable extent, so parents would do well to keep an eye on this. It may be advisable not to leave them in charge of younger siblings, especially if the younger ones complain afterwards.

When Aries is the youngest, they can find their failure to win in competitive games extremely frustrating – Aries children like to be best at everything they do. Not being top is a tough one for Aries, so this is a hard lesson learned very early in life. Parents might want to make sure that older siblings don't humiliate their younger Aries sibling, although they can brave out a fair amount of normal sibling teasing.

It is important to have established a good working relationship with an Aries child way before puberty kicks in, as this phase can push parents to their limits. This child is defiant at the best of times and parents need a track record of trust and compromise as well as agreed and negotiated ground rules, on both sides, for this phase to be managed smoothly. If earlier developmental stages have been dealt with successfully then, when the hormones start to run riot, parents have set a precedent that they can fall back on.

The authoritarian parent will have a particularly difficult time as an Aries teenager is likely to rebel all the harder at this point. Imposing rules absolutely won't work anymore. Being authoritarian is the opposite of having authority, and such a parent loses their credibility through attempting to dominate their child. This can only ever be a short-term option and adolescence signals the end of it. At this point, there is a fast learning curve for parents and child if communication is not to break down entirely. Parents have to learn to listen and respect their child's autonomy if they are to stand a hope of regaining their trust, which may be seriously damaged by a legacy of ruling by might.

One of the joys of Aries children is that they are spontaneous and straightforward. These children do not lie or conceal – they let parents know how they feel and what they want in an open and honest way. Others know where they stand with them. They are life's innocents, who may act tough but actually aren't. They are competitive, strong-minded and wilful but also transparent. They have no guile. This doesn't mean they won't bruise easily, as they are not thick-skinned, but if they are treasured for their gifts they will shine.

2

Taurus
The Bull

April 20th to May 20th

A fixed earth sign, ruled by Venus

Introducing Taurus

Taureans can be recognised by their charm and consideration. These are delightful individuals who emanate inner satisfaction and contentment. Never loud or brash, they have sophisticated social skills and a quiet certainty about them. They are grounded in their physical senses and, as such, know where they stand on most things. With their creative and practical approach to life, they deal with all matters from this standpoint, finding pragmatic solutions to problems as opposed to abstract or intellectual theorising.

Taurus is ruled by Venus, the planet associated with love and beauty, and these natives are blessed with easygoing, amiable natures and good looks. Even when not conventionally beautiful, and many are, they have an attractive and pleasing manner that takes them a long way. With a knack of drawing to them the things and people they like and want, life may appear to be effortless and hassle free for them.

Like Librans, the other Venus-ruled sign, Taureans seek

49

to establish harmonious connections and relationships with others and to this end are accommodating, friendly and inclusive. In social situations, they focus on the common ground between themselves and others, minimising and avoiding any differences or areas of contention. Taureans are calm and pleasant individuals, with a steadiness about them – they don't rush or flap about – their motto could be 'when in doubt, do nothing'.

In fact, Taureans have a considerable capacity to do nothing. More than most signs, they can simply sit and be still. They have a placid and peaceful nature and take their time, resisting any sense of rush. This is a fixed sign and as the name implies, these people can really dig their heels in and refuse to budge. The more pressure others exert the more likely a Taurean is to stall. Partly this is because when under duress they go blank and may not know what they're feeling. Whatever the reason, they tend to deal with stress by shutting down and withdrawing.

For those confronted by this Taurean trait, it's sensible to back off and give them some space. No one will ever get a result from a Taurus by issuing an ultimatum. Their reputation for stubborn obstinacy is true from others' points of view, but often misunderstood; they hate being in a hurry or hurried because any decision is considered long and hard and this requires time. However, once they make up their mind, they won't waver but remain committed to a course of action.

As the first of the earth signs (the other two are Virgo and Capricorn) Taurus produces sensible and down-to-earth individuals whose attitude to life is creative, practical and realistic. They have their feet firmly on the ground and do not get swept away by possibilities. Their take on life is like a finely-tuned, sensitive yet objective overview, in which there's no place for abstract ideas. They deal with the concrete facts and actual details when considering a situation.

What Taurus can overlook are the opportunities, as they focus on what is, rather than what might be. Some see this as a lack of imagination, whereas it's more that they do not speculate or project into the future. These people prefer to wait and see what actually transpires. They live in the moment.

At home with the physical realm, Taureans are extremely sensual and innately tactile, taking delight in all of their five senses, especially touch. They make physical contact as some make conversation, offering those around them soothing caresses and occasional strokes in a casual and undemanding way. Just as some people will automatically stroke a cat in passing, they find it hard to pass a loved one by without making some physical contact – it's an instinctive form of interaction. And as this is something they particularly like themselves, when in a relationship, long lazy cuddles are plentiful and not just a prelude to sex.

This non-verbal communication is deeply reassuring and comforting to all the earth signs and to Taurus in particular. For this reason, they need a relationship and don't thrive that well when on their own. Even in an unsatisfactory relationship they are loath to leave, often suffering in silence and trying to tolerate the difficulties, possibly choosing not to see them, rather than give up physical intimacy. They know how painful being on their own can be and need the emotional security that regularly sharing a bed at night gives them.

Taurus may not rate words as a means of self-expression, however they frequently have remarkable voices and musical talent. Even their speaking voice is often melodic and easy to the ear. Some go on to develop this gift in a singing and musical career, in which they are able to communicate deeply and profoundly. Yet even those who do not take the professional route can gain considerable pleasure from their ability, possibly as part of a local choir or band and in entertaining their friends at impromptu musical evenings.

When run down or stressed or with low immunity for whatever reason, the throat is Taurus' weak spot, too, and they are particularly susceptible to throat infections. If they get a cold it often goes to their larynx and they lose their voice. Sore throats are frequent and can come and go, depending on their general well-being. Their voice-box may be blessed but it's also vulnerable and tends to be the point of least resistance. Some suffer from stiff necks produced either by tensing up because of inner pressures or from swollen glands.

The body is an area in which Taureans have innate expertise – they know which muscles tighten up, how to gently ease the sore spots and release the knots. Comfortable in their own skin, they have a no-nonsense, matter-of-fact attitude to bodily functions and are not squeamish in the least. This is one of the least hung-up signs of the zodiac. In their eyes, cellulite is no big deal, everyone perspires, periods are a fact of life and blackheads exist to be squeezed. Through their non-judgemental, accepting attitude, they often help to put others at their ease.

Taureans are not afraid of commitment and are reliable and dependable. Once emotionally involved they enter readily into a deep and binding relationship. They expect absolute fidelity in return – this is not an individual to dally with and is the most possessive sign in the zodiac. More than most, they are acutely security-conscious, so a potential partner's ability to offer them either financial or emotional support can feature in their choice. I'm not saying they're necessarily gold diggers; it's just a very attractive attribute to them. They tend to value emotional and material security equally but some prioritise one over the other.

Sexual contact is always going to be important to a Taurean, so they do not do well in periods of celibacy.

They enjoy sex for its own sake, which may not always feel that romantic, as they need sex purely for the physical and emotional release it provides. With their primitive, no-frills, caveman/woman approach, they can be a bit basic and crude to other, less earthy, souls. Probably the worst thing a partner can do to them is to withdraw sex. This is a sign with a lusty appetite and while they can remain faithful when satisfied, they are tempted to stray when not. They are quite capable of having a lover on the side and keeping their 'main relationship' ticking over happily. And they won't necessarily feel any guilt or remorse either, seeing it as their right. Taureans can be blind to normal considerations when it comes to getting their needs met.

However, were their partner to be unfaithful, this would be so catastrophic for Taurus that it would signal the end of the relationship. Yes, they have double standards and what is acceptable for them is absolutely not so for their mate. They see a partner as their possession. Infidelity is experienced as a violation of their territory. While this may not be a very attractive attitude, they're unlikely to have words to express themselves anyway; they'll be stuck in primordial rage. Their reaction to a partner straying is primitive to put it mildly.

A lot has been said about Taurus' sensuality, which can have a liberating effect in a relationship. The level of acceptance they offer a lover can heal many of the wounds caused by the more rejecting attitudes to the body that are prolific in our society. Here is someone who doesn't baulk at flesh, who positively revels in it and can enable their mate to feel pride and love for themselves. They really do cherish and prize their lover, warts, blemishes, spare tyres and all.

Taurus' sensuality means that they are motivated by the pleasure principle and have a penchant for the fine things in life, food, wine, clothes, the home they live in and the kind of holidays they take. And they tend to fall into two distinct categories, those who prefer the basic and wholesome and those who are drawn by the expensive and luxurious. The first type go on camping holidays, wear cotton, linen and wool, have a comfortable home, eat healthy organic food and enjoy their wine. With their solid, down-to-earth values, they prefer to live in a simple and unadulterated way.

The second category of Taureans also goes for the feel and texture of natural fabrics but extends this to include more luxurious fabrics such as silk and cashmere. And this group can have staggeringly expensive tastes. They buy the designer labels, attracted by the workmanship, style, quality and finish. This is never an ostentatious display, as others may have no idea how much they lavish on their clothes. With or without a big budget, these are individuals capable of making a strong fashion statement.

These Taureans also appreciate cordon bleu cookery, eat out in the best restaurants and possibly are excellent cooks themselves. If anyone ever wondered who pays the fabulous prices that some top-quality mature wines sell for, it's most likely to be a Taurean, because they have the taste buds to appreciate it. Again, it's not bought to impress and they won't make a show of it. These individuals have highly sophisticated tastes.

Some may cook for a living as Taureans love food, have the requisite sensitive palate and like to entertain, so cooking for lots of people on a regular basis suits them perfectly. Their food may be on the rich side but equally they are responsible for marrying unusual flavours to produce astonishing and original results – like black pepper and rhubarb. If this is the profession they follow, they may turn out to be a world-class, innovative chef.

Taureans appreciate art and those who can afford it may be collectors. Their home is likely to contain beautiful and valuable furniture of either antique or classic modern designs, pieces that appeal to their tactile sensitivity. Those lacking a high income still create a home that is both tasteful and comfortable. With an eye for what works, they create harmony around themselves.

Often found working with art or antiques, some Taureans are dealers, while others may be artists, either painters or sculptors or in the design and fashion industry. Their ability to perceive in an accurate and literal way, akin to having a photographic memory, along with a keen aesthetic sense make them ideally suited to this arena. For those who don't develop their artistic talents professionally, this remains a gift that they put to good use with their own sense of style.

Another hobby or profession that Taurus is keen on is gardening or horticulture. They may well have green fingers, love flowers and their eye for colour and form is put to good use in these arenas. With the steady patience to raise seedlings and cuttings, they don't mind hard work and some soil beneath their nails. They revel in the smell of the earth, newly-cut grass and all the wonderful scents from a garden. A garden with a greenhouse in which to raise seeds and protect delicate plants over winter is likely to be a space that Taurus wiles away many an hour. It de-stresses them and gives them endless pleasure to simply potter away.

Alan Titchmarsh is a well-known Taurean gardener, popular on television for his good looks as well as his horticultural skills and even accused by his co-workers of dodging some of the hard work. More will be said on the reputed lazy side of this sign in negative Taurus; for now, it's enough to say that, while they aren't necessarily afraid of hard work, they don't see the point in over-exerting themselves.

Taureans have an affinity with nature in all its multifarious forms and thrive in a natural environment. When there is a choice between a rural or urban lifestyle, then rural is going to offer greater satisfaction. A home with plenty of land, possibly enough to keep the odd horse, sheep, goat or ducks suits this sign perfectly. Their bond to animals is remarkable – one Taurus friend of mine slept in the stables with her horse for the few days leading up to her producing her first foal, there to help when the need arose. Although her work was elsewhere, her priority was her horse.

Some Taureans are experts on wildlife. They may be bird watchers or have knowledge of wild plants or an empathic attunement to domestic, farm and wild animals. Some are amateur weather forecasters, with an ability to recognise the changing weather patterns and a keen understanding of cloud formations. Many simply draw pleasure from the countryside, going on rambles and hikes. Farming suits this sign, too, even though it is a hard life.

Whatever arena Taurus ends up working in, and they are definitely not limited to the ones outlined above, they bring certain attributes to the job. This is the sort who in an office environment, will bring in the odd pot plant to brighten the place up and replenish the biscuits if no one else does. They are easygoing, cooperative, fair-minded and pleasant to work alongside. Their strength is that they relate well to others and as such are good in a team; they are inclusive of others and concerned about others' well-being. It is to their credit that they are sensitive too and can be badly affected by friction in the workplace, which includes tense undercurrents that others might be oblivious to. They thrive in a congenial atmosphere.

Taurus has gained a bad reputation for its materialistic side, so perhaps this has to be explained from their point of view. For them it's all to do with primitive feelings of safety. Possessions help them to feel secure in the world. Add to that their aesthetic appreciation of beautiful objects and their acquisitive nature becomes transparent. They acquire things to shore up their sense of themselves;

much of their identity is invested in what they own. Even those living in an extremely simple way cherish the few possessions they have.

As a Venus-ruled sign, Taurus tends to take the line of least resistance and dislikes conflict and disharmony. Yet the bull, a pretty ferocious and frightening animal when riled, is the symbol for this sign and similarly when in a rage a Taurean is a very scary sight. They don't blow their top often but when they do it can be earth shattering for them as well as those around them. They take a long time to cool off and their whole system is upset for days even weeks or months in some cases.

One Taurean man, whose sexual relationship with his partner was over, was nevertheless in a rage for two years when she got involved elsewhere. Remember what I said about their possessiveness? This sign is slow to anger and can then quietly simmer for a long time – a bit like the bull pawing the ground prior to charging – before they, too, explode with fury. The extent of their anger is a measure of how much they've not reacted during the time leading up to the blow up. Like a dormant volcano, they are far more dangerous than those who have more frequent and predictable eruptions and find it difficult to express anger coherently.

Notwithstanding the above, Taurus is a peaceable sign; it's just that their aversion to any kind of discord and disunity can build up and cause a far worse problem. They have to realise that it simply isn't possible to go through life avoiding confrontation and that stubborn resistance to pressure is not always the best solution. Sometimes, it's necessary to make a stand.

On the plus side, Taurus' capacity to sit things out, to simply endure means they can weather considerable hardship. These are stoical individuals, who have staying power in seemingly impossible situations. They do not get beaten or give up, on people, projects or their dreams. Once they emotionally commit to an undertaking they work steadily and consistently – it's the builder in them – and bring whatever they are doing to completion. They don't leave things half finished and are not daunted if it takes a long time. For better or worse, they are persistent.

Part of their ability to withstand and resist whatever life throws at them is simply because Taurus hates change. They have a 'better the devil you know' attitude and prefer to stick with what is rather than risk what might be. Change of any kind can threaten their sense of security and stability, so they can become stuck in a rut, with an entrenched pattern of existence. If anyone is going to go to the same place for his or her holidays, year after year, it's a Taurus. For them, knowing where they are going to takes all the stress out of the equation and they don't rate the excitement or anticipation of travelling to somewhere new.

This preference for predictability doesn't mean they have their lives planned out ahead, many Taureans don't and have unusual lives that do actually contain a fair amount of upheaval. However, this always comes at some emotional cost to them and with a fair amount of complaint. Moving home, changing jobs or ending a relationship is a very big deal and is considered long and hard before they act. Once they've made their mind up, though, there's no going back. It's irrevocable and they don't tend to look back, taking an unsentimental stance.

Famous Taurean actors include George Clooney, Jack Nicholson, Ryan O'Neal, Al Pacino, Michelle Pfeiffer, Uma Thurman and Debra Winger. All have been helped by their good looks. Jack Nicholson in particular is known for his skill in utilising his physical presence to great effect and has portrayed many characters with few words. They share an inner certainty, which comes from being grounded in their bodies and in the physical realm that they are able to draw upon professionally in the roles that they play.

Queen Elizabeth II is perhaps one of the best examples of a typical Taurus in action. During her reign she has brought stability to her kingdom and has remained constant, making any changes in protocol only when absolutely forced to by popular demand, such as at the time of the death of Diana, Princess of Wales. She illustrates the value of remaining steadfast in a changing world, which is, no matter what their circumstances, a Taurean strength.

Negative Taurus

While any of the general characteristics of Taurus can degenerate into negative traits, they are most susceptible to problems of the flesh. The sensuousness that makes these individuals so attractive can lead to over-indulgence, sloth and debauchery. Typically, Taurus savours and enjoys fine wines and excellent cuisine, but the very pleasure this affords them can be sought as a comfort when life is hard. The couch potato that has stocked up on crisps and chocolates has to be a Taurus. Most on that slippery slope will step back and regain some balance in their life, but will nevertheless have binges every now and then when they abandon all moderation. However some fail to recognise when they have slipped too far in that direction and adopt this as a lifestyle, which they then find difficult to turn back from.

This can be seen as a lopsided expression of Taurus' natural appetite. Perhaps as a result of being unable to get their needs met by others, they find ways in which they can sublimate them and gain direct satisfaction. When this is a reaction to the pain of a sexual rejection, then this particular route becomes ever more attractive. This way they are in control and can meet their own needs – even if it's just to eat a chocolate bar. They avoid having to risk being rejected. Whatever the underlying causes, comfort over-eating and a consequent weight problem is a cross many Taureans struggle with.

Taurean Liberace struggled publicly with his excesses. His love of beautiful clothes and jewellery became an ostentatious statement and, although part of his act, it arguably detracted from his music being taken as seriously as he might have wished. He was undeniably talented and yet became a parody, with his over-the-top lifestyle.

While over-indulgence is a problem for some Taureans, denial, suppression and asceticism is a reaction to their sensual natures that they may also adopt. Don't expect them all to be overweight; just as many are slender and live by a strict dietary regime, as if they are forever afraid that their natural appetite will take over; they are determined to be in control of their sensual appetite. These individuals may not be much fun to share a meal with, as this need for control can result in adhering to the latest food fad and pernickety ideas about what's meant to be 'good for you'. If anyone is about to go on a brown rice and herb tea diet, it'll be a Taurus.

Taureans' asceticism can extend to all areas of life, where they may follow a strict but obscure spiritual practice, live in the equivalent of a monk's or nun's cell, fast regularly and eat macrobiotic food. Not that there is anything necessarily negative about any of these practices – far from it – but there's something about the extremes that some Taurus individuals go to and their 'holier-than-thou' attitude that others may find perverse and obnoxious. They are cultivating a stance that is diametrically opposed to their nature and through suppressing and denying their sensual desires they assume a position of superiority, as if this were something to admire.

On the one hand, Taurus only trust the experiences of their senses – what they can taste, touch, see, smell and hear – and, on the other, they are fascinated by the non-tangible level of reality and desperate to forge a relationship to it. What they lack is the *apparatus* with which to do this and in the process they reject their five senses and all the good common sense these give them.

Taurus seems to have a fatal attraction to religion in all its varieties. Many are found on a spiritual or religious path, which they follow in a fanatical way. They are impervious to reason, having rejected this in favour of something they perceive as higher. This allure for the very thing they are least equipped to evaluate gets them into situations that others would not be vulnerable to. They may become a devotee of a particularly suspect guru or be susceptible to cults and dubious lifestyles that promise deliverance. In their search, they do literally abandon their senses.

Two infamous Taureans who exemplify some of the negative characteristics of this sign are Adolf Hitler and Karl Marx, ironically politically a million miles apart, yet both extreme and dogmatic in their opinions. They illustrate how fanatical Taurus can become and in both cases they were driven by a kind of religious zealousness, although Marx was diametrically opposed to religion per se.

A more recent Taurean phenomenon is David Icke, whom some would describe as mad, but who nevertheless espouses a philosophy that attracts followers and uses his personal charisma to hold sway.

Jim Jones was yet another Taurean religious fanatic. He was the leader of a cult called the 'The People's Temple' which ended with a mass suicide in 1978. Those who didn't choose to die willingly were forced, so in effect were murdered. He must have held considerable persuasive power over his followers to get them to commit such acts.

However, not all Taureans who have a developed religious dimension are mad or bad, as Buddha, who is thought to have been a Taurus, exemplifies. This sign can yearn for a connection with the transcendental and, although this does sometimes go spectacularly wrong, it's not always the case.

Shirley MacLaine, the Taurean actor, is someone who has grappled with this dimension in the public domain. She has written several books on her spiritual and metaphysical journeys and has perhaps become as well known for these as for her acting.

There are glimpses of this dynamic in many Taureans. Spiritual and religious practice is ordinarily a positive choice, it's just that this earthy sign can't always handle it that well and becomes obsessive. Physicality is their issue, so in traditionally religious terms it becomes a focus for struggle and is sometimes misdirected. So, for instance, fasting, which can lead to altered states of consciousness, can become too extreme. In their attempt to transcend the limits of the body, they may actually neglect and harm it. This is after all the vehicle within which all we mortals have to exist while here on earth and it pays to look after it reasonably well.

Taurus, usually so enviably at home in their body, can reject it and its needs, not in the careless way a fire sign might, but cruelly and persistently, as if the very denial gave them pleasure. Such an individual may eventually manifest physical complaints that demand that they take on board the needs of their much-neglected body. This can arise from psychic disavowal, too, in which an attitude of denial of certain painful feelings gives rise to physical symptoms.

It can be argued that a serious illness can take years and years of neglect to cultivate, so once in the body it is going to be hard if not impossible to make sense of it. In this way the messages of the body become incomprehensible and mysterious. Unravelling the psychic component or predisposition is not going to produce a cure, although it is no doubt helpful; the illness needs to be dealt with on its own terms but a recovery will stand a better chance of being maintained if the psychological causes are also addressed. Even the temperamental sore throats that this sign is famous for do well with a spot of introspection, along with the throat lozenges.

Taurus' ability to be calm and at peace has been commended, however this can degenerate into lethargy and unresponsiveness. Their steady manner is simply sluggish and obstructive. These individuals resist any pressure by grinding to a halt. Metaphorically as well as literally they dig their heels in and refuse to budge. And they often feel under pressure in circumstances and situations others would not. It is not possible to get a Taurus to hurry up because they deal with pressure by slowing down and while this can be a problem for them, it is totally infuriating for those around them. Perhaps their reputation as patient and placid has to be put in the context of exactly how much they can try the patience of others.

Taurus is a fixed earth sign, and in nature fixed earth is rock. There is nothing as impenetrable and impervious as certain rock formations, so this is an apt metaphor of what others are up against when dealing with an obtuse Taurean. Their resistance to certain kinds of activity can be seen as laziness, something they often get accused of, so it's important to understand this psychologically. Their motivation in life is always pleasure, so unless an undertaking promises this, they won't find it an attractive proposition. They don't act out of a sense of duty; should and ought are not part of their vocabulary. Other more hyperactive signs can only marvel at Taurus' ability to do nothing. They possess a languorous and sensuous nature, which is never far from sloth, yet there comes a point when 'taking it easy' does turn into 'bone idle'.

The Taurus individual finds it hard to confront others in a straightforward way and often agrees to requests that they really don't want to comply with. In fact, all Taureans should have a sign up reminding them that it's okay to say 'no' or, failing that, 'I'll think about it'. At least that way they buy some time to consider what they really want and break the compulsion to agree first and wriggle out of it later, because, by not saying 'no' when they need to, various complicated and convoluted scenarios ensue. One is that they blame the other person and feel angry that they've been put in this position in the first place and truly believe that they shouldn't have been asked. They fail to see it as their shortcoming.

The blame culture we now live in helps Taurus to think it's acceptable to accuse others of causing their inner difficulties. It enables them to avoid their struggle with self-assertion, as all they have at their disposal is their wordless resistance and non-compliance. It's not that this sign is a pushover, far from it, they definitely won't do anything they don't want to; it's the way they refuse that's problematic, that and their tendency to make this someone else's fault.

Taurus can also gain a bad reputation for being too nice. While this may be hard to imagine, it is exactly the accusation levelled at British Prime Minister, Tony Blair, a Taurean. People often wonder if a man who smiles that much can be trusted. His smile is considered too congenial and his pleasant manner treated with suspicion and mistrust. How can he possibly be genuine, what does his easygoing nature mask? A man with sophisticated social skills is not seen as authentic, and it's this specifically Taurean trait that the media has focused on.

It's also true to say that this sign is very good at distancing others with their impeccable manners and embracing smile, never betraying anything of their deeper feelings. Taurus' ability to hide behind a polite mask and fixed smile is a clever, non-confrontational way of dodging intimacy and of extricating themselves from awkward situations relatively gracefully. The problem is that in avoiding conflict and masking their true feelings they can be seen as untrustworthy and phoney, which in that moment they are. The 'I'm slithering out of this' smile is an elegant solution for those who are fundamentally accommodating, always seeking the common ground and trying to avoid recognising differences or discord.

Taurus' dislike of anger or aggression means they tend to suppress and deny these difficult feelings, which results in them seeping out in indirect and covert ways. This is one reason why those intimately involved with a Taurean can be tipped into blind fury. While it's not fair to blame Taurus for this, there is something about all that control and repression that can topple a more expressive partner. Such a partner somehow becomes infected by the unexpressed and possibly even unfelt feelings of their Taurean mate and are inexplicably reduced to behaving in an appalling way. In the worst-case scenario, Taurus can deliberately exploit their partner, provoking them to express these unpleasant feelings for them. Taurus' identity is bound up with being nice, so they get someone else to do the dirty work. For those involved with a Taurean, reflect on whether this is a dynamic in the relationship and if it is, try to disengage from this role. It's not an attractive deal.

Taurus dislike of change and over-all passivity can become negative. At times, they tolerate circumstances that others would challenge or walk away from. They can have a marked fear of upsetting the apple cart, preferring to stick with what they know – however bad – rather than risk the unknown. This means that some stay far longer than is good for them in unhappy and unsatisfactory situations, suffering in silence and not daring to do anything about it. In a loveless relationship, many will wait to be left, sometimes provoking this, as they can't bear to bring about an ending themselves. Such a decision can weigh too heavily upon them, so they prefer to dodge the responsibility.

None of Taurus' faults are that dire. They are simply the flip side of their strengths, which are the qualities that their nearest and dearest love and appreciate them for. Their downside is part of the package and for those involved, there's a lot to be said in favour of these kind, tolerant and laid-back individuals.

The Taurus Man

The Taurus man is charismatic, charming and elegant and easily recognised by his magnetic presence. This is the strong, silent type. When he does speak, his every word is listened to – he readily commands the respect of those around him. He is an extremely attractive man with impeccable taste, pleasing manners and often found wearing quality clothes and sporting finely manicured hands. He has a solidity about him that exudes trustworthiness and reliability.

This is a practical man, who thinks in a pragmatic and realistic way and approaches life on these terms. Not good on abstract topics, he is dismissive of what he calls airy-fairy stuff. He trusts his five senses and is limited by the information they provide him with – this is his domain and beyond that he's on shaky ground. This is a no-nonsense kind of guy, with oodles of common sense and a level head.

Whether or not he is classically good looking – and the majority of Taurean men are – he will have a pleasing demeanour and tremendous sex appeal. His attractiveness also lies in his attention to detail. Well groomed, he takes care of his appearance and the way he presents himself. His clothes will be immaculate and coordinated and his shoes polished. He'll have an air of confidence about him that comes from all this preparation and adds to his allure. Whether his dress is smart or casual he'll look great and know it. Some Taurus men have been accused of being a dandy and most will have a vain streak. Not all will manage the whole grooming package but will nevertheless give special attention to some aspect of their appearance. They may take exceptional pride in the way they shave their sideburns for instance, which will always be impeccable, or they'll be one of the few men who exfoliate and use face creams. Whatever, it betrays the relationship these men have to their reflection in the mirror. It's not that there is anything wrong with this; perhaps more men should develop the care regime Mr Taurus has adopted.

The footballer and England captain, David Beckham, exemplifies these aspects of Taurus, with his expensive designer clothes and frequent changes of hairstyle. He is certainly concerned with his image as well as his fitness and this winning combination has enabled him to secure some lavish sponsorship deals not to mention female – and male – attention.

However, not all Taurus men care about their appearance to this extent. They come in several varieties including a more traditionally macho type, who only shaves every other day and enjoys his stubble. This man exemplifies the no-nonsense attitude to life and is totally unpretentious and without guile. He doesn't like fancy food or wine and prefers plain, wholesome fare. He's a steak and chips bloke.

The Taurus man's practical skills means that many develop trades, such as building, painting and decorating and carpentry, where their tactile and design sensitivity are put to good use. In these jobs they find the physical effort and results satisfying – an illustration of the down-to-earth attributes of this sign. Many are artists, designers and craftsmen, too, who enjoy seeing their creations take shape and take pride in their realisation.

The Taurus man has an appreciation of wood, its grain, colour and vibrancy and many become expert in how to use it. As a furniture designer/maker or carpenter his feel for his materials puts him in a league of his own. His standards and finishing touches come from his fine aesthetic sensitivity.

As an artist, the Taurus man's speciality may well be

sculpture, as he understands and is aware of form. Carving and chipping away at stone or wood suits him temperamentally. Equally, he can be found working in one of the many applications of design or in the fashion or music industries. Brian Eno, David Byrne, Steve Winwood and Roy Orbison are all Taureans who have had considerable and long-lasting musical success.

Dance and choreography are other possibilities, as Taurean men can move gracefully and may well have a good sense of rhythm. Hairdressing is a further option that can suit him well, as it relies on an aesthetic yet practical eye. Not that he's limited to the above by any means, he could just as well work in other spheres, even as a banker, where he relies primarily on his pragmatic, sensible attitude. Whatever path he follows, he has at his disposal a practical mind, a keen tactile awareness and an appreciation of texture, colour and style.

Such a man is very attractive to the many women who see men who can put up shelves as 'real men'. Even those Taurean men who don't work with their hands can usually manage enough DIY to impress their loved ones. He is happy to oblige with this kind of stereotypical expectation.

Ferminism and women's equal rights have bypassed the Taurus man. This is definitely not the 'new man' who is supposed to have emerged out of the women's movement. If, for instance, he helps around the home, it's because of his good manners, not because he's heard it's now politically correct to do so. This is among the least liberated signs and he is likely to hold traditional assumptions regarding his role in life. Unless his consciousness has been forcibly raised he has a conventional view of the division of labour within a live-in relationship too. Certain tasks he sees as his and the rest is up to his partner and simply not part of his agenda.

When it comes to a sexual relationship, the Taurus man operates on a primitive level. It's not that he lacks sophistication, it's just that he is extremely possessive and territorial around his partner. Territorial implies conquered land and that is how he sees a mate. He's wooed and won and now she or he belongs to him. A gay man will by and large exhibit the same characteristics in his relationships as a heterosexual man. He expects total loyalty and fidelity and is unable to abide anything less.

The Taurus man is jealous with a capital J and there's nothing that can trigger his rage more than if he suspects his partner of infidelity. Were a partner to be unfaithful this would be sheer torture for him and would continue to distress him for months even years after. It is very unlikely a relationship would survive what is for him a devastating betrayal. Yet all this upset may not feel very flattering to his partner, who is seen as a violated possession, rather than as someone in his or her own right and separate to him.

While the Taurus man sees complete fidelity as his right, in fact as a basic requirement, he may not be one hundred per cent faithful himself. He has some interesting definitions of fidelity, which are rather one-sided. However he is faithful in certain respects, his partner remains central to his life and he doesn't place that in jeopardy, no matter what he gets up to elsewhere. For him, regular sex is a necessity but there doesn't have to be an emotional involvement. Sex and love may well be intertwined in his main relationship, but he can usually separate them from one another and enjoy sex for its own sake elsewhere and, because love is not involved, he deems it doesn't count.

That said, a partner can insist on a pledge from the Taurus man that he is capable of respecting, especially if it is made very clear from the outset. He is loyal it's just that *exactly* what that covers needs to be spelled out. He may not see an occasional one-night stand as a problem unless he's told very specifically that it is. If his relationship is unhappy and sexually unfulfilling and yet he decides to stay, usually for reasons of security or stability – although he will also stay for his children – he is then highly likely to have a long-term additional relationship in the wings. He would not survive without it. A close physical relationship is as essential to him as the air that he breathes.

Besides having strong sexual desires a Taurus man also has a developed sensuality and enjoys stroking and caressing his loved one. He knows what pleases and is a considerate lover. His attitude to the body, both his own and his partner's is matter-of-fact. He understands muscle tension and what is needed to release it; he may actually work with the body, as a masseur, or in some other kind of body-work and is more than comfortable with all shapes and sizes, blemishes and imperfections. He's a realist and is not fooled into thinking, by the airbrushed pictures in magazines, that this is how anyone actually looks. This can be liberating for his partner, who can find his attitude of acceptance enables them to relax.

Notwithstanding the provisos above, a Taurus man does make a steadfast and devoted partner. When in a happy relationship he is emotionally constant and available and stands by his mate through thick and thin; he is not one to be daunted by difficulties. In fact, if his loved one is having problems, he is more there than ever. He is supportive and involved and a genuinely 'good sort'.

For those looking for a mate to have children with, the Taurus man is a particularly good prospect. His creative side comes into its own as a father and he fosters his children's creative interests, encouraging them with artistic projects that he'll be more than willing to help them with. He's a dad who likes nothing better than hanging out with his offspring; inventive and stimulating when it comes to things to do, he takes them to art galleries, museums and the theatre as well as the football. Even when they are tiny, he does his share of the child care. His steadfast nature means that whatever happens in his relationship, he maintains a relationship with his children. This father won't walk away. In fact, in the event of a split, he might well fight for custody. He's more than capable of heading a single-parent family.

An ideal family man, the Taurus male is affectionate and patient with his children. The fact that he's rarely in a hurry, which has its drawbacks in some areas of life, means he has plenty of time for his family and is there, in his solid, steady way, when he's needed.

The Taurus man is not that forthcoming with words – his communication is often of the non-verbal kind. That's one of the reasons why sex is so important to him – it's emotionally deeply reassuring. He is kind and thoughtful and shows his partner affection in concrete and tangible ways, by doing things that he knows pleases and by offering gifts. He may lavish a new love with expensive presents as a demonstration of the depth of his feelings. Similarly, he appreciates this reciprocated, as evidence that the feelings are mutual. Words do not impress him much. Love tokens don't necessarily have to cost huge amounts, but they must be well thought out and need to speak volumes.

Taurus is a placid sign and this man doesn't get riled easily. He holds his own in a quiet, unobtrusive way and very rarely finds it necessary to raise his voice or make a more vehement stand. However, on the infrequent occasions that he does get angry, he can be really frightening. It takes a lot for this to happen; he might claim he has been extremely provoked, but whatever the circumstances he can seem threatening and intimidating. Partly this is because he's not used to dealing with this kind of extreme feeling and so doesn't manage it well. Once he's cooled down it becomes possible to speak about the incident rationally. This post-mortem is important for everyone – he may want to go silent but he mustn't be allowed to get away with it. He needs to unravel and make sense of his anger, too.

More typically, the Taurus man deals with difficulties by being stubbornly uncooperative. He avoids conflict but refuses to comply in his inimitable fashion. This man is the consummate expert in passive resistance, which often has the effect of driving others to distraction – his nearest and dearest will be in a rage while he remains infuriatingly self-controlled. Then he occupies the moral high ground, without recognising how provocative he has been or that others may even be expressing his anger for him.

The Taurus man can also provoke loved ones through his behaviour by leaving a mess or 'forgetting' certain chores, which are meant to be his responsibility. That's always quite a conundrum to unravel; everyone is ultimately responsible for themselves and their own outbursts, but if a Taurus man finds himself regularly on the end of others' fury, it may have something to do with him. And for those involved who are possibly expressing his disowned anger, this is not an attractive role to be manoeuvred into so try to step back, evaluate and change the situation.

Venus, a feminine planet, rules Taurus and men born under this sign have to establish a male identity that includes attributes traditionally considered feminine, such as a kind and gentle nature, a love of beauty, an aesthetic and sensual sensitivity and strong physical desires. Negative emotions compromise his idea of himself, so he has found strategies to deal with them. He handles love and affection easily; he is an expert in these arenas. This man is reasonable, pleasant and steadfast without in any way being a wimp. Whatever his sexual orientation, this is a manly man, albeit with grace and charm, who is very certain of his masculinity.

The Taurus Woman

The Taurus woman emanates inner serenity and contentment. She is calm and contained and refuses to rush or get into a flap. She epitomises common sense and has a down-to-earth approach to life and people. With her feet firmly on the ground, she can deal with whatever life throws at her – not a lot fazes her. In many ways she is the archetypal earth mother, taking care of everything and everyone around her in a quietly matter-of-fact way. This is an extremely capable and competent woman.

This is one of the most physically attractive signs and the Taurus woman has many admirers. She may be blessed with classical good looks, although her attractiveness may be as much to do with her pleasing manners and ability to relate to others. Her allure also lies in her sensuality and self-containment – this acts as a magnet no matter what her physical attributes actually are.

Unlike some of her sisters, the Taurean woman doesn't seek challenges and is not particularly ambitious. Rather, she is motivated by the need for security and stability in her life. Her identity is bound up with the material world and she invests much of herself in the things she possesses. To say she is materialistic is an understatement and fails to address exactly what material objects represent to her. The objects she owns offer her a sense of security that is her bedrock. She relies on her home and the things in it to provide an emotional anchor; they reflect back to her who she is and are an extension of her identity.

Alongside this, the Taurean woman has impeccable taste and an aesthetic sensitivity, which may not come cheap. Money is attractive to her because of what it can provide. Her attitude to money is realistic; she's not extravagant in a flamboyant way although, because she has a connoisseur's eye, she can spend huge amounts. She recognises and prioritises quality and is not interested or tempted by a bargain if it compromises her standards.

Luxury silk underwear was invented for the Taurus woman, as although other women may buy it too, she really appreciates it and wears it for her own pleasure. Even if she's on a tight budget, she'll have expensive lingerie. She's not impressed by labels as such, but is happy to spend her money on the finest she can afford and appreciates the cut, finish and fabrics of designer clothes. This woman is a class act and invests time, money and thought into her appearance. She'll be on intimate terms with her hairdresser and frequent beauty salons to help make the best of herself.

Comfort and relaxation are important to the Taurus woman and she creates a home environment that provides this for herself and her visitors. This is someone who takes delight in entertaining, who enjoys gathering friends and family together and throws lavish dinner parties. A lot of thought and attention to the practical details go into making her guests comfortable and at ease. The food is exquisite, the table beautifully decorated and the ambience relaxing. It's always a pleasure to be invited to her occasions as nothing is too much trouble. She similarly takes care of her houseguests' every comfort and need, so an overnight stay is always a treat. She is the consummate hostess.

This talent makes the Taurean woman a real asset in her relationships. She offers support and makes social obligations run smoothly, seem effortless and most importantly enjoyable. If heterosexual, her husband may well get promoted on the strength of her dinner parties, which whether or not business-related, are always elegant and gracious. In this way, even if not bringing in an income herself, she contributes to her partner's earning power.

The Taurean woman's choice of a mate is almost certainly influenced by their income, as, for her, this is definitely an added attraction and allows her to have the kind of lifestyle to which she feels entitled. However many are just as interested in generating the money they need for themselves. They are not necessarily expecting a partner to provide them with financial security and there is no way they can be bought. They may crave a comfortable lifestyle but they are quite capable of living simply and humbly if that's all they can afford and still be happy.

Once the Taurus woman's security needs are satisfied she is motivated by the pleasure principle. This is a woman who knows how to relax and enjoy herself and can help those around her to do this, too. She has a talent for putting others at their ease, is amiable, charming, sensuous and tactile, genuinely enjoys the company of others and expresses her affection through touch. One Taurean woman I know always seems to have someone's feet in her hands. She gives foot massages to her nearest and dearest to soothe their stress away, along with her own. For her it's an important avenue of self-expression and communicates her feelings of affection to her friends very directly.

While some Taurean women may work with massage professionally, others simply use it as a natural part of their everyday relating, offering the occasional backrub as a gentle and unobtrusive way of checking in with their loved ones. Once they have their hands on another, they can tune in to how they are.

Although the Taurus woman is found in all walks of life, she is particularly happy when she can use her natural talents. Careers in art, design, fashion, music, cooking and gardening all draw on her strengths. However if she chooses to go in another direction, these aptitudes still remain hers and may be expressed tangentially in her work as well as in her private life.

The Taurus woman doesn't rush into a relationship, mainly because once she has made a commitment she remains extremely loyal. She takes an involvement seriously, is always careful of others' feelings and likes to get to know a prospective partner slowly over time. Until she is certain, she bides her time. She expects to be courted and responds well to tokens of affection. Words do not impress her much; she judges others by how they behave and expects tangible evidence of love.

For Taurus, expensive jewels and gifts symbolise how much she is valued, along with the traditional flowers and chocolates – only make sure they are beautifully-wrapped flowers and luxury chocolates. She won't think much of the kind you can buy in the supermarket.

Once wooed and involved the Taurus woman remains constant in her feelings. Having taken her time, she is among the most steadfast of women and sticks by her partner. Being in a relationship suits her and she settles in for the long haul. As she is an extremely sensual, tactile being, she needs the reassurance of a close physical connection. This includes sexual intimacy as well as lots of lounging around together, wrapped around each other and casually touching while reading, listening to music or watching television. The worst thing a partner can do to her is to withdraw physical affection. While arguments won't destroy her love, being shut out might. Excluding the Taurus woman undermines her confidence and leaves her feeling insecure. She is prone to jealousy at the best of times – this is a very possessive woman. It's not because she distrusts her mate; it's simply her nature to hold on tightly to the things and people she loves. She recognises the extent to which her emotional security is invested in her relationship and is not about to jeopardise this. It's a basic survival instinct for her to guard and protect those things that she relies upon.

This is a fixed sign and as such the Taurus woman doesn't like change. She prefers things to stay as they are and any kind of modification can unnerve her. In particular she objects to others imposing their innovations upon her. She objects if her routine or schedule is disrupted and she minds the furniture being rearranged, let alone other more radical alterations, like the house being redecorated and new items being introduced. She feels safe and secure when the things around her remain as they have always been. Change may be the spice of life for some people, but it threatens our Taurus woman and fills her with dread. She thrives on sameness and predictability.

The Taurean woman's reliability and dependability has to be understood with the above in mind. A partner needs to know the extent that her psychological well-being rests on her life being stable. She is steadfast because that's what she needs. She won't let her mate down, but can he or she promise the same? That's the deal she seeks.

An unhappy or unfulfilled Taurus woman is prone to weight problems. She can struggle with her size anyway, simply because she loves food, and rich 'bad for you' food to boot, but her vanity ordinarily helps her keep the pounds off. However, it doesn't take much for whatever regime she has to collapse and once she gets despondent she may find herself on a downward spiral. Her main difficulty is that she uses food as a comfort. In her favour, the plump Taurean is still going to be attractive and at least she is not suppressing her appetite, it's just a little misdirected.

Some Taurean women do exist on a strict diet; it's the only way they know how to control their tendency to over-indulge. But while they may keep their slim figure, they are far less relaxed to be around. By denying the sensual pleasure food affords them, they can become uptight in other areas of their lives, too. Before getting involved, take her out for a meal and make sure she clears her plate. However, the majority does not fall into either of the above categories and have a healthy liking for wholesome food.

Taurus is a fertile and productive sign and this woman is likely to see motherhood as part of her destiny. More than most women, having children is an important aspect of her creative self-expression. As a mother she comes into her own. Her fortitude, patience and tolerance make her innately equipped for this role. From babies in a scream-ing paddy through the tantrums of the 'terrible twos' to the belligerent teenager, she remains calm in the face of challenging behaviour and takes each awkward phase in her stride. Her pragmatic approach is ideal; she can cope with her offspring's various demands and provides constancy and stability, giving them a secure base.

The Taurus mother is likely to be a stay-at-home mum. She immerses herself wholeheartedly in her children's upbringing and welfare, investing a huge amount emotionally in their lives. This becomes her life and most children thrive on the attention she offers, especially in the early years. Later, as her children mature and no longer need her in the same way, she may have problems adjusting. She may well go on having children, spread out over many years, to stall this problem.

Nevertheless, the Taurean woman is confronted by the 'empty nest syndrome' at some point and may well suffer acutely at this time, especially if she hasn't worked or had much of a life outside of her family, and she will struggle with feelings of redundancy until grandchildren come along. Then she is back in her element, ever available to help out making an ideal grandmother.

This does not mean that the Taurus woman has to have children to fulfill her potential. Those who choose not to have children direct this powerful creative force in other ways and may well achieve a great deal in some artistic endeavour. Family life suits her, she's a great homemaker and mother and an asset as a wife or partner but all these skills get far more recognition in the world of work, where she is likely to excel too. Never underestimate her – as we've already seen, this is a very capable woman.

Famous Taurean women include Cher, Barbra Streisand and Audrey Hepburn. All beautiful in their different ways. Cher seems to believe that her looks define her worth as she periodically goes under the surgeon's knife to enhance her attractiveness and attempts to halt the ageing process. She has publicly spoken of how much she dislikes growing older. This is not that typical of this sign, as ordinarily one of their gifts is to be happy in their own skin but then, in her profession she is subject to some extraordinary pressures to stay looking young and beautiful. Barbra Streisand has reached the top of her profession and her expensive taste is clearly visible. Both Cher and Barbra Streisand have remarkable singing voices, a Taurean gift that they have made the most of. Audrey Hepburn had the steady gaze, self-containment and sensuality typical of Taurean women and was blessed with exceptional beauty. While not all Taurus women will have the talent or opportunities that these three have had, they do typify the grace and elegance of those born under this sign.

For those thinking of getting involved with a Taurus woman, remember that this will be no light-hearted dalliance; this is serious and she really is quite a catch. The stakes are high because she expects a lot and has an awful lot to offer.

The Taurus Child

The Taurus child is likely to be particularly adorable. These are good-natured, placid children who get on easily with others. Genuinely cooperative, they fit in happily with other family members. They are kind and want others to think well of them – they need to be liked. As well as having delightful personalities, they are often blessed with chocolate-box good looks; their features being symmetrical and well balanced. Every parent thinks their own child is gorgeous, but in this case others will concur. These are the winners of the beautiful baby competitions, with the potential to be child models.

Taurean children are charm personified and use their powers of persuasion to get what they want, however they lack the assertiveness of some of the other signs and rely on others responding positively to them. The saying 'Love makes the world go round' is the inner assumption they are born with. Their basic surmise is that the world is a benign place and that it will provide for them. Many adults spend hours chanting such positive affirmations, but this child comes into the world with it already in place and it takes a lot to dislodge this confidence. It's their gift.

Born under a Venus-ruled sign, the planet associated with love and attraction, the Taurean child instinctively seeks to connect and relate to others. They are an asset to any group as they minimise conflict and strengthen the harmonious strands; bringing emphasis to what is working in the group. This is an innate talent that stays with them throughout their life. They aren't aggressive or competitive and depend on their ability to draw to them the things and people they want in life.

Taurean children's main strength when it comes to dealing with adversity is their endurance. They can tolerate a lot and simply sit out the bad times and wait for the good ones to return. They are stoical and put up with a lot without their fundamental belief in the goodness of life being dented. This is all part of their calm and easygoing temperament.

With a steady and dependable air, Taurean children develop their above-average common sense early in life and can be trusted not to behave in a silly or irresponsible way. They have a practical and realistic outlook that allows them to assess situations and not to take foolish risks. Parents can trust them to behave sensibly and to keep to agreements. They go about tasks in a methodical way, taking their time – they hate to be rushed.

They say, statistically, that girl babies smile sooner and more often than boys, indicative that the cultural gender divide kicks in very early in life. The Taurus girl uses her smile to draw a favourable response from the word go, realising right from the start that she's on to a winner. She can wrap her father round her little finger. Aware of her feminine charms, which she exploits, she possesses girlish guile and is mindful of her effect on others and how to solicit attention. Appreciative of clothes from a very young

age, she may well prefer pretty dresses to more service-
able jeans. She's likely to show a precocious interest in
make-up and spends hours with her friends in front of the
mirror, experimenting with hairstyles and looks. For her,
this is a creative activity. She decorates and adorns herself
and becomes skilful at creating a favourable impression.

Not all girls born under the sign of Taurus become obsessed
with their appearance. And while some boys have a vain
streak too, this is likely to develop in boys well after puberty
begins. This is a self-conscious time for all adolescents, but
because these youngsters have already come to depend on
their looks, it's not surprising they mind more than most
when the teenage spots erupt, the hair goes lank and greasy
and all the other awkward signs of hormonal development
are visible. Once a teenage Taurus becomes sexually aware,
then they do all they can to enhance their sex appeal. They
recognise the value in being found attractive.

Much has been said of the Taurus child's calm temperament, but they can occasionally lose their temper and cause
a spectacular scene. This won't happen often, but when it
does it may leave them upset for some considerable time.
In fact, like the bull that represents this sign, once enraged,
they find it hard to stop. The bull is a placid creature and
doesn't charge often but when it gets going and picks up
speed it just keeps going. As with the bull, stand clear if
they are on the rampage and leave them until they are
spent. Even with a two-year-old, if at all possible leave him
or her to emerge from their tantrum in their own time.
Whatever their age, they'll be keen to make amends, once
the catharsis is over.

Many Taurus children are nature lovers and enjoy
gardening, animals and the outdoors. If it is possible, allow
them their own patch of garden in which to grow flowers
or vegetables of their choice. Many ask to own a pet, which
they are fairly good at looking after, although they may
not be that reliable when it comes to the less pleasant

aspects of keeping a pet, the things that rely on a sense of duty and responsibility, rather than pleasure. What they love is to groom a pet – they enjoy the physical contact and emotional bond of owning an animal. So, something warm and furry is recommended, rather than a reptile, for instance. A pet is showered with affection and these children are amply rewarded by the way their beloved cat, dog or guinea pig recognises and acknowledges them.

Taurean children may also show a keen interest in other aspects of nature and enjoy country walks, collecting seeds like conkers and acorns – even getting them to sprout; identifying birds, trees and butterflies; keeping caterpillars and bugs and watching them develop and metamorphose. This may become a lifelong pleasure and is to be encouraged with age-appropriate books to assist this process, possibly by even having a nature table at home.

Taurean children are both creative and practical and may enjoy all kinds of artistic activities. Offer them paints, crayons and large sheets of paper to make pictures; scissors, glue, household cartons and coloured paper to make collages and model-making; clay and Plasticine for modelling with; and a sandpit with lots of toys to use in it. They have a natural affinity with colour and design, relish squelching clay through their fingers and may end up later in life working with one of the above media.

The Taurean child may also have a musical ear, so provide them with instruments to play and be prepared to pay for lessons if they show aptitude. Introduce them to a wide variety of music throughout their childhood and encourage them to sing. Dance, too, could be an important avenue for their self-expression and something they have a real feel for. Again, foster any latent talent, as this, too, may be something they later do for a living. Even if they don't grow up to follow any of these interests, they are likely to enjoy them throughout their life.

More than most, Taurean children like to own things

and have control over their possessions. These children do not want to share their toys and object strongly if anyone touches their things. Even as a baby, they can make a huge fuss if another child picks up one of their toys. From the beginning, if it is at all possible, they need a room to themselves. And as they get a bit older, it's important to them that nobody enters without permission or interferes with the way they have arranged their bits and pieces. If someone else cleans their room, they need to remember this.

The Taurean child's things, even if they are sea shells found on the beach, all lined up in a particular way, or feathers in a jar, mean a lot to them. They invest feelings of security in these objects and feel threatened if they are moved. Later in life they may well collect other objects that have real monetary value but the point remains the same – their things are of value to them and this should be respected.

Many families do require a certain amount of give and take and think it's important that their children learn to share but, with Taurean children, what's important is that they have choices. They need to be persuaded to share and to see that it's to their advantage, if it all looks like one-way traffic they won't be keen. It's also important to them that others use their possessions respectfully – they take great care of their things, so won't take kindly if others trash them.

The Taurus child doesn't cope well with change of any kind. They derive safety and security when life remains the same. Regular meals and bedtime and predictable activities help them to feel they have some control over their world, at a time when they don't actually have that much.

Depending on their age and the circumstances, moving home can be traumatic for a Taurean child. As items are packed away they can feel as if they are losing them forever and become distraught. The best way to ease this passage, which is likely to be a time of high stress for parents, too, is to involve them as much as possible beforehand. Take them to see the new place more than once if this is at all feasible and include them in discussions. Don't assume that because the new home has advantages, like a bigger or better room, or garden, that they'll be pleased; they may well need to grieve over the loss of their old home, no matter what the future benefits may be.

It's a good idea to give the Taurus child pocket money fairly early in life. These children covet material possessions and enjoy spending, so they can learn a lot by having a small amount of money to manage. It's important that parents don't condemn their acquisitive nature as, for good or ill, it's an intrinsic characteristic. Encouraging them to collect and treasure the things that they can afford and to save up for the big items that they have their eye on teaches them some financial sense and helps them to recognise the costs involved.

Taurean children can easily equate their value and self-esteem with owning the best bicycle in the neighbourhood, so it's essential that these issues be dealt with sensitively. Parents have to strike a happy balance between not pooh-poohing their feelings, while not incessantly giving in to their demands. Parents can feel tyrannised by the constant 'I want', especially when it carries such a strong emotional punch.

Most teenagers want the 'right' brand of trainers or certain desirable labels, which can extend to all manner of things, like mobile phones and watches as well as clothes. This is often led by peer pressure, which has in turn been influenced by advertisers. For the Taurean teenager, a lot can be at stake here and there are some hard lessons to learn, not least about values. The prestige from owning certain items can make them quite desperate to have them.

Parents may have to tread carefully here, while not being railroaded into spending unseemly amounts. A good compromise is one in which parents pay the amount that they would ordinarily, for a comparable non-designer item, and the Taurean child in question pays the balance. That way, they can begin to question the desirability of such goods without feeling deprived.

All children need cuddles, but the Taurus child needs them in abundance. These are particularly sensual, tactile children and need the constant reassurance of physical affection. Words are not enough. Parents are advised to let them climb on to their lap as and when they want and occasionally allow them into their bed at night – they can't be given too many snuggles. They will return this affection in bucket loads and mature into confident and loving adults.

Take care with a Taurus child that they don't develop too much of a sweet tooth. These little ones love their grub and have a healthy appetite, usually for the things that are actually good for them but if they are offered sweets as a reward, then problems can arise. They have a tendency to become over-fond of food so it's important not to do anything to encourage this. Once sweet things become associated with love, later difficulties may emerge in life.

Those who do gain weight are usually compensating for some lack in their life; this Taurean child may feel a deficiency of physical affection. So, give them massive doses of affection, as early inoculation will give them lifelong protection against over-eating. Again, for the parents, a delicate balance has to be struck as an anxious attitude to the amount of calories consumed can also cause later problems. It's hard in our society, with its fear and loathing of fat, not to be infected by culturally unhelpful attitudes to the body and pass these on to children.

Taurus children need harmonious surroundings and feel distressed by quarrels and rows. If they are born into a situation where the parents are volatile, they can find this particularly difficult. Obviously parents have the right to self-expression but avoiding World War Three in front of these children will undoubtedly help them. In a scenario where one parent is passive, while the other chucks the plates, they tend to identify with the quieter parent and feel estranged from the more dramatic one, blaming them for all the strife. Such a child can grow to fear this parent, even if there is no threat of actual violence. All children suffer in a violent home, but the Taurean child can react badly to even a mild discord as it challenges their fundamental inner belief that the world is a happy and safe place.

In fact, the Taurus child dislikes all kinds of friction. They make a stand in the most unobtrusive way, using non-confrontational methods like simply being resistant. These children are as stubborn as they come and can successfully refuse to cooperate – just because they dislike a showdown doesn't mean they are a pushover. They have a way of staying pleasant no matter what and manage to get what they want through a quiet insistence.

When there is a conflict of interest, Taurean children are more likely to become silent and withdrawn than to shout. They adopt an unrelenting persistence in the pursuit of their desire; they won't give up or let go. Whereas some children can be distracted and soon forget, this won't work with them. Finding a compromise is the key. If an agreement is reached, they will accept this provided they have input and are listened to. Don't assume all is well if they go quiet, make sure that they really have come to terms with the settlement.

This is a Venus-ruled sign and boys are not necessarily going to want to play football and partake in traditional male activities. Encourage boys to develop their so-called feminine side and, along with the girls, they may well end up working in a creative medium that does not compromise their masculinity one bit. This is a fertile and productive sign and, as such, both boys and girls have tremendous aesthetic and artistic potential – surely something to foster and be proud of.

3

Gemini
The Twins

May 21st to June 20th

A mutable air sign, ruled by Mercury

Introducing Gemini

Geminis are recognisable by their quick wit and quirky, individualistic take on life. They possess a wonderful sense of humour and are known for their outrageous, offbeat responses. Their humour rests in part on their ability to see situations with a degree of detachment – from an out-of-the-ordinary perspective. With powers of observation that cut through any pretentious niceties, their comments can be sharp, revealing, accurate and extremely amusing. Never bound by the normal restraints of polite society, they are irreverent, playful, mischievous and great fun to be around.

With a highly-strung, restless, nervous disposition, Geminis are alert, bright, quick on the uptake and have a low boredom threshold. Above all else, they seek mental stimulation and a varied existence and like to keep on the move, circulating and mixing with a wide range of people. They have friends across the ages and from all walks of life and a packed social calendar.

Mentally agile and naturally inquisitive, Geminis

brighten up any social gathering and draw out the shyest of guests. While they themselves may be shy, they nevertheless strike up conversation simply because others fascinate them. They always have questions to ask and comments to make. It is their abiding interest in others that in turn makes them interesting. There is a quality to the way they listen and the attention they offer others that makes them very attractive.

However, Geminis' curiosity can be misconstrued. Because they cast such a tantalising light on any person or topic that they choose to focus on, others may not know how to interpret this. It may well be found exciting. They can ask awkward, penetrating and personal questions, probing more than is customary in a casual conversation, which can slightly unnerve others, who often respond by opening up and revealing more of themselves than they might ordinarily. When this occurs, others can feel that a special kind of intimacy has been established, which may or may not be justified.

For Gemini, this kind of connection is an everyday occurrence. People do end up confiding in them and telling them their innermost thoughts – they just seem to have that effect on others. But unless Gemini, too, has opened up, then it's probably safe to say they are not actually feeling emotionally involved. It is easy to mistake their curiosity for more than it is, especially when an emotional attachment would be welcomed.

Geminis like to keep up to date with current debates in the news and media. They are undoubtedly knowledgeable and well informed. They have an extensive interest in the arts and will often visit art galleries and exhibitions, the theatre, ballet, opera, concerts and the cinema. Whichever of the arts absorb them, and it's likely to be several, they will read the reviews and know what the critics think of the latest exhibition and performance. Not that these opinions stop them forming their own, but they like to stay abreast of the consensus of opinion, which they can then pitch themselves against.

A desire to know the facts, about others and about the world around them, is a motivating force for Geminis. They are great gatherers of information, some serious and to be used at some point in an article they plan to write, and some that's trivial but of special interest to them. Just as the squirrel gathers and stores his nuts, possibly mislaying the stockpile, possibly never returning to it again, but gaining satisfaction from the garnering, Geminis enjoy collecting data. Some keep files of newspaper cuttings on various subjects, which they rarely refer to, but like to have on hand and available, just in case they need them one day.

Similarly, Geminis collect reference books, so that whatever they need to know is at their fingertips. Many personalise these and they'll be full of markers, taking them back to important and relevant points. Some Geminis resemble a walking encyclopaedia, as they retain myriad facts in their brains. Games like Trivial Pursuit, which rely on a wide general knowledge and quiz shows, like the TV programme *Who Wants to be a Millionaire?* are made for them.

Whatever generation they hail from, Geminis take to new technology with enthusiasm and interest. Thoroughly modern and up-to-date, they are never afraid to embrace the latest ideas and keep abreast of new developments and remain conversant with the latest terminology. They welcome anything that supplies them with information and allows them to communicate with others more easily. Their homes contain many of the latest gadgets, they have sophisticated electronics and, unlike some, they know how to use them. They may well have their own website and certainly appreciate the significance of the dot com industries.

Geminis are afraid of feeling bored and rely on a variety of media with which to make sure that doesn't happen. Avid readers, they usually have a novel or two on the go, which they carry around with them. Typically, they'll carry a portable CD player, too, in order to listen to their favourite sounds on headphones. Besides this they carry a notebook and pen, just in case they want to make a note of something or other.

When driving, the car stereo will be on and, as they have wide musical tastes, they have a large selection available, usually well organised, too, so they can readily locate whatever they are in the mood to hear that day. They enjoy the radio as well, including plays and may listen to story tapes when undergoing a long journey.

Dreadful gossips, Geminis love to exchange news and bits and pieces of tittle-tattle. Never tell them a secret, as they can be like a sieve when it comes to holding a confidence and it's bound to get passed on, even if only to their best friend – which in their mind doesn't count. They love being the one in the know but in order to demonstrate this they have to spill the beans. They want to be the one who holds all the information, even if it's nothing important. If they are not kept up-to-date with the latest on the office scandal or family row they feel excluded and marginalised.

Geminis can be hard to pin down. Agreements that others might see as final are renegotiated at the eleventh hour. Their plans change minute by minute and arrangements can be left hanging, as they like to keep their options open. This may not be for the reasons others fear – that they're waiting to see if they get a better offer – but simply because they hate feeling boxed in unnecessarily.

Those born under the fixed signs (Taurus, Leo, Scorpio and Aquarius) can find these last-minute changes upsetting and annoying. However, for the Geminian, who can adjust to a new plan at the drop of a hat, this kind of juggling act is the staff of life. This is the most agile sign of the zodiac and while some may be actual gymnasts, most demonstrate their gymnastics in their lifestyle and in the mental sphere.

Speaking of lifestyle, Geminis notoriously cram their schedule to bursting point. They run themselves ragged, trying to fit more into one day than some signs would attempt in a week. When out and about, they go from one social arrangement to the next and think nothing of it. A shopping trip, followed by a lunch date, followed by a visit to a gallery and then the cinema with friends is not uncommon. They barely allow themselves time to breathe and do not consider that they might need time to process and digest each experience before they go on to the next. And they suffer for it.

Being around a Gemini and trying to keep up can be exhausting. It takes them a long time to learn to pace themselves and to recognise that such a thing as overload exists, let alone that it might be causing them stress. However, even when they have understood this, they still tend to overstretch themselves, trying to get certain chores, errands and social obligations 'over with' so that their time is then their own, but wearing themselves out in the process.

When cooped up or restricted, Geminis can experience 'cabin fever' and a desperate need to stretch their legs and get out. They are good at hovering; at the ready to be off, unsettled which in turn can be unsettling for those they live with. The air we breathe circulates all the time, that is its nature, and as an air sign, Geminis similarly need to move freely and circulate. Owning a means of transport, even if it's a pair of rollerblades or a bicycle, gives them a sense of freedom. Being able to come and go as they please and not have to answer to others is also important.

It follows that Geminis are particularly good at multi-tasking. It's the logical extension of their flexibility. Their normal mode of operation is to have three or more activities on the go at any one time, turning to whatever's most urgent and prioritising it in that moment before shifting gear and focusing their attention elsewhere. They tend to have a short attention span, so this switching back and forth between various activities suits them. It maintains their interest and keeps their low boredom threshold at bay. The idea that there might be too much going on at once is foreign to them and they are completely at home in the quick changing world we now inhabit.

The symbol for Gemini is the twins and many born under this sign feel a longing for their mythical 'lost twin' and spend much of their life searching for this elusive soul mate. Those who do find their 'other half' have a long and happy life together, however these are in the minority because it's a bit more complicated than that. Even those who appear to be happy and settled from the outside are aware of this inner ache for their missing soul mate.

Geminis in a committed relationship can feel plagued by these feelings of dissatisfaction and struggle with their yearnings for something more, something wondrous. It's easy then for them to focus on the shortcomings in their current relationship and wonder whether to break up and continue looking for a better match. At some point they have to realise that this ideal 'other half' doesn't exist – it's a fantasy – and stop the search. Those who keep looking can suffer from melancholy, as their quest is endless and never satisfied.

A partner is invariably pained by this dynamic, feeling acutely his or her own insufficiency. It's hard not to get caught up in Geminis longing and most partners simply wish that they could provide the magic elixir and fulfil the dream. Unless Geminis are able to contain their disappointment, they can find that their relationships fall apart.

These Geminis can go through several failed relationships before they realise the problem is not 'out there' but an inner one of discontent. It's not that there is something necessarily wrong with their successive partners, just their own inability to commit to something real and available. They can't bear the anguish of sacrificing the fantasy of a perfect love. A life scattered with broken partnerships is ironically a less painful option, as that way, the dream remains intact. Some prefer a lonely existence rather than risk a compromise, as they see it.

Compromise is arguably an attribute of maturity, a recognition that relationships are not quite as depicted in the fairy stories; that they involve give and take and hard work. Geminis inability to compromise can be seen as a refusal to grow up. They remain idealistic and shy of too much reality. While this may all sound a bit dramatic, these individuals do have a penchant for the Gothic romantic melodrama.

Gemini is a dual sign and they have a capacity for more than one love, simultaneously. This is as likely to be an interest as another person, so they may love tennis or the novel they are writing and a partner may experience these interests as rivals and feel excluded. And their involvement elsewhere, albeit ostensibly non-threatening, can be passionate and all-consuming. The key to all this is that it's more likely to be a 'mental affair' as opposed to a physical relationship.

Geminis can dedicate their life to the search for knowledge. Some are perpetual students, going from one course of study to the next. Because they enjoy learning it's no hardship, although it can have financial consequences, particularly as they often fail to capitalise on their qualifications and their subsequent earning power. Before the course they are on has finished, they may already have their sights set on what they'd like to study next, which may not be a natural progression from the subject currently being studied – it may be at a complete tangent. They are not necessarily academic or intellectual either; they could be studying almost anything, horticulture, shiatsu, aromatherapy . . .

So, typically, Geminis do not follow a conventional career path. It may take financial responsibilities to get them to stick at any one job, as without these, they won't see the point. They value their time and freedom over and above any money they can earn. Often, they'll be in a situation where they need a job that allows them to have time off in order to pursue other activities, so prefer to work part-time. There is nothing wrong with this but they are less likely to get promoted. Work is not their priority, doing the things that interest them is, along with having sufficient funds to afford these activities.

Geminis are neither materialistic nor goal-oriented. They live in and for the moment and the idea of making sacrifices for some nebulous future does not appeal. They can manage with surprisingly little money and still not appear poor, as they are good at juggling their finances. They are not against having money in the bank but it is not something they need in order to feel secure. Their priority is to create an interesting life.

So, what with chopping and changing their work, studying subjects that do not provide career opportunities and only working part-time if they can afford to, Geminis may not have a glittering career. Inadvertently, they can be extremely successful when they are involved in something they love, but achieving goals is not what life's about for them.

Any position that requires the dissemination of information and relies on communication skills suit Geminis, as this is what they excel at. Because they find it hard to sit still for long periods, they do not do well in jobs that require this – they will be forever inventing excuses as to why they need to leave their seat. A job that is varied, involves travel, contact with others and flexible hours is ideal.

Geminis are good in any work that involves exchanging ideas with people. Depending on their level of education and qualifications, they can work as a broadcaster, journalist, editor, teacher or lecturer, librarian or in a book shop, as a pilot or air steward, receptionist, in public relations, in IT, as a TV presenter, a travel guide or as a translator, to name just a few.

Geminis do not usually find themselves in the role of employer, it's far too much responsibility. However, if they do end up for one reason or another in this position, they make undemanding and flexible bosses, who care about their employees lives and are prepared to discuss any special requirements they might have regarding working arrangements. What they need themselves they are more than happy to offer to others. They help to create a lively and relaxed workplace. While they may not hold authority in the conventional sense, they do command respect, as they are well liked.

As an employee, Gemini pushes the boundaries regarding everything imaginable, from timekeeping, to lunch breaks, to designated holidays and how these are counted. They are rarely wholeheartedly involved in their work; it is usually a means to an end and as such, they can be quite a challenge to manage. They may well be very good at their job, as they are quick on the uptake and can adapt quite easily to the demands of any particular position. Their boss would do best to view them as a very able employee, who may not stay for that long but will brighten and liven up the place while they're there.

Whatever Geminis end up doing, they bring to their work a wide and broad-based knowledge, so their views can open up new possibilities of how to carry out any particular task. They are inventive and original and bring a cross-fertilisation of ideas from other disciplines to their current position.

The Gemini TV presenter, Cilla Black, typifies this sign. Mature in years yet still young in spirit, she remains high profile and relies on her wit and intelligence. She is a little risqué but, as a presenter on prime-time television, stops at anything too rude. The late Bob Monkhouse, who wrote most of his own material, is typically Gemini, with his sprightly irreverent humour. Gemini Sandra Bernhard, the US comedienne, pushes the boundaries of what is acceptable that bit more and while some find her quite hilarious, she's too outlandish for mainstream tastes.

Not all Geminis want such a profile but these multitalented individuals, with their enquiring minds and openness to whatever comes their way can reinvent themselves many times over and create an out-of-the-ordinary life. Variety and stimulation matter most and work is only ever a small part of this. Their family, friends and interests are always going to be more important. Don't be fooled into thinking that they've simply not got their act together. They may well have worked it all out far better than most.

Negative Gemini

Any of the Geminian characteristics already outlined can tip towards a negative expression but what dogs their reputation most is Geminis mercurial nature. These individuals have always suffered a bad press regarding their honesty and, while this is frequently undeserved, they still remain one of the least trusted signs. Partly this is because they have the capacity to unsettle others through their elusive, playful manners – and no one likes not knowing where they stand. Others may feel played with, as the butt of the joke rather than part of it and feel wary of Gemini on these grounds alone.

Sometimes, a small white lie just trips off the tip of Gemini's tongue and is used as a harmless excuse mainly when they can't be bothered to go into the full story. For them it's expedient. It's not malicious, they just don't always feel a compulsion to explain themselves. It does mean others don't always feel secure around them; they know something doesn't quite add up but don't know the extent of it. Some Geminis lie by omission, they can be evasive, allowing others to believe what they want to believe and, if it suits them they'll allow a misconstrued understanding to remain in circulation.

While most Geminis are fundamentally honest or bend the truth in a subtle and non-malicious way, some do deliberately conceal the truth and can be spectacularly dishonest. The worst of this type lies for gain, deliberately misleading others in order to exploit them. The con artist, with a silvery tongue, who talks others into parting with their money for an improbable and unlikely product or scheme and is most convincing in the moment, is an example of these negative traits taken to the extremes.

Most Geminis have the gift of the gab and when this is coupled with an unscrupulous and immoral streak, they can become experts at ripping others off. Those who take this path can usually justify what they are doing through their strange, convoluted thinking, whereby they deny the truth of their behaviour to themselves. In fact they are self-deluded and can hold a distorted view of what rightly belongs to whom. In extreme cases, their grip on reality may be tenuous – they become fantasists, living in their own made-up world. However these are a minority. Geminis have an inventive and original way of thinking, which can be used for good or ill. Most channel this talent into socially acceptable outlets.

This Gemini talent is demonstrated by the conjuror, pulling rabbits from a hat and producing doves seemingly out of nowhere and the card sharp, who with sleight of hand produces the desired Ace of Spades. No matter that most do not perform tricks, this serves as a metaphor of the deft skill often possessed by those born under this sign. They have a touch of the magician about them and can cast a magical allure.

Geminis thrive on good communication. Although, on the whole, they make good listeners, they can also inter-rupt, especially when excited by the conversation. They can't always contain their quick responses and may miss the point others are trying to make by finishing their sentences for them.

Geminis can have problems, too, in admitting that they don't know the answer to a question or solution to a problem and will invent one on the spur of the moment, rather than admit their ignorance. Just as in some cultures, when travel directions are requested, it's considered rude not to oblige, so travellers may be directed in entirely the wrong direction.

Occasionally Geminis can assume that anything they find interesting is necessarily of interest to a partner and so share their observations unreservedly regardless of how mundane and banal they might be. Not everyone will appreciate being read snippets from the local newspaper. Such an individual monopolises a loved one's mind, filling it with trivia. It's ironic, given their own low-boredom threshold, that at times they can be rather boring themselves.

Geminis pride themselves on their intellect and their capacity to behave rationally, to keep a perspective and to be able to think things through. They evaluate people and situations with their minds and brains, rather than with their instincts and feelings. This can get them into difficulties in areas where detached thought is no longer required, such as matters of the heart. Within their relationships they can have problems with the feeling realm.

More often than not, Geminis experience an erratic connection to their feelings, with their emotions often overwhelming and destabilising them, rather than their feelings being an inner certainty that they remain constantly aligned with. Either they are cut off and disassociated or awash with emotion. Ask a Gemini what they are feeling, and they'll reply, 'I think I feel . . .' They approach their feelings via their minds, which can create interpersonal problems.

Geminis need to *know* can equally become a negative trait. They can be the know-alls, who know nothing, in so far as they have the facts but no real comprehension. And they can delude themselves into thinking that facts are all that's important, rather than a deeper understanding. Instead of a conversation, they can relentlessly fire questions at others, gathering information as a substitute for intimacy. They confuse knowing things about someone's life with intimacy and, provided they are up-to-date with what's going on for their friend, they believe they are close.

At their worst, Gemini can pursue what amounts to a form of interrogation while revealing virtually nothing of themselves. It is used as a ploy to deflect others getting near to them. Even when not carried out in an obviously aggressive manner, Geminis are capable of keeping the focus of attention away from themselves, fending off close contact. This can happen at a conscious level, where they have decided they want to keep a particular individual at bay, or it can be unconscious and irrespective of whom they are relating to.

After such vigorous questioning, others can feel stripped down, like an onion that's had one layer after another peeled off until the core is exposed. This is by far the most negative expression of Gemini's idle curiosity.

Those Geminis who are more psychologically sophisticated can couple their inquisitive nature with their analytic mind to powerful effect. Friends may rely on them for their insightful comments and yet there may be a feeling of emptiness in these supposedly close relationships. The task for Gemini is to learn to open up and reveal themselves equally in their friendships. However witty, entertaining and helpful they may be, if the emotional connection is missing or underdeveloped then relationships will ultimately be unrewarding.

A Gemini caught up in the 'lost twin syndrome', may unconsciously employ this distancing tactic, confirming to themselves the hopelessness of their current relationship and the need to keep searching for their soul mate. In fact, this is exactly the opposite of what they ought to do; for greater psychological health, they must become more emotionally available and acknowledge and show their needs, by opening up to those around them.

Gemini is not a sign with a great track record when it comes to fidelity, as they remain essentially free spirits, committing in the moment rather than into eternity. Perhaps the most important criteria when it comes to a partner is that they remain interesting. Not that it's a partner's responsibility to entertain and amuse their Gemini mate, but if life becomes too predictable and humdrum, then trouble looms. A lack of stimulation is experienced as claustrophobic and they may well look elsewhere.

Gemini is both fascinated and repulsed by someone who is more attuned to their inner world and, when intimately involved with such a person, some interesting scenarios ensue. A partner may know what their Gemini mate is feeling before he or she does, picking up the signals and interpreting them. This is something Gemini may become dependent upon, yet resent at the same time. When a loved one can read them so easily, they feel both exposed and reassured. In many ways, the ideal choice for Gemini is someone who can demonstrate another way of being and help them to become less threatened by feelings. Geminis have met their match with such an individual and, if they are so minded, can learn a lot from them. However, they may use their superior ability at rationalising to undermine their partner and they can, if they do this in a sustained way, make a very good job of it. If they feel their way of being is under threat, they revert to what they do best and may then never learn how to tune in to and listen to their feelings.

Gemini's playful nature means that they can also have a tendency to use wit to avoid intimacy, playing the clown, who on the one hand courts attention by being funny, while simultaneously avoiding any real intimacy. Their idea of fun can be cruel and at others' expense, such as making personal comments on the mannerisms, clothes and appearance of others. On these occasions they use their acute observational skills to publicly humiliate. Those who are better connected to their own feelings won't indulge in this, but the variety of Gemini that is woefully out of touch may.

One of Gemini's strategies for coping with emotional difficulties is to become disconnected. They simply split off when it's all too much for them. They may not even realise that this has happened; they just recognise that they've become a bit absent, a bit far away. Usually, they find their own way back, as the emotions subside they can re-inhabit their skin and planet earth. Geminis are sensitive and highly-strung and need to be handled with care. Closeness is not necessarily what they need; they may only be able to tolerate it in small doses.

While in this disassociated state Geminis are impossible to connect with, they avoid eye contact and set up distractions. They can excel at displacement activity at the best of times; finding something to do just as a meal is being served, being late for appointments because they never leave enough time to make the journey comfortably. They always delay leaving the house; there seems to be some last-minute anxiety about the transition into the outside world, which means they 'forget' things or have to go back and check on something. Not surprisingly, this has considerable impact on a Gemini's loved ones. Their lateness can drive a partner to distraction. Even when a mate offers sympathetic understanding and doesn't take it personally, it's hard to manage the inconvenience.

When a Gemini is in a disassociated, cut-off state, partners may find themselves burdened with all the unprocessed, unmanageable feelings, which permeate the atmosphere but do not reside, as it were, where they belong. A partner may find themselves experiencing the disowned feelings of their Gemini mate and no longer know where they begin and their partner ends. This kind of muddle happens to some extent in all relationships, but it's hard when the partner in question is in denial. Be warned, a Gemini can be hard work.

Most Geminis flirt, some more so than others and for them it is no more than light-hearted, playful banter. Recipients usually feel flattered and enjoy the special attention they are receiving. Typically, they flirt with the waiter or waitress in the restaurant, the receptionist, the car mechanic and with anyone and everyone with whom they cross paths in the course of their day. This may not be gender specific; it can be indiscriminate and is an intrinsic part of their social interaction. A partner needs to be aware of this and find ways to manage the jealousy that it can trigger.

This can damage Gemini's significant relationships, causing hurt and distress. Loved ones may feel undermined and unimportant and doubt the strength of their Gemini mate's feelings for them. It can be devastating for a partner to witness their Gemini's twinkling eyes directed at someone, a connection that had made them feel special, being dished out to all and sundry.

Although to a bystander it can look like an addiction Geminis never concede that their flirting is anything more than harmless fun; Geminis crave the fix, the feel-good factor flirting generates and won't give it up easily. They are adept at denying anything is going on, which is almost certainly true, but this doesn't help reassure their partner. The more psychologically aware among them will at least not flirt quite so outrageously and will take on board their partner's feelings.

Often, Geminis are not conscious that they are flirting and are not necessarily even attracted to this person, who may understandably be confused by the message they are receiving. This can be dangerous and can get them into tricky situations with those who take them seriously and don't like being messed around.

Gemini's curiosity can also land them in trouble. Just like that cat who even with its nine lives will eventually come a cropper, so Geminis can venture into dangerous territory as part of their need to know. They have this compulsion, which can be summed up by the phrase, 'I wonder what will happen if . . .' This is one of their most delightful characteristics too, but frequently they come unstuck. They pry and delve into places they shouldn't; they ask impertinent questions; they read things not meant for their eyes and don't necessarily respect others' personal boundaries or rights to privacy. They find things out that they'd rather not know, out of context and not meant for them. And once something is known, there's no going back.

Besides this, Gemini's curiosity can mean that they never settle. Their interest darts from one thing to another but is never sustained. Instead of becoming expert in any one field, they become a 'Jack of all trades but master of none'. They have no problem in becoming fascinated by a subject but lack staying power and soon drift on to the next thing that grabs their attention. They may have a broad-based knowledge, but no qualifications, or if they have qualifications, they may fail to become experienced in their particular field.

Some Geminis collect qualifications but have no aptitude to practice. Partly this is because they become bored easily. They need variety and plenty of stimulation. Once they become good at something it no longer holds their interest and they move on to something new. They aren't seeking new challenges, but new stimulus and, as they aren't motivated by ambition, then there is nothing to hold them.

On the whole, Geminis find it hard to finish things. Within the home, they often leave things undone. They get distracted. Some find it hard to concentrate and break off what they are doing and wander off to do something else.

Domestic chores are abandoned, washing up is left half done, clothes are sorted into piles but not put into the machine, the shelves are put up but never sanded and varnished and when decorating the final coat of paint is never applied. They may leave a string of tasks half finished and struggle to bring any one thing to a conclusion. So, their talent for multi-tasking can just mean lots of chaos, especially as they may not be very good at tidying up after themselves.

Geminis' restless, taut, highly-strung disposition can mean that they resemble those suffering from attention deficit disorder or hyperactivity. Typically they find it hard to sit still and fidget, jiggle, tap their feet and drum their fingers, as a way to dissipate the build up of nervous energy. They need to release it and activity helps. This is one of the reasons they usually stay slender – they burn up huge numbers of calories doing very little. Time spent playing sports and athletics and at the gym offers an alternative way to discharge tension that won't irritate others.

One of the criticisms made of Geminis is that they are superficial. While this is far from true, they *can* be light-hearted and take an interest in trivia. They don't have pretensions and even those with highbrow or academic involvement still have time for ordinary and everyday inter-actions. Rather than accuse them of lacking depth, it may be important to recognise how egalitarian and inclusive they are. This is among the least snobbish signs of the zodiac.

Every sign has its difficulties and Geminis are no worse than any others. Their faults are easy to understand, once you try to look at life through their eyes and understand what it's like to be in their shoes. Which is, surely, what those who love them want to be able to do.

The Gemini Man

The Gemini man is recognisable by his youthful demeanour. He grows old gracefully, has boyish manners and often retains the slender body typical of adolescence well into later life. Whatever his actual age he remains young at heart. This is the Peter Pan of the zodiac, who never really grows up and keeps his delightful, playful, spontaneous qualities but with a sophisticated experience of the world – an irresistible combination.

One of Gemini man's most attractive characteristics is his sense of humour, which is second to none. With his witty, irreverent outlook, he can turn even the most mundane event into a sparkling, fun happening. He possesses a special kind of charm and magic, which lights up dull places and makes him a sought after companion. At times, he can flirt wildly and outrageously, making those who come into his orbit feel special. While this can land him in trouble, it also gives him a kind of reckless appeal.

Entertaining and amusing, the Gemini man is a gifted communicator. With his own idiosyncratic ideas and take on life, he is happy to converse about anything and everything; whether it is deep and serious or idle gossip, he loves to talk. He has been known to dominate a conversation but others rarely mind, because he is so well informed and interesting.

When first in love, the Gemini man bombards his new lover with a mass of communications. Expect texts, cards, emails and phone calls. He's skittish and playful but much is sent to amuse, rather than to say anything serious. He's articulate, though, and when he wants to declare himself he does so with eloquence and style.

Once involved and sure of his feelings, the Gemini man moves at quite a pace. Playing hard to get is not his style; he wants to progress a relationship on, so there's no doubt when he wants more. He involves a new lover in his everyday life, including them in all things that he ordinarily does, whatever that may be, such as, going to the cinema, art exhibitions or other cultural activities, playing tennis or other sports and even the supermarket shop. He clearly enjoys a new partner's company. He may also organise weekend trips away, especially city breaks, which are full of stimulating cultural things to do and exciting for new lovers.

Commitment does not come naturally to the Gemini man; it's the antithesis of his habitual way of being. This is an individual who thrives on spontaneity; it's part of the essence of who he is. He likes to be fancy free, to follow his impulses and go where the flow takes him. This doesn't mean he can't be faithful or loyal, but his commitment is something he recreates and re-evaluates regularly, rather than a static fact of life. It is not something he can in all honesty promise forever and ever.

More than anything the Gemini man has to be faithful to his spirit and to where that takes him. Clearly, this is worrying for those hoping for a more conventional commitment, which he may offer when smitten but actually not be able to deliver long term. Partly, he's too curious, which includes his sexuality and he enjoys newness and variety. Some might argue he's simply shallow, lacking emotional depth and seeking excitement as a substitute, but they'd be biased. Much of his attractiveness lies in his elusive quality, the fact that he belongs to no one – can't be owned – and is a law unto himself. It's strange but true that a partner will often try to change the very characteristic that drew them to him in the first place.

Part of the Gemini man's reluctance to make a commitment is his yearning for a soul mate and the sense he carries within him of the existence of a lost twin, who's out there in the universe waiting to be found if only he searches long and hard enough. This immediately makes anyone actually available and present not 'the one', because deep in his psyche, his perfect partner is mythic and unobtainable. This is a tough one to deal with, for him and his partner, but recognising the dynamic helps.

In a solid and secure relationship, the Gemini man's

restless longings can be recognised and tolerated for what they are and run alongside the ups and downs of everyday life. An emotionally sophisticated partner will accept that he has this unrealisable fantasy and humour him. Where it is more dangerous and destructive is when this elusive, ideal mate is actively sought as if he or she actually existed in reality rather than in the imagination. Those caught up in such a search are probably insecure and unhappy, with this eternal yearning a symptom rather than the cause.

The Gemini man is not helped by the fact that he relies on his intellect and quick wit to negotiate life and struggles with the feeling domain – for him this is an unfathomable mystery. While he makes a delightful and fun partner in many respects, being tenuously connected to his own inner world means he can be a bit like a rudderless ship, with insufficient emotional anchorage.

And, when it comes to emotional matters, the Gemini man does not make a good listener. He's more of a talker anyway and not generally about personal or intimate matters. While he is curious and interested and his comments may be helpful, he's unlikely to offer much empathy. He can view others' emotional states as novel and with too much detachment rather like the way a scientist examines his specimens.

Even though the Gemini man has difficulty with his feelings, he usually recognises this at some level and is attracted by those who have what he lacks. As a consequence, he is drawn to those who have easier access to their emotions. Provided he respects such a partner's strengths, this is a creative and helpful union, which can be of mutual benefit. He can teach his partner not to take everything quite so personally and can learn about feelings at close quarters. However, when he feels threatened or insecure, he can resort to being overly rational, using his superior logic in a destructive way to analyse and dissect others and their motives, rather than to look at himself.

Gemini man's partner has to find a way of not being intimidated by his rationalisations and to stick to their guns, even if they are made to seem mad. It's very easy to scrutinise and pull apart a feeling type but he has to realise this is an empty victory and that he's with this person for a reason – to learn. Not that this is necessarily the *raison d'être* of the relationship but it's nevertheless an important part of the attraction.

Typically, Gemini men have a problem growing up. On the positive side, they stay light-hearted and retain their infectious sense of fun. What can be more problematic is their reluctance to make commitments and take on responsibility. Witnessing a middle-aged Gemini man still pretending he's a teenager can be sad, especially if it means he's missed out on the benefits associated with commitment, like a family and home. Not that he sees it this way – he's glad to have escaped all of that, seeing it as a trap that would have enslaved him.

The Gemini man may not have a lot to show materially but he has a considerable knowledge of life. When he does have money, he tends to spend it on non-material things – on experiences – rather than on possessions. He is likely to prioritise concerts, the theatre, trips abroad and similar activities. He often travels lightly through life, preferring not to weigh himself down with financial commitments. This is not necessarily some lapse on his part but an important statement about what he values.

The planet Mercury rules Gemini so keep mercurial qualities in mind when trying to fathom the Gemini man. He adapts quickly and easily to new situations, changes arrangements himself on the hoof and expects others to be able to adjust as effortlessly as he can. His agility is key; he is mentally and physically quick, flexible and alert. Both metaphorically and possibly in reality, he's a sprinter rather than a long-distance runner, as stamina is not one of his strengths. Often edgy and of a nervous disposition, with a wired body and mind and fast reflexes, he has problems unwinding and relaxing.

In a domestic situation, the Gemini man expresses his restlessness in a variety of ways. It's hard for him to stay still and he may even eat some of his meals standing up or walking around. He changes the TV channel frequently and hogs the remote – not that he minds getting up to change the channel, either. He thrives on a lot of simultaneous stimuli and has been known to have the television set on without the sound, with music on the CD player, while reading. Prospective partners be warned.

The Gemini man overloads his nervous system, may well suffer from insomnia and tends to be a night owl. He tunes the radio into odd stations that only come on at certain times, so when others put the radio on it just crackles. He wanders around the house, fiddling with one thing or another, but never finishing anything. A master at leaving things nearly done, tidying up and finalising a task is anathema to him.

If the Gemini man gets around to doing any DIY – and one of his problems is that he's always too busy – he's likely to leave a mess in his wake. Partners are meant to be grateful that he's attended to the task at all and he can be crestfallen if they happen to mention that it's still not quite finished and all his tools are left lying around. He doesn't see the point in putting them away because he intends to go back. It's just that this could be days or even weeks later. With his short attention span, he's already on to the next thing that's grabbed his interest. Rather than concentrate on one thing at a time, he deals with several tasks at once. That way he doesn't get bored.

Once a relationship is firmly established, a partner must recognise and hold on to the fact that, even if he denies it, the Gemini man is dependent on their relationship. If he refuses to acknowledge this, it is because he fails to realise it himself, but that's his issue. Occasionally, reluctantly, he admits he needs his partner and it's important they keep this in mind as he flits about giving them every reason to feel insecure.

The Gemini man thrives on spontaneity and something dies in him if he's tied down – he needs to feel free. However hard this is, a partner has to trust him and not attempt to get him to account for his every move. When cross-examined he becomes evasive and a vicious circle ensues. A mate, understandably, becomes suspicious and once mistrust is shown, he becomes even more secretive. It's more than likely that there's nothing going on to be worried about, he just hates having to explain himself and is very good (with no malice intended) at getting loved ones to feel paranoid. Their task is not to be. Those who want to forge a lasting relationship with him should allow him a long rein, as otherwise he really will take off.

The Gemini man who does settle down and have a family offers his offspring an exciting and tantalising glimpse of the world. As a father, he prioritises their education and makes sure his children receive one that is wide and inclusive. Ever ready and available to discuss the big issues in the world, be it culture, politics, war, religion, philosophy, he credits his children with an independent mind and thereby fosters their development.

As a father, the Gemini man may not always be age-appropriate and could cause his offspring some embarrassment (as all parents do at some stage). He's the dad who wants to join in with their youthful activities, such as rollerblading in the park, tagging along when he's no longer wanted, like an overgrown kid himself. His reluctance to grow up has to manifest somewhere. He may not be the most responsible of parents but he makes up for this with his lively involvement and genuine interest in his children.

Work-wise, the Gemini man thrives in an environment that can utilise his adaptability. Routines don't suit him. He prefers a work schedule with a changing pattern of shifts rather than a nine-to-five. An early start to his working day is not an attractive proposition for him, whereas working until two am does not pose any problem.

The Gemini man can change directions entirely, possibly more than once, if he becomes bored with his current work. So he may have had several different careers. The trouble is that once he gains expertise in what he does, he may no longer find it stimulating or exciting. Once it becomes routine and easy, he looks for new horizons, where he can continue to learn and discover. A job that challenges him intellectually and offers variety and scope suits him best. Some accumulate an array of qualifications and find themselves over-qualified for the work they are interested in, which may not worry them but a prospective employer could be concerned, as it's clear from their CV that they may not stay in the position that long.

Although being self-employed is an attractive option, in so far as it offers a degree of flexibility, the Gemini man doesn't usually take that route. He needs the involvement and interaction of others and does best when working as independently as possible within an organisation. He's not a loner and those who, for instance, write, can find that a hard choice – he may be good at it but he doesn't enjoy the solitude that inevitably goes with such a career.

Famous Gemini men include Bob Dylan, Clint Eastwood, John F Kennedy, Paul McCartney, Prince and Donald Trump. John F Kennedy exemplifies several Gemini characteristics; besides his inspired oratory, his flirtatious charm brought in the votes and endeared him to the female electorate, which helped him to become president and, it later transpired, he had a fickle side as his womanising became public knowledge.

Paul McCartney has an excellent track record when it comes to relationships, proving the point that many Gemini men are capable of this. He has retained his slender physique and remains extremely youthful in both appearance and outlook. His marriage to the much-younger Heather Mills, after the loss of his first wife, Linda, affirms that he is only as old as he feels. The lyrics he has written, from his time with the Beatles and since, demonstrate his gift with words, another classic Geminian trait.

Sixties' icon Bob Dylan was above all else a poet and exceptionally mercurial, with his ironic sense of humour, his ability to juggle with words and play mind games. Eighties' phenomenon Prince played on his sexuality, flirting outrageously and using risqué language. The duality typical of this sign is apparent in his change of names and his elusive, playful qualities are also typical of this sign. In fact, both men vividly demonstrate classic Geminian characteristics.

The Gemini man comes in a variety of packages, but what they all have is an indomitable spirit of youth. More than anything, he is a fun, lively companion. Don't ask him to be old and sensible as he finds growing up very, very hard – he'll get there in the end and lead all a merry dance along the way. Enjoy the journey with him.

The Gemini Woman

What do Joan Collins, Marilyn Monroe and Kylie Minogue all have in common? They are all Gemini women, albeit of different generations and with their own way of expressing their quintessential Gemini characteristics. Joan Collins has a mischievous expression, is famous for her quick, bright, funny remarks and interviewers have said it's hard to get a word in edgeways. Whatever her actual age, she remains young at heart and retains her looks.

Marilyn Monroe made good use of the flirtatious side of Gemini and possessed a sharp wit and lively intelligence. Kylie Minogue flirts outrageously, too, especially with the camera and has a playful, skittish and vivacious personality that is typical of this sign.

The Gemini woman comes in many guises; in fact, that

is intrinsic to her character. She is not easy to define, as she is changeable and adaptable and fits into whatever environment she finds herself, yet in her own distinct way. What marks her out is her light touch, the convivial way she approaches life and her irrepressible humour. Don't ever mistake her for an airhead though, as however frothy she may appear to be, this woman has a good brain. It's just that it may sometimes suit her to play this fact down.

The Gemini woman is almost certainly brighter than she lets on, as she has learned it pays for her not to advertise this in today's world, despite the advances of feminism. She knows she has a choice between appearing intelligent and being popular and usually plumps for the latter. It could be argued that this is actually a clever move on her part. All it takes however is a serious conversation to realise she has a mind of her own and has thought long and hard about a number of issues.

The Gemini woman has a keen interest in people and the world around her, which she expresses by asking questions and by an alert attention to what others say and how they conduct themselves. She possesses sharp powers of observation and deduction, which can be a bit unnerving to others, who can feel themselves watched and analysed. She has a quizzical nature and a lively curiosity, but may not give much away about herself. The spotlight is firmly focused on others while she remains an enigma.

Even if the Gemini woman doesn't offer to reveal personal information about herself, she does love to talk. Whether it's an intellectual debate, a cultural critique or plain old gossip, she positively seeks dialogue with those around her. Conversation and words are important to her; she listens carefully to the content of what is being said, taking in information and facts. This gives her an astute intellect, but her thinking and understanding can be too literal.

Like the Gemini man, she can have problems with the feeling domain and relies on her rationality. In conversation she may overlook the tone or feeling with which the words are spoken and thus miss the undercurrents. She is not very good at picking up subtle nuances and non-verbal communication. She relies on and responds to what is said and assumes that others are saying what they mean, as she does. However, she usually has better access to her own inner world than her male counterpart, so even though this isn't her strength, she's rarely as out-of-touch as he can be.

An avid reader with wide tastes in literature, poetry and non-fiction, the Gemini woman may well belong to a library, although ultimately she likes to own books. Books are treasured and kept and re-read. She has her favourite authors and is able to speak knowledgeably about their body of work.

Even when on a tight budget, the Gemini woman allows herself to buy a book – she may collect sets of books or be interested in antiquarian books. Her shelves are groaning as she finds it virtually impossible to ever discard a book; they are like friends to her, holding sentimental memories of how she was feeling when they 'met'. She may well believe that she is led to the particular book she needs to read at any given moment, so the book then holds a special meaning for her.

Besides reading, the Gemini woman likes to write, especially writing of a personal nature. Diaries, journals, recording her dreams, she's likely to build up a fair body of her own work over the years. It's an important dialogue that she has with herself. Through writing down her thoughts, perceptions and feelings, she establishes clarity and insight. While she may use modern technology for this, she's as likely to use traditional methods and if her bag is investigated, along with her book, there'll be a notepad and pen, just in case an idea comes into her head that she'd like to write down.

The Gemini woman's love of words extends to relationships, where words play an important part. She needs things to be said, spelt out and does not make assumptions when unspoken gestures are made that traditionally carry special meaning to lovers. It's not that tokens of love such as flowers, chocolates and presents aren't welcome, but the note that accompanies them is just as important. She treasures any letters, cards and e-mails, which she prints out and keeps – if anyone is going to save every scrap of communication from a loved one and bind it all together with a red satin ribbon, it's a Gemini woman. Not only does she hold on to all communication from her loved one, but she keeps the messages left on her answer phone, theatre tickets and programmes and other mementos.

At the start of a new relationship, the Gemini woman offers and expects a constant stream of dialogue. She wants postcards, notes, phone calls, text messages and emails – she needs words to affirm and reassure her. These don't have to be declarations of love and commitment – in fact she might get alarmed if they were – what she needs is to stay connected throughout her day. The messages back and forth can be light-hearted, playful banter; what she can't bear is a long silence where she will wonder what's happening, imagine the worst and withdraw. Depending on the stage a relationship is at, all this could happen within a two-hour time span. So, for those who want to keep this woman interested, don't ever leave her waiting for a response for too long. She'll have moved on.

The downside to all this, of course, is that she relies too heavily on the spoken word and when emotionally involved she can have real problems dealing with her and her partner's feelings. For her, feelings can be threatening, so she analyses them to make them less so and in the process can come across as cool and detached. Other people's distress makes her uncomfortable and rather than offering her partner the sympathy and empathy that they need she may have a tendency to get them to think rationally about what's going on.

If the Gemini woman's loved one has been in an argument, she offers the perspective of the other person, believing that by explaining the opponent's position, this will help. While this may be useful a day or so later when some of the hurt and upset has subsided, this is almost certainly not what's needed in the immediate aftermath. She copes with her own upsets by trying to understand and rationalise what has caused them, rather than actually experiencing these difficult feelings. She may not see this as a problem at all, but those who are close to her will almost certainly find her approach too detached when they are in emotional pain.

As an air sign, the Gemini woman is predominantly cerebral and tends not to trust her instincts, unless the data they provide fits in with her preconceived ideas. So, for instance, she may miss the opportunity to have a baby, rationalising that the time is not right. She ignores her deeper instinctual longings that tell her now is the right time, never mind the practicalities. This is a worst-case scenario, but one she should guard against. Learning to listen to strange stirrings and not to dismiss them out of hand is an important part of her personal growth. Just because they don't fit in with her grand scheme doesn't mean they don't have their own logic.

There will be times when the Gemini woman is unable to deal with her emotions and is completely overwhelmed by them. Like a weak swimmer out of her depth, she fears she is drowning and finds the whole experience very frightening. Her best defence against these difficult emotional episodes is to become a stronger swimmer. Then she can't be knocked sideways by the waves of feelings that will surely sweep her off her feet if she continues to deny, repress and disconnect from her feelings. As she dares to acknowledge and allow her feelings, she can develop a facility to make the journey back and forth between her inner and outer world and truly link the two, becoming master of both, if only she finds the courage. Most find themselves travelling along this path.

What the Gemini woman brings to her relationships, more than anything, is her sense of fun and playfulness. She brightens and lightens her partner's day and life. She can be serious, but she never gets over-serious and with her humorous take on situations she makes everything feel easier. This is quite some gift.

Those hoping to have a long-term relationship with a Gemini woman must give her space and take the time to really get to know her, not just take the jewels she offers and accept her at face value. She takes some getting to know, because she's not what she seems, even to herself. Anyone who buys into her enigmatic silence and accepts it unquestioningly will never actually engage her. Because she doesn't reveal herself, others can project whatever they want on to her and, because she enjoys their infatuation, she allows it to continue. She may well have a coterie of admirers, all with their own notion of who she is, which bears little resemblance to what she is really like. They may be besotted, but they've not penetrated her facade so haven't begun to reach her emotionally.

It's worth remembering, too, that the Gemini woman is probably the world's worst or best flirt, depending on how you look at it. She sees it as harmless fun and she loves to play, so she will often have a string of suitors who have all misinterpreted her flirtation. A relationship with her only becomes deep and meaningful when she opens up and starts to share her inner thoughts and feelings. Until then, it's a game and the more insecure she is, the wilder her flirting will be. Her need to be desired, which reassures her, creates a powerful undercurrent.

When involved, the Gemini woman can fail to recognise the ways in which she is dependent and what her needs might be and consequently may not offer her partner much appreciation – a bit like the way a cat may grace you by sitting on your lap.

Once in an established relationship, it's important that the lines of communication stay open and stimulating. The Gemini woman wants to be able to have interesting conversations with her partner, not just settle into a domestic routine. Simply talking about your day will not suffice. She wants to talk about politics, culture and topical issues and without this she becomes restless and dissatisfied and judges the relationship to be lacking.

Despite her need for companionship and how lively and sociable she is, the Gemini woman can choose to spend considerable time on her own. She's not desperate to have a relationship, in fact she has a fair amount of ambivalence to cope with when in a relationship and may like going home alone at the end of the evening. She has a packed social calendar and is never short of friends, so is unlikely to feel lonely.

More than most signs, the Gemini woman may choose not to have children, perhaps because she fears their dependency on her and the restrictions they will impose on her lifestyle. Becoming a mother involves being 'a proper grown-up' and she never feels she's got there. She has to dispel this notion and realise that she has as much right as the next woman to have a child if she so wishes and that there aren't necessarily any external criteria that she has to measure up to in order to do this. This isn't to imply that deciding to be child-free isn't a valid choice for her, because of course it is.

As a mother the Gemini woman offers her children plenty of stimulation and is happy to ferry her little ones to this class or that. More than most mothers, she values the extra-curricula activities that are on offer and won't find the running around stressful; she needs it herself and positively thrives on all the interaction available with the other parents who cross paths with her on a regular basis.

The Gemini mother takes a keen and genuine interest in her child's schoolwork, always willing to help with homework and offer enthusiastic support and back up. This encouragement enables her child to develop his or her intellect and interests to the full. She won't mind if their interests change, if they drop one thing in favour of another, she's been there, done that and understands the need to experiment.

The Gemini woman's flexibility and adaptability means she can cope well with most aspects of domestic life, but what she struggles with are the strictures on her autonomy. For this reason, she does best with some live-in help, if this is a possibility, whether from a relative, an au pair or a nanny. She can cope with someone else sharing her home; what she finds hard is not being able to leave it as and when she wants.

Work is an important part of the Gemini woman's life, not because she's particularly ambitious, but for the stimulation and variety it offers her. For this reason she's likely to remain working when her children are small, possibly part-time and to continue full-time as soon as she's able. She enjoys rubbing up against others on a daily basis and doesn't do well if isolated, so working at home alone, for instance, doesn't suit her.

Being her own boss doesn't suit the Gemini woman either, because that by its nature is a lonely position and she prefers to have colleagues and be among equals. If she is the boss, it is important for her to have links with others in a similar position.

The Gemini woman is a real gem. For those who are involved with one, don't give up on her lightly. Tricky she may be, but she has much to offer, not least her intelligence and a light-hearted, playful sense of fun.

The Gemini Child

The Gemini child can be recognised by his or her lively, alert and cheeky manner. They may well possess an elfin quality, with a mischievous face and an impish manner. Even when innocent, these children can look as if they're up to no good. They are born with a great sense of humour and find life amusing – in fact they make it so, always able to see the funny side of things.

Gemini children love playing tricks, clowning around and cracking jokes. They are irreverent and just as likely to send themselves up as others. A natural mimic and impressionist, they are able to use their finely-tuned observational skills to humorous effect.

All children ask why, but young Geminis do this even more than most. They possess an innate curiosity about life and the world around them and ask awkward questions as soon as they have the verbal skills. Their grasp of language is precocious and they quickly develop a sophisticated vocabulary, way ahead of their peers.

Gemini children are a teacher's dream – quick to learn and positively hungry for knowledge and information about the world around them. Parents, too, can be gratified by the lively curiosity this child expresses and continue to enjoy stimulating and interesting conversations with their offspring throughout their life.

Multi-talented, Geminian children do well in all areas of life that depend on a sharp wit and speedy responses. They rely on their mental dexterity and are extremely quick on the uptake, usually getting the point well ahead of their classmates if, that is, they are paying attention.

Gemini children's downfall, when it comes to school, is that so often they aren't concentrating on what is going on, as their mind wanders the moment they are bored – which doesn't take long. They need plenty of stimulation and if that isn't provided they can play up, distracting other pupils with their tomfoolery. They can become a disruptive influence in class, which can give them a notoriety that they enjoy. This is a dangerous precedent, as they can find this so rewarding that they maintain it and learn very little at school. It has to be emphasised that this is rarely because they lack the mental apparatus but almost certainly because they're not being sufficiently stretched.

More than most, the Gemini child needs intellectual challenges. They love to learn and discover and do well on projects where they can explore a topic independently and draw their own conclusions. They thrive in a stimulating, educational environment. They need to flex their intellectual muscle and one of the worst things that can happen to this child is to be in a dull and underachieving milieu. This isn't to say all Gemini children are necessarily especially brainy, but what they have is a bright, sharp, inquiring intellect and, initially at least, an eagerness to learn.

As well as a quick mind, the Gemini child is likely to possess a flexible and lithe body and may well be good at certain sports and athletics. They are particularly suited to gymnastics and any activities that rely on gymnastic ability, like diving, ice-skating or rollerblading. They can usually run fast and often have good eye/ball coordination, which makes them good at sports like tennis, basketball and netball. As a parent, offer these youngsters encouragement to pursue their interests, possibly even coaching, (without turning into a pushy parent). Not all are the next Steffi Graf, Venus Williams or Bjorn Borg, all Geminis and champion tennis players, but some just could be.

Besides these avenues, other less conventional outlets may appeal to, and suit, the young Gemini. They are well suited to become contortionists or jugglers and could excel in other circus acts that depend on physical agility, like the trapeze. Most youngsters enjoy hanging upside down and attempting these kind of tricks, but the Geminian child may actually go on to make a career out of it. Whether or not this transpires, flexibility remains an asset, for as well as being a physical accomplishment it is a state of mind. These are adaptable children, who adjust easily and are not fazed by an erratic routine. Whatever they grow up to do, they neither expect nor need life to be predictable.

Expect the Gemini baby to be mobile especially early. They are highly motivated to move in some form or other, and once able, they'll be in to everything they can possibly get their hands on. This is a sign that loves to explore its world and the baby does this initially through placing everything in its mouth. Parents be warned, keeping an eye on this little one is a full-time occupation. They are especially curious, not only in finding out what their world tastes like but later, in toddling off. Parents need to be particularly vigilant and careful that their Gemini baby doesn't venture into hazardous situations. They are quick, agile and inquisitive, a potentially dangerous combination.

At all ages, Gemini children demand plenty of variety to keep them interested. They get bored quickly with the same old toys and need new games and things to do. Even babies like to go out and take great interest in the world around them. The Gemini toddler thrives in a nursery school or playgroup – all those interesting activities and other children to mix with is a perfect combination. These are particularly sociable and gregarious little ones and enjoy the company of others from a very young age.

While Gemini children need plenty of stimulating activity, parents would do well also to encourage quiet times. Too much stimulation can aggravate the tendency to hyperactivity and over-excitability. Diet may play a part in this, too, and parents are advised to keep additives known to increase hyperactivity to a minimum and limit these children's sugar intake. Attention deficit disorder is a serious condition and any steps taken to discourage its onset are recommended.

There are several ways a parent can help a young child to calm down. Baby massage is recommended for all babies, as it always sedates and relaxes them, but is especially good for Geminis. Whatever their age, stroking them will always pacify them and they can then be led towards quiet activities that absorb them. Sensual activities, such as modelling with clay or dough, having a sandpit or tray and being allowed to play with water (a large washing-up bowl, sleeves rolled up and collection of things that can be dunked) are all calming and help to ground a manic child.

Books are Gemini children's mainstays. Provide them with plenty, starting with rag and board books when they are babies, and continue to supply them with age-appropriate books throughout their childhood. When telling the bedtime story let them join in, finishing and embellishing. Introduce them to the public library system and allow them to subscribe to their favourite comics and magazines.

For those who own a home computer, give Gemini children access, even if for limited hours, when they are still quite young – they'll almost certainly make good use of this facility. The internet may be a marvellous source of information that can assist them with their homework and assignments but, given this signs inquisitive nature, they need adequate protection and some parental controls are essential – possibly banning chat rooms, where they are most vulnerable to being exploited.

Provide Gemini children with a television in their rooms, too, with access to the Discovery and Knowledge channels or similar educational and informative outlets. Obviously care must be taken to monitor their use as some more introverted children can retreat into a fantasy world, where reading, television, computer games and internet access play an unhealthy and significant part. If they lack friends and fail to participate in normal social activities, it's important that parents help these children find an outlet where they engage with others too.

A drama class may suit these less gregarious Gemini children, as playing a role can mask their shyness and their sensitivity is an asset, enabling them to put themselves wholeheartedly into the characters they portray. Pre-school, a fancy dress box is recommended, as this provides scope for their vivid imagination. Even before an age when drama groups are an option, these children enjoy acting and creating interesting 'stages and backdrops' at home, with sheets draped over the table or the bunk beds and such like, if given the chance.

Gemini children's ability to mimic gets them plenty of recognition at an early stage and accents are never a problem for them. As they become interested in literature, then their knowledge and experience in drama is an important adjunct. While this might be their future career, it's more likely that it's an important part of their socialisation.

Board games such as Scrabble can also be an enjoyable family activity that Gemini children particularly relish, not because they are necessarily competitive, but because they love honing their skills. In fact, in Scrabble, they are more likely to make a long and interesting word that gives a lower score, than a higher scoring but less satisfying word, so winning the game is not as high a priority as demonstrating their love of words.

As they grow up, and even before the hormones kick in, Gemini children can be naughty, rude and provocative. It's just that their mischievous streak coupled with their strong curiosity can get out of hand. They question the limits set by adults, pushing against the boundaries. In fact, from their point of view, telling them not to do something or other is tantamount to a challenge to do it. In order for them to accept any rules, they have to see the reasoning behind them, so full explanations are essential. Obedience does not come naturally to them – they need to know why.

Adolescents are notoriously difficult to manage and above all else, Gemini children hate being restricted; they want to find things out for themselves. As a parent, try to give them as long a leash as possible, in order that they can satisfy their curiosity. They crave opportunities to explore life, so send them on trips and excursions. Exchange holidays are ideal; they get to see a foreign culture and different way of life as well as improving their fluency in the language.

As Gemini children become old enough to travel independently, they may well want to venture further afield, maybe to places that, as a parent, you'd rather they didn't visit. The more experience they've had, the more streetwise they are, the safer they will be. See the earlier jaunts as preparation for the later travel.

The travel they undertake is an important part of a Gemini child's education. They are likely go on to further education too, as they are never happier than when learning, so again, as a parent, it's worth bearing this in mind and budgeting accordingly. How long into adult life parents are willing and able to support their offspring is a personal decision, bearing in mind that a Gemini can easily become a perpetual student.

Geminis love to chat and once they are able to use the telephone, they can hog the line. There's nothing they like better than chatting to their school friends, dissecting their day and helping out with homework. The fact that they have just spent all day with these friends doesn't deter them from lengthy conversations in the evening, installing a second line can be a godsend.

There are probably fewer differences between Gemini girls and boys than there are between the sexes of other signs. Mercury, the planetary ruler, is an asexual planet, so this is neither a strongly masculine nor feminine sign and both sexes can equally well embody the traits. Typically those born under this sign are physically slight, slender and agile and often have an asexual quality. However, this doesn't mean this child's gender is in any way indistinct: Marilyn Monroe and Clint Eastwood are cases in point.

Because of their cerebral nature, Gemini children are not tuned in to practical matters. They may not be that good at organising themselves. Creating homework schedules can be problematic and their rooms can be a mess. Rather than criticise them, parents would do well to offer them practical help to master these things and to make it clear that doing so is important. The Gemini child must be encouraged to acquire basic domestic skills to equip them in later life. If these are seen as a part of a learning exercise and rewarded, then they are going to be keener to comply. In later years, they will be grateful that they can finish a task and have at least got some proficiency in practical matters.

One of the more challenging attributes of Geminis is in their desire to learn, they can become 'know-it-alls'. This is difficult enough in adults, but in a child it's insufferable. No one likes a twelve-year-old lording it over them – at least an adult has some experience and gravitas. This kind of attitude is often found in those who, ironically, lack confidence and feel the need to impress. Parents are advised to reassure these children of their worth and value, irrespective of anything else and never make them feel stupid or inferior for being unaware of something.

The parents' own competitive streak can be triggered by their Gemini child's thirst for knowledge, which inadvertently becomes a threat to them. Parenting is never an easy task but these children need to be supported and encouraged to use their minds and hopefully to go on to a high level of education.

All parents want the best for their children. With a Gemini, give them clear explanations, keep them informed, talk to them and debate with them. Offer them plenty to do but foster quiet and contemplation and reflection too. That way, parents can help their live-wire Gemini to grow up to be a well-rounded and centred individual.

4

Cancer
The Crab

June 21st to July 22nd

A cardinal water sign, ruled by the Moon

Introducing Cancer

Cancers are caring, nurturing, creative and imaginative souls, recognisable by their enigmatic and slightly dreamy presence. It's as if they're not quite paying attention to what's going on in the moment because their focus is turned inwards. These are self-contained individuals, who can be rather inscrutable and hence hard to read. They are very much in control of themselves and, unless they choose to, don't give much away. They prefer to keep their thoughts and feelings private and only share them with those they are close to. It's important not to mistake their reticence for shyness, as although some Cancerians may be shy, this is not necessarily so.

Cancerians possess a zany sense of humour. With a rather wry, slightly skewered take on life, they approach things from a different angle to everyone else. This is both disconcerting and thoroughly charming and makes others sit up and take notice. They can be relied upon to have an idiosyncratic point of view.

Alongside this, Cancerians are particularly good storytellers and can hold the attention of any small gathering with their quirky tales, which usually involve them. They laugh at themselves and don't mind revealing their own vulnerabilities and even disparaging themselves. They manage to be self-effacing in a way that endears others to them. It never actually works against them and allows others to reveal aspects of themselves they might otherwise keep hidden. In this way they have a knack of bonding with people and establishing intimacy.

This is the first of the three water signs, the others being Scorpio and Pisces, and those born under these signs are complex individuals. Cancer is the most straightforward of the three and at first acquaintance, easy enough to get along with. Sympathetic and empathetic, they make good listeners and, unlike some signs, do not feel overwhelmed by others' difficulties. In fact, they are fascinated and like nothing better than open and revealing conversations. They need to feel met at an emotional level and to have their feelings acknowledged. Their inner world is the main focus of their attention, hence the enigmatic atmosphere, and for any contact with others to be considered significant by them, more than a surface connection has to have taken place.

Like the sea, there is something unfathomable and mysterious about the Cancerian. Their 'emotional weather' is subject to sudden changes and they can be at the mercy of undercurrents. They obey an unseen force, their feelings, so they do not appear to be the most logical of signs. They base their evaluation of people and situations almost entirely on their gut reactions. All their decisions in life are based on their personal preferences – they don't think things through, as an air sign might and this makes it hard for them to explain or justify themselves, so in the main they don't bother to attempt to do so.

This ability to know and be in touch with how they feel gives Cancerians an inner certainty. In that respect they are sure of themselves. Because they don't think things through in a rational, detached and objective way themselves, many will actively mistrust the world of ideas and see it as full of opinionated intellectuals. This is both a weakness and a strength.

The moon rules Cancer and, in its orbit around the earth, the moon changes shape as it progresses from new moon to full moon to new moon again. Similarly those born under the sign of Cancer are changeable. In fact, they possess an odd mix of constancy and fluctuation. At a deeper level they are constant and reliable but on the surface they chop and change all the time.

In its gravitational pull on the earth the moon affects the tides and all life here on earth. Humans are composed of sixty per cent water, so the moon's pull also affects human life. Cancerians seem to be particularly attuned to this and are sensitive to the full and new moon. Their moods ebb and flow and they are notoriously moody for no apparent reason – certainly there's no rational cause. When in a mood they are capable of generating an almost tangible atmosphere – the black cloud hovering over their head is virtually visible. This atmosphere can permeate a whole house, seeping like a fog, the home becoming clogged up and stifling. All this, because our Cancerian probably needs to have a good cry. They have a knack of communicating non-verbally and this is one of the ways in which they do this.

Words derived from the moon, la luna, like loony and lunatic, can also apply to Cancerians. Not that they are any more susceptible to mental illness than any other sign, but they can behave in a loony way, especially around the time of the full moon. There's a Dionysian undercurrent that surfaces and their behaviour may be extreme – partying very hard and generally letting their hair down. There can be something a little wild in their sense of humour, too and they can appear a tad unhinged. They have a wide emotional range and can cope with extreme states perfectly well but those around them may find it threatening. Their antics can topple loved ones into deeper waters than they feel safe in.

Always keep water and its nature in mind when trying to understand Cancerians. Water takes the path of least resistance; watch a stream finding its way around boulders and similarly Cancerians will look for the easiest route. On the other hand, never underestimate them; just as water will erode the hardest rock over time, so this is a persistent sign and does not easily give up or let go of what it wants.

The crab, a creature that has a reputation for its tenacity, depicts Cancer. Like the crab, who walks sideways, these individuals approach what they want in an indirect way. Watch out for the sideways, wary look Cancerians have, too. They are accused of being manipulative and, while this may be true, often they don't actually know themselves what their intentions are. They act on instinct and may not have any conscious awareness of where they are heading. Hence, when they get there, they are often surprised. If they look closely at their actions, they can see in retrospect that there was an unconscious driving force that steered them in the right direction. This comes back to the fact that they trust their instincts and are guided by them. One Cancerian friend absent-mindedly picked up and bought a set of white-board marker pens before she had a use for them. It was the first clue she had that she wanted to teach and yet within a few months she had her first teaching job and her marker pens were being put to good use.

The crab is a primitive, timid creature with a soft and vulnerable underbelly and a tough, hard, outer shell. Cancerians are pretty much like this too. Some have a more developed shell, so you really don't get a sense of their vulnerability, while others may not have enough of a shell and seem painfully unprotected, as if they really aren't viable in the world. The latter are very good at finding others who are happy to take on a protective role.

This sign has powerful associations with the mother and mothering and can be roughly divided into those who offer this and those who seek it. Many Cancerians are extremely maternal (yes, men too) and take care of others in some way. The helping professions contain a large number born under this sign. Their instinct is to nurture and protect and they choose to work in a field where this is part of the job description. Others are perennial girls or boys, looking for a maternal figure. With their childlike demeanour and air of helplessness, they solicit the desired response.

Some Cancerians vacillate between the mother and child position and embody both at different times. For instance, a woman who works as a nurse, yet still acts like a girl in her private life. Or a man who holds down a responsible management job, yet has his shirt collar awry and tails half tucked in, in such a way that he's communicating, 'I can't look after myself'. These non-verbal signals can tug on others who feel compelled to step in and take care. For those who find themselves irresistibly drawn, be sure this is what you really want to take on.

This maternal streak means that the family, for good or ill, plays an important part in the life of all Cancerians. They are likely to maintain strong ties to their family of origin. Those who don't may have had painful experiences in childhood, which has led them to seek other alternatives, perhaps where they can exercise more choice, such as a 'family' of friends. The influence of parents on their offsprings' psychological health and well-being is well established and, as an adult, a Cancerian stays involved more than most signs and attempts to resolve any difficulties that exist. While not all will be immersed in family life, for many it is central, providing them with emotional anchorage in their adult life.

Cancerians live with an awareness of the interconnectedness of life; of a substrata that somehow connects all human life. This has to do with their watery nature and the way that the water table is continuous. Unlike some, other people's pain and suffering affects them personally: they can't shut it out or distance themselves. In a sense, they are tuned in to the wider family, sensitive to their place in the larger picture and of how they fit into society. Their compassion comes from their capacity to feel for others, even those they have never met and who live in a culture very different from their own. They have no mechanism to detach, so suffer alongside others.

The need to belong is a Cancerian trait, which is another reason why the family is central. As adults they can decide what exactly they want to belong to. Being excluded or shut out in any way is extremely painful for them. They have an innate need to feel included and to be assured that they are a part of any group. Even if joining a political party or ideological group, the sense of community and the emotional bonding with other members is essential.

Whichever political party they actually support, Cancerians are conservative with a small c. They hold traditional values, based on the importance of the family and the relationships between kith and kin. One Cancerian woman, who needed a favour, suggested approaching a relative she had never even met, with the words, 'He's family'. In her book you're meant to look out for each other. This idea of family duty is firmly rooted in the last century but holds considerable sway in the psyche of modern-day Cancerians.

Along with family values is an attitude to conservation. At many different levels, Cancerians are conservationists. The countryside, historic buildings, values, ways of life, and much more, Cancerians will be busy trying to protect. They see the value in preserving traditional methods that have been tried and tested and shown to work and do not embrace progress readily. Feelings of safety and security are invested in the past and anything new is threatening.

One way this can work out in practice and at its most prosaic is that Cancerians hoard. Nothing ever gets thrown out. Old yoghurt pots and margarine tubs have their storage uses; they save stamps for worthy causes, they recycle anything and everything, old string and odd buttons are kept, you name it, they save it. This is in many ways admirable; but it's just that they can't bear to ever throw anything away. Open a typical drawer or storage box belonging to a Cancerian and you'll find it stuffed full of bits and bobs that 'will be useful one day'. Their homes become clogged up with all the paraphernalia they are saving, and loved ones will find the amount of junk, to use a less polite word, quite overwhelming. Those who are minimalists, stay clear!

Saving things is another manifestation of Cancerians' nurturing attitude. Wanting to be able to provide whatever's needed in an instant, they try to make sure that they have the resources at their fingertips. They hate to run out of anything and will stockpile household essentials, so that they are never caught short. This they would find quite shameful.

Cancerians are careful individuals, some say canny and although far from mean, they like a bargain. Not for them the highly-priced designer clothes, as labels don't impress them one bit. They'd rather shop at the market and get excited by the savings they're making. They make what money they have stretch a long way and are good at staying within their budget. Even when on a low income, many manage to save. They keep in mind the proverbially rainy day, not noticing that it might be raining right now. They make prudent choices in how they spend their money and see extravagance as a form of stupidity.

It follows that if anyone is going to have a good pension, it's a Cancerian, although this could be in the form of property investment. They trust bricks and mortar and make sensible decisions over the years, building up a fair amount of wealth in a discreet way. It's just them being security-conscious. To these ends, they'll spread their savings over various schemes, seeing it as safer not to have all their eggs in one basket. A Cancerian would find it distressing and anxiety-provoking not to have money in the bank and quite terrifying to be in debt. Not for them the increasingly twenty-first-century way of living on credit: they need a financial cushion for their emotional well-being.

When in love, a Cancerian is most influenced by the non-verbal levels of communication and the behaviour of their loved one. For them, words are fairly meaningless. How a potential lover behaves is what counts. And whereas with some signs, gifts are important, these won't wash either – although they won't object to presents, they won't hold much sway. What matters is the care and consideration and thoughtfulness of a partner. Small gestures that demonstrate these qualities mean a great deal, such as running them a bath and remembering their favourite bath oil or giving them the seat near the window on the train. Nothing flamboyant, as that fails to impress, what they seek is a quiet attention to their needs. This is in turn reciprocated and a partner's well-being is paramount.

A relationship with a Cancerian is never flashy. It's serene and private; a soul union where words are redundant. The emotional atmosphere becomes all-important and this can sometimes lead them into difficulties. At times, especially when they are feeling insecure, they may find it difficult to differentiate between a partner coming home tired and being tired of them. They rely on the feeling connection to a loved one and this can be experienced as demanding and even intrusive by a less watery mate. An air sign, desperate for space, can at times feel drowned and stifled in such a relationship.

Yet, the air signs are particularly fascinated by such

watery folk. Cancer has all the attributes they lack as well as all those they most fear, so such a coupling is not uncommon. Opposites do attract. If they can respect each other's strengths and if the Cancerian in question is not hypersensitive or insecure they have much to offer each other. Cancer can learn to say what they want occasionally and not to dismiss language as a way of communicating. They especially appreciate a loved one who remembers the shape of their day, talks to them about it and is attuned to any emotional interactions and sticking points that it may contain. And they can teach their airy partner to appreciate the non-verbal levels of communication.

Cancerians exhibit some contradictory traits when it comes to sexual fidelity, which makes them hard to fathom. On the one hand, once emotionally involved a Cancerian remains so. Feelings can't be turned on and off, so their connection is maintained. However, this is no guarantee that they'll be faithful. Remember, they obey this unseen instinctual force, which means that they can stray with relative impunity, while remaining in their main relationship. In this case, they are committed to their *feelings* rather than to another. Yet there are times when such a strong sense of belonging to another is evoked that they will be absolutely faithful, to roam would then be a betrayal and violation of their own feelings. In other words, they please themselves and do not hold a consistent position.

Cancerian's need for family means they make great parents. Most want children and won't find other creative outlets an acceptable alternative. Their ability to tune in at a non-verbal level means looking after a baby is a cinch. During the early years they are in their element. Where they may run into difficulties is when their child wants a bit more independence. This they can find threatening. Depending on the child in question, an almighty tussle can develop. Such a parent can find this extremely hurtful and the whole growing-up phase will be a tough transition.

Those with work and a life outside the home will manage better than those who have completely immersed themselves in family life.

Cancerians are active in many areas of life, including, as we have seen, the caring professions, taking in all branches of medicine, social work, counselling and psychotherapy as well as the whole spectrum of complementary health care professions. Their nurturing and empathetic nature also draws them into the hospitality industry, not just as chefs, but hotel and restaurant management too. Equally they may be drawn to work that involves nurturing others in more symbolic ways, such as fostering and supporting talent.

Besides these arenas, Cancerians are often drawn to the media and the arts, where these imaginative and sensitive souls can equally feel at home. Various avenues are open to them under this wide umbrella. Their empathic nature means many can act; they are well able to step into the shoes of another and know how it might feel.

Writing is an option that suits Cancerians, especially plays, movie scripts and fiction, where they can use their vivid imaginations along with their ability to observe life and comment upon it wryly. Iris Murdoch, is one such Cancerian writer, who since her death and release of the biographical film *Iris* has been shown to be an extremely untidy and messy individual, too. Her problem seemed to be in part typical of all Cancerians, in that she couldn't throw anything away. Ernest Hemingway and Barbara Cartland are examples of two other very different Cancerian writers.

Cancerians are good in PR, management and human resources. They value people and the interactions between them, they are good at relating and soothing away difficulties but are at the same time proactive. They tend to be trusted so they can usually gain others' confidence and support.

The Cancerian businessman Richard Branson, who set up the business empire Virgin, which owns an airline, record label, record shops and trains, exemplifies many of this sign's traits. While he is extremely successful, he has an image of a caring and involved boss, who appears to be far more 'hands-on' than he probably is.

Cancerians are good at all the touchy-feely stuff; they have what is now called 'emotional intelligence' in bucket-loads which takes them a long way in life. Whatever work they do, and they are by no means limited to the above, they bring to it a caring, sharing attitude.

Negative Cancer

Any of the traits described in the introduction can become negative but we'll start with Cancer's close bond to mother. As this manifests differently in men and women, it will be discussed separately. There is plenty to admire about a man who maintains a close relationship with his mother. He shows his caring, feeling side by being solicitous of her welfare and by running errands and doing chores for her. The downside to this can be that he is overly attached, remaining dependent on her emotionally in a way that is not appropriate as an adult. His partner will undoubtedly complain that he does things for his mother that he neglects to do for her.

The mother–child dynamic is a powerful force in the psyche of all Cancerians and in these instances the man has identified with the child and stayed bonded to mother. He hasn't grown up. Many recreate this pattern in their relationships. They expect their partner to mother them while they remain essentially a boy – not an attractive proposition. Such a man may marry a much older woman. He may have plenty to offer by way of empathy and consideration but fail to take responsibility for himself and the relationship.

Even worse is the man who doesn't manage to leave home at all. He stays with his mother and hovers around her, being helpful. She comes to rely on him and doesn't give him the push out into the big wide world that he needs. She colludes and lets him stay. Her husband, his father, may mind, but is loath to make a fuss and come between the two. They make an odd kind of couple. Any woman attempting to get involved with this kind of Cancerian man genuinely does have mother-in-law problems because of the dynamic she walks into. His attachment to his mother takes precedence and his dependency on her doesn't give a relationship a chance.

In a gay relationship, a male partner may be able to find a place for himself that does not challenge the status quo in the same way. The Cancerian man may feel he's got the best of all worlds – his mother's eminent position unassailed and a partner who is not threatened by this and accepts it.

This mother–child pair manifests differently in the Cancerian woman. She can identify with either the mother or the child position and adapts her stance accordingly. Those identified with the mother are extremely capable and tend to mother the world, for example, by being in a pivotal role in which large numbers of people look to her for guidance. She excels in supporting others' talent and nurturing and facilitating their development. There's not much of a problem here, unless her fostering of others sacrifices her own creativity.

The opposite pole, a perpetual identification with the child, is far more problematic. This is the woman who when in her thirties still dresses like a schoolgirl with shrunken cardigans and pigtails. Like her male equivalent she gives out the message that she's not fully grown-up and needs to be taken care of. And this pose is not entirely unsuccessful. Some men and women will take her under their wings and offer her protection. Yet ultimately, it's

138

impossible for her to create a mature relationship if she is stuck developmentally at the age of eight. She is full of her own unfulfilled needs. This may work for her in her twenties, but as she grows older she becomes increasingly out of synch if she doesn't adopt a more age-appropriate stance.

Such a woman may well miss out on becoming a mother herself. This would enable her to connect to this role within herself and could be healing for her. Of all the signs, Cancer has the strongest maternal instincts, so to spend her life seeking this rather than embodying it is a tragic loss. This is not to say that Cancerian women are obliged to have children to be fulfilled, but they do need to express the creative, maternal side of their nature.

The Cancerian propensity to be identified with the child has a positive dimension, too, as it can be argued that they are in touch with their 'inner child'. Various types of personal growth work are in vogue that aim to get adults in better dialogue with their inner child, which is seen as a source of creativity and spontaneity, so those who have become conscious of this aspect of themselves are streets ahead. The problem, often, is that there's an *identification* with this child aspect of themselves but there's not a great deal of dialogue or awareness. Unless this connection occurs, they are simply being childish.

It could equally be argued that Cancerians have special access to qualities of innocence, trust, renewal and creativity, all extremely positive. This is perhaps the biggest bonus and does enable them to remain youthful and hopeful throughout their lives.

A difficulty that all Cancerians face is their moodiness. This is a moon-ruled sign and intrinsic to the moon, from our earth-bound point of view, is the fact that it is constantly changing shape. Poets have remarked on this throughout the ages and there has been a long association between the moon's changing faces and its subjects' changing moods. More than most signs, Cancerians have to cope with their own fluctuating feelings; they can go to bed perfectly happy and wake up in the depths of despair. When they can remember their dreams, this may explain their change of mood, but more often than not it's impossible to make sense of them. Because they don't know what's wrong, they pretend that nothing is, yet convey the opposite by their mood. It's not surprising that those trying to live alongside them are sometimes exasperated.

Such a Cancerian, when asked if something's wrong, will reply that everything's fine. This has to be translated as 'I don't have a clue what's wrong'. Clearly something is but, as they don't have the wherewithal to explain, they deny it, while exuding an atmosphere that communicates the problem non-verbally. Loved ones are baffled and struggle to understand what's going on. It's very easy for loved ones to get paranoid around such an atmosphere, to feel accused of causing the difficulties and even to assume the blame. This won't help the Cancerian in question; it just adds to their difficulties.

While Cancerians may be victims of their own inner machinations with others being affected by this, sometimes, they are much more deliberate. They purposely and deliberately upset those around them. They know perfectly well what's going on and refuse to discuss it. Maybe they are upset, maybe they are angry, but by withholding and sulking, they are in effect blaming others for their difficult feelings and attempting to make them suffer.

Emotional blackmail is one of the most unpleasant tactics that Cancerians resort to, and one at which they are expert. Despite possessing inner depths, they are not always able to cope with their own tumultuous feelings. They then attempt, albeit unconsciously, to make others experience their difficult feelings for them. They also attempt to control others, in order to avoid certain unwelcome feelings. Sounds complicated? It is, but anyone who has had a close relationship with a Cancerian is likely to have wondered what on earth was going on from time to time. It's easy to lose sight of where you begin and end in a close relationship, what exactly belongs to whom, and this is what a Cancerian exploits – and in an extremely subtle way.

A Cancerian mother can manage to make it feel a complete impossibility to say 'no' to a cup of tea. The cup of tea on offer somehow comes to stand for much more that she doesn't have the language to express. Her very being feels rejected if the tea she offers is rejected! Her child picks up on this and can't fathom out what's going on; this is the emotional soup in which she or he has grown up. All they know is that they feel inexplicably guilty if they refuse this proffered cup. Something life-threatening, something catastrophic gets evoked. Such is the power of the undercurrents – of what is not being said.

There's no easy way to untangle this kind of emotional knot but ultimately, as the mother has clearly not been able to come to grips with what is being triggered in her, it's down to the adult offspring to disentangle. Being able to see the dynamic for what it is creates an immediate sense of mental freedom and space. And, eventually, by saying 'no' to things that they don't want in a non-defensive and compassionate way, they can help the mother to withdraw her investment in such things. But even if they never quite manage that, knowing that it's 'her stuff' always helps.

While we are on the subject of Cancerian mothers – and much can be said in praise of them – it also has to be said that they can be over-protective to the point that a child feels suffocated. There's a line between the innocent request to 'wrap up warmly' and an implied but never stated fear that, if their child doesn't, he will catch cold, die and thereby abandon her. And a child will pick up on this fear even if he, too, can't put it into words.

This is a knotty problem with which Cancerian parents

must grapple. Cancerian fathers also have their over-protective side, but that's more likely to kick in later, in adolescence and to focus mainly on their daughters. In fact Cancerian parents cope better with younger children, who are dependent, and have difficulties at the stage when their child wants more independence, which threatens them. Depending on how fearful they are as parents, they can thwart their child's developing autonomy, stifling them and making them fearful too.

Caring Cancerians can in fact be extremely selfish. They are in touch with their own basic survival needs and do their utmost to get these met but they are not that good at seeing what others need, especially if there's a conflict of interest. In such moments they can be blind to how mercilessly they pursue their own agenda and consequently won't feel any remorse or guilt. They completely fail to see how ruthlessly they behave. Ruthless is not a word ordinarily associated with this sign, but the crab is a cold-blooded creature and they, too, have this capability. When the going gets tough this comes to the fore.

Cancerians get accused of being manipulative – and rightly so. Like the crab that moves sideways, they head for what they want in an indirect way. This is intrinsic to their nature and innocent enough; they are simply following their instincts. But it can also be done more deliberately, when they feel too vulnerable to ask for what they want in a straightforward way. They won't risk being rejected so try to get their needs met via round-about methods.

It's not always easy to see the line between deliberate manipulation and a quirky way of going about things, but there is one and those on the receiving end know the difference. Loved ones, who are cued to behave in certain ways, understandably feel manipulated. To refuse to respond to the cues is unthinkable and there is an underlying threat that something unspeakable will happen – the sky might fall in or the Cancerian might drop dead – and the loved will be responsible. Improbable as this clearly is, what's being communicated is how terrified the Cancerian is of not getting their needs met. Their viability in the world is in peril on an emotional level. And they have a capacity to muddle others unwittingly into this.

Cancer's mistrust of words and difficulty in thinking things through contributes to these problems. Their well-being depends on maintaining a positive connection with loved ones, so they won't risk any feelings that might disrupt that. Anger and hurt are extremely threatening and so are expressed indirectly, through their dark moods. Similarly they'll employ their cunning tactics of manipulation in order to get what they want and so avoid feelings of rejection.

Moaning and whingeing is another rather unattractive characteristic that some Cancerians resort to. Instead of expressing negative emotions directly they seep out and can leave others feeling uncomfortable. In a conversation, if everything they have to say is gloom and doom, then it's more than likely that they are actually furious about something, possibly with you, but not saying so.

Cancerians may well feel angry and resentful if they need a favour because of how vulnerable and dependent this leaves them feeling. This comes through in their voice, which can have a 'poor me' undertone, designed to confound the listener and make them feel guilt. At the very least, others can feel ungrounded by such a request and unable to think clearly. When Cancerians feel they have the right to ask for something they can nag – another indirect way of expressing anger.

Cancer's hoarding instinct can pose problems. There is a line between keeping useful items and a home that looks like a storage depot or even worse, a tip. Occasionally a story hits the headlines of someone living in complete squalor and never throwing anything away –

this is probably a slightly deranged Cancerian. Even if all these possessions are stored in a fairly efficient way (and usually their homes are rather chaotic and messy), the fact that their home is crammed to the hilt can create a suffocating atmosphere. This is fine if they only have themselves to consider, but in a shared space they rarely improve. Tidiness is just not something they can achieve. Probably it would stunt their creativity. Be warned.

One of the characteristics of the crab we've yet to address is their pinch. This is not a creature that attacks unprovoked but when threatened it has a mean pair of pincers that it deploys in its defence. All of this applies to a typical Cancerian, not least their ability to nip. Often this is done verbally in a fairly subtle way, but nonetheless those who have been pinched feel it. And because Cancer can be a tad oversensitive, they can feel endangered by something relatively minor and mount an out-of-proportion offensive. Remember, this is, of course, all conveyed in an indirect way. Those on the end of such a complicated attack find it impossible to get to the root of the problem and may never know what they did to cause offence, although they're left in no doubt that offence has been taken. A typical Cancerian has vendettas going back years that are seemingly insoluble.

In a close relationship this kind of game playing can go on interminably. It's a kind of dance, whereby the crab attempts to out-manoeuvre their loved one, never coming clean about their agenda. They probably aren't actually conscious of it themselves – they're just acting instinctively. Anyone hoping for a more open and honest relationship is in for a rude awakening.

Like a crab, Cancerians have a tendency to hang on with their pincers and refuse to let go. This has various implications psychologically, but one is that they hold on to old hurts and nurse their grievances. This is not a sign that forgives and forgets – once wronged, they'll remember it for life. In an argument they'll not stay with what's currently on the agenda but return to old scores and bring up unresolved incidents from way back. It's somehow never possible to get beyond the past and into what's happening now. This is deeply frustrating for loved ones, who want to move on. There's no such thing as a clean slate with a Cancerian.

Cancerians are also known for their resilience, getting what they want through their persistence. They wear the opposition down. They may appear to give up but actually this is all part of their strategy. A new approach is being hatched, although again it's important to emphasise that this may not be consciously thought out as they operate in a primitive, instinctual way. Because these individuals appear timid and unassertive, it's easy to underestimate the power they exert and their capacity to get their own way. Think what the sea, over time, does to the rocks.

The Cancer Man

With his quiet charm and enigmatic presence the Cancerian man has a powerful allure. He is recognisable by his ability to convey emotion. His face often has a fleshy softness to it and his feelings are readily visible. He has a moody, broody charisma. Part of his attractiveness is his sensitivity, he's easy to talk to and genuinely listens. This is a kind and gentle soul who cares about how those around him are feeling and shows it. Others are drawn by his attentive manner, open up to him and value the understanding and empathy he exudes.

The Cancerian man likes women and has a lot of female friends. He enjoys their company, their conversation and is genuinely interested in them and their lives. It's not that he doesn't have male friends too, but he'll have far more of the opposite sex. The Cancerian male is able to talk about his doubts and fears so in many ways he fits in with and feels more at home with women. His own feminine side is well developed and he doesn't have to mask or deny it when in female company where it's actually really appreciated.

This sensitivity also creates many difficulties for the Cancerian man. It is perhaps the most difficult sign for a man in a society where showing feelings and emotions is considered weak and where macho behaviour is valued. Just like the crab with its tough outer shell, many develop a hard exterior to protect and defend themselves. They learn to hide their vulnerability and only ever display the carapace. These men experience difficulties establishing close satisfying relationships and by cutting off from their inner life they cut themselves off from all that nourishes them too. They've imposed a metaphorical tourniquet on their lifeblood. This is a dreadful price to pay in order to fit into Western culture.

Most Cancerian men manage to strike a balance, whereby they have a hard shell that they can retreat into when threatened but will come out and relate and connect to others in a meaningful way. They learn when and to whom they can reveal their vulnerability and one such time is when in love.

The Cancerian man is a woman's dream. She will never have met a man so able to tune into her and know her inner being. She'll drown in him. Not only does he understand her feelings and emotions, he positively welcomes them – a latent side of his nature has an outlet at last. He offers a lover a connection at a deep feeling level. When in love he also offers his beloved a sense of certainty. This is the domain in which he has confidence, he can make a commitment based on how he feels and knows he's on solid ground.

However, if the Cancerian man is not smitten he can still seem very involved to his lover who may believe she's met her ideal man, while *he's* just dallying. Because he's so adept at tuning into a woman he makes an accomplished lover, he's considerate and attentive and emotionally open, so it's easy to misread the signals. He may well leave behind him a string of broken hearts, wondering what went wrong. For him, nothing went wrong as such, they were just not the one. Unlike Gemini, who may never find 'the one', Cancer does. Before too long he settles down into a relationship and wants to have children. This applies whatever his sexual orientation. Of all the gay partnerships, one that contains a Cancerian man is most likely to look at how that might include children.

As a partner, a Cancerian man is superb. He can cook, is domesticated, emotionally available and absorbed in family life. He needs to be needed and endeavours to make himself indispensable, which makes him dependable and reliable. He seeks and offers steadfastness and security and does what it takes to protect and safeguard his relationship. This is his anchor in life; it underpins his ability to function in the world about which he has no illusions. Once he's given his heart he wants it to stay safe.

This doesn't mean the Cancerian man is guaranteed to be faithful. He may have the odd affair, but he won't risk his mainstay relationship. His affairs, if he has them, happen by accident. He always has close friendships in which he has an unusual degree of intimacy and if the opportunity presents itself this can break through the normal bounds. He's relatively inscrutable when he chooses to be, so all his partner may register is that he's a bit uncommunicative and moody. He'll continue to shower a partner with love and attention so that any playing away won't be that apparent. He gets away with it.

On the whole, even if he occasionally strays, the Cancerian man's sexual interest in his partner won't diminish. He has a strong libido and whereas some men are able to separate sex and love, for him they are invariably intertwined. Which is why, once in love, he's in the main faithful. For him, sex is a moving and deep exchange with a loved one. It's also deeply emotionally reassuring and part of his sexual drive is in order to obtain this reassurance. Much of his inner confidence and feeling of self-worth rests on being wanted and if a partner wants sex less frequently than he does, this can threaten him at a fundamental level. So, although he's a great lover, his sexual demands can feel quite loaded to a loved one, who knows how much is at stake for him and the extent to which he suffers when turned down.

There are occasions (perhaps when the Cancerian man's main partnership is going through a bumpy patch) when he turns elsewhere for solace. He doesn't cope well with any level of rejection – it makes him feel excruciatingly vulnerable. This kind of liaison is rather different to his 'accidental, opportunistic affairs' as it does pose a threat to his partnership. He's in danger of becoming emotionally involved elsewhere and facing an excruciatingly painful choice further down the road. Where there are children involved a Cancerian man will be extremely loath to leave, however dissatisfied or unhappy he is in his relationship and he will tolerate considerable difficulties in order not to be separated from his children.

The Cancerian man is par excellence a family man. He makes a great father as it's the perfect outlet for his caring, protective side. Depending on his and his partner's respective earning power and circumstances, this man has the makings of a house-husband, but if that's not to be he's a hands-on dad and extremely helpful and supportive around the house. He's particularly keen on cooking and shopping (he likes to choose his ingredients) and will happily take on that role full-time, leaving his partner to do other things. However, he's not the tidiest of people; all that creativity in the kitchen can generate quite a bit of washing up so a dishwasher is probably a good investment.

Besides the cooking, if the Cancerian man is not at home

taking care of the children, he'll endeavour to make it home in time for their evening bath and bedtime story. As his children grow up he remains interested in the nitty-gritty of their lives and is a reliable and dependable father and his offspring will feel able to confide in him. His active involvement is a real boon for his partner, who gets plenty of emotional support.

When things are not going well for the Cancerian man he communicates it through his moods and it has to be said that men don't cope as well as women with their inner emotional fluctuations. Men have even less of a handle on what's going on, take even less responsibility for the thunderclouds they emanate and expect loved ones to rescue them from the muddle they are creating. A degree of moodiness can be attractive, but too much and the atmosphere can permeate a whole house and everyone in it is affected. Such a moody man can in a passive way control and tyrannise all those around him. It's important to confront him and not to let him get away with it. He needs help to unravel what's causing his moods, so challenging him will ultimately be of use to him, too. This is the price he pays for his sensitivity.

One of his endearing characteristics is his sense of humour. A little wacky, he has this oddball perspective that can be quite hilarious. His standpoint is always highly personal, he has a way of including himself and relating situations back to himself, which is both interesting and charming. He doesn't tell jokes or hold forth and he's not an entertainer but rather his humour is intimate and involves those he's actually talking to.

If space permits, a room that's his alone reduces domestic stress. A study, a den, or even a garage or garden shed, somewhere he can store all his bits and pieces and somewhere a loved one can dump things that he leaves scattered about the house. Cancerian men are not going to be the tidiest and they collect and hoard to boot, but with some forethought and planning this can be managed. For those about to set up home with such a man, think storage – plenty of it.

Cancer men also direct their creative, nurturing, caring side into their work and the helping professions are densely populated with these men. We've already admired his culinary skills and this is another avenue he can pursue professionally, he's at home in the kitchen and a natural chef. If, however, he decides that nurturing others in this literal way is not for him, then he can apply his talent for nurturing in a symbolic way. He's excellent at fostering others' talents and excels in a supportive role. Managerial positions and a business career are further possibilities. This man has flair and imagination so he can also be found working in the arts which provides a fulfilling and rewarding option for him. His receptivity makes music, art, theatre and film all potential areas for success.

Working with animals, as a vet, farmer, breeder or rescue worker is another road the Cancer man might take. This is a kind, gentle man and if he chooses to follow a career that involves animals he has a special magic that he brings to it. He's able to tune into an animal and connect to it in a sympathetic and helpful way. The Horse Whisperer must be Cancerian.

The Cancerian songwriter, singer and musician George Michael exemplifies this sign. He's undoubtedly creative; he has a moody, emotional presence and values and protects his privacy. He also takes things personally and his feelings are easily hurt, as his songs and videos reveal.

The Cancerian actors Tom Hanks and Harrison Ford have both played a wide range of roles and are particularly gifted at portraying the inner feelings of the characters they play. Tom Hanks, too, possesses the ability to appear ordinary – he has the 'common touch' – another Cancerian talent.

Cancerian actor Sylvester Stallone, who is well known for his physique, has perhaps developed a shell to protect his sensitive nature. Maybe his well-honed body also serves as a carapace. He shows that, no matter how sensitive this sign is, men can still have a macho appearance.

The US president, George W Bush, is a high-profile Cancerian who demonstrates many characteristics of this sign. He witnessed the terrible assault on the American people in the attack on the World Trade Center, which would impact profoundly on a Cancerian. His war-mongering has been motivated by further perceived threats to America and whether or not these turn out to be justified, this is typically Cancerian. They always want to protect their own.

Another prominent Cancerian is Prince William, who, like his Cancerian mother, Diana, Princess of Wales, appears touchingly shy. His obvious vulnerability is endearing and he exudes sensitivity and emotion. As Prince William's rapport with 'ordinary people' develops he has every chance of being as well loved as his mother was and becoming 'the people's prince'.

For those who are involved with a Cancerian man, don't expect him to play the macho role, as even though he can, it's not really his style. Appreciate the soft underbelly of this crab and he'll never stray and will be yours for life. He's not perfect but as an involved, supportive and caring partner it doesn't get much better.

The Cancer Woman

The Cancer woman is recognisable by her gentle, caring and sensitive nature. She's self-contained and self-possessed and although not necessarily reserved, she's never pushy or loud. When she does speak, others listen, as she has an innate authority, which comes from the fact that she only ever ventures an opinion on things that she knows about. She can therefore be relied upon to speak sense.

The Cancerian woman holds traditional values and

prioritises her private life. Whether or not she has a career, and many do, those she cares about come first. She's very much rooted in her family and remains an involved daughter, not out of sense of obligation, but because of her protective nature and the emotional bonds. One of her interests may well be in her family tree, as she appreciates her ancestral lineage and the sense of continuity this provides.

History, and in particular how people lived in the past, fascinate the Cancerian woman. When she picks up a novel, it will more than likely be one placed in an historical context. Her taste in furniture and furnishings tends to be antique and traditional, with the emphasis on comfort. Her house is probably pre-1900, as she appreciates the character of an older building. She enjoys visiting stately homes and admiring all the beautiful artefacts. It's not that she wants to live in the past, it just helps her understand her place in the whole scheme of things.

The Cancerian woman is famous for her humour, which is zany and off-the-wall. Entertaining and endearing, with her anecdotal stories and self-deprecating wit, she helps others to feel accepted and included. In fact, she's a master at using her own experiences to disarm others. She has a way of being intimate and personal without actually giving too much away. An asset at any gathering, she enables those around her to relax and feel comfortable.

The Cancerian woman is not at all threatening. She does her utmost to make others feel safe and at ease because this is something she also needs. She's attuned to her own and others' emotional well-being and recognises slights that other less sensitive souls would miss. As a consequence she is easily hurt by unintentional insensitivity and is always careful of others' feelings, imagining herself in their shoes.

One of the consequences of the Cancerian woman's sensitivity is that she is no good at dealing with conflict. If she has a difficulty with a loved one she deals with it indirectly. Her technique is similar to that of the crab: move in a sideways direction and maybe give the odd pinch. She's not above throwing a mood either and her emotional weather is something to behold.

The storm clouds that the Cancerian woman generates may be deliberate or may be something she has little control over. Usually, she has some choice. What's discernible is that the atmospheric density increases around certain people. No one is in any doubt that there's a problem, although getting to the bottom of it and sorting it out is another matter. Just as she can be tipped into a mood without really knowing why, so her disposition can miraculously change for no apparent reason.

These moods of the Cancerian woman can be quite hard for those who live with her, because there's no knowing if it's directed at them or not. It's very easy for them to feel blamed and imagine that they've somehow caused offence or inadvertently hurt her. Loved ones can be plunged into feeling guilty with no understanding of what exactly it is that they are meant to have done wrong. And it may have nothing to do with them. Putting someone on a guilt-trip is not the most admirable way of dealing with difficulties, and the best way for loved ones to deal with her moods is to never assume responsibility, that way she has to attempt to find a different solution. Encouraging dialogue is also recommended, as putting her grievances into words is as much a revelation for her as it is for those around her.

That said, moods are a part of the Cancerian woman and won't ever go away. This woman is rooted in her own inner depths and although she can't always explain herself, she's not about to abandon her way of being in the world. This is not a rational woman; she follows her instincts. She doesn't think things through, she feels things through and this can take a while and be a temperamentally demanding process. Stand back and give her the space. A lot of the problems arise because loved ones take her disposition personally.

The Cancerian woman doesn't quite fit into the introverted or extroverted category. Essentially introspective and
private, she likes time to herself and enjoys periods of
solitude but also needs company. She doesn't like to spend
too long on her own. Her preference is to be surrounded
by loved ones. She takes pleasure from social occasions
that have real meaning and significance for her. Celebrity
hobnobbing won't impress her; she loves family occasions
like birthdays.

For those captivated by this woman, a few pointers
follow. The Cancerian woman evaluates people and
situations according to how she feels, so this is how a
potential partner will be judged. Wooing her means
showing her consideration. She'll appreciate the small,
thoughtful gestures that demonstrate a lover has her in
mind. Remember the shape of her day and the things that
are important to her and make time for her. She expects
emotional involvement and support, and practical help
won't go amiss either, in so far as it demonstrates tender
loving care. When enamoured, she offers this kind of
solicitous attention too.

When in love, nothing is too much trouble for the
Cancerian woman. Her loved one is her number one priority and she invests all her creativity into the relationship.
She is decidedly the marrying kind and, if lesbian, she'll
still be looking for a long-term partner to settle down with.
She values emotional security and looks for a partnership
that has a future – one where she can imagine growing old
together. To her the upset and upheaval of a separation
doesn't bear thinking about, so she'll make a prudent choice
of mate, keeping dependability, reliability and the long haul
in mind. Even if she's very taken with a beau, if what she's
looking for is not on offer, she'll move on. She's not going
to waste her time if there's little scope for a committed
relationship to grow and develop.

In this sense the Cancerian woman doesn't trifle, she's

serious about her future. However, once that's secured, on a day-to-day level she does play games. She might not see it as such; perhaps it's just that she's at the mercy of her inner feelings. Whatever, she can lead a partner a merry dance as she fluctuates and changes. So there's constancy of a sort on offer, but not of an entirely unchanging variety. Keep the shifting shape of the moon in mind. It's actually always there and in reality doesn't change, but from our point of view here on earth it's constantly changing shape. She's pretty much like that.

Cancerian women are possessive and territorial. When young, they don't manage the flat-sharing phase that well, as they have a rather matriarchal, dominant streak to their nature, which means that, unless they are lesbian, they don't much like sharing space with those of the same gender. She's ahead of her peers, too, with her nesting instincts and will surprise flat mates by buying things like a washing machine and expect a contribution from them when they are still perfectly happy to use the launderette. This woman likes to run her home her way and be in charge. She's more attached to her possessions than most because of the emotion she invests in them.

These possessive feelings extend to partners. The Cancerian woman is keenly aware of what she could lose and endeavours at all times to protect her own interests. She's not particularly jealous in nature, as compared to, say, Taurus or Scorpio, but she deals ruthlessly with anyone who threatens her safety and security. This is when her talons are drawn and she won't fight by any rules, she simply fights to win – to survive. Never underestimate her, as despite her kind and gentle nature she can be tough when it's needed.

When things are going well, she offers love and attention in abundance to her loved ones. The Cancerian woman is the nurturing type and she thrives when in a position where she can take care of others. She's likely to choose to have children and, as a mother, she's in her element. If, however, she decides to direct these qualities into her career, then she can do very well for herself.

A Cancerian mother finds it difficult to juggle both family and career, which doesn't mean she can't have some kind of meaningful job but it does mean she won't invest her all into her work. If she opts to have a child this will bring her tremendous fulfilment and satisfaction and be her priority while her career will take a back seat. Ideally, if she can resume her career a few years down the line, this will be best for her and her family.

One of the dangers for the Cancerian mother is that she invests so much of herself into family life that, as and when her children grow up and fly the nest, she is left feeling completely bereft. Or she makes it very difficult for them to leave, hanging on to them in all kinds of subtle and manipulative ways. Her need to be needed means she thrives when her children are little and dependent but finds it hard to relinquish them and allow them age-appropriate independence. For this reason alone, she may have several children, fairly well spaced out, so that over a protracted time she always has a baby to care for. The point at which her youngest reaches school age is a time when she may well get broody and want another. For those involved, if another child isn't what you want, suggest alternative creative outlets and make sure she isn't the one responsible for contraception – accidents do happen.

While the care and protection the Cancerian woman offers young children is just what they need, there comes a point when they may find her over-protective and smothering. Her partner, too, may find their relationship a tad claustrophobic at times. She demands emotional closeness and needs to repeatedly affirm her connection to those she's close to, so everyday living can be rather intense. If her partner then pulls away because they want some space, she'll feel insecure and become more demanding. The more settled and secure she is within a partnership the less likely she is to throw an occasional emotional tantrum.

The Cancerian woman who decides not to have children has an abundance of creativity at her disposal. This is a woman who can rise to the top of her chosen profession as she has much to invest. Especially if she is single, she will be looking for a great deal of satisfaction from her work. Besides the obvious careers in the hospitality industry and the helping professions, which actually may suit a Cancerian with children rather better, she can do very well in business. She's good with people and understands commerce in an instinctive way and has a lot of energy and drive to boot. She's excellent at nurturing a small enterprise and watching it grow and flourish. And her empathy and relating skills means that she can draw the best from others, gaining their support with her endeavour.

A career in the arts or the media is another option open to Cancerian women. Their ability to establish a sense of intimacy quickly means they make great interviewers, whether working in radio, television or journalism. They have a knack of drawing others out and getting their interviewees to confide in them.

They may choose to act as they often have a gift in portraying inner states of mind. Meryl Streep is a Cancerian actress known for her emotional range and subtlety. She brings to her roles a depth of feeling that touches the audience. This is the gift of all Cancerians.

The suffragette and feminist activist, Emmeline Pankhurst, was a Cancerian and through her, and others', militant action in the early 1900s, women eventually won the right to vote. Although militancy is not necessarily typical of this sign, Cancer women, like Pankhurst, can become so when sufficiently outraged.

Elizabeth Kubler-Ross was another extraordinary Cancerian who did pioneering work on the care of the dying. Her book *On Death and Dying*, published in 1969, opened up this taboo and often much-neglected subject and brought into the public domain greater understanding of the grieving process. But more than anything she helped to bring greater dignity and respect to the care of the terminally ill, especially children.

Cancerian Tracey Emin, the controversial British artist, shocked the art establishment with her exhibit at the Turner Prize exhibition of an extremely untidy unmade bed. Soiled and in disarray, this is an intimate and personal exhibit, that disturbs by bringing strangers in to a private place. Much of her work is revealing and has the power to cause discomfort and embarrassment to viewers.

But perhaps the most famous Cancerian of all was Diana, Princess of Wales, who did a tremendous amount of charitable work, with children her priority. Even before she became a princess, she was working in a nursery. Diana's compassion and empathy illustrates the best of this sign. That she may have been emotionally hungry herself does not detract from this in any way.

The Cancerian woman is a caring, kind and gentle soul, who can be whipped up into a fury when her survival needs are not met. She is temperamentally complex and challenging. She brings an emotional depth and richness to those whose lives she touches. Treasure her.

The Cancer Child

The Cancerian child is imaginative and gentle and maybe a little timid. These impressionable and sensitive souls pick up and reflect back whatever's going on in the environment – especially within the family. If this baby regularly has colic at six in the evening and this coincides with their father coming home, it may be there's tension when he arrives or it could simply be they mind no longer having their mother all to themselves.

Cancerian children are and remain strongly attached and possessive of Mum and may see Dad as a rival from a very early age. One eleven-month-old baby, in bed with both her parents and feeding on her mother's breast, glared at her father, as if to say, 'What are you doing here'. Way before the usual developmental stage when little boys imagine that they will marry their mothers when they grow-up, this tiny chap can harbour these ideas. These children are undoubtedly Mummy's boys and girls. Father will get a look in, but not until they're a bit older.

Cancerian children are highly attuned to their personal safety and security and the image of the toddler, peeping out from behind mother's skirts, fits these little ones. They come out and greet whomever, as and when they are ready. It's best to allow them to take their time and not to make a fuss, as coaxing them is not going to help. All it will do is draw attention to their predicament and make them even more self-conscious. Like the hermit crab that can retreat into its shell when threatened and venture out when the coast is clear, so young Cancerian children wait until they feel safe.

So, Cancerian children stick close to mother. She's the centre of their world and essential to their well-being and they are acutely aware of this fact. They know they need her and their attachment lasts right into adulthood. Throughout their childhood they remain more dependent on her than most children of a comparable age. The mother of such clingy or seemingly needy children can worry and wonder if she should be brutal and force more of a separation upon them. The answer is no. While it can be trying for her, especially if she's had other more independent children, this little one needs to move away from her as and when they can manage. They'll be damaged if they are pushed to separate before they are ready and it will actually only make them more insecure.

Let go of all preconceptions and give Cancerian children

unconditional love when they are little and they will grow up to be self-reliant and confident. Their mother need have no fears about over-indulging or spoiling them as they thrive on tender loving care, internalising the message that they're valuable and worthwhile, which in turn gives them self-esteem in later life.

Cancerian children's sensitivity means that they show their emotions easily. If they're hurt, they cry and they cry readily. It's important not to imply that there's anything wrong with this, their upsets should be accepted, and parents need to acknowledge their feelings in a matter-of-fact way while not making their tears into a drama. Treat them as a normal, everyday occurrence, which they will be, and don't blow them up out of proportion. That way, they learn to take their feelings in their stride neither cutting off from them and denying them nor wallowing in them.

Cancerian boys have a harder time than girls, as boys are more likely to be teased. This can do untold damage and should be resisted by parents, especially by the father, who may find uncomfortable feelings are evoked by his sensitive, emotional son. Girls may find that turning on the waterworks is a means to getting their own way. So, while it's important to acknowledge these youngsters' feelings, it's equally important to carefully monitor the outcome. Such a daughter may have her father well trained, especially if he's desperate to have her calm and composed again. These manipulative skills are clearly not to be encouraged.

When little, Cancerians enjoy helping mother and like to be given a task alongside whatever she is doing. They'll help with the washing up, making it into a fun game, sloshing water around. If Mum or Dad bakes, they'll pester to be allowed to make cakes and biscuits too. While they may be slow to become independent, they'll be way ahead of their contemporaries in being able to cook a meal. Given that this may be a career option for them and certainly something they'll enjoy, let them loose in the kitchen as soon as they are old enough.

Both sexes like to play house and with dolls and, again, this should be accepted. Don't expect a Cancerian lad necessarily to want to play football. He may well be keen but equally he may be drawn to play that is traditionally considered feminine. Dressing up, making up sketches and plays and creating dens around the house will appeal to boys and girls. These children have rich imaginations and colonise all kinds of everyday household items to create an imaginary world for themselves. Foster the creative and artistic streak in these youngsters and they may end up famous one day.

The Cancer child's heightened sensitivity is a real asset when it comes to their appreciation of music. Play them a wide variety of music and give them access to musical instruments and lessons if they show an interest and aptitude as they may well have a musical gift.

Take young Cancerians to art galleries and exhibitions and provide them with paints and crayons and modelling clay. Although, as children, their attention span may make the visit a bit frustrating for adults, they'll be stimulated and inspired. If possible, it's worth making a separate visit that's especially at their pace. Put their drawings and paintings on the wall. Admire and praise their efforts and they'll learn that their creativity is worthwhile. This is just one of many outlets for their imagination as although not all have artistic talent, they are all creative in some way.

Cancerian children need help from early on to be tidy. Making them responsible for their own room when still quite young is recommended. Offer them help when it degenerates into chaos. That way, they start to grapple with the problem and will emerge as adults knowing that if they simply dump stuff down it stays there. If parents tidy up after their messy offspring they never learn. There's no need to be fierce about this. Plenty of help can be given, but at their request. That way, they learn about the consequences of their actions and to be responsible.

Cancerian youngsters have a gentle and caring nature and definitely benefit from having a pet. In this respect, they show an innate sense of responsibility and maturity. Their empathy enables them to tune into an animal and be a considerate owner. Obviously not all families can accommodate a pet and it needs to be borne in mind that this child will form a strong and close attachment to any pet, so one that has a short life, like a mouse, may be a tad traumatic. However, any pet is better than none – whatever the family can manage.

A dog or cat is ideal. Be warned though, that the Cancerian child, if given half the chance, will want it sleeping in their room, even on their bed. A friend of mine's child had a black Labrador dog that would regularly sleep right in her bed. If this is absolutely not on, then be clear from the start, otherwise their bed will resemble a kennel. This child can spend many hours grooming a pet and, if they have a dog, training it, too. The emotional bond these children form with an animal is formative and sustaining. For the mother who needs a bit of space from a rather clingy child, this could be the answer.

Cancerian children become attached to their possessions, too. They hate throwing anything away, even if they haven't used it or played with it for years. Things have sentimental value for them and being separated from their favourite toy, shirt, or dress, even if it no longer fits, can be traumatic. And they'll remember this and hold it against the perpetrator, too. This is a tricky dilemma for the parents. Ordinarily no one would suggest being sneaky and getting rid of stuff when they're not there to witness it but this may be the only way. If it's possible, do it in two stages. Move things out and keep it somewhere out of sight for a while and see if they notice. This stage should last as long as possible, as a Cancerian child has a long memory.

Eventually, if nothing is missed, then it's safe to let it go completely.

However, on the plus side, the Cancerian child is an early collector of what may be an important collection one day. They like to save things, be it stamps, or thimbles, or special cards. It doesn't have to be anything valuable, they could save shells from the seashore or press wild flowers. These acquisitions are important to them and as such should never be interfered with, in the way suggested above. There's a considerable emotional investment on the part of the Cancerian child into their collection. This, too, enables them to develop feelings of self-worth.

Pocket money, which they may well save, is another way to foster feelings of independence and self-reliance in the Cancerian child. It gives them some autonomy and allows them to buy certain items that they want very badly. Even if their pocket money simply covers their comics and a bit more, it is a good idea to start it at a young age. Later, a small clothes allowance could be part of it, which will help them to manage their finances. Parents should make it clear, though, from the start, what their money is meant to cover, as they have been known to save all their money and expect parents to still buy all their everyday requirements.

The Cancerian adolescent is not nearly as difficult as many of the other signs. If they've been given the support and encouragement that they needed when younger, then this stage of burgeoning independence will be welcomed by the parents and go relatively smoothly. They're not likely to run wild.

Cancerians need to feel they belong and for a teenager the focus of their belonging begins to shift from the family to their peer group. Increasingly their emotional security is invested in their school friends. Typically, they'll be part of a social network who hang out together and listen to music. They'll want to be included in whatever it is their friends do, so a parent should be vigilant as to what their friends get up to. If their mates are up to no good then it's ten to one that they're up to no good as well. Not that these youngsters are easily led – they are strong-minded when it's needed – but they do want to be accepted and included and that holds considerable sway.

When it comes to school specialisation, if all things are equal, then Cancerian youngsters are more likely to prosper and find it useful to opt for the arts in general, including literature and languages and creative subjects, like art, drama and media studies. Cancerians are happiest when engaged in areas that use their rich imagination, however, if they show great promise and aptitude in the sciences then don't discourage this, as their caring side may take them into medicine or nursing or the caring professions.

University may be the beginning of an independent life, a halfway position during which they come and go, maintaining the safety of their room at home, while venturing forth and testing the waters in the outside world. Encourage them to choose a university away from home and to work during the long holidays. Those who don't take up a university place may need a similar opportunity to ease themselves out of the comfort and security of life at home.

Dependency is something Cancerians grapple with all their lives. Make sure, if you have a Cancerian child, that they are encouraged to have confidence in their own abilities. As they grow up don't always rush in to help them, allow them to flounder and fail and recover by their own efforts. That way they develop the resilience they'll need for later life. And, if they haven't left home by their early twenties, give them a push – they'll thank you for it one day.

5

Leo

The Lion

July 23rd to August 22nd

A fixed fire sign, ruled by the Sun

Introducing Leo

Leos are recognisable by their warm, sunny disposition and confident demeanour. The lion, which represents this sign, is the king of the jungle and Leos have a royal presence. Like the lion, they have a dignified bearing, with an inborn sense of their own significance along with an innate pride and poise. Not all can actually be king or queen but, nonetheless, they act as if this position were their inalienable right. They take centre stage and are commanding individuals.

Queen Elizabeth the Queen Mother, who lived to 101, is a shining example of a Leo. Although not actually born a royal, she possessed all the characteristics and later became Queen Consort by virtue of her brother-in-law, Edward VIII's abdication. She was loved for her Leo qualities, her warmth, generosity of spirit and polished dignity. Leos bring a sense of occasion to any gathering by their sparkling presence.

The lion is courageous and fearless and Leos similarly have these qualities in abundance. They are honest, have integrity and are reliable and principled. They never shrink from speaking their truth, so others always know where they stand. And they feel entitled to their opinions, which they voice with absolute certainty. They have this innate sense of responsibility and authority, so whatever their actual position in life, others automatically take notice and show respect.

As a friend said when out to dinner with a Leo, 'If the restaurant was on fire, you would spring into action and take charge, seeing it as your job to lead everyone out to safety'. She agreed and said the problem, if that's what it is, is that she sees in a flash what is required in any given situation and then automatically takes on the task. And this is what she does in all areas of her life. Not surprisingly, like many Leos, she is successful.

Leo is the second of the fire signs (Aries is the first and Sagittarius the third) and all the fire signs exude warmth. These are naturally friendly, involved individuals, who are spontaneous and big-hearted. With their intuitive take on life, they often find themselves in the right place at the right time and appear lucky. This is something they take for granted, trusting that fate will be kind to them.

This is arguably one of the most popular signs of the zodiac. Leos are renowned for their generous spirit and gallant, expansive, inclusive attitude. They give a tremendous amount and expect it back in equal measure. They believe that what goes round comes round and live by the principle of abundance. Never petty or mean, they won't lower themselves to behave in this way and if someone is nasty or underhand towards them, they walk away. They are far too dignified to demean themselves by responding.

As they are not afraid to take charge, they are often found in positions of power and authority. They carry this role lightly and, as leaders, are usually well liked. Former US President Bill Clinton was enormously popular during his term of office and is a good example of a Leo in power.

Leos' noble and magnanimous intentions are clearly visible for all to see and they emanate a sense of integrity, which inspires confidence. They are trusted as well as loved.

166

As a leader, they have vision and are not afraid to make radical changes in the way things are done. They use their personal power to good effect and do much good on behalf of others. Although it can go to their heads, as they're not above a touch of egoism, they usually rule, whether in politics or business, in a benign way that really does bring benefits to others. Not all Leos can occupy elevated positions but in less spectacular ways all Leos show these characteristics.

Napoleon Bonaparte, emperor of France showed the courage typical of his sign with his military daring and prowess.

Physically, Leos have particularly straight backs and hold their heads proudly. They are, however, susceptible to back problems, as it's the spine, literally the backbone, which feels the burden of all the responsibilities they take on. And back pain can be seen as the body's cry for more back up, more support; an indication that the individual is being challenged by their physical limits to do less.

However this vulnerability is viewed, Leos must take special care of their backs and gentle strengthening and stretching exercises are recommended. The stomach muscles support the spine, so strengthening these will help, as will many of the yoga exercises that keep the spine flexible. The Alexander technique is another useful system to master, as it enhances an awareness of movements and actions that place an undue strain on the spine and teaches how to move in a way that flows with the body's structure.

The sun, which is the centre of our solar system, rules this sign and Leos can expect others to revolve around them, like the planets orbiting the sun. They have an underlying sense of their own importance and, while they don't in any way presume that they are more important than others, their confident demeanour means that others tend to fit in with them and their plans. Leos have a gift at getting things on their terms. They possess an enviable mixture of a happy disposition, friendly outlook and an assured manner that is a real winner.

Introverted Leos do exist; not all are outgoing, and the more introverted individuals tend to exemplify, in a quiet and understated way, the pride and dignity of this sign. They have carriage and bearing. Others still gravitate towards them, sensing they have something special, even if it's not so obviously on display.

Leos appear to have a strong sense of identity but this is something that continues to grow and develop throughout their lives. The question 'Who am I?' is of fundamental importance to them and something they spend their whole lives answering. So, in fact, their quest is to *discover* their identity – it's not something they feel they have as a given. Many of their antics have to be understood with this in mind. They are continually experimenting to see who exactly they are. The pop star, Madonna, is a classic example of this kind of Leo behaviour. She continually reinvents herself as if she's saying 'I can have many identities, I can be this or that.' She doesn't feel confined to one image and her outer changes may reflect her inner search.

Leos are attention grabbers and heads turn as they enter a room. At any gathering they steal the limelight, upstaging others simply by their presence. At times this may be a deliberate ploy on their part but often it's something that simply happens. They take being the centre of attention for granted and thrive on being a showstopper.

Jacqueline Kennedy Onassis was one such Leo, who didn't consciously court all the attention she received. Her poise and bearing meant that all eyes were riveted on her wherever she went. She became a style icon, too, as others tried to copy this indefinable quality that she possessed. She maintained her dignity throughout her life, an example of a self-contained Leo who had dramas happening all around her but was in no way a drama-queen herself.

Leos need lots of recognition and acknowledgement.

Depending on how well this has been satisfied in childhood, some are hungrier for it than others as adults. Even in everyday conversation they have a tendency to exaggerate. They are naturally colourful and vibrant individuals who can make those around them appear dull and inspid. They don't necessarily set out to be noticed and can feel really hurt when others mind that they have been eclipsed, finding it hard to believe that they are not being deliberately upstaged. In this sense Leos are a little naive and as they mature they develop more sensitivity towards others and learn to take a back seat at – say – friends' special occasions.

With their innate sense of drama it's not surprising that many Leos are drawn to the acting profession. They thrive on the applause of a theatre audience and the fame and celebrity status that goes with a successful television or film career. But whatever arena in life they find themselves, they have a way of making those around them into an audience for their performance.

This sign is naturally proud and as a consequence Leos do need to actually achieve something of real significance that they can justifiably feel proud of. That way, they gain the recognition they seek in an honourable way. They are more than capable of rising through the ranks of any business or institution to take the top job and to carry it with aplomb. Never underestimate their capability as this causes a huge affront to their dignity and only fuels their determination. This sign is not easily beaten.

Ambitious though Leos may be, this is probably the most generous and warm-hearted sign, too – this is what makes them so well loved. They respond immediately and with obvious sincerity to a loved one in distress and will go to no end of trouble on their behalf. This is certainly not a fair-weather friend; they are loyal and steadfast and stick by their friends in times of difficulty. Perhaps because they recognise and identify with those in crisis, they know how important it can be to offer some timely undivided attention and to remind a loved one of how special they are.

Leos make reliable and trustworthy friends and lovers. Unlike some signs that generate excitement, they offer stability, too, and will go to the ends of the earth for those they hold dear. When in love, they are colourful and dramatic and create a dizzying whirl of energy that knocks a potential lover off their feet. When a relationship gets underway they offer a constant stream of affection and are not afraid of commitment. They don't play mind games and are upfront and this in itself is disarming and successful in terms of getting what they want.

However, the constant drama can become a bit wearying. A partner soon finds out that everything surrounding Leo is larger than life. This is not going to change; it goes with the territory.

What Leos offer is also a good indicator of what they need, so while wooing them it's important to shower them with attention. There is no such thing as overkill with a Leo – the more over-the-top and flamboyant the better. Shout your love from the rooftops. Propose on air or national television and announce it in the newspapers. They are happy that the whole world knows and they love the grand gesture. Just remember though, this is something they need forever, not just at the start of a relationship.

Leos live by a high moral standard and have considerable integrity. They can't be bought and react badly to anything underhand. They like things to be above-board and are honest folk. What they are vulnerable to is flattery. Lacking guile, they can't always tell whether or not others are sincere and consequently get taken in. They, wrongly at times, assume others are as honest as they are. Leos never deliberately mislead or play with someone else's feelings. Their need to be appreciated means they trust even the insincere flatterers. So, if a potential lover sets out to impress, they can be swayed.

Once involved, Leos need to be reminded regularly of how important they are to their partner. One of the worst things you can do is take them for granted. They expect to be treated as if they were a prince or princess. So, if the relationship is to survive, make a fuss of them. Leos appreciate gifts and gestures that make them feel special; these need not be expensive if they make the point. That said, expensive always makes the point – they like a present that has involved some sacrifice.

There will never be a dull moment living with a Leo. Their sense of drama infuses all that they do so that even the most mundane occurrences become colourful. However, they do have their quiet, reflective times, too, when they recharge their batteries. They can be self-contained when they choose to be. But, by and large, these are sociable individuals who surround themselves with friends and family. Their friends are varied and diverse, so they are also likely to bring people together who might not ordinarily cross paths. This contributes to the lively atmosphere that surrounds Leos.

Despite Leos' apparent easygoing nature, when actually living under the same roof they may not be quite so laid back. Unless they instigate it, they are not that good with change and like things to be done their way. They'll be surprisingly set in their ways and expect others to fit in with them. They have a stubborn streak that has to be encountered to be believed. When not getting their own way they can resist in an obtuse way. Even the most petite Leo can suddenly become a solid, immovable hulk, occupying space way beyond their actual size and seeming to weigh far more than they actually do. They simply won't budge.

This sign is particularly associated with creativity and, as having a child is the creative act par excellence, this is a natural and expected occurrence. Leos make proud parents. Their children thrive on the attention they lavish on them and imbibe the feeling that they are special and valued. So, a Leo parent communicates to their offspring that they have rights and are worthwhile. They invest their child with all the things that they crave, which, at its best, gives a youngster an opportunity to develop self-esteem that will hold them in good stead throughout life.

Leos love to play; this is intrinsic to their nature and more than anything, this is their greatest gift as a parent. Fooling around, horseplay and general tomfoolery comes naturally to them so their child feels he has a playmate. Play is associated with childhood but is ultimately about being creative; it's out of play that many great ideas are born. Leos retain this ability throughout their lives and can readily enter into their child's world. Whereas for some parents play is obligatory and a duty, for a Leo parent it is always a joy. This participation is a tremendous asset and enhances the scope of their child's imagination.

Not that the Leo parent can't be authoritarian at times, too. Their bossy and controlling side can be problematic but a plus is that they give their child clear boundaries so they know where they stand. There's no liberal, pussy-footing around with a Leo parent.

Leos' natural sense of authority and command means that they often boss others around. Born to delegate, they make good managers because they are so good at asking others to do things for them. But he warned: that royal, imperial streak can get out of control.

Alongside this, Leos have vision. This is an intuitive, future-oriented sign, which has a finger on the business pulse. They have a nose for knowing where it's at and are impressively convincing. If anyone is going to get a business loan for some madcap scheme, it's a Leo and it will almost certainly prove to be successful, too. They have faith in their own convictions and inspire confidence in others.

There are many arenas in which Leos can make their mark, from the business world, working as entrepreneurs and managers and directors, to a whole range of careers within the arts, where they also excel. Notice that in the commercial field they gravitate to the top jobs and that they probably didn't start at the bottom either. They don't suffer fools gladly and when in a position where they have to answer to another, if they don't respect that individual then there will be serious problems. Leos challenge those in authority and aspire to this position, genuinely believing they could do it better. Wherever possible, they do best when able to make decisions and organise others. With their flair and panache, they readily gain the respect of those who have to answer to them. They make humane and warm bosses who can get the best from their workers.

In the arts, besides performing, they also make good directors. Again their vision and organising ability stand them in good stead. Many will have artistic and design ability and could be working in these arenas. Whether or not they follow this as a career, many make a design statement wherever they go. Often turning themselves into a work of art, they take considerable trouble with their appearance and create a strong impression.

One Leo who became extremely well known as a fashion designer is Coco Chanel. Her style was chic and distinct and she was among the first designers to include accessories. Her bags and belts and shoes and scents are as famous as her clothes.

Whatever work Leo does, they need to be noticed. This is not someone who is ever going to tolerate being overlooked, so if they are an employee, recognise and acknowledge their talents or they'll leave for pastures new. In the right environment, they make great employees, investing tremendous enthusiasm into their job. With their sunny, friendly disposition, they brighten up any workplace.

Negative Leo

Many Leo characteristics can become negative. The fact that they have an inborn expectation to be popular and adored simply means their fall from grace is that much harder. When not getting the attention that they feel they deserve they can be outrageous prima donnas. Taking being overlooked quietly is not an option for them. They can throw a tantrum like no one else.

Part of the difficulty for Leo is that if they are not at the centre of things, and being shown that they are special and important, they can feel as if they don't exist. They feel annihilated by other's indifference. So their temper tantrum is a way to assert that they are a force to be reckoned with, as their very identity is on the line. It's a fight for survival. However, not many of those around them will realise this and they are pretty intimidating when making a scene.

Some signs, like Virgo or Capricorn, would die rather than make the kind of fuss of which a Leo is capable. In this respect they seemingly have no shame. Making a public spectacle of themselves does not faze them in the least. If they are annoyed, no matter that they're dining in a quiet intimate restaurant, they'll raise their voice and won't care who hears. It's all part of them feeling that they occupy centre stage and that what they feel in any given moment is of the utmost importance. Loved ones of a less flamboyant nature can find their outbursts excruciating. This is the down side to their spontaneous and colourful temperament.

Leos' need for an audience can also be problematic, especially if they aren't performers of some kind. In a personal relationship they can hold forth as if their friend or partner were the audience. Such a Leo will launch into what they have to say, regardless of the state of the other person. They have a desperate need to express themselves, no matter, and often fail to relate or connect to whomever they are actually speaking. They might just as well be on a soapbox, giving a speech.

One such Leo would arrive home and even if 'his audience' was ill and lying prostrate on the floor, he wouldn't notice until he'd said his piece. These individuals can be so full of themselves and find themselves so interesting that they assume others will be equally riveted. When they are on a roll they barely stop to draw breath.

Understandably, Leos get accused of being selfish and self-centred and in so far as they place themselves at the centre, they are. However, even the most egocentric Leo will respond if a friend or lover says, 'What about me?' They somehow expect others to be able to take the space they need, in the way that they can. There's nothing malicious about a Leo and they feel shocked and hurt when others, who don't fight their corner, blame them for it.

Leos can be very sure of themselves and express their opinions in a rather dogmatic way. In response others can feel put down, especially if they are not quite so sure where they stand. Some signs see the nuances and greys, while for Leo things tend to be black or white. There's nothing wrong with this, as such, but it doesn't leave much room for anyone else's opinions. Leos simply overlook the fact that not everyone is as seemingly cocksure of themselves or as assertive as they are, and expect others to match them.

This certainty that some Leos present is a cover-up but it's so convincing that others are taken in. For some reason they expect themselves to know – to have the answer – and put themselves under considerable strain to come up with something. So they act in a high-handed way, to fend off criticisms, which in fact attracts them. What will help is if they can learn to tolerate uncertainty and not knowing.

Leos' need for attention may start to resemble a narcissistic personality disorder. Narcissism is a wound to the sense of self that arguably comes from a lack of the right kind of attention as a child grows up and results in a voracious need for attention in adult life. Such a wounded Leo will drain those around them, as no amount of tender loving care fills the empty void. They differ from other Leos in the degree to which they make excessive demands on loved ones and the extent that they are completely self-absorbed. Everything revolves around them and is referred back to them as if nothing else exists. They have lost any comprehension of others' reality. They have gone beyond being a drama-queen, which has its own difficulties, into something far more extreme.

Most Leos don't cross this line, even if loved ones occasionally accuse them of behaviour that borders on the pathological. These are just bossy individuals and when it becomes too much, it's often driven by a fear that if they don't stay in control and tell everyone what to do, nothing will get done. Many secretly find the responsibility that they are expected to carry a strain and a burden.

This type of Leo has lost the ability to delegate. In order to delegate, Leo has to recognise an inner king or queen part of themselves and believe that there are others in this world to wait on them. This can go too far in the other direction but without it, they end up trying to please this inner tyrannical aspect of themselves and carry the whole world on their shoulders.

A bossy Leo may well be anxious and stressed and longing for someone to take charge, someone they can respect and rest assured that the task in hand will be accomplished as they would do it. And therein lies their trap. It's the 'as they would do it' that causes the problems. They can't or don't trust others to do a job as well as they would and this can become all too apparent. They hover over others and either inwardly or outwardly criticise their efforts. It's a *Catch 22* situation that Leo has – usually unknowingly – set up in which no one will ever be able to get a job done as well as them. Any Leo caught up in this has to allow others to fail and learn and has to find a way to let go of the reins. Leo is the original control freak – something to which even Madonna admits.

This side of Leo can make them overly authoritarian as parents. Their playfulness gets pushed aside by the need to feel in charge and, at worst, their homes can resemble a boot camp, with them the sergeant-major. No child responds well to being ordered about, so such a parent will have an almighty rebellion to deal with somewhere along the line. The more fearful Leos are of feeling out of control, the more repressive and tyrannical they become.

The Leonine need to be centre stage can be hard for their children. Of course, parents set the agenda and children do have to fit in with them but equally a child needs to feel they are at the centre of their parent's world. When a parent is too narcissistic, instead of demonstrating that their child is worthwhile, the opposite happens. Such a child can feel exploited – that they are in the world to fulfil their parent's needs, rather than the other way round.

Leos can be forceful and dominating individuals, especially when no one stands up to them. It can be a lonely position. This type can be miserable about their isolation and long to be challenged by someone who is not intimidated by them and who doesn't back down. However, this is not the answer – they have to learn to respect the rights of others and not to run roughshod over them, it's not ultimately up to others to give them appropriate boundaries.

Some Leos consciously indulge in power trips and have no idea why happiness and contentment subsequently eludes them. They probably think it's someone else's fault – these individuals are very good at blaming others. The fact that others are terrified of them doesn't register. Those around them may express awe and this is interpreted positively by them, such is their egocentric view. All the positive characteristics of Leos become distorted by those chasing power.

What drives Leo is their need to be loved. This is behind their ambition and control and even their delightful qualities like their sunny disposition, generosity and warmth can be cynically viewed as a bid to be loved and adored. This is what makes this sign so popular – they feed on the love they are so generously bequeathed by others and in turn give it back. It's only when a Leo is damaged and doesn't have the self-confidence to generate the love that they need that things turn ugly.

This kind of Leo can also be grandiose, believing themselves to be far more important than they actually are. A C list celebrity demanding preferential treatment and saying 'Don't you know who I am' is a prime example. Even when someone is important, a touch of humility doesn't go amiss – swaggering around is never going to be endearing. Grandiosity is just one way of masking feelings of inferiority, which may well be the result of not getting enough unconditional love in childhood. Leos need this in bucket loads; they need constant reassurance when young that they are valued and worthwhile – becoming arrogant and self-important is one consequence of it being in short supply. Not that feeling sorry for them helps when they are behaving in a thoroughly obnoxious way but some understanding of the psychological dynamics can make being around them more bearable.

Many of Leos more negative characteristics become apparent in a live-in relationship. They may well take up more space than their partner on all kinds of levels. They are very good at claiming their territory and don't go in for concepts like equality. If they need three-quarters of the wardrobe then they'll take three-quarters. If they have a picture they'd like to hang in the sitting room, they'll replace the one that's there. Leo finds it hard to imagine that loved ones won't agree with them and think they're right.

This unflinching self-belief is perhaps one of the most difficult Leo traits for a partner to live with. Leos are rarely swayed. They are utterly convinced of their own infallibility and will argue a point to the death. Getting a Leo to back down or admit that they might be wrong is nigh impossible. The most important thing for a partner is to be able to hold their ground and agree to differ. That way, a partner is not undermined and a chink of doubt may register in Leo.

Not all Leos are extroverts and the more introverted, while

not being as demanding or as likely to make a scene, have their special difficulties. They find it harder to get the attention they seek and are even more prone to arrogance. They can take on a haughty superiority. One Leo, who rings occasionally, never leaves a friendly or chatty message on my machine, just an 'It's X, can you call me'. It sounds like an imperial royal command. She'd probably be shocked and appalled to know how she comes across and is no doubt trying hard not to be demanding, but her tone gives her away.

This is a proud sign and some Leos develop a false pride that is vulnerable to injury at the least slight. Particularly the more introverted Leos, who, less able to command the attention they crave, can feel wounded and plot revenge. Others may not even realise that their pride has been hurt and wonder what's hit them when the return salvo is launched. Leos are prepared to suffer for their pride and this is a contributing factor in their inability to back down. Even when they know they are in the wrong about something, they can't bear to admit it and, as they see it, lose face.

Clearly Leos can succumb to delusions of grandeur. These individuals think and act on a grand stage, so if life does not provide them with this it can be a problem. Take a Leo man who is below average in height and he's more than likely to have a complex about it. While many men invest masculine pride in such things, the Leo man makes it a huge issue, to the extent that it becomes unmentionable. If he's short, then it's a taboo topic. He'll wear built-up shoes and only go out with women who are shorter than him. He can't bear to feel exposed and as he sees it, a woman who is taller shows him up.

Women have other issues, their vanity will be exercised by how perfect or not their bodies are, the size of their breasts for example – the way women are judged in Western society. Pamela Anderson is one such Leo woman, who is probably as famous for her breast enhancement surgery as anything else. So both Leo men and women have expectations of themselves to measure up to society's stereotypes and feelings of inferiority in areas where they fall short. It doesn't occur to them that not everyone shares these opinions.

But perhaps the most common and difficult Leo trait is their expectation that the world revolves around them. This is apparent in even the most self-aware Leo. Try making arrangements with one and it'll almost certainly be on their terms – others feel compelled to make concessions – concessions that they wouldn't make for anyone else and they may not even recognise that they have. Leos just have a knack of getting away with it. This is their gift and it infuriates and captivates those around them in equal measure.

The Leo Man

The Leo man is recognisable by his popularity – he's the guy that everyone is listening to. He seems successful and sure of himself, with an air of confidence that marks him out in the crowd. It is apparent that others instinctively defer to him, which he takes for granted. This man is masterly and masculine.

The Leo man has a spontaneous warmth and generosity. He responds immediately and makes decisions quickly. He gives the impression that he is – by and large – a happy and contented man and emanates a sense of conviction and satisfaction with his lot. He trusts his intuitive take on situations, which happens in a flash and he bases his choices in life on that. This is his cornerstone; it's how he operates.

His intuition is both the Leo male's strength and weakness. He's future oriented and his sense of what lies ahead enables him to see round corners. His accuracy at assessing others is unparalleled and he knows immediately whether he can trust someone and whether he can work and relate to them. All of this certainty adds to his self-confidence.

The downside is that the Leo man can't justify or explain

himself. Because he relies so completely on his intuition, he has no idea how he arrives at his decisions and can't back them up with facts or figures. When things go wrong he has only himself to fall back on. It also means he's not that grounded in the moment, he's always ahead of himself and focused on what's next.

The Leo man is very good at getting a sense of the big picture, but not so adept at filling in the practical details. He's not that good at implementing his grand schemes and needs others to help him out in the execution of his ideas. This can be annoying, as he'll want to claim all the credit, when actually he couldn't have done it without others' assistance; he has a canny way of stealing the glory and not acknowledging those who have been equally involved. He justifies this on the grounds that, as it was his idea in the first place, he has ownership of the project or concept: without him there would be nothing. While this may be true, it is a little disingenuous. It's his need for recognition that distorts his clarity – he wants the praise and to be the main player and that often overrides genuine fairness.

When it comes to love, the Leo man has a lot of masculine pride to take care of. He's not about to risk a rejection, not because he's sensitive in the way the water signs are, but because of how this would effect his ego. His ego is bound up with his confidence and self-esteem, so he has to protect it. He looks for clear signals that his advances will be welcomed before he makes a move. Once he gets the green light, he enjoys an extravagant courtship and wines and dines a prospective partner in style.

The Leo man is generous too; he'd never expect his date to share the expenses and is happy to pick up the tab. Displaying his wealth is all part of his masculine pride. There is something of the peacock in his character, especially when it comes to courtship. He likes to show off his resources and wants to impress. When out and about he takes charge in a masterly way. In a restaurant he snaps his fingers and the waiter responds – he readily commands respect. He plays the traditional masculine role and, if heterosexual, expects his girlfriend to complement him by playing her feminine part.

The Leo man's longing to be loved and appreciated means he's vulnerable to flattery and can be seduced by praise. Anyone who makes enough of a fuss of him has him purring away, more like a pussycat than a lion. This susceptibility means he doesn't necessarily see past appearances and the strokes his ego is given. He can look for a partner who enhances him and often that boils down to appearance – whatever his sexuality, he can go for a 'trophy wife'; he sees his partner as an extension of himself rather than a separate individual in his or her own right.

When involved, the Leo man can believe that, like the lion which has a whole pride of lionesses, he too should not be restricted to a monogamous relationship. He could well believe in polygamy. This may be no more than a fantasy but is not very flattering or reassuring to a partner. Whether or not he acts this out will depend to a large extent on his partner's attitude to monogamy. It's not even that he necessarily has a high sex drive. His partner may wonder where he's about to get the energy from to satisfy other lovers, when they might be happy to partake in sex more often. Perhaps it's the idea of a harem and what that does for his ego that appeals, rather than the reality of more sexual demands. However, a Leo man is essentially loyal and the more he acknowledges these desires the less likely he is to have illicit affairs. For those involved, if fidelity is important, then spell it out very specifically. He's unlikely to break a promise. Just make sure what exactly has been avowed is crystal clear.

The rock star Mick Jagger is a high profile Leo man who has a reputation as a philanderer. From media reports it's hard to know what the truth is but he has undoubtedly fathered children by different women, some while supposedly within a committed relationship, which seems to suggest he has some of the Leo tendencies just outlined. But he also maintains a close friendship with Jerry Hall, the mother of several of his children, so in this respect he demonstrates Leo's capacity for loyalty too.

Jagger seems to have good relationships with his grown-up children and is often seen in public with them, in social situations and supporting their creative endeavours. He is happy to be photographed at these occasions and is clearly a proud father – displaying positive Leo characteristics. However, perhaps Jagger's greatest passion and creative outlet is his stage performance, where he is in his element.

Sexually, the Leo man is not exactly adventurous. He may seem exciting out of the bedroom, where he displays considerable panache but once in it he's rather conventional. He's not a particularly sensitive lover. In common with the other fire signs, sex may be approached as if it were an athletic performance – one in which he strives to excel. As this doesn't necessarily involve him emotionally, it's not going to pass muster with a discerning lover. He may be accomplished, but his lack of deep engagement gives the game away. He's competitive too and when single and fancy free is not above scoring notches on his bedpost. That way he proves to himself how desirable he is.

Once in a committed relationship, the Leo man is more a creature of habit than one would normally suppose. He likes his routines and his days may have a familiar pattern to them. This is a fixed sign and as such he offers stability and reliability to a partner. In this way, he's extremely reassuring, being where he says he'll be and arriving on time. He emanates a kind of certainty, without ever being the least bit boring. He's sure of himself and what and who he wants in his life and is not afraid to demonstrate that.

The Leo man can be extremely generous, but it's very much on his terms. He likes to be the magnanimous one and to be seen as benevolent, so he'll give when he wants to but woe betide anyone who actually asks him for something. The problem with requests is that they make him feel mean and he hates that. He wants to be in control. The only way to get something from the Leo man is to somehow get him to think it's his idea. Then he can feel altruistic and chivalrous; his sense of identity is intact and everyone is happy. For a partner who is relying on him for financial support, this can feel a bit humiliating. He makes sure that they know in no uncertain terms that he has the financial power.

The extent to which the Leo man's generosity is bound up with his identity produces other problems, too. Sometimes he's bountiful with strangers rather than his nearest and dearest. He obtains more kudos from the unexpected acts of charity he performs and is gratified by the liberal thanks he receives. With those closest to him it's less rewarding. This can be enraging for a partner, who has to witness him being Mr Nice Guy with others, while not necessarily delivering the goods to him or her. That said, this is a kind and well-meaning man who is never deliberately mean or withholding. His particular brand of masculine pride means he expects to take care of all those around him and endeavours to do so.

The Leo man's pretensions to royalty must be mentioned. The fact that he's not king and could be anywhere on the social scale doesn't detract from the way he carries himself and the expectations he has of himself and others. He takes on responsibility for others and situations way beyond the call of duty and never shirks the difficulties inherent in being a leader. It's his calling, which he responds to whenever the need arises. Others can rely on him to take charge and show leadership and are grateful that at least someone has come forward to carry the responsibilities that they don't want.

The Leo man's leadership qualities can be tinged with ambition and issues around power and dominance can creep in, so he does well when he occupies this position legitimately. Then his title and the authority that others have invested in him back up his innate authority. He makes a great manager or director of a company as he's good at making decisions, can delegate effortlessly and is a superb organiser. Much of his creativity is directed into his organisational skills, at which he excels. His flair and vision can provide employment for a large workforce.

Off duty, the Leo man has a playful side to his nature, too and this is particularly evident when he has children. While he may find it hard to abdicate being head of his family, in a controlling way, he does enjoy having fun and being light-hearted. He's likely to introduce his offspring to cultural activities, taking them to the theatre and art galleries from an early age. These are activities he derives pleasure from and wants them to enjoy too.

If he plays sport, then the Leo dad is happy to do so with his children although his attitude may be a bit too competitive for younger children, who like to feel they are in with a chance, but teenagers can hone their skills with him. At least he doesn't patronise them by allowing them to win and enters into the game enthusiastically.

As a father the Leo man is encouraging and supportive, warm and involved, but he can also be quite strict and authoritarian. He certainly sets high standards and expects a lot from his children. He takes pride in their achievements and offers praise where it's due. With their future in mind, he's ever ready with suggestions as to the direction in life that they should take. Some of his own ambition, of which he has plenty, may get channelled into them. When this is the case it probably means he has unrealised potential that he is hoping to live out via his children – a complicated and potentially damaging burden for them to carry.

An unsuccessful Leo father, judged by his own criteria of what constitutes success, is a dangerous thing. He would do well to try to fulfil his own ambitions and back off from his children. Nevertheless, his involvement, even when a tad overbearing, has to be better than being a remote father. Children thrive on the fantasies that are woven around them, and he has these in abundance.

The Leo man is powerful and potentially forceful, with strong ideals and beliefs, for good or ill. He always thinks he's right and often sets out to prove that. Those who end up in politics use their considerable personal charisma to their own advantage. While their rule is often benign – Bill Clinton is an example – some are undoubtedly dictatorial and cruel. Fidel Castro and Slobodan Milosevic are Leo leaders whose records in power are still being assessed. Whatever the verdict, what is certain is that they have both exerted a massive influence on their countries and the rest of the world.

However, the Leo man's desire to make an impact is more likely to take him in other, more creative directions. Robert Redford, Dustin Hoffman, Antonio Banderas and Arnold Schwarzenegger are all well-known Leo actors who have made their mark in films and Redford has gone on to direct, so he literally gets to call the shots. Schwarzenegger's entry into politics as governor of California has brought many, so far unsubstantiated, complaints about his past sexual behaviour. While this could be damaging to him, it didn't stop him being elected, so he now has real power and control over the lives of others.

The Leo man never does anything by halves, so whatever career he follows, he invests his all into it. He brings to his work his inherent pride, authority, creative flair, intuitive genius and organisational ability. He's ambitious and dedicated and gravitates to the top of whatever field he's in at a dizzying speed. Whatever he sets his mind on, he can do.

For those who are thinking of getting involved, keep the lion in mind and remember what a magnificent, gracious animal it is. Along with being loved and adored, the Leo man needs plenty of strokes and, behind closed doors, he'll turn into a big pussycat. Don't be fooled into thinking this is a domestic animal, though, he still has a ferocious roar and sharp teeth and claws. Respect that and he'll keep purring.

The Leo Woman

The Leo woman is unmistakable. Regal and warm, upright and confident, she gives out the message, 'Here I am, notice me'. And everyone does. She's quite impressive. She stands out in the crowd and knows how to make an entrance.

For the Leo woman, life is one long performance, which doesn't mean she's not authentic, but it does mean she's always aware of her audience and the impact she's making. No one is as conscious of herself and how she comes across as a Leo woman. This resembles an art form for her. She has flair, style, panache and presence, is colourful and vibrant, which is why she gets noticed.

What can be particularly striking about the Leo woman's appearance, is her hair, which can resemble a lion's mane. Not all can be natural blondes, but many lighten their hair or have it 'sun-streaked' and more importantly, whatever the colour, their hair is often big and proud and very much her crowning glory.

Besides this, Leo women carry themselves well, with a particularly straight back and their head held high. They walk as if they are someone important and have a right to be proud. The lion is a noble beast and so are these women.

The Leo woman's confidence in life, which is considerable, is based on an innate conviction that in all matters, she is right. For those around her, this can be either infuriating or charming, depending on whether they are in agreement or not. She is absolutely rooted in her own belief in herself and in this respect she's unequivocal. And even if proved wrong, she contrives an excuse and doesn't back down. By the time anyone realises that she might be wrong, she's moved on anyway and is no longer even interested in the debate.

The Leo woman is big-hearted and gives of herself in an enthusiastic way. Her responses tend to be larger than life as she displays all her emotions, and those around her are in no doubt as to what she thinks or feels about them. She doesn't expect others to take offence; she is reasonably robust herself and expects a fair bit of cut and thrust as a part of everyday life.

When in love the Leo woman is extremely romantic and idealistic. In fact, reality is in short supply. Even if her beau has an appalling track record, she believes that with her it will be different and all will be well. Partly this is because of her over-brimming confidence, partly an omnipotent streak with a dire shortage of common sense. She is so convinced she's special, which indeed she is, that she gets quite carried away.

What this means is that the Leo woman can get badly hurt and let down, although she recovers relatively quickly from what might devastate others. Her recovery is assisted by the drama she makes, which acts as a catharsis so she is never left with bottled-up feelings. Whereas some signs would fester inwardly, she's emotional and expressive, talking things through with those close. She is also very forgiving. Some might wish she didn't forgive and forget so easily, at least not forget, as she goes on to make the same mistakes again. It's as if she never learns. She has an innocence and simplicity that is positively beguiling. Friends look on in wonderment at how, having had her heart broken, she can open it up to another in the trusting way that she does.

The Leo woman doesn't bear grudges and, as her recovery from any injury is rapid, when a relationship fails she bounces on to the next one. She's not usually short of admirers, so there'll be somebody waiting in the wings, upon whose shoulder she'll cry before – lo and behold – she's in the grip of her next grand passion.

Leo

The Leo woman's life is punctuated by her dramas, each one bigger than the last. Her friends are gripped by the details of her life, which she shares, in confidence, with them all, one by one. One friend of a Leo woman I know introduced herself as 'one of X's many best friends'. Each friend is made to feel special and in her mind they all are. When she has large gatherings, some of her friends can be dismayed to find how thin she spreads herself but soon forget, as she is such good company.

The Leo woman loves to entertain and makes a great hostess, bringing all her many friends together. Whatever the size, her parties are lavish and she's particularly good at creating the party atmosphere – hers are the parties that go on into the wee small hours, with dancing and games until dawn. Everyone wants an invitation, which is another reason why she has so many friends – people keep in with her in order to be included in her colourful social life.

Even at her parties, the Leo woman's ability to delegate is evident. She'll have various cronies in charge of things, like the music, or the food, or the drink, while she keeps the overall picture of the event in mind. She manages to bestow an elevated status on those helping, so that they are more than happy to assist. Getting others to do things for her and run around after her is an art form that the Leo woman has mastered.

This organisational skill means that the Leo woman does well in a career where she runs the show, either as her own boss or as a manager. She doesn't follow other people's direction very well, unless it happens to coincide with her own views, that is.

So, as an employee, the Leo woman can be difficult unless she is given the authority and autonomy over her patch, whatever that entails. Once she has that she'll work extremely hard. In fact, that is in part her problem as she throws herself into her tasks so wholeheartedly and gets so deeply involved that she becomes completely immersed in her job. With so much of herself invested, she clearly wants a great deal back. And more than anything, what she seeks is the power to do things her way and to have her say. So, while she doesn't make a good employee, she makes a great boss.

As the boss, the Leo woman can galvanise her workforce to give of their best and she generates enthusiasm and commitment. She's loyal to her employees and wants the best for them and from them. She won't tolerate slackers but is reasonable and understanding and never expects of others anything she isn't willing to undertake herself. Initially she feels hurt if an employee doesn't pull their weight, for she experiences it as a personal affront but whatever her private feelings she'll confront the situation and act in a decisive way. She's not afraid to flex her muscles or wield the power she has and rises to any occasion.

Apart from romance, where the Leo woman doesn't always see things so clearly, she has a good handle on what's what. She always holds the big picture in mind though she's weaker at dealing with the immediate details. This is partly because details bore her and she can't be bothered with them. She doesn't see them as important and so delegates that chore to someone else to deal with. The grand vision suits her temperamentally, while crossing t's and dotting i's is perhaps too menial for her – although she'd be loath to admit that. Don't forget that whatever her station in life, she is a princess, expecting there to be a servant on hand to do the chores.

The British royal family is populated with Leos. Besides the late Queen Elizabeth the Queen Mother, both Princess Anne and the late Princess Margaret were born with the sun in Leo. Princess Anne displays the imperious and aristocratic side of her sign and, for a Leo, is not particularly popular. Princess Margaret was in many ways more typical, with her penchant for parties and the good life. She avidly supported the arts and some have said that she really wanted to be queen. In her early life, when it came to a choice between her love for the 'commoner', Peter Townsend, or remaining a princess, she chose the latter, which may have been a decision she lived to regret.

Madonna has to be a shining example of this sign. As a performer, she's been trashy and showy and classy all at the same time, quite a combination to pull off. Her arch rival in the early Nineties, Whitney Houston, is another Leo who possesses a similar magical allure. Both have a magnetic presence that stops others in their tracks.

The performance artist and musician, Laurie Anderson, is also a Leo. She may not be as well know as Madonna and Whitney, but she brings a uniquely creative style to her work that makes it stand out. Quite out of the ordinary, she has a loyal fan base and continues to create exceptional and unusual recordings. What all three have in common is a gift for performance, in which they push the boundaries of what's possible in a live show.

For those who have become involved with a Leo woman, she has much to recommend her. She is loyal and stead-fast and although a bit theatrical, she doesn't play games. She's honest and authentic in this respect and, despite all the drama the surrounds her, she's looking for stability. She thrives when her main emotional needs are taken care of in a secure relationship. Then her crisis can be about minor things, like what to wear.

Once in a settled relationship, provided she's heterosexual, the Leo woman's thoughts are likely to turn to babies. A child is the perfect outlet for her creative drive but she's unlikely to choose to be a single or a lesbian mum. If she can't make a baby with the person she loves she'll direct this drive elsewhere. For her, having a baby is about creating something tangible out of the love she feels for her partner. Once her first child arrives she has no problem in loving him for his own sake, but the initial drive is to cement her love. After her first offspring, she'll almost certainly want a second and even a third, as that's what constitutes a proper family to her and if she's doing the family thing she wants to do it properly.

As a mother the Leo woman is in her element and brings in to play all her organisational skills. The physical mess created by her baby's early years doesn't faze her, especially as she's so good at getting on top of domestic chaos. She's efficient and strong willed, gives her children clear boundaries, fosters their creativity and is very good at running a home like a business, well organised with plenty of the chores delegated. She sees that the children get to all their extra-curricula activities, whether or not she's the taxi service, and that the fridge is well stocked and the house clean even if she simply orchestrates the whole show. This she may do, with the help of a nanny or au pair, while working full-time, too.

Depending on what the Leo woman has achieved to date with regards her career, she's unlikely to give it up when she has a child. Those who are full-time mothers are in danger of investing too much of their own ambition and creativity into their children, so going back to work is recommended. If any woman can have it all – be a superwoman – it's a Leo woman.

One of the characteristics of the Leo woman that can be both infuriating and charming is her utter conviction that she is right. She is absolutely rooted in her own belief in herself and in this respect she's unequivocal.

For those thinking of getting involved with this exciting and impressive woman, here's a checklist of the credentials required. They'll need to be able to hold their own with a fiery temperament and recognise the inherent vulnerability behind her seemingly egotistical and selfish demands. She needs plenty of reassurance, ranging from deep insecurities about her worth and value, to superficial praise that she looks good tonight. Never neglect her; like an exotic and high-maintenance plant, she shrivels up and dies if not given the right kind of regular attention. Keep that sense of importance and that royal connection in mind. She's not that complicated. Appreciate her, she's worth it.

The Leo Child

The Leo child is a complete joy. Sunny and easygoing, this child has everyone wrapped around his or her little finger from the word go. They come into the world with the expectation that they are meant to take centre stage and proceed to claim this position. Leo is an entertaining, delightful and adorable child.

All parents think their child is special but, in this case, others will agree. Even when very little, Leos shine and have an ability to pull others into their orbit. Their magnetism captivates those around them and these winning ways will take them far in life.

Leo children have a dignified and regal demeanour even when very young. Most babies don't mind if they have sticky fingers but one Leo baby I knew would sit in her highchair, wave her hands in the air and shout to get them wiped, like a little princess. This particular baby failed to learn to crawl; it was as if even attempting this was beneath her dignity. Instead she went straight on to walk.

Missing out the crawling stage is not uncommon among Leo babies. They have no urgency to be on the move and are quite happy to sit and have others fetch and carry for them, which is something they have no problem in obtaining. And, as soon as they can sit, they hold their backs up straight and when out and about, look out from their pram or buggy, as if surveying their land.

Leo children's leadership quality shines through and in nursery, games like 'follow-my-leader' instantly appeals as long as *they* are the leaders. They quickly take charge and assume a central role in play activities, bossing other children around if given half the chance. Because they are popular and everyone has such a good time under their direction, they get away with it. In fact, this is a role they seem to get thrust into – others just expect it of them.

Leo children, like all those born under a fixed sign (Taurus, Scorpio and Aquarius are the others), have a stubborn streak. Way before the 'terrible twos' these little ones try to get things on their terms. Even when babies they can throw spectacular tantrums if they don't get their own way. For the parents, who don't know quite what's hit them, remember this a lion cub with a strong imperial will.

A mixture of deft avoiding action along with surrender when the fuss is about something that is unimportant is recommended to parents of Leo children. Give in when it doesn't actually matter too much and try to pre-empt situations that you have learned trigger a scene. It is very easy to feel completely out of control with such a child and believe that it's essential to assert some authority. Parents may well have fears for the future about how such a strong-willed child will grow up if not thwarted. Actually, they'll be fine, there's no need to worry and there's no shame in giving in. These children become far more easygoing as they begin to feel more in control of themselves.

The very fact that they lack independence and autonomy is why Leo children are so prone to temper tantrums – they just don't cope with this phase very well. They know they are somehow meant to be in charge and run the show and they just can't wait to exercise this power. As they mature, parents are advised to give them as much freedom as possible to follow their own volition and make choices about their life and future. On an everyday level, try to include them in all decisions that relate to them and when this is not possible, negotiate with them rather than being in any way dictatorial.

Leo children will rebel, big time, to anything that's imposed upon them as a fait accompli. However, this kind of parental attitude can do damage to their self-esteem.

These are proud little souls and to lose all sway over their own affairs is humiliating. Simple choices like what clothes to wear and possibly even when to go to bed, which can become land-mined territory, can be handed over to them, along with the consequences if they misjudge. They respond well to this and repay the trust placed in them by behaving responsibly.

With a Leo child, time and time again, parents have to ask themselves, is this really important or not? On reflection, all sorts of matters are simply done because of convention. One young Leo, no more than three or four years old, regularly goes out with her mother to the supermarket in all kinds of fancy and, some might deem, inappropriate dress. It works a treat. No traumatic scenes about getting her dressed to leave the house and she gets all kinds of attention that she thoroughly enjoys when out.

Most children want to be admired, but Leos positively crave it. As they develop, their catch phrase is 'Look at me'. It's 'Look at me' standing on my head, 'Look at me' skipping, 'Look at me' doing just about anything. A parent can't help wonder if all this is healthy and whether their offspring won't turn into an out-and-out show-off if their demands are indulged. In fact, the opposite is true.

The more Leo children are indulged when little, the less likely they are to grow up craving attention. If their need is satisfied, it quietens in them. Children who have been denied the attention they seek are hungrier as adults and hence more demanding. So enjoy their antics and praise them to the hilt. They'll soak this up and mature into an assured and confident adult.

Leo children are particularly creative and imaginative and love to perform. A dressing-up box is recommended, with all kinds of glittery and colourful items of clothing with which to improvise. Special cowboy, Superman, princess and ballerina outfits and the like are of course welcome, too, but they can do just as much with a selection of feather boas, sequinned hats and sparkly material. Their performances, in whatever shape or form, should always be applauded and encouraged. This may be a future star.

Whatever talents Leo children demonstrate, they should be fostered. They are impatient to excel and may not realise that this requires sustained practice. They may well think they should be brilliant without having to work at it, so show appreciation from the start while encouraging continued practice. If they don't receive enough recognition, their efforts can tail off and they may fail to develop their gifts. See it as an investment for their future.

Leo children benefit from extra-curricula involvement in the arts, as whether or not this turns out to be their path in life, it develops their character in positive ways. It fulfils a deep need to express their creativity and is a rewarding outlet for their 'Look at me' tendencies, giving them a legitimate and challenging opportunity to perform.

Parents would do well to enrol their Leo children in drama classes as well as allied activities like dance, music and singing. Of course, this can prove to be quite expensive, but perhaps if they do one or two options at a time, over the years, that allows them to test out their aptitude and gives them an outlet. In urban areas a choice of ballet, tap and freestyle dance are usually available and any or all might appeal. Even when they are not necessarily that good, it can give these children tremendous pleasure and satisfaction. Yes, even the boys may like to go to dance classes. In rural areas the choice may be limited but whatever is available is better than nothing, for if they take to it, they can specialise later on.

Leo children can cost a small fortune and parents may well make sacrifices in order to give them certain chances in life. However, these have to be in proportion to the needs of the whole family as otherwise this puts too much pressure on this child to succeed. They are meant to be having fun and while they may one day be super-successful, equally they may not. As they get older, maybe the cost of some of their classes can come out of their own money.

When it comes to pocket money, Leo children want and can get through large amounts. It goes with their generous nature to splash their cash around, so they are likely to spend it on their friends, too. Even in junior school, they may take a big bag of sweets with them, in order to hand them round. They like to impress and to be seen as having plenty to give. It helps them to feel worthwhile and adds to their confidence. So money can easily get equated with self-esteem. However, parents should not part with more than they can afford.

When there are brothers or sisters, they may develop problems with their attention-grabbing, popular Leo sibling but will nevertheless be charmed too. Like anyone who spends a lot of time with a Leo, siblings have to resist becoming a satellite, as this can lead to later resentment. Parents have the task of making sure that each of their children is valued equally for their specific talents and strengths.

Whatever school they attend Leo children are likely to excel in drama and English and may well go on to follow a career in the arts and humanities, although, if they show aptitude in other areas these certainly shouldn't be ruled out. Subjects that support a career in business and commerce will also stand them in good stead. This may be a future managing director in the making. Even a very young Leo demonstrates organisational ability – and they are excellent at delegating. They manage to get others running around after them and if parents don't want to turn into slaves they must set limits.

In schools that stream children according to ability, Leo children do better when they are near the top of their class. Teachers sometimes want to move those doing well into the stream above but, unless they are seriously under-stimulated, it's not a good idea to put these children up. If their position in a higher stream is not in the top few places and they find themselves halfway down or less, they lose motivation. Even though they may enjoy the status of being in a higher stream, on a day-to-day level, if they are struggling, they won't be as happy as coming top in the class below.

One of the consequences of Leo's popularity is that they have lots and lots of friends. They surround themselves with friends, some of whom are genuine and some who are tagging along because this is where the party's at. Leo won't object as they enjoy having admirers and won't question the composition of their entourage closely. Parents might want to, though.

Once Leo children are old enough to go out alone and can travel by public transport, they usually go about in a group, which they lead. This hones their organisational skills, as they are the one who decides where they are going on a Friday or Saturday night and work out all the logistics. Given the size of the crowd, this can take most of the day on the phone. Some signs, the water and earth signs in particular, would find all this work tedious but not Leo, who likes to be at the centre and in charge. Their social life is a major preoccupation into which they invest a tremendous amount of creative energy.

Leo teenagers, arriving home late at night, may well bring back a crowd of friends to stay over, who proceed to eat everything in the house. This can be extremely trying for parents, to put it mildly, especially if they've gone to bed that night with the fridge well stocked, only to find there's nothing left for breakfast. Their Leo offspring loves to be generous, so they are delighted to play the host, but they're not yet footing the bill. Parents need to provide some guidelines for their teenagers about their visitors' conduct.

By the time a Leo child is approaching the age at which he or she could leave home, parents may feel as if their life has become totally eclipsed by their child's. The Leo child's life may be colourful and vibrant and full of activity while the parents feel old and worn out and staid. Such is the impact of being around a Leo who is living life to the full. It's time this child moved out so that some balance can be restored.

None of this is intentional and Leo children in particular can not be held responsible. They are destined for prominence and their family home is their training ground. Just because they command so much attention doesn't mean they aren't vulnerable. Part of why they have so many friends is because they need to be needed.

It may appear to more cynical bystanders that it's ego strokes that Leos crave but actually it's much deeper than that. By being central in others' lives they validate their own existence – what would the sun do if the planets and asteroids didn't revolve around it? It is a matter of their identity. And much work goes into cultivating a lifestyle that supports and affirms their incipient sense of self. Remember, it's not a given, it's an ongoing search. A young Leo is actually surprisingly fragile and the light that they radiate can be easily snuffed out. However wearying and over-demanding some may seem, they need all the back-up they can get.

Leo children's popularity means they may well be honoured and made form or team captain, rising through the ranks to be school or games captain eventually: all excellent experience for what's to come later in life. If they don't pull this off, then there may be a problem and of course not all Leos can manage it. Make sure that, no matter what, they are always seen as special and important in their family. That way, whatever happens in later life, they carry with them the inner certainty that they are loved and adored and their capacity to love is untarnished. With that in place, they can conquer the world.

6

Virgo
The Virgin

August 23rd to September 22nd

A mutable earth sign, ruled by Mercury

Introducing Virgo

Virgos are discreet, refined, self-contained individuals, recognisable by their practical stance and helpful attitude. These are realists who don't have much time for illusion or delusion. Like all the earth signs, they are unpretentious and have their feet firmly on the ground.

Humble and self-effacing, Virgos don't display a great deal of self-confidence and tend to underestimate their capabilities. They set themselves unrealistically high standards, striving, as they do, for perfection. They have a picture of the ideal that becomes their norm and is impossible to maintain on an everyday level. For them, perfection means completeness and wholeness – a concept derived from the symbol of the Virgin, which represents this sign – and is a powerful motivation in their life; it is their driving force. Their idealism is attached to all sorts of mundane activities and can become a kind of tyranny, as they search for this sense of wholeness even in inappropriate places. Nevertheless, the high aspirations and their link to virginal purity and chastity must be kept in mind when trying to understand this sign, as they are fundamental to their character.

With all this perfectionism, it's no wonder Virgos have a reputation for being critical and fussy. While this trait can become negative and, perhaps ironically, attracts a fair bit of criticism, essentially it is a neutral characteristic that can be used positively too. Virgos exercise discernment and judgement in all they undertake and can be relied upon to notice faults and errors in themselves and others, as well as in their work, for example in editing, quality control and teaching. Wherever exacting skills are required, Virgos excel.

This sign is also associated with the need to be of service and so those born under Virgo enjoy being useful, often in pragmatic ways, offering advice, help and support. They are very good at coming up with practical solutions to problems, particularly other people's. Their modesty means they like being in the background or in a second in command position and, when they don't have to worry about the outcome and it doesn't directly affect them, they are at their best. For this reason they excel in jobs that involve problem-solving.

The Virgoan need to be useful is readily apparent in many areas of life. In a meeting, it'll be a Virgo who volunteers to take the minutes and offers to make the tea, the minutes will be perfect *and* delivered ahead of time. Because they are humble beings with an appreciation of all things small, no job is too menial. In fact, they understand the true meaning of being of service and unlike many, don't equate it with being servile. There is a very real difference and a Virgo brings dignity and respect to the notion of service.

A particularly attractive Virgoan quality is their brand of humour. There is a mischievous and playful side to them that is witty and irreverent and very entertaining. They are gifted mimics and have an ability to poke fun at situations and others, gently teasing – sometimes not so gently – and casting a perceptive and intelligent light. Their humour lies in their ability to see things for what they are and expose them as such. These are unassuming individuals who can readily see through others' pretensions and bring them down to earth, not unkindly, however, as their humour is rarely cruel; what it reveals more than anything is how astute they are.

Virgos' observation skills are coupled with an ability to listen carefully to others. They can pay close attention, are compassionate and caring, and are able to see practical solutions that really do make a difference. Their analytic abilities are extremely useful as they can think things through in ways that more emotional signs can't – they have a well functioning brain that won't go to pieces in an emergency.

Like Gemini, Virgo is ruled by the planet Mercury, and both signs have a developed curiosity. Whereas Gemini's interest tends to be more abstract and mental, Virgo likes to know how things work and fit together and is more practical. Both are interested in ascertaining facts and information but Virgos are more likely to make use of these in tangible ways. Virgos are altogether more purposeful.

Virgo is a mutable sign, which means they have an adaptable and flexible nature. But although they cope well with change and variety, they are quite attached to their routines and find them reassuring. Their routines can resemble rituals, which perform an important psychological function, acting as a container for their anxieties and helping them to feel safe. Sometimes their routines can become entrenched and inflexible, revealing how threatened they feel at that time. As they come to feel safer, they loosen up.

Virgos are receptive to others' opinions and ideas, which they take on board and adjust their position accordingly. Life isn't black or white for them as they can see, all too well, the many shades of grey. Some would say they bend in the wind because they aren't ever that sure of themselves, however, their ability to comprehend and adjust to the subtleties and nuances of situations is one of their strengths.

Virgos are sensitive and highly-strung individuals, often with a lot of nervous energy. They can be extremely restless and anxious, especially when under pressure. Finding a way to settle themselves and their nerves is important and something that restores calm, like walking, yoga, swimming or meditation is recommended.

When stressed, Virgos are susceptible to digestive problems and stomach complaints that have no obvious cause or remedy. Avoiding the triggers and situations that cause them stress is important as is recognising that they have a delicate system that can react violently to strain. Virgos may expect themselves to be able to manage more than they actually can. In that way they become their own worst enemy, overloading themselves and suffering physically as a consequence. It can be helpful for a Virgoan to see digestive problems as a communication from their body that all is not well on other levels. Trying to befriend their body, rather than feel persecuted by it, and trying to decode its messages is a positive attitude to adopt.

As part of their search for perfection, Virgos strive to create order. While this is not always entirely successful, various aspects of their life will be extremely ordered and sorted. It could be their CD collection, which is in alphabetical order, or similarly their books. Some signs appear to have a tidy home, but, if a drawer or a cupboard is opened, there's really a mess lurking beneath, with things stuffed in willy-nilly. To a Virgo, however, any mess is visible and a testament to how they are feeling. Their cupboards are well organised and their drawers have a system. Even their tools and dusters are tidy, with everything in its place.

On an everyday level, Virgos struggle with chaos, which

threatens to overwhelm them both emotionally and practically. Part of their striving for order is in an attempt to keep the inner feelings of chaos at bay. Being tidy is actually an attempt to create a calm environment in the hope this will bring inner tranquillity – they long for inner peace. And this inner chaos does usually intrude and manifest in some way in their immediate surroundings. Even those who remain tidy at all times are gripped by their fear of disorder and of being engulfed by it. As you can imagine, they are not exactly relaxed to live around. Although many Virgos are mystified by the idea that their sign is meant to be tidy, even those who live with messy surroundings still often have pockets of their homes that are surprisingly well organised.

The order-versus-chaos dilemma is an ongoing theme in the life of most Virgos, changing and evolving to reflect their current state of mind. Perhaps what's most important is to realise there's no right or wrong here, that tidiness is not necessarily a virtue and untidiness is nothing to be ashamed of and that theirs is not a superficial concern; it is connected to deep underlying issues for Virgos.

Like all the earth signs, Virgoans are tactile, sensual individuals. Touch is important to them and although they are shyer and more reticent and don't have the ease that a Taurean might, they thrive on plenty of physical contact. Once emotionally involved their sensuality is evident and their sexual relationship underpins their well-being. It's their corner stone and anchor. Their self-contained and refined air hides just how tactile they are, so a pleasant surprise lies in store for a new lover – it's one of their best-kept secrets. However, getting involved with a Virgo may be tricky and takes time and effort. A prospective partner is carefully scrutinised and their suitability assessed as they slowly become acquainted. Think in terms of a long and protracted courtship, in which various tests are set. Virgos have some fairly rigorous criteria as to whom they will be involved with. Many are ruled out instantly. Income and status are important, as are job prospects, along with reliability. They take relationships seriously and, as their comfort matters to them, they want a partner who will be an asset to them, someone who will enhance their standard of living not detract from it. Some of their criteria may seem extremely hard nosed and materialistic but anyone determined enough can bypass it – it's just an initial hurdle.

Once through these first stages and into a relationship, Virgos value a partner who is helpful and useful to them. This criteria ranges from those who are willing to share the chores – someone who puts the rubbish out unasked gets a zillion brownie points – to someone who has the right connections to enable them to get ahead. This isn't as mercenary as it sounds as this sign expresses love in tangible ways – it's how they communicate their feelings. They equate help with love, which they in turn reciprocate. So a partner is offered all kinds of support and back up, from cups of tea, to typing up and checking their CV, in fact, whatever's needed. All Virgos' practical and pragmatic skills are at the disposal of their partner.

A partner is judged more on how they behave, than what they say – although words do matter. Virgoans are an odd mixture as they take what's said absolutely literally and expect it then to be followed up by action. If there's no action in support of what has been promised, then no amount of sweet talk persuades them to believe or trust this individual, they are never taken in by clever talk.

Virgos are curious, some might accuse them of being nosy, as they like to keep abreast of what's going on. In part their need to know is to settle some unspoken anxiety within them. They have a habit of compartmentalising things, a kind of mental filing process goes on and if some thing or some piece of information is not filed they can find that disturbing. It's their way of ordering their world and is essential for their peace of mind. It can mean that they get overly interested in facts as if this is the route to calming down difficult feelings. Those Virgos who have a tidiness obsession are essentially acting out the same drama, trying to put everything in order on an external level in an attempt to feel less chaotic internally.

One such Virgo, on hearing that a couple she was close to had separated, demanded to know all the practical details about the new living arrangements, as if knowing these facts would help her to digest the shocking news. She barely asked her friend how she was feeling, she was so emotionally rocked herself and struggling to stabilise. In a sense she bought time to process the news by keeping the conversation factual.

Along with this desire for inner and outer order, Virgos need to know how things work. This can be a curiosity about inner, mental and emotional processes as well as about how an object works, too. So these individuals range from being psychological detectives to mechanics and engineers. As mechanics, whether qualified or not, they enjoy fiddling with machinery and taking things apart to see how they are constructed. This covers taking the back off a clock, to taking apart a car engine, the video, washing machine and computer. For those involved with a Virgo, expect things to be dismantled and be warned – they are not always so good at putting things back together. So, despite their penchant for tidiness, there can be a fair old mess as things are taken apart and abandoned for a time. Often an essential screw is lost, or some small part needs to be replaced to have the machine working again. Whether or not the appliance ever works again is dubious although these individuals are good with small intricate things. They make good electricians, lacemakers, seamstresses and carpenters, too, all skills that require attention to detail and precision. Virgos make especially great editors as they have an eagle eye when it comes to grammar, spelling and punctuation and may actually find it a soothing task.

Virgo

The work of Agatha Christie, the crime fiction writer, with its deftly woven and intricate plots and meticulous attention to detail, is typically Virgoan. They are methodical and have considerable skill in synthesising ideas. When producing written work, Virgos are good at creating an overall structure for a piece initially, even if they tend to lose sight of this once they get immersed in the piece. However, they set themselves such high standards that writing can become a tortuous process. As a consequence of their focusing in on the details Virgoans find it hard to keep the bigger picture in mind and often get bogged down in the minutiae.

Typically, as students Virgos hand in excellent work that's caused them no end of angst to produce. They always underestimate their ability and are surprised when they do well. Rather than hand in something sloppy or shoddy, which other less particular signs might consider perfectly acceptable, they'll stay up all night (missing their deadline isn't an option for them either). Once their student days are over, this tendency persists in other contexts. The fact that they've done extremely well doesn't affect their attitude. It could be argued that it is because of this attitude that they continue to excel in the tasks they undertake.

Despite Virgos' impeccable track record, they aren't usually found in the top jobs. For them, the anxiety that this position would generate means that they prefer to be the boss's right hand man, a position that involves responsibility but is not as visible. This suits Virgos' humble and self-effacing qualities. As an employee, they extend themselves way beyond the call of duty, working diligently and with thoughtfulness and care.

Virgos excel in many fields, albeit in a quieter way than some signs. The actor, Sean Connery, is one very well-known Virgo, probably most famous for playing James Bond on screen, who stepped down from this role when at the height of fame, ostensibly because he wanted to play a greater variety of characters. Because of their natural humility, Virgos are more likely to make excellent actors who have no interest in being a celebrity.

Virgos have a need to be of service and to do something useful and worthwhile and so gravitate to careers where what they do really does make a difference. The helping professions, which includes all branches of medicine and social work as well as complementary therapies are ideal. They are comfortable with the physical domain – the body and its functions – and aren't squeamish. If anyone's going to be at ease working with colonic irrigation it's a Virgo! In particular, jobs in nursing, dental hygiene and nutrition suit their innate characteristics.

Just as Virgos are temperamentally more suited to being an employee than being the boss, they don't do that well self-employed either, mainly because the precariousness of working for themselves can create too much anxiety. They like to know what their income will be and to plan accordingly.

When the boss, Virgos lack the assertive edge, and tend to lead by example. Frequently, they put in more hours than any of their employees. By working this hard they communicate non-verbally what they expect of others. This reluctance to be explicit can feel uncomfortable for those who have to answer to them, especially if more than their job description is being expected of them. Virgos always give over-the-odds and need help to ensure they do less – when they are the boss, there's no one to do this.

Virgos' hobbies can include various crafts, where their penchant for accuracy and intricate detail are called for (and where they can make some 'spare cash'). These individuals maintain many of the old-fashioned cottage industries and whether or not they do actually weave, knit or make picture frames, they are well suited to these pursuits.

Virgos also have considerable business skills and are especially good in the retail and hospitality industries where service and customer care count. With their practical, common sense stance they make good decisions that are realistic and workable.

One other broad area that may appeal to Virgos is horticulture, nature and the environment, either as a career or as a relaxing hobby, where they can replenish themselves and draw nourishment. Some may become experts, advocating sustainable practices, aware of the political implications.

Whatever their path in life, and Virgos are by no means limited to those above, they bring to it their fastidious attention to detail, hard work, a humble attitude and a striving for excellence. No small order and no mean achievement.

Negative Virgo

Being overly critical, of themselves and others, is probably the negative trait that Virgos are most associated with. Their critical faculty can extend widely to cover what they will eat and the way it is cooked, to the clothes they wear and the way they are washed and ironed, to personal cleanliness and the way they approach their work. In fact, it covers everything.

Some Virgos have a few areas that they particularly focus on and are less particular in other areas. At its worst these individuals are a complete pain with their perfectionist standards. And make no mistake, it is perfection that they aim for and want as a norm. When this is simply applied to them, it's only their own life that they make a misery. However, whatever standards they set themselves they tend to expect of others, too – especially their nearest and dearest.

Virgos have a tendency to hover, ready to pounce on a loved one's shortcomings. A partner can feel perpetually on trial and all too aware of how they are failing. Virgos are, by and large, hardest on themselves but for those who are intimately involved and aware of the standards they set themselves, it's easy to feel judged. After all if they are this meticulous, they are hardly going to appreciate it when others aren't. They can be positively ferocious if others are sloppy and even when nothing has been said, others often sense Virgos' criticisms and become all too aware of their failings and imperfections. These are usually task oriented rather than personal, although it can extend to dress. Virgos obsess about practical matters.

What many Virgos fail to appreciate is that, even if by the standards they set themselves they are failing, by the rest of the world's standards they are doing just fine. No one else expects as much of them.

When it comes to DIY, something many Virgos enjoy, they attempt to do the job to a professional standard and take great pride in their achievement. When decorating, they'll do all the preparation that the experts recommend and more. But who exactly cares? And is it worth all that angst? It is to a Virgo. They have staying power and can see things through to completion although the final part of a task is always the most difficult and they may well leave some small and insignificant bit unfinished. Quite why is not clear but it may be because they're dissatisfied with the job – in some way they've not achieved the desired perfection. This then nags away at them and much to their loved one's horror, they are quite capable of deciding to strip it down and start all over again.

Virgos can be hygiene freaks, which may not sound a bad thing, but can be really oppressive to those who live in close proximity. They are super aware of germs and, as such, make those around them equally aware. These Virgoans scrub and disinfect tirelessly and scrutinise others' hygiene habits, as if others are attempting to deliberately pass on some infectious disease. Very few pass the washing-up test. The upshot of this is that Virgos often take on sole responsibility for this task. In fact, some have a dishwasher for this very reason – they deem them more hygienic, although this is a moot point and other Virgoans may see them as not hygienic enough.

Taking charge applies to many other domestic chores, too and others may not realise that the reason Virgos always rush to start these tasks is that no one else is trusted to do them properly. This concern with cleanliness may seem a bit of a joke, but it can become obsessive. Checking that the fruit and vegetables have been washed thoroughly is hardly a crime, but it does place undue importance on these matters, and it highlights Virgos' extreme fussiness.

For those living alongside such a hygiene-obsessed Virgo, keep reminding them that germs can also be good for you and that cleanliness is not necessarily next to godliness!

Virgos may well claim it's not just germs that they worry about, but pesticides too. It's a similar story, as the thing is still invisible to the naked eye. If anyone is going to buy organic produce and be keen on environmental issues it's Virgo. And they may well save the planet – it's just that too much fussiness can be exasperating.

The actor Jeremy Irons has the classic neat appearance of this sign. This ironic report appeared in the Guardian newspaper on August 9th 2002: 'The mildly eccentric Mr Irons, whose flight to Cork had been diverted to Shannon due to fog, found himself at a loose end in the airport's famously messy bar area, whereupon he was seized by an attack of public fastidiousness . . . He helped himself to a dishcloth and wiped down a few tables to pass the time.' Pure unadulterated Virgo!

The pop star Michael Jackson is a famous Virgo who exhibits several of the negative characteristics of this sign. Besides his music, he's known for the extensive plastic surgery he's undergone, in an attempt to achieve his idea of physical perfection. Rumours about his bizarre lifestyle abound including that he spends time each day in an oxygen tent, or that he has specially adapted oxygen breathing equipment. Whether or not any of this is true, this kind of faddy concern about health is typical of negative Virgo. And Michael Jackson is regularly seen wearing a facemask in public, presumably a health precaution. He exemplifies the more eccentric concerns regarding health that many Virgos struggle with.

Another problem that Virgos have, paradoxically, is their unique ability to create a mess. They blitz a room and it's perfectly tidy, only for it to become strewn with things in no time. Sometimes it's because they don't tidy up as they go along, sometimes because the tidiness they aim for is unrealistic. The pristine order that they strive for, they utterly fail to maintain.

This illustrates the inner dynamic between chaos and order with which Virgos constantly grapple. For some, there is so much inner chaos that the very idea of something being out of place is too much for them. It reflects their chaotic feelings and is unbearable. In an attempt to create inner calm their outer life has to appear ordered. This is a highly-strung, nervy sign and these people are forever trying to settle themselves. One of the ways they do this is to make their surroundings as calm as possible. So, it could be argued that Virgos who can tolerate messy surroundings are no longer overwhelmed by their feelings.

Another foible of Virgos is that they are always on the make. It's something to do with not being particularly intuitive, so perhaps feeling they are missing out on opportunities. We're not necessarily talking about selling their granny for a profit – not with that sensitive conscience – although they do have an exploitative side to their nature that is quite shocking when it puts in an appearance. Usually their materialistic streak extends to no more than good common sense and it's only when this becomes extreme that they seize any opportunity to make a quick profit. This characteristic is more often found in Virgo men than women, perhaps because men feel under more pressure to make money. Typically, too, women have more empathy and stay more related and in contact with how others might feel, and it's harder to rip others off if you feel a connection to them, it takes a degree of detachment as well as ruthlessness.

A Virgo friend of a friend, who came from a poorer country, and was visiting England for the first time, looked at everything from a financial point of view. All he saw were opportunities to make a profit – how much things cost, how much they could be sold for, how much money was involved in various enterprises. He worked in tourism in his own country and had fallen prey to a particularly unattractive trait – his thinking was entirely that of a hustler.

This 'hustler mind-set' can also be seen as a defence against being exploited themselves. It is the 'dog eat dog' attitude. Virgos are sensitive, humble individuals who are vulnerable to being used. They are innately helpful, with a need to be of service to others, which can easily be taken advantage of and there's a fine balance to be struck whereby they don't become either the exploited or the exploiter.

This dynamic is evident at work and in the home, where Virgos typically show affection by doing practical and helpful things for those around them. It's easy for others to take them for granted and not recognise the goodwill that is invested in the deeds they perform. If, for instance, they make the tea nine times out of ten, it may be important for those around to offer to make it more often, too, or at the very least to acknowledge that the situation isn't equable. Virgos simply have a knack of seeing what needs to be done and doing it.

Some Virgos offer help as a kind of insurance policy. For them it's a shady deal that they make, so that at some point in the future they can call in the favour. Lodged in their mind is a list of all that they've done and, as a consequence, feel is owed to them and come payback time, they expect help to be reciprocated. So while it gives them the confidence to ask for a favour in return the real point of helping has been destroyed – there's no generosity of spirit.

Virgos who suffer from low self-esteem can become compulsively helpful. They mistakenly believe that they will be judged more worthwhile if they are useful. In fact, the opposite can be true, as they become a kind of dogsbody, who others don't value at all.

Those Virgos who find that they veer in this direction would do well to question their altruistic impulses and analyse their underlying motivation. If it is to gain acceptance and approval, then it's doubtful that this will ever actually be achieved this way. The first step is to acknowledge the desire for acceptance and the emotional pain felt at its lack. Then a decision about how much assistance to offer becomes clearer. So often, on committees, especially of a voluntary and unpaid kind, it's Virgos that carry the brunt of the work. Frequently, they do all the hard slog while others steal the glory. While the rest of the committee may appreciate how essential and fundamental a Virgo's contribution is, the rest of the world probably doesn't. Such a Virgo must regularly ask himself or herself whether they are content with this scenario.

This dilemma is a tricky one, as it could be argued that the world is a better place because of the attitude of Virgos and it's the rest of the world that is out of step and needs to change. Provided they are happy and don't feel used, that's fine, but so often they are actually suffering in silence. Learning assertiveness skills could be a revelation.

Virgos can be overly sensitive and prone to stress-related complaints. Stress is always an indicator that they have taken on too much. Just because someone else can cope with X, Y or Z doesn't mean they can or should attempt to do so. Even if they aren't able to complain verbally when feeling overloaded, their digestive system is likely to protest. If left unchecked over a protracted period of time they could end up with something like irritable bowel syndrome. Irritable bowel syndrome has no known cause or absolute cure but seems to be triggered by stress and certain dietary factors are thought to have bearing, too. The problem involves digestion and assimilation. Perhaps Virgos, with their delicate systems, need more 'digestion and assimilation time' than most, in order to process psychological matter as well as food.

Another negative Virgo trait is the 'not seeing the wood for the trees' syndrome. Their analytical bent means they excel in working with details but lose sight of the bigger picture. They focus too much on dotting i's and crossing t's and, it could be argued, get their priorities wrong. This happens with projects where the overall aim is forgotten and too much attention is diverted into the myriad constituents. It happens in writing reports and essays, where the point they are trying to make is often lost in favour of too much information – they argue their point finely but it lacks emphasis and impact so dies on them like a damp squib. Virgos can find writing quite tortuous, as they are such perfectionists. Usually their grasp of grammar, punctuation and spelling will be worthy of a copy editor (which many are), but where they may struggle is in sorting out in their own mind what it is exactly that they are trying to communicate. They become bogged down in the particulars.

One thing that all the earth signs share is the fear that they are boring. This has come about mainly because they are pragmatic and hence not seen as exciting in the way some signs are. Nevertheless, some Virgos do appear to be rather dull. The British tennis player Tim Henman is a case in point. No matter how good his tennis may or may not be, he lacks charisma. His neat good looks are typically Virgoan, but he doesn't have that special something to make him attractive.

The Virgoan comedian the late Peter Sellers thought he was dull and without character and that was in part what inspired his comedy. He saw himself as hiding behind the characters he invented, to obscure the fact that he was uninteresting. His fear that he was boring motivated him. And it worked; he is widely regarded as an extremely funny man. Not all Virgos are able to go to these lengths to make up for this perceived deficit.

Lastly, one other rather unattractive characteristic that certain Virgos develop has to be commented upon. They can pry; particularly when they are agitated or distressed. They garner information about a person or situation, as a way of helping them to feel settled and secure. By being able to put things into a category of some sort, their world feels less chaotic and hence less threatening. However, the way they go about this can be grossly insensitive and at worst they can resemble an interfering busybody. Their intention is to quieten their own inner turbulence but those on the end of their questions would be hard pressed to realise this.

Virgos sometimes process emotional issues via what looks to others to be a complicated and convoluted route. So, for instance, trying to make arrangements to meet up with a Virgo, can, for no apparent reason, be frustratingly full of seemingly practical difficulties. And trying to offer solutions is to no avail, as they are all turned down. An emotional issue has become rooted and is being enacted in this particular way. The Virgo in question may have no idea why they are throwing up all these obstacles but gradually they come to realise that they are blocking the meeting. Like the knots their stomachs get into when they are under stress, external knots appear that are impossible to disentangle, too. It is best to give a Virgo who is generating these kinds of problems some space, as they will then sort it out within themselves.

It can not be over-emphasised how sensitive and

highly-strung Virgos are and that they cause far more suffering to themselves than to others. Their negative traits are without exception mild in comparison with some signs and wreak far more damage on themselves and their nervous system than on others.

A few words of advice for the partner of a Virgo who is behaving in a dysfunctional way: reassure them of their worth, try to help calm their nerves, never withhold information from them, not because there is anything wrong with that but because it drives them to distraction. Indulge their foibles and what may seem like petty ways, because it matters to them. Eventually they *may* get over it . . .

The Virgo Man

The Virgo man is recognisable by his quiet, modest and self-contained manner. He holds back only coming forward when he has something of real value to contribute. No matter that others jostle for position, he is happier out of the limelight which also means it's harder to spot him.

Perhaps what distinguishes the Virgo man most is his genuine humility. He exhibits the kind of deference and courtesy which is in short supply these days. This sometimes gets attributed to his lack of confidence and while this is partly true, it's also an innate characteristic. Even the most confident Virgo man is still going to be polite and discreet in his bearing and manner.

One of the Virgo man's greatest strengths and difficulties is his highly critical nature. He has rare analytical ability and little capacity for self-delusion; he can see himself, others and situations for what they are. This doesn't always make him popular but it does mean he's trusted to give an honest and tactful opinion.

The Virgo man usually manages to cloak any caustic and close-to-the-bone comments with humour. He veers towards the irreverent and ironic, as it's his style to downplay his observations while uttering throwaway lines that those without a keen ear can miss altogether. He has an intelligent wit which he uses to say things he might ordinarily find hard to say. He's extremely perceptive, observing as he does the minutiae of life and commenting upon it in an understated and dry way and accurately pinpointing others' motivations. However, this man usually saves his witty asides for those he feels close to. He doesn't generally hold forth and entertain the crowds, it's a personal and intimate communication. Those he confides in are privileged to be privy to his thoughts.

When it comes to relationships, the Virgo man doesn't rush into an emotional involvement. He takes his time, getting to know a potential partner over a series of meetings and outings, which may not even be obviously dates. That way he's covered himself should he decide not to pursue a relationship. Despite his reticent manner, he's still very much in the driving seat and the one who does the choosing. He just doesn't reveal his intentions until he's reasonably certain; he's not one to wear his heart on his sleeve. He's discriminating and selective in his choice of a partner, which means he may spend periods of time on his own, during which he's likely to remain celibate.

Such periods of celibacy are not particularly difficult for the Virgo man. He's fussy about who he sleeps with, so unless he has a partner, that's his preference – he doesn't sleep around. This doesn't mean that he has a low sex drive, though. The Virgo man is extremely sensual and when emotionally involved his sexual appetite is awakened. He just has the ability to allow his desires to lie dormant when there's no one special to direct them towards.

The Virgo man falls in love slowly, checking a prospective new partner's credentials as he gets to know him or her. He has strict criteria and sets exacting standards for a long-term mate, which may include pragmatic considerations, like their usefulness to him. He values practical back-up and help, so someone with skills he lacks can seem very appealing.

Once all the tests and hurdles have been passed and the Virgo man has given his heart, he is truly romantic. This may seem a bit of a contradiction, when he's approached love with such caution but perhaps all that is simply to protect his idealistic side. And idealistic he is. He also has a tendency to put a lover on a pedestal and worship them. Possibly this is because he's so grateful they have stuck around while he's prevaricated! A partner goes from being decidedly mistrusted to idealised and adored in quick succession.

In this romantic phase, the Virgo man is wonderfully attentive and thoughtful. He notices all the small things that make a big difference and gives a quality of attention that makes a loved one feel valued. If he buys flowers, they'll be his partner's favourites and with any gifts, he takes care over the details. But more than that, he gets involved in the minutia of his partner's life, and offers helpful suggestions that make their life easier. He will go to no end of trouble on their behalf, researching, for instance, what new car or stereo or camera is the best buy for their particular needs and presenting the information in a tidy folder.

The Virgo man is reliable and does and says what he promises. There's no spin or false hopes raised – he can be counted on to be who he says he is. In fact, if anything, he undersells himself so a partner is in for some pleasant surprises.

Perhaps the Virgo man's best-kept secret is his sensuality. He is extremely tactile and uses touch to express his affection, frequently caressing and stroking his lover. This is deeply reassuring for him and his partner, conveying as it does his love and commitment non-verbally. Not that he's ill at ease with language, as he's perfectly eloquent when he wants to be, but the direct communication that physical contact provides is his mainstay.

The Virgo man can lack confidence, however, as a lover. Partly this is because he may lack experience and, to shore up his uncertainty, he may rely on technique. While technique has its place, he may underplay the importance of his feelings, not recognising how important the emotional connection can be for good sex. However, despite his initial hesitancy and insecurity when it comes to sex, as his technique improves, so does his confidence and he simultaneously allows his deeper feelings more expression. He may mistakenly believe things have improved because he's become more expert, whereas actually it's because he's loosened up.

Even those Virgoan men who have considerable past experience still have a chaste quality to them. This is the sign of the Virgin and it could be argued that they approach each new relationship as if they were virgins. And there is much to recommend this attitude, as each new relationship becomes a fresh journey of discovery, with nothing taken for granted.

Once Mr Virgo has found his mate, he still has commitment issues that take some time to sort out. He's hard to pin down and puts off marriage or its equivalent as if it's a threat to his identity. This can be blamed on his mercurial nature – something he has in common with Gemini. There's something of the eternal boy in him that remains a bit elusive and unaccountable and he imagines that a commitment inevitably means this is sacrificed. This boyishness doesn't have to be and is one of his attractive characteristics, keeping him mysterious.

The actor, Hugh Grant, exhibits many classic Virgoan traits. The screen persona he's most associated with is the hesitant, foppish, well-mannered gentleman, made famous in the films *Four Weddings and a Funeral* and *Notting Hill*, which seems to be inextricably interwoven with his public persona. He's also famously unmarried, having dated (and had a live-in relationship) with Liz Hurley for many years; some might say he's marriage shy.

Acting may seem an unlikely career for these self-effacing men, but Virgo has a mercurial ability to observe others accurately and to mimic which is undoubtedly helpful in this profession. Those who do take this path, like Sean Connery and Jeremy Irons, do so on their terms and without all the celebrity razzmatazz that some signs seek.

Despite his apparent reluctance, the Virgo man does eventually settle down, although he may leave it rather late, perhaps as late as his forties. What can happen is that he suddenly realises all his contemporaries are married and have children and he panics. Anyone who meets him around this time will find he is very much the marrying kind and may be mystified as to why he's still available. It's because he's just had a psychological breakthrough and woken up to the fact that there are fates worse than making a commitment – like being the only bachelor left on the planet. So, if he is heterosexual, he'll eventually get married and if he's gay, he'll set up home with his partner and revel in a new-found domesticity. For those who are living in hope that their particular Virgo man will soon reach this stage, there's no rushing him, there's no cajoling, but hang on in there and he should get there in the end.

For those Virgos who marry late, one of his motivations will be to have children – he wants the whole package. And once there are children, it's hard to imagine the Virgo man ever wanted anything other than family life. So from a reluctant and unpromising start, he goes on to become an involved father and is hands-on right from the start. As an earth sign, he's not squeamish when it comes to bodily functions, so will do his fair share of the nappies and manage the mess babies create in a matter-of-fact way. He has a calm steadiness that makes him particularly good at dealing with small babies and, having done his share at this early stage, those all-important emotional bonds are in place.

As his children grow up the Virgo man particularly enjoys doing practical things with them, showing them how to do and make things. He is generous with his time and more than willing to spend hours on tasks that are for his children's benefit. His children provide him with the perfect excuse to indulge in less productive activity and play. This is a rare man, as he has the patience and interest to help his children with their projects. By demonstrating to them how things are done he teaches them skills.

Having procrastinated about family life, the Virgo man is now in his element. Not only is he good with his children, he's house-trained and is helpful and useful around the home. He's more than willing to do his share of the chores and enjoys cooking to boot. Perhaps he knew that he was a good catch and held out for those reasons; wary of being exploited. This is a domesticated man – his second best-kept secret.

When it comes to his career, the Virgo man is not particularly ambitious. He is extremely conscientious in whatever he does and as an employee, is greatly valued, but he puts other things ahead of promotion. The responsibilities that go with each step up the career ladder weigh heavily on his shoulders, which is why he's not necessarily seeking to climb it. He measures his success by wider criteria than the amount in his pay packet, prioritising his total well-being.

The Virgo man does value comfort though and seeks a reasonable standard of living, so tends to gravitate to the better-paid jobs. Despite his modesty and humility, he doesn't come cheap. This can be all the more surprising to those who imagine he'll undervalue himself financially. He doesn't.

Whatever career path the Virgo man chooses, and there are many different directions that suit his temperament, he brings to it his exacting standards and efficiency, his helpful attitude and concern for others' welfare. His contribution to a team endeavour is immense – always above and beyond the call of duty.

The Virgo man's career is not necessarily something he's passionate about and may have been chosen because it pays the bills – his interests and recreational activities are far more important to him. Those who are able to find an interest that will also provide an income will feel particularly blessed.

Because Virgos are good at paying attention to detail, they often end up in jobs like accountancy or in research, which are not necessarily going to be that fulfilling. Others value how meticulous he is but he may feel boxed in. He is more likely to derive satisfaction from an involvement in one of the natural sciences.

The Virgo man is at heart a country boy and thrives in a rural environment, although those who opt for an urban life can always escape at weekends and holidays. Without some connection to the natural world he feels alienated and cut off from an aspect of life that nourishes and sustains him. If he has to live in the city, then a garden where he can potter and unwind is a priority.

Nature appeals to Virgo's earthiness and when it provides him with an opportunity to classify different species, he's a contented man. He'll enjoy activities like hiking, trekking and camping, possibly taking the whole family along and pointing out things of interest. He loves to plan routes and is in his element with a map and a compass. When driving, too, he knows all the short cuts, having studied his map and then checked them out. He's an expert when it comes to planning trips and leaves nothing to chance, covering every eventuality.

The Virgo man loves gadgets and gizmos, from a state-of-the-art Swiss Army knife to the latest piece of technological wizardry. He appreciates well-designed equipment and is quick to utilise it. Unlike some, where interest in these things is short lived, he masters its intricacies and continues to enjoy it. So anyone not sure what to buy him for a present has no excuse now!

Perhaps one of the Virgo man's most appealing characteristics is that he invests most into his personal life and his nearest and dearest undoubtedly get the best deal. He is an essentially private man and those who are closely involved with him and get to know him are the fortunate ones.

The Virgo Woman

The Virgo woman is recognisable by her self-contained and modest demeanour. These women are quiet and self-possessed, so don't stand out in the crowd. They tend to sit back and watch and when they do pass comment it's considered, perceptive and astute. Their powers of observation are second to none and coupled with their ability to analyse people and situations, their take on things is quite impressive. They notice all kinds of details that others miss, which they fit together like a jigsaw, creating a picture that is the basis of their understanding. Because they are practical, pragmatic beings, this is always grounded in good common sense, never fanciful. So while these women may not draw attention to themselves by being loud or expressive, they are respected and their opinions are sought.

There is something impregnable about the Virgo woman that draws others to her. This is the sign of the Virgin and before Christianity's interpretation of virginity, it actually meant 'belonging to no one'. The pagan prostitutes who worked in the pre-Christian temples were thus seen as virgins as they 'belonged to themselves' rather than to a husband, as most women did. This can cast a whole new light when it comes to understanding the Virgo woman.

First and foremost, the idea that they belong to themselves

and not to a partner explains that difficult to define but unmistakable attitude so many Virgo women exemplify. Whether or not they are in a relationship they are very much their own person and answerable to no one else. For instance, when asked to do something, they rarely run the invitation by their partner; they make their decision independently. They neither hide behind a partner nor seek his or her permission. They act autonomously.

Twiggy, who as a model was known as the face of the Sixties and Claudia Schiffer, a super-model of the Nineties and beyond, are both Virgos. They share a refinement and a kind of modesty that many Virgo women emanate and that has its origins in the virgin, pagan, temple servants that represent this sign and is part of their mystery and allure.

Sophia Loren and the late Greta Garbo and Ingrid Bergman are cinema icons who possessed that earthy aloofness that is so typically Virgoan. Few follow Garbo's extreme example and seek the seclusion she opted for but most choose a fair degree of privacy. By being essentially private the Virgo woman remains an enigma and rather enticing. She firmly believes that by not revealing all, she remains more interesting. This operates on many levels, so for instance, the Virgo woman is unlikely to wear clothes that expose her body or to go topless on the beach. For a start she wouldn't feel comfortable herself (her own comfort is a priority), plus she's naturally understated and subtle.

Whatever intellectual ability a Virgo woman has, she possesses an astute and sharp mind. Like all the earth signs her understanding is of a no-nonsense kind. She cuts through waffle to get to the point and isn't impressed by those who over-intellectualise. She sees it as a cover-up as she knows full well that anything can be expressed simply and clearly, which is how she communicates. This doesn't mean that she can't grasp complex ideas, because she can, she excels at that, but she sees no need to make anything more complicated than it is already.

The Virgo woman's ability to think in a clear and logical way is one of her greatest strengths. She is a natural analyst, able to take apart and examine the components of a situation or individual and then synthesise these into a conclusion. This skill, coupled with her feminine instincts, make her a formidable force to be reckoned with. However, she's not one to challenge others – she doesn't readily speak her mind. This isn't because she lacks courage; she's simply too modest and self-effacing. What she does is to confide her insights to those to whom she's close. In this way she's an invaluable confidante.

Her analytic ability is a talent the Virgo woman applies to all areas of her life and especially to herself. If anyone is going to make a pros and cons list when trying to make an important decision, it'll be her. She may even go further and dissect the pros and cons. She leaves no stone unturned in her search for an answer.

The Virgo woman has a quirky and original sense of humour, based on her acute observational skills. She has a light-hearted, playful, irreverent side that enjoys repartee and quick quips, at which she is very good. She can be extremely funny in her depiction of others and situations, daring to say the unmentionable. She notices and picks up on inconsistencies in others and, in effect, sends them up, only she's not cruel – just accurate. She reveals through her humour that she's nobody's fool.

What can be a bit daunting for a prospective partner is realising that a Virgo woman has an accurate assessment of them right from the start. And before they get a look in, they'll have to measure up to her strict set of criteria. This criteria gets reviewed and updated regularly and is based on her experiences in life so far. When first becoming acquainted with a new beau, she'll have in her head, even if not on paper, a pros and cons list regarding his suitability. And, although she's certainly not a gold digger, a partner's income and potential earning power will matter. She doesn't want to waste her time on someone she sees as going nowhere.

The Virgo woman is in many ways quite pragmatic when it comes to choosing a partner. She knows that the romantic phase doesn't last and she's looking for a relationship that survives beyond the first flush of being in love. So, she looks for a mate with whom she has much in common, good communication and shared interests. The meeting of minds is extremely important to her and gives her relationship a solid foundation. She wants her partner to be her best friend and confidant, not just her lover.

This doesn't mean the Virgo woman lacks passion. This is a sensual woman and once emotionally involved in a relationship, her passion is released. She's comfortable with her body and knows what works for her sexually – she's no shrinking violet at this stage of a relationship. She expects her partner to satisfy her and if necessary, she'll show him or her how to. Being this down-to-earth can be quite threatening to a lover, who may not be up for instructions in technique.

All this may seem rather at odds with how shy the Virgo woman first appears. This is actually her innate reticence to get involved with anyone until she is sure she wants to. Unlike some signs, she's very able to be on her own and to be perfectly content. She doesn't need a partner to enable her to feel complete; she feels complete by herself. This self-sufficiency gives her bargaining power – she's not dominated by her needs. And even after becoming committed, she retains this position. It's not that she's in any way aloof, because that's simply not her style. She embodies the belief that her relationship can be on her terms.

If the Virgo woman decides to have children, it will also be on her terms. She's pretty realistic about what having a child will mean and only goes ahead if she is in a position to offer a child stability and security. Which means she needs to feel she's found a partner she's staying with, who will support her through the pregnancy and early years. She may choose to return to work, but she doesn't want to feel forced back by financial necessity. She doesn't enjoy being a superwoman, her anxiety levels run too high for that, and she's not bothered by political correctness, either. Once she has had her first child, she may well decide that she likes being a mother so much that she decides to carry on and have a few more and is occupied for some considerable time with full-time motherhood. Domesticity could become her career.

Unlike Cancer, who is extremely maternal, what the Virgo woman enjoys is domestic life, of which children form a part. She is in her element when being useful, helpful and supportive. She is efficient and capable and can run a home that is both well organised and relaxed. Much has been said about Virgo and tidiness and her home may well not be very tidy, but it will have a sensible orderliness to it, with everything having its place.

If the Virgo woman is heterosexual, she is a great asset as a traditional wife. Not that she's exactly conventional in that role, as she's still very much her own person. However, her husband benefits from her reliability and groundedness and the amount that she automatically takes care of on an everyday level. Whether or not she works, the home runs smoothly. He's expected to contribute, too, she's no doormat, she just oversees and manages their domestic life very competently. In a lesbian partnership she may play a similar role, although unless there are children and she's the main carer, there won't be such a clear division of labour.

In terms of a career, the Virgo woman's desire to be of service affects her choices. She may be drawn to the helping professions, which includes nursing, social work and complementary therapies. She may also be drawn to secretarial work and if so makes a brilliant secretary or personal assistant. Her tendency to underestimate her abilities means she can work in a job that doesn't stretch her. When she's working below her capacity she doesn't necessarily get bored, as she enjoys feeling on top of the job. She won't, however, stay forever and does eventually move on to something more stimulating. Later, she may wonder what took her so long.

Whatever career the Virgo woman pursues, she brings to it a professional attitude and impressive competence. She's never afraid of hard work and fulfils her tasks efficiently and with good grace. She's helpful and supportive and a good all-rounder to work with. She can work equally well as part of a team or on her own. Her only drawback, if it can be called that, is that she won't suffer others' inefficiency lightly. It will cause her stress and problems.

If the Virgo woman has the opportunity and can afford to, she may well work part-time, whether or not she has children. Those without children can easily occupy themselves and enjoy having a lifestyle that isn't too pressurised. They thrive when they have regular 'down-time' and can potter about, doing what takes their fancy, rather than working to other people's schedules. It's the antithesis to all their super-efficiency and creates a balance that calms and de-stresses them. For the Virgo woman who has to work full-time, then having 'me-time' is essential for her health and well-being. She needs her weekends to be free of plans – even social events can be taxing.

Virgo women have an innate understanding of how the psyche and the body intertwine, influencing each other, and they try to look after both. If they feel physically ill, they automatically think in terms of any psychological stress that has affected their well-being and contributed to this current bout of malaise. They keep themselves well informed with up-to-date ideas regarding health and nutrition and may follow a special dietary regime. They probably take vitamin, mineral and herbal supplements that make various claims to improved health and vitality. They'll invest in complementary therapies and have regular appointments with their homeopath or acupuncturist and the like. This is not necessarily just something they turn to when ill, it's seen as preventative and as money well spent. They may well be practitioners themselves, so they know what they are talking about. And they don't need to be taught a holistic approach, it's inborn.

This means that the Virgo woman never takes anything at face value; she always investigates it that bit further and finds deeper connections and meanings. Sometimes these get a bit muddled up with her own preconceptions but she is an interesting woman with her own unique stance and a great deal to contribute. This is why she commands the respect and attention of those who are close to her. They know her true worth, even if she never really does.

The Virgo Child

The Virgo child is sensitive and helpful and easy to get along with. These are self-contained and thoughtful little ones, who may seem timid; certainly they are not brash or brimming with confidence. Their confidence develops as they gain mastery over various tasks and builds steadily throughout their life. They may not be born with it but when handled gently they acquire it and grow up to be quietly self-assured.

Virgo children's modesty means that they don't exaggerate and they are not good at self-promotion. If anything they undersell themselves and make light of their achievements. Most parents ask their children how they got on at school and what sort of day they've had and must learn to interpret the response they get from their Virgo offspring. They are more likely to talk about their failings and difficulties, rather than their successes.

Virgo

To get a realistic picture of how Virgo children are doing, talk to their teachers, while keeping in mind their child's version, as this describes how they feel and experience life. Parents have to find a balance in which they acknowledge their reality and don't play down their anxieties, yet also don't take them too seriously either. They can and do manage very well indeed. These children are humble and self-effacing, a rare and not particularly fashionable quality in today's world, but one to treasure.

Because Virgo children are sensitive and highly-strung, they are prone to developing worries and anxieties. These need to be dealt with in a pragmatic way. It's important that they are given the time and space to unwind as without this they won't get to their deeper concerns, which do need to be addressed. Ideally, too, they need calm, unflustered parents in order that they can safely confide their troubles. With overly anxious parents there's no one there for them to turn to, to allay their fears. Give these children some quiet, reflective time on a daily basis. Too much activity does not suit them and a busy schedule over-stimulates their nervous system.

As a Mercury ruled sign, there aren't huge differences between Virgoan boys and girls. Mercury is an asexual planet, so both sexes can express the characteristics of this sign equally well. However, the way society responds to gender differences means that girls are more likely to be exploited for their helpful natures. Even as children, Virgos enjoy being useful. The best way to protect a daughter is to make sure she isn't taken advantage of within the family. This is her training ground. By properly valuing her and what she has to offer she learns her own true worth, which she has a propensity to under-value throughout her life. This can be equally true for boys. What is more, there are cultural expectations for boys to be a tad more macho than the average Virgo boy usually is, so girls have an easier time in that respect and he may need to be valued and shown appreciation for his gentler nature.

All children ask why but Virgo children probably do so more than most and what's more, won't be fobbed off with incomplete answers. They like to have things explained properly and continue to ask questions until they're satisfied. They are quite sophisticated in their ability to understand complex ideas and concepts and, as they're innately extremely curious, explanations go down well. What's more, when they're taken seriously, they feel respected and this helps their self-confidence.

The intense interest Virgo children exhibit is a characteristic they share with Gemini, also ruled by the planet Mercury. Like Gemini, these children notice things that would pass by other, less alert children. Their powers of observation are acute and accurate and these children pick up on details and particulars, which means they can be quite challenging.

As an earth sign, Virgo children have a practical and pragmatic outlook and like to make sense of their world in these terms. They need to know how things work. As a baby, they'll like toys that fit together and can be taken apart, like the posting box shapes and later simple jigsaws and Duplo. As they mature, give them more complicated construction toys, like Lego and Meccano. Provided that it's safe for them to do so, give them access to discarded household items in order that they can investigate how they work, too. They'll thoroughly enjoy taking the back off an old clock or having an old radio to take apart and examine. They may grow up to be an engineer.

A Virgo child's imagination works best when given a concrete and tangible medium through which to express it. One Virgo child I knew made complex tunnels and roads in his sandpit, into which he also introduced water, small cars, soldiers and animals that were all part of a rich and elaborate environment he created. He made a fair old mess but was deeply engrossed for great swathes of time.

Clay offers a different kind of sensual experience, which Virgo children enjoy. Although there are plenty of newer modelling materials on the market these days, nothing is quite as satisfying to an earth sign as clay. The mess, which puts some parents off, is actually quite manageable and is part of what makes handling clay so enjoyable.

Besides working with clay, Virgo children may well be more conventionally artistic. Most children are provided with paints and crayons, and Virgos will enjoy collage and mosaics, too. They have a penchant for making things and are good at dealing with small, tricky parts. Some paint or draw from a bird's-eye perspective, a bit like aboriginal artists do, often including plans of buildings. Possibly this is a future architect or town planner in the making.

Patience is one of the virtues Virgo children possess, as well as an interest in detail. If anyone is going to build an object out of matchsticks it'll be a Virgo, although perhaps not until they're grown up. In the meantime models of aeroplanes will appeal and keep them occupied.

Virgo children often develop an early interest in nature. They enjoy collecting things for a nature table, from conkers and acorns when very young, to more unusual items when they grow older. Identifying fossils, stones, trees, birds and wildlife are all likely to appeal to their curious nature. Besides, they enjoy classifying things. Owning objects as such doesn't matter to them; they want to know about them. So, for instance, a bird table and a pair of binoculars are a good investment.

Most children benefit if they have a garden but Virgo children do especially enjoy, and are thoroughly absorbed by, the way plants grow and fruit and flower. If there's a patch of garden that can belong exclusively to them, they'll spend much time digging and building and creating there. Expect large holes to be excavated and even a small pond to appear. They'll end up with a lot of earth beneath their nails but they'll sport a healthy glow. For those who don't have access to this, then the bean that grows in the jam jar and sprouting mustard and cress give them a glimpse of these things. Again, classifying the plants and understanding their propagation interests them. They want to know facts and sequences and they store this information away.

These are adaptable children. Virgos adjust to a new situation relatively easily and although they like their routines, they don't object if presented with a new schedule. It means, for instance, that as little ones they travel reasonably well, if that's what's required of them.

They will object, though, to a change of diet. Even a Virgo baby is a bit fussy and fastidious. They're particular about what they'll eat and show definite preferences early in life, which should be respected. They'll acquire a taste for a wider and more varied diet as they mature. As they'll have a sensitive digestive system care should be taken with weaning. Breast-feed them, if possible, for as long as you can and consider waiting to introduce any solid food until they're six months old. This gives their delicate digestion the best possible start and minimises their susceptibility to assimilation problems.

From early on, Virgo children need encouragement and support. Be especially careful when criticising them, as they take it to heart. They are self-critical enough and anything more is overload. If they have to be censured, do it as gently as possible and make sure they realise it's their behaviour that is being admonished, not them, themselves.

It's important, too, not to urge the Virgoan child to attempt to do things they are not yet ready for, as that gives out the message that more is expected of them. Rather, do the opposite, and try to soften their expectations of themselves. More than anything they need to be accepted, which lays the foundations for self-acceptance in later life. Help them to be less critical. Parents would do well to focus on what they get right and play down their mistakes.

Virgo children's perfectionist streak means they can struggle and suffer with their homework. Whereas another, less particular child might send in a piece of work that's good enough, they strive to get it to a standard that they can be proud of, whether or not they can actually manage that. Their judgement is exacting. For better or worse, they are aware if their work is not up to standard and they mind.

The level of excellence that Virgo children strive to attain may actually elude them and be beyond their reach. Although the work they hand in is the best they can manage, this may not be obvious to their teachers, as their work may in fact look quite messy, with lots of alterations and corrections. Although they've laboured long and hard, their supreme effort may not be recognised as such, which only adds to their frustration. In the meantime, it's important that their parents do praise their efforts and recognise their hard work.

Virgo children may be a little timid. They lack the confidence of other more thoughtless and boisterous signs and need to be handled with sensitivity. They are helpful by nature and strive to be useful. This means they'll readily help with chores and do their bit around the house. The Protestant work ethic is inborn, they're industrious children, happiest when busy with a task. They're quite content to work for their pocket money, which is perhaps not the best way to go with this particular sign, as the Virgo child needs to be protected from ever feeling exploited. Parents would be advised to reassure them that they're wanted and valued just for being themselves – they don't have to earn love – in fact they can't earn love. It's important that they realise that not everything has a price and certain things can't be bought. So, it may be a good idea to keep the pocket money they receive a separate matter to the chores they do around the home.

Allow a Virgo child to have a pet, if this is at all possible. This doesn't have to be a particularly demanding pet, as a mouse, gerbil, hamster, rabbit or guinea pig are all ideal, although a cat or dog is also an option, depending on what suits the whole family best. These children will form a strong attachment to a pet and it satisfies their curiosity to learn about an animal and its nature. They particularly enjoy petting and grooming and their down-to-earth temperament means they can deal with the less pleasant tasks associated with them. There are also psychological benefits, in taking care of a small animal that is dependent upon them, as it helps in the development of self-mastery and self-assurance.

Much has been said about Virgoans' struggle to maintain order and the fallacy of their reputation for tidiness. Virgo children are no exception and thrive in a household that is well organised. They are classification freaks and like their possessions to be kept in a way that makes them readily accessible. Storage solutions that have clear labels work extremely well. Their attitude is pragmatic, rather than aesthetic. When their rooms become messy, they feel overwhelmed and need help to regain order.

In adolescence, the Virgoan self-contained manner means they manage this phase relatively well, at least outwardly. They aren't obviously moody and obnoxious. Again, the problem is more likely to be their insecurity. This is a difficult time at best, with great growth spurts and physical developments that leave children feeling awkward and self-conscious. Sport or dance are activities that can help them to feel more at home in their bodies and, as such, are recommended – allow them to take up anything that might ease their transition into adulthood. These are not wild and irresponsible young people so parents can afford to encourage them and allow them the freedom they need to build up their self-confidence.

By the time Virgo children have to make a decision about

which subjects to specialise in at school, their interests should be apparent. Until then, they do well to keep their options wide open, as they could easily follow several different directions. They will undoubtedly have technical skills, but may not wish to become a technician or designer. They could equally choose an arts or humanities path to the sciences. Subjects like biology, geography and geology may well be useful to them on their career path. Despite their liking for categorisation, they're not easy to categorise themselves.

Virgo children tend to underestimate their abilities, which could limit their options in life. While being an overly ambitious parent is not the way to go and suggesting they could do more may not be exactly helpful, a gentle quizzing as to what they would most like – what their dreams are – won't go amiss. As parents, keep in mind that these children are modest and humble and are probably better than they realise at everything they do. When it comes to the all-important exams, they're likely to get higher grades than predicted.

Virgo children are not the most conspicuous, not the loudest or the ones who try to grab the attention. If they have siblings, make sure they are not eclipsed by their more vocal demands. Just because they are self-contained doesn't mean they aren't equally in need of tender loving care and could easily feel sidelined where there are younger siblings whose needs come first. Parents would do well to give them some time on a regular basis that is theirs alone, where they don't have to compete with others for attention. It may be a bit of a surprise what comes to the surface in these private moments. And even if nothing major is spoken of, Virgo children need this quiet intimacy throughout their lives. It's in these moments that they truly reveal themselves. It would be tragedy if a parent were to miss out on that.

7

Libra
The Scales

September 23rd to October 22nd

A cardinal air sign, ruled by Venus

Introducing Libra

Libra is arguably the most attractive, charming and agreeable sign of the zodiac and these individuals are easily recognisable by their good looks and pleasing disposition. Even when not classically beautiful, and many are, they have an aura of grace and elegance that draws others to them.

This sign is ruled by Venus, the planet associated with love and attraction and, for those born under Libra, love is what makes their world go round. These individuals are relationship oriented; they enjoy interacting with others and are gregarious, sociable folk but finding a partner is their priority. They are romantic and idealistic and are looking for the, 'Then they lived happily ever after' fairy tale ending. A tad unrealistic and starry eyed, they hold high aspirations about how life could be and their intention is to make the world a better and happier place. They genuinely look for and bring out the best in others.

Diplomatic and tactful, Librans have a sensitive way of saying even the most difficult things, which means they rarely cause offence. They are easily offended themselves and couch their comments as if they were on the receiving end. Their discretion can mean that they avoid awkward and contentious topics, staying clear of anything that might cause upset or controversy.

The symbol of this sign is the scales and Librans seek to establish balance and harmony. This is one of the most important dynamics to keep in mind when trying to understand these individuals, as it runs through every aspect of their life. Their pleasant manners and good taste all emanate from their attempt to maintain equilibrium, both inner and outer.

Most obviously, this applies to Librans' appearance, hence the care they take in presenting themselves in the best way possible. They may well have a wardrobe to die for, with designer clothes tastefully colour coordinated. They go for subtle shades that make a quiet statement and natural materials like silk, cotton, linen, cashmere and wool. Care and attention is taken with storing and looking after their clothes – expect costly dry cleaning bills and everything hung in protective covers. Having bought the best they can afford, they look after their investment and because they go for classical cuts and designs, their clothes don't date. Some items may be the latest fashion, but most won't be.

Libras' surroundings and home are likely to be aesthetically pleasing; as with their clothes, the colours they choose harmonise and the atmosphere created is tranquil. They go for neutral shades, as they know they will not date the way a stronger statement might. Any colour is added in ways that can be easily changed, such as cushions or flowers. Their taste tends to be classical, modern and minimalist, rather than antique, as much antique furniture is too fussy for them. Comfort is also of paramount importance, so their minimalism won't ever be extreme; it's more that when a room is too busy or cluttered it distracts from the calm that they like to create.

Some may wonder if the above applies equally to Libran men, and yes, it does. Both sexes dress well, have impeccable taste and invest much time and energy into their appearance and their homes.

A more cerebral way that Libras' concern for balance and harmony manifests is in their political conscience. They don't necessarily get involved in mainstream politics, but evenhandedness and fairness are concepts that mean a lot to them. They lose sleep over issues associated with justice and will fight for what they perceive as injustices. These are extremely principled individuals, often found working in areas to do with the law and coming from an egalitarian position. The idea that life is simply not fair is something that they are never able to come to terms with.

Bob Geldof, the organiser of Live Aid, which raised millions of pounds for the starving in Africa, exemplifies this Libran characteristic. He is incensed by the injustice of the inequities in the world and uses his position as a pop star to take action. He has become something of a crusader, also speaking out about cancelling Third World debt. In Britain he has been recognised for his charity work with the award of an honorary knighthood.

Librans are characteristically pacifists and, when mounting a fight, use methods of resistance and persuasion. Typically, anger is an emotion they have difficulty with; it upsets their equilibrium. These are placid, peace-loving individuals and even a relatively small exchange of angry words upsets them and can leave them struggling to recover their inner harmony for some considerable time. Hence, they have developed these impressive and sophisticated verbal skills which circumvent as much as possible the need to ever directly confront others.

Fundamentally accommodating, cooperative and easygoing, Librans can be put upon. When asked to do something, they find it hard to say 'no' as their automatic response is 'yes'. Part of the difficulty is that they want to please others and, because of their penchant for putting themselves in others' shoes, they imagine how they would feel if they were refused. They have to learn that they are entitled to say 'no'. Once they recognise they have a problem they can begin to develop strategies. A notice over their phone, 'I'm allowed to say no' is one. Writing in their diary, 'My time, keep free' is another. For those who can't manage 'no' straight out, then buying time is another. By saying 'maybe' or 'I'll think about it', they have the chance to consider and can then gather themselves and work out a gracious refusal – one that they don't find distressing to deliver.

Part of Librans' difficulty is that they are genuinely nice, pleasant people who can't bear others to dislike them. More than any other sign they care what others think about them and can get themselves into a right tangle trying to keep everyone happy. It's not only their nearest and dearest whose opinions matter, as the bus conductor, the waiter, the shopkeeper all hold equal sway. Their need is for others to reflect back to them a pleasing image of themselves.

Librans are famous for their indecision; they find it almost impossible to make their minds up. This is because they take decision making extremely seriously and carefully weigh up their options. Typically they go back and forth, vacillating as the scales tip first this way and then that. Each time they literally hang in the balance – shall I, shan't I? – until finally they make their selection. Even then, they can backtrack and change their mind.

Friends and colleagues who are on the end of this – those waiting to know what Libra has decided – are advised to schedule in plenty of time; Librans can't be rushed. Check in occasionally as to where they've got to, but it may be best to avoid the detailed explanation. Getting involved in their decision-making process is time-consuming and involves endless, circular discussions on the pros and cons. Leave that for their nearest and dearest who have less choice in this matter.

Part of why it takes Libras so long to arrive at a decision is their tendency to put others first and try to keep them happy. This means it takes them a while to know what they want and they find it particularly difficult to work this out in isolation. They need others' input. Those who are closely involved should expect to play this role. Some decisions take days, weeks or even months but at the very least a Libran should always sleep on it, to see how the scales balance after the unconscious has had its say.

Although, at times, Librans expect a lot of others, it's no more than they'd be willing and ready to offer themselves. These are sociable individuals, who enjoy the stimulation of interacting and engaging with others. They'll count among their numerous friends some pretty diverse types and they take pleasure in meeting new people. Vivacious and gregarious, they thrive when their social calendar is hectic, full of gatherings, outings and parties.

However, not all Librans are extrovert by any means. The more introverted types still participate in a lot of social activity but find it all a bit more of a strain. The invitations keep arriving because they are so socially adept that others rarely realise they find it hard going. What they actually prefer is contact with those they feel close to on an individual basis and, at gatherings, they'll be engrossed with the one or two people they have a special intimacy with for most of the time.

Whether introverted or extroverted, one-to-one relationships are what matter most to Librans, as it is through this close interaction that they come to know themselves. They need the feedback that others give them and without this they can feel lost, as if they don't have an identity. It's akin to feeling as if they only exist when they can see their reflection in the mirror and others are that mirror. They invest a huge amount of energy into relationships and find it hard to understand that perhaps not everyone needs to be part of a couple, in the way that they do. Even when spending periods alone, they're reviewing the relationship they've recently come out of while obsessing about and on the lookout for their next mate. Some spend a considerable amount of time on their own, appearing to have a contented solo lifestyle. This is in fact rarely the case. With or without a partner, they remain partnership oriented.

Considering how dependent on a relationship Librans are, they are far from pragmatic. In many ways they are in love with the idea of love and get swept away by romance. They love wining and dining and candlelit dinners, giving and receiving flowers, poetry and walks along moonlit beaches. Note this includes none of the everyday stuff. Most people get intoxicated by those special moments; it's just that Librans often want their whole life to resemble a fairy tale. So, although relationships are vital to them, their unrealistic attitude means they are far from trouble free.

Once involved, Librans have to confront the everyday business of actually sharing their life with someone. No more dreams and fantasies, they now have someone whose actual physical presence may be a bit of a shock. This is a cerebral sign and Librans do live in their heads a great deal; at their worst they are accused of being airheads or fluffy-minded. They are not the most practical of people, not terribly well grounded in their bodies or physical reality, hence can be quite scatterbrained and untidy. Their aesthetic sensitivity does not necessarily object to surface mess if it belongs to them – they would see it as part of their creative process. So, however wonderfully cooperative and accommodating they may be, living alongside them is not without its difficulties.

Besides this, Librans are also not that good at dealing with their feelings and can be surprisingly cut off and remote, which is more of a jolt to a loved one than their mess. It's hard to square their detachment with their strong romantic tendencies but these are in fact no indication that they can handle deep emotions. They find strong emotions quite distasteful as well as threatening to their finely-balanced aesthetic sensibilities. Any intensity destabilises them and hence is to be avoided and one way they attempt to do this is with a cool disapproval directed at anyone who emotes anywhere near them.

Librans have a strong sense of proper and appropriate behaviour and this is frequently brought to bear on their private life. For instance, intense emotional exchanges may be censored, as they break the bounds of what is considered civilised and polite. And loved ones may be expected to observe all kinds of niceties and refrain from less genteel behaviour. Their standards intrude on intimacy and loved ones can feel, in a living-together situation, that there are just too many rules. This is all a ploy on Libra's part to keep a distance, as intimacy is threatening, even when it's also what they long for.

Librans are complicated in that they exercise a push/pull hold over those who care about them. For those who experience this as a control trip, it may help to understand that this comes from their own need to maintain equilibrium, which draws others into playing out a part for them. Imagine a see-saw with only one person sitting on it; clearly it needs someone to take the opposite seat, to get the game in motion. Similarly Librans need another to complement them, to spar and challenge and create a balance. Nevertheless, they have considerable ambivalence, as they are never quite sure if the equilibrium they seek is actually to be found through this particular partner or not. They vacillate and imagine that with a new and more ideal partner the balance they seek would be there automatically. While at other times, they recognise that no matter who they are with, it's inner balance they have to establish.

Librans have so much going for them, including oodles of appeal and allure, that others fall over themselves to become involved and then find there are 'no go' areas – like expressing negative emotions. And without being able to share deeper feelings, intimacy is compromised. This is as much a disappointment for Libra, since when their relationship fails to live up to their expectations, they are left with a sense of loss.

How Librans deal with this is crucial and depends on their level of maturity and perhaps, too, on how many times they've been in that position before. There are only so many times that they can convince themselves it's their partner's fault and not an inner state that needs investigating. Yet, their tendency is to move on and search for someone new, where the 'in love' phase can be experienced all over again. While this initial phase in a relationship is intoxicating and blissful, it's not real intimacy, which comes from knowing someone and loving them for who they are.

Some Librans will try hard to avoid taking a look at their difficulties in establishing ongoing intimacy. This involves letting go of the fairy story and unrealistic expectations. Once they are able to take their fair share of responsibility in making a relationship work, they'll stand a chance of finding one that endures and offers a steadier happiness.

Despite their own problems, or possibly because of them, Librans excel at helping others with their relationship difficulties. Their difficulty in taking sides in others' quarrels has its positive side. Their detachment and perspective are exactly what's called for here and their rare ability to see both parties' point of view and to value each equally makes them ideally suited to mediate. Although friends and family call on them to perform this function, it's perhaps best to invest this talent in a more neutral situation. Couple counselling, mediation work, public relations, customer care and related professions are all suitable career options.

Librans also make great managers, handling others with

consummate skill, using the kid glove approach, where others barely recognise they have just been directed to do something. They are good bosses to work for; fair and principled, they take the welfare and working conditions of employees seriously. They're good listeners, able to think about the needs of the workforce, recognising and valuing their contribution to the success of the company. With them in the driving seat, the morale in the workplace is high and they are good at maintaining a happy and relaxed atmosphere.

This doesn't mean the Libran boss is a pushover, though. Fair they may be but stupid they are not. Anyone who takes undue advantage of their good nature is in for a nasty shock. When they feel someone has overstepped the mark, they can be positively ruthless, terminating employment with immediate effect. All their egalitarian principles go out of the window when they are on a self-righteous roll. It's as if they suddenly have permission to be angry and they are furious. This applies in all areas of life, not just as the boss.

As an employee, Libra contributes much to a workforce. These are team players who excel at working cooperatively. Not only that, they bring out the best in other members of a team as they facilitate harmony and can help to encourage creativity in others. Their moderate position helps in disputes and generally oils the wheels of social interactions, so that everyone gets along better. Where there is conflict, they have a gift in being able to help resolve it in an unobtrusive way. Whatever the standard of their actual work – and their work is likely to be good – they remain a huge asset in the workplace in keeping good relations.

Librans pull their weight and get involved in intellectual arenas. This is an air sign and these individuals enjoy using their mind and are good at generating ideas, particularly in a collaborative setting. Playing with concepts, testing them out and getting feedback is right up their street.

Although Librans are well suited to these careers, they don't necessarily find a creative outlet in them. This is one of the most artistic signs of the zodiac and in order to feel fulfilled these individuals need to express themselves creatively, whether through their career or through recreational interests. Many love music, especially the melodic and refined kind, and enjoy singing, whether professionally or in an amateur setting, perhaps in a choir or operatic society. Many go to art school and progress on to work in art or design. Some establish themselves without any formal training and others derive much pleasure and satisfaction from working with oils, watercolours or pastels as amateurs. Careers in design cover a wide spectrum, from fashion to graphics to interiors to jewellery. They bring to all these arenas their innate sense of balance and harmony. Even when not pursuing design professionally, friends and family may well turn to them for advice and copy their ideas, too.

Film and photography are also options that Librans gravitate towards. Their skill in dealing with people is an asset in both these professions, as they are deft at getting others to do exactly what they want.

Where Librans may not fare so well is being self-employed. They need the social interaction and stimulus of working alongside others, so working as a sole trader could be a lonely and isolating experience for them. If, as a self-employed individual, they brush up against others even slightly then that could suffice, for instance, as an artist or designer who shares studio space with others.

Whatever job a Libran ends up in they bring to it their concern for balance and harmony and their keen aesthetic sensitivity. These are cultured, polished individuals with sophisticated tastes who influence, for the better, those around them.

Negative Libra

Many of the Libran characteristics that have been introduced can become negative. Especially when stressed,

Librans famously go 'out of balance', lose their poise and equilibrium and actually become quite extreme. Most find that they only achieve the balance they crave fleetingly and that they spend a lot of time crashing up and down like an out of control see-saw. On the whole, this is more distressing for them than for others, who may not even realise how out of kilter they feel.

Librans see themselves as unselfish and will comment on the selfishness of others. However, they overlook the fact that often, when they accuse someone else of being selfish, it's actually because they can't persuade them to do what they want. In effect, they put moral pressure on others. Yet, because being unselfish is part of their identity, to accuse them otherwise would challenge them to the core and be deeply wounding and threatening to them – and they probably wouldn't see it and would definitely deny it. This can be extremely frustrating to the people close to them.

Because Librans live by a rather strict moral code, they believe this is how life should be. While they may have a good argument here, they overlook the fact that this contradicts the rights of others to live according to their beliefs. They are big on protocol and manners and can hold an extreme, bordering on tyrannical, position as to what is and isn't acceptable behaviour in others. This ranges from the obligatory thank-you cards, not just after receiving a gift but to thank the host or hostess for all manner of events and occasions; to it being deemed an offence to use the wrong cutlery when eating; to much more serious breaches of an unwritten code of behaviour in polite society.

If all this smacks of a kind of class snobbery, then yes, Librans can be very class conscious and afraid themselves of stepping out of line. Hence their condemnation of others when they do break the invisible boundaries. They make sure they are well versed in what is expected of them.

Libra

Debrett's *Etiquette* is a book all Librans know off by heart – without necessarily ever having read it. Those who are unfamiliar with or fail to abide by its strictures on social courtesy are seen as uncouth and threatening. From Libra's standpoint civilised society could end if everyone behaved in this way.

There can also be, with all Libra's refinement, an elitism that looks down on others who don't share their tastes. Of course, they come from all walks of life, but there's an educated, intellectual snobbery that many adopt, no matter what station in life they were born into. This position signals insecurity but by taking it on they manage to get others to feel inferior and insecure instead. Sadly this can result in others avoiding this ultra-sociable person.

For those who have been on the receiving end of such a Libran, remember it's actually their problem. Avoid getting caught up in an odd kind of competition when it comes to knowledge about cultural and historical matters. They have a way of saying 'of course, you know . . .' and thereby wrong-footing others, as there's an implication that anyone and everyone knows this piece of information and that there's something seriously wrong with you and your education if you don't. Unless you do happen to know, then the only way to disentangle is a reply of 'no I don't.' Those who pretend in order to cover up for their own feelings of inferiority become ensnared in a game of intellectual snobbery.

All of this elitism goes against the grain of the egalitarian position that Librans adopt, so is not something of which they are proud, or even conscious. It's a shadowy area, where their genuine interests get muddled up with a competitive streak that they deny they have. They judge competitiveness as 'not nice', so it gets relegated to the unconscious, where it pops up in various rather less pleasant guises. Instead of being straightforward, it's complicated, covert and altogether nastier. When Librans

249

can accept that they have a competitive side to their nature, along with the rest of the human race, they can express it in a more honest way.

Librans think of themselves as considerate, especially when it comes to others' feelings. They put themselves in the other person's shoes, as it were, not always recognising that this is a convoluted way of going about things and can create much confusion. They fail to see that they don't actually know how others feel: it's their fantasy – in fact it's how they would feel were they in that position, which may not faintly resemble how the other person actually feels. Remember that this is an air sign, so not as empathetic as, say, the water signs. There is a kind of tyranny in all this, where Librans see themselves as being eminently unselfish, yet are actually engaged in a complicated inner dialogue.

Here is an example of a frustrating conversation with a Libran woman that concerns what film to go and see that evening. When asked for her choices, instead of just naming two or three films that she'd like to see, she responds by asking which film her friend would like to see. Trying to get her to answer is nigh on impossible. She erroneously believes that were she to disclose her preference, her friend would feel obliged to go. She'll insist on knowing what her friend wants to see and then make her selection based on that information. This Libran woman refuses to put her cards on the table. Presumably, if her friend names two or three films he is interested in seeing and she selects from those, these may or may not contain one of her top three choices. She sees herself as unselfish and fails to realise how she drives her friend to distraction. He just wants a straight answer and can't fathom out why it's so difficult.

This kind of scenario comes from Librans' general difficulties in making decisions. They are notoriously indecisive and, some would argue, uncommitted. Each choice they have to make is tortuous, as it seems to bring with it so much to think through and consider. Whereas other signs would miss these implications, for Librans they are all too apparent and have to be properly explored. They procrastinate, going back and forth, until eventually they get there. So, to say they are uncommitted is actually unfair, although the time they take making their minds up can be exasperating to those waiting. And for a sign that prides itself on being unselfish they can inconvenience others while they vacillate and, in this respect, they put their need for time first.

So there are occasions when Librans can seem rather hypocritical. Putting their needs first is clearly something they are entitled to do, it just doesn't sit well with their stance of putting others first. They are in a paradoxical position. They somehow have to get others to agree to and want to give them what they want. This can mean those who are waiting on tenterhooks for a decision that will affect them end up reassuring Librans that they can take their time.

This is a Venus-ruled sign and as such Librans are identified with being 'nice people' which means that they often have a problem with anger – nice people don't get angry. This has its pluses and its minuses, as it's because of this that they have developed such a skill in dealing with others, without ever needing to get angry. However, there are times when anger is appropriate and called for and this is when they come unstuck. Unless they believe it's absolutely justified, they try never to allow themselves this feeling. Now a feeling is not actually something any of us have control over. What we have control over of is how we behave when we have a particular feeling. Librans find it hard to differentiate between having a feeling, which is personal and private and to which they are entitled, and expressing it emotionally, which somehow becomes compulsory in their mind once a feeling has been acknowledged. This gives them no choice in how they behave, so their only way forward is to suppress the feeling entirely, unless they are in a position where they are willing to reveal themselves. They only allow themselves to feel anger when they believe it is justified and then they take decisive action.

This sequence leads to Librans taking the moral high ground when they believe they are right. They have finally found a legitimate release for all their previously suppressed anger and they come down on others in a heavy-handed way and come across as self-righteous and pious. Yet they fail to realise that the reason they are in such a strop is because they are reacting to so much more than the actual 'wrong deed' of the moment.

Libra's life is peppered with shoulds and oughts. They are hypersensitive to what others think of them and impose a tough ethical code upon themselves that can be quite daunting to live up to. What they sometimes fail to recognise is that they, too, harbour harsh opinions and can be scathingly judgemental of others and yet no one worries more about what the neighbours think than Libra. Again, this is convoluted thinking on their part and comes from a mechanism known in psychology as projection, whereby disowned aspects of ourselves are attributed to others. This is a normal and natural occurrence but what is always interesting is what gets projected. Their concern about what others think may actually be something they secretly think but can't acknowledge. After all, it's all in their imagination.

This can make things complicated inter-personally, especially when, as is often the case, Libra manages to find others who do think and feel as they imagine. There is always going to be someone to carry their projections, which, nevertheless, remain a denied part of themselves that perhaps needs to be reflected upon, especially for those who feel unduly restricted by what others think. Most people struggle at times to know where they begin and end, especially in close relationships, but Libra has a particularly difficult time.

Libras need others to bounce off and provide essential feedback and are aware of their dependence on others and of how society is based on inter-dependencies. It's only when the scales tip too far in the dependency direction that others' opinions become unduly important and influential and Librans stop recognising their own independence and autonomy.

Libra's desire to be seen as a 'nice person' can mean that they sometimes come across as an odd mixture of prim and sickly sweet. Libra actor Julie Andrews has suffered from this association, based on her roles in the films *Mary Poppins* and *The Sound of Music*. It could be argued these roles called for this and her ability to convey these qualities is why she was chosen for the part, but equally, the fact that she is Libran meant she could draw on these attributes. It's interesting to note that she has remained associated with these characteristics, despite playing a variety of other roles subsequently,

The sickly-sweet adjectives are more often applied to women and the male equivalent is probably smarmy or superficial. Either way, it's at some cost that they keep up their nice person image. It can mean, too, that they attempt to be all things to all people, adapting to fit in with whoever they are with and feeling lost as to who they genuinely are. Over-adapting to be liked by everyone comes at a price and such an individual needs help to be able to tolerate not always being liked and to start valuing themselves.

This particular Libran trait can result in the 'goody-two-shoes' type, who has their halo in place and desperately wants others to be convinced of how pleasant, nice and caring they are. They interfere in other people's business, in their capacity as the upholder of virtue, telling others how they should be conducting private matters. When the judgemental side of Libra kicks in, they can seem patronising and condescending as they dole out their good deeds.

Not surprisingly, those Librans who bend over backwards to be thought well of, often don't actually like themselves very much. That's why they spend so much time proving what a nice, worthwhile person they are and why someone else's dislike becomes unbearable. They have to find a way to care less about what other people think, believe that they matter and take back some of the power they have given away so indiscriminately.

There is an opposite position to this that some Librans develop, where the scales tip in the other direction, and they become more like Aries – their opposite sign – than Aries are. Whereas an Aries can usually get away with being selfish and direct because of a certain innocence and naivety, Librans lack this and come across as heavy-handed and self-centred.

The former British Prime Minister Margaret Thatcher exemplifies this type of Libran. Much was made of how afraid others were of her during her term in government and the extent to which she was a disciplinarian and overly authoritarian. Her voice, with its artificially modulated tones, was often seen as insincere, another negative trait that some Librans develop when trying too hard to be convincing. In many ways she became a parody of what is usually understood as Libran, perhaps indicating what a strain the job was.

Both Aries and Libra have a selfish/unselfish dilemma but perhaps Libra has to find a way to be healthily selfish. Making themselves more important than others won't work any more than making themselves less important – they have to make themselves equally important. It is about honouring and respecting their own needs, just as they would those of others.

Once Librans are in a secure relationship the sense of loss that some experience is a kind of identity crisis. Their sense of self is established by the myriad reflections they receive from all those around them so that once in a relationship with just one person they begin to feel hollow and empty inside. Their dilemma when looking inside to discover who they are, as opposed to being defined by others on the outside, is that they don't actually know what they need or want. They are so used to adapting and fitting in to what others want of them that they've lost touch with an essential part of themselves. They have to rediscover how to be authentic and true to themselves and how to get their own needs met.

For such a peace-loving sign Librans can be surprisingly argumentative. Ironically, it's to do with their need for balance, so when one point of view is aired, they feel the need to present an alternative position. There's a kind of perverse reasonableness at work here, a balancing of the scales. However, this can be extremely annoying for others, who mind being opposed in what for them is casual conversation. Others may not be up for an energetic debate, which Libras sometimes seem to provoke and enjoy.

This contrary side to Libra seems to be at odds with their need to find agreement, yet it is actually exacerbated by this trait, as not only do they present an argument, they persist in trying to get others to then agree with them. Others can feel wrong-footed and unwillingly engaged in an argument that they have no real interest in and without any idea how they got into it. All because, in the need to maintain equilibrium, Libra has waded in with an opposite view.

Librans are gifted communicators and can, if they choose, put a spin on what they have to say to make themselves highly convincing. They are not prone to outright dishonesty but they can polish and distort the truth. Depending on their field of work, these people make excellent spin-doctors as they are extremely plausible. There's no way, if they decide to be economical with the truth, that those on the receiving end will be any the wiser. Be warned!

At the end of the day, none of Libra's negative characteristics are that dark or terrible. In fact, Librans try harder than almost any other sign to get on with others, to be fair and to take responsibility for themselves. All this and charm, too – worth a few arguments or what?

The Libra Man

The Libran man is recognisable by his classical good looks, charm and magnetism. His features are often symmetrical and well balanced and he's likely to be aware of his attractiveness. In fact, he may be a bit vain. It comes from all the attention he gets because of his looks, which in the end bores him. In order to impress him, pretend not to notice that he's drop-dead gorgeous. Pay attention to some of his other attributes, especially his ideas and opinions.

This can be difficult, as the Libra man clearly invests a lot of time, money and attention into looking good. He's likely to be among the few men who have manicures and use moisturisers. His grooming will be impeccable and his clothes immaculate. He'll have exquisite taste, too, buying the best clothes he can afford and genuinely appreciating the cut and quality. All of this makes quite an impact when first meeting him and can feel a bit intimidating. It's hard to concentrate on his mind when he so obviously cares a great deal about his appearance.

Yet, the Libran man is also a great conversationalist. He quickly puts others at ease, with amusing and light-hearted banter. He's open and receptive to what others have to say, too, so makes a good listener. Besides being adept at small talk, he has a serious side and cares deeply about injustice in the world and he may well be a member of Amnesty International or Greenpeace.

At heart, the Libran man is a pacifist; he doesn't like angry words, let alone war. Yet he mounts some pretty impressive fights, but on his terms. He can be extremely persuasive when he has a mind to be and can get others on his side. He uses skilled argument and conviction to get his point across and can mastermind a crusade. Mahatma Gandhi is a shining example of these Libran characteristics.

One of the Libra man's vulnerabilities is his need for approval. He wants to be liked and thought well of and as a consequence can never be impervious to what others think about him. The opinions that get to him most echo his own uncertainties and insecurities and mean he is forever striving to be a better person. His own inner judge is in constant dialogue with him, a rather harsh judge, so that his attempts to be exemplary inevitably fail in his own estimation.

Because the Libran man cares how others view him, he is gullible when it comes to flattery. He's unable to distinguish whether others are being sincere or not, especially when they are saying what he wants to hear. He's an odd mixture of self-confidence and total uncertainty and those who try can manipulate him for a time. He will realise, sooner or later, that he's being strung along and free himself from such subterfuge, but it means that he sometimes trusts the wrong people in the first instance.

Besides being exceptionally handsome, the Libra man has impeccable manners and a suave sophistication. He's what was once called 'a ladies man' in that he appreciates old-fashioned courtesies, opens doors, gives up his seat and is generally very considerate. Partly he is obeying an unwritten code of how to behave in polite society and partly he is genuinely kind and thoughtful. Sometimes it can be tricky working out which of these is behind his actions and those on the receiving end may want to know if they are getting special treatment or not.

The Libran man is far from straightforward, so it's not surprising that others find it hard to work him out. He's so caught up with proper behaviour that discerning what his true feelings are can be difficult, not least to him. He says and does the right thing, but may not be entirely present. He can try to please others in a rather compulsive way, as if a lot rides on him obtaining their love and acceptance, only for them to find out after they've given it that he doesn't actually love them in return. And *he* may be shocked and dismayed to find this out, too.

This dynamic has earned the Libran man the tag of womaniser – and gay men are equally accused of this – flirting and letting others believe that they are interested and available when in fact they are not. For this reason, he can be seen as shallow and as one who plays with others' feelings, which isn't his intention. He's driven by his own need to be accepted, regardless of whether or not he wants a relationship. His difficulty is in not knowing his own mind.

When a Libran man is wooing or pursuing a love interest he is probably the world's most romantic man. He understands romance in a way that no one else does and what's more, is happy to indulge in it. He sends flowers and love notes and chocolates and champagne. He wines and dines and springs surprises that delight. He's in his element when in pursuit. This is a Venus-ruled sign and love is what he's best at.

Although his sign is ruled by a feminine planet this doesn't mean he's effeminate – the Libran man can be quite macho in his appearance but it does mean he has a well-developed feminine side, along with poetic and idealistic notions about love and life. And whether or not he's heterosexual he gets on well with women and enjoys their company and conversation. His closest friends are usually female which can present problems for a female partner, who may feel insecure. In fact, there's probably no need to be. Although he's not one with a great track record when it comes to fidelity, he doesn't usually compromise his friendships in this way. This may be of small comfort to his partner, but at least she can be reassured that when he's out with a close female buddy nothing untoward is likely to occur.

When a Libran man does fall in love, he's taken by surprise. Until then it's all been an elaborate dance that he enjoys without realising the implications. He goes through the motions and then finds he's emotionally involved. He does better with a partner who doesn't pursue him, who allows him space. The minute he's pursued he runs away. A partner has to stand back and allow him to either develop deeper feelings for them, or not, as the case may be. It's not something that can be forced.

The Libra man has a horror of some of the darker and more difficult emotions like jealousy and possessiveness. He simply can't handle them. He denies they exist within him and distances himself from a loved one who expresses such feelings in his presence. They touch on something he finds threatening but how he deals with that can be rather unpleasant. At such times he may trivialise or make light of a loved one's feelings by trying to laugh it off or change the subject with a charming remark or even quietly leave the room. Not surprisingly the loved one can feel emotionally abandoned, making it all far worse. He can only manage 'nice' feelings and cuts off from those that he deems distasteful or uncivilised.

The Libran man may well be drawn to a partner who has easy access to these more difficult feelings, simply because he finds what he most fears equally fascinating. This may sound problematic, but it is actually quite a good option for him, as via his partner he begins to establish a relationship with these 'taboo' feelings. Such a partner needs to be able to hold his or her own in the face of his disapproval of their emotional outbursts – and take comfort in the fact that this is exactly what he needs.

The other option that the Libra man may go for is to hook up with a pleasant man or woman who is equally detached emotionally. Together life may be harmonious but it will lack dynamism and, quite possibly, sexual depth. In such a scenario he may well roam, looking for the exciting intensity that he denies he wants. This then becomes a far more destructive situation, in which he creates justifiable feelings of jealousy and possessiveness in a partner who is as much out of their depth as he is with these feelings.

So, when it comes to predicting how likely the Libran man is to remain faithful, the occasional stand-up rows are recommended. He may say how much he hates arguments and how bruising to his sensibilities he finds them, which is likely to be true, but they provide him with access to parts of himself he didn't know existed that are vital for his well-being. And the quarrels keep him energetically engaged with his partner. Otherwise he can drift away into a kind of apathetic uninvolved place, where being unfaithful becomes no big deal. At least with an emotional partner, he's reminded that it does and will matter.

The Libran man will always be a flirt, it's part of the way he makes conversation and this is something his mate has to accept. Those who don't understand him accuse him of being superficial and fickle, which misses the point. When he's emotionally engaged he's an honourable man even when he's playing the flirt and he may be completely unaware that others are getting hurt. Those who care about him should ascertain where they stand.

Once the Libran man has made a commitment, he takes it very seriously indeed. Those who have affairs after this point in their relationship won't be doing so lightly, as they will be tortured by it. He lives by a high moral code and finds it hard to lie; it goes against an inner dictum. So, provided his relationship remains vibrant, he has as good a chance as the next of remaining faithful.

The Libran man probably doesn't have strong feelings either way regards having children, but enjoys them once they arrive – particularly daughters, whom he spoils rotten. He makes a rather indulgent father as he's too relaxed and laid-back to be good with discipline, which is often seen as the father's role. He's not that good with the sticky fingers, messy eating stage, either. After all, he does have his designer clothes to consider. As his children mature he takes more and more pleasure in their company, as he can then share with them some of his own interests. This means lots of cultural pursuits, as the Libra man is often artistic or musical or interested in the theatre. He may be professionally involved in one of these areas of life or it may just be recreational, but he'll be knowledgeable and informed and expect decent conversations from his children. He'll introduce them to the cinema and will encourage them to discuss the various directors and their body of work.

The Libran man is interested in how his children are getting on academically and will foster their education, being more than willing to pay for extra-curricula activities. He recognises the importance of vocational subjects, so his children don't have to be academic for him to be impressed and proud of them.

His own career may not follow a conventional route, as Libran men play hard when young and often skip some of the stepping stones that many careers depend on, like university, art or drama school. He's more likely to find his own way artistically or creatively. A list of Libran musicians includes John Lennon, Will Smith, Sting, Chuck Berry, Bruce Springsteen and Bob Geldof. Several of these men have been associated with idealistic causes (John Lennon with world peace, Sting with saving the rain forests and Geldof with feeding the world). John Lennon's romantic nature was visible, too, in his love for Yoko Ono.

Those Libran men who follow a creative path draw on their feminine side. They often gravitate to careers that allow them to have an intimate and privileged involvement with a client group that is mainly female, such as fashion design and hairdressing. In these positions they are privy to women's self-doubts and insecurities and can handle this well, using their relating skills along with their aesthetic judgement to help them make the most of themselves. When it's a professional relationship, as opposed to a personal one, they aren't so threatened (it's their own feelings they have difficulty with) and can cope admirably with their client's feelings.

Other Libran men pursue a career in fine art and design, using their skill in creating balance and harmony in the work that they execute. Not all have the talent or opportunity to make this their career but having some kind of creative outlet remains important to their happiness.

Those Libran men who choose a more academic route are particularly suited to careers that draw on their diplomacy and fair-mindedness. Law, the diplomatic service, conciliation work and public relations are all possibilities. Whatever this man ends up doing he brings to it his creative flair and considered, balanced point of view.

This is pre-eminently a reasonable man who gets on with others, has accomplished social skills and can carry himself well in all walks of society. His good looks can be a mixed blessing as he wants to be listened to and taken seriously and often gets mistaken for a pretty boy. For those involved, remember he's fragile, too, and despite his sometimes contrary nature, finds real arguments hard to take. This is a cultured and cultivated man, idealistic and principled who definitely needs and wants a mate. He may seem a bit fickle but actually he's far more serious than he lets on. It's his best-kept secret.

The Libra Woman

The Libran woman is recognisable by her beauty, grace and charm. She's elegant and refined, with impeccable taste and polished manners. She's the kind of woman who can go anywhere and look good, fit in and appear at ease. She moves well, with the deportment of a model or dancer and carries herself with a cool assurance. All of this contributes to her air of sophistication and a quiet, understated confidence.

It's not just the Libran woman's looks and demeanour that are attractive; she has accomplished social skills that contribute to her popularity. She enjoys social occasions and gets on easily and effortlessly with others. Like all the air signs, Gemini and Aquarius being the other two, she is interested in the world of ideas and has her own opinions on a wide range of topics. Her conversation is lively and stimulating and she listens attentively to what others have to say. She offers supportive and involved responses, yet manages to introduce her own independent thoughts and cast new light on others' concerns. She can be both empathetic and challenging, depending on how she feels and who she is in dialogue with. The Libra woman has the rare gift of being sensitive in the touchy-feely domain as well as having detachment and perspective.

Because of all this, the Libran woman is well liked and in demand. Others enjoy her company, not least because she is careful not to cause others hurt or offence. She is the epitome of tact and discretion and has a way with words that is impressive. She can verbally manoeuvre her way through the most land-mined territory and emerge unscathed. This is a skill that she puts to good use in many areas of her life.

One of the reasons Libran women are so well liked is that they seek to establish the common ground between themselves and others. Even in casual conversation they quickly establish a shared interest or involvement which is mutually enjoyable to discuss. If they fail to find such a topic they are still able to give others a quality of attention that flatters them and leaves them feeling that they are interesting. They are especially gifted at what is called 'light conversation,' which can be disparaged but is in fact an enviable social grace. This also means that when the

Libran woman does take up a contrary position others are taken aback, which gives her an immediate advantage.

The Libran woman sees herself as a paragon of unselfishness, which may or may not be true, but is important in so far as this is the position she comes from. She does look at things from other people's point of view and she is kind and considerate but, as we've seen, Librans have a particularly convoluted way of going about things. What matters here is not whether or not she's unselfish, but the fact that she wants to be seen as such and cares deeply about what others think of her. Anyone who dares to suggest otherwise must realise she will be insulted.

The Libran woman can't stand being disliked; it is quite unbearable for her. Her need to be seen in a favourable light is why she is so nice. Currying favour, as she does, can be hard work as she puts considerable energy into maintaining her well-liked position. Occasionally this backfires and someone takes exception to her, often because she's so pleasant and inoffensive that they don't trust her. Her sincerity is challenged. This is a tricky one for her, as she has little defence; she desperately wants to be thought well of and besides, sincerity is an important component of her self-image as a person of principle. Other more robust signs, like Aries, with a more 'take it or leave it' attitude, simply don't understand where she is coming from. In fact, her tact and diplomacy are wasted on a large section of the population, who have no idea how considerate of their feelings she is being.

However, the Libran woman is certainly not weak and has her own resilience. Her strategy is to avoid confrontation and use her considerable skills of persuasion to smooth her passage in life. She has a persistence that others may find quite surprising as when apparently defeated in an argument, she returns to the issue again and again. She presents subtle nuances that she purports cast a new light but she is, in effect, albeit with a deft touch, simply wearing the opposition down.

Venus, her planetary ruler, is associated with love and attraction but was once also thought of as a planet of war. It's the flip side of the coin; love and hate are never as far apart as we imagine. It's just that the Libran woman has a real problem recognising that she might have strong negative feelings; they are a taboo area for her, and often being contrary is as close as she gets to fighting a war. She's happy to make a stand for a principle, such as recycling or renewable energy, and argue passionately about the state of the planet, but when it's personal and to do with her feelings she flounders.

When it comes to relationships the Libran woman is extremely idealistic. She likes a romantic courtship, where a prospective partner follows a surprisingly old-fashioned code of behaviour. This woman really does want a chivalrous suitor, who woos her. Anything too rushed she finds uncouth and will withdraw from. The pace is all-important because she doesn't really want the courtship to end; that's what she enjoys most and, if she had her way, her whole life would consist of the first flush of romance. The next phase of a relationship, whether getting married or living together, can be too ordinary and mundane for her.

Nevertheless, most Libran women enjoy the companionship of a live-in partner and so manage to progress to the next stage of a relationship, while looking back on the earlier period with nostalgia. The best way for a partner to counter this is to keep the romance alive by making romantic gestures on a regular basis. Never take her for granted. She loves flowers and girlie gifts – perfume and all things scented go down well, as does expensive lingerie and champagne and chocolates, provided they're top of the range. And jewellery is always acceptable! It doesn't have to cost a fortune or be solid gold, so long as it's got class and is stylish, such as costume jewellery by a well-known designer.

In some ways, the Libran woman doesn't want to inhabit

the world of normal life. She wants to live in a fantasy world that's always happy and where nothing ugly exists or occurs. While there's nothing wrong with wanting to be happy, the extent to which she tries to deny other states can be problematic, not least for her. And for her partner, trying to engage with her on deeper levels can prove difficult. By showing disdain for a partner's emotional outbursts, she can effectively cut them off in mid-flow. She's very adept at blocking exchanges she finds threatening. There's something of a Seventies flower child in the Libra woman and she doesn't want to face up to the harsh realities of life.

Once the Libran woman is involved and settled in a relationship and the ground rules are established, she's prone to bouts of dissatisfaction. However hard her partner tries, her idealistic, romantic notions are unlikely to be fulfilled. Whereas some signs relax into taking their partner for granted in a positive way, and enjoy the feelings of security that this gives them, the Libran woman baulks at this. She pines for the candlelit dinners and dancing afterwards – she wants occasions to dress up for. These things are an essential part of her life which she won't give up without a considerable inner struggle. Naturally, visits to the opera, ballroom dancing classes and other gracious pursuits can keep the cravings at bay, but they're still not a substitute for an eternal courtship.

For all these reasons, monogamy may not suit the Libran woman terribly well. When in a committed relationship, she is susceptible to straying as she looks for romance with a new love. She may have a string of extra-marital liaisons, which may in fact just be flirtations but could become full-blown affairs. Unlike many women, she is capable of having more than one relationship at a time and feeling she is doing justice to all concerned. A discreet lover or two or an intense platonic relationship could be what it takes to keep her happy and a long-term partner may decide to turn a blind eye to her affairs, in order not to lose her.

The Libra woman may be fairly disinterested if her partner has the odd affair, too, provided it doesn't impact directly on her. She won't tolerate any public humiliation, but if the additional relationship is low-key and operates within certain parameters, she may not like it but she may well put up with it. What allows her this degree of liberality is her reasonableness, which prevents her making a fuss.

The Libran woman's tolerance may not be that good for her psychological well-being. If the affair threatens her relationship or her lifestyle it's off limits and then she'll lay down an ultimatum. Others might judge that she did too little too late and at some cost to herself. A partner's affair is bound to damage her confidence and self-esteem and her apparent nonchalance means she could end up losing someone she really cares about.

Having children is not a priority for the Libran woman as she's not one of those women who have to have a child in order to feel fulfilled. She often leaves it to fate and allows herself to become pregnant 'accidentally', rather than making a conscious decision. This may be to protect herself from the disappointment if she fails to conceive or it may be because she is truly ambivalent and can't make up her mind. However those who remain childfree rarely have regrets and enjoy the benefits, such as more money and freedom, and find other ways to have a creative and interesting life.

Perhaps the real reason the Libran woman opts to remain childfree is that her main love and preoccupation is with partnerships. This is how she defines herself and whereas she can't live without a mate, having a child is more of an option.

For those who do become mothers, and many do, the Libran woman's approach to motherhood is more cerebral than instinctual. She finds it hard to trust her instincts and so becomes acquainted with all the theories around child rearing, in order to evaluate them. At the end of the day, her instincts guide her but she likes to have these confirmed by a pedagogical authority.

The Libran woman's firm beliefs in equality are put into practice in her domestic life and she expects a partner to do their fair share and offers her children a rare amount of respect, particularly with regard to their autonomy. She's a truly liberal parent, willing as her children grow up to discuss matters and to take their opinions seriously. With her, everything is negotiable. She doesn't act in an authoritarian way and because what her children think and feel is taken into account in all decision making, they grow up feeling empowered.

However, the Libran woman can put her foot down and, when she needs to, can lay down clear boundaries for her offspring. She doesn't allow them to run amok. Her principles regarding what's fair and what's not mean that her children are taught to consider others and their feelings and that includes hers. They have polite, pleasant manners and behave courteously because that's what she expects of them. She's deeply offended by rudeness, so can have problems with adolescents who refuse to tow the line but, provided the lines of communication remain open, they'll appreciate her qualities of fairness and equal mindedness and she won't lose their affection permanently. She can also become rather controlling and manipulative at the point where they want more freedom. Having invested so much in a one-to-one relationship with each of her children, she finds it hard to let go of them.

Whether or not she has children, the Libran woman is likely to want a career. She needs the variety and stimulation of work and if she can afford to, will employ a whole raft of domestic back-up help to enable her to continue working while raising her children. She's not a superwoman but she does want it all. Of course, this depends on whether she has managed to find a career that is creatively satisfying in the first place. She believes she's destined to work with her brain rather than her hands, although this doesn't include crafts, and any kind of manual work she may well see as demeaning.

Many Libran women are practising artists, writers, musicians, actors, filmmakers and photographers. Others find their way into related fields where their appreciation of these arenas is essential, such as art history and art criticism, the world of design, teaching in academia or as a curator in a gallery. Whatever field of the arts they choose, their taste tends towards the refined and harmonious – no kitchen-sink dramas or sustained discords for them!

Those who don't work in the arts in some capacity may concentrate on their diplomatic and inter-personal skills. Whatever arena she's found in, this woman is an asset in enlisting the cooperation of those she works alongside. Not only that, she's the one who improves the workplace – she'll bring in flowers, nice mugs or a picture to make the working environment a more pleasant place for everyone.

The Libran woman is not necessarily political with a capital P but she is concerned about fair play and justice. She will stick her neck out and can be counted on where blatant discrimination is apparent, whether that be in the workplace or in her private life. She has high moral standards that she expects others to have, too and is deeply upset by obvious injustices.

If a sportswoman, she plays fairly and wants to win on her performance. The Libran tennis player, Serena Williams, would have found the suggestion that she and her sister Venus fixed their matches, deeply insulting. Her ethics would not allow her to do that, let alone her own desire to win. This sign is well suited to sports like tennis where there is a direct exchange, but they are equally capable of playing team games where their cooperative spirit is called upon. However, they may well prefer less competitive and more aesthetic physical activities such as dance or yoga or pilates, which work on creating inner peace, balance and harmony.

Famous Librans include the actor Kate Winslet, whose Botticelli good looks typifies this sign. Despite her professional success there is almost as much coverage in the tabloid press about her private relationships as there is about her films. Gwyneth Paltrow is another well-known Libran actor whose love life is equally the focus of media gossip. Given that this sign has a capacity to obsess about relationships, it's interesting that the public also seems inordinately curious about this aspect of their personal life.

Brigitte Bardot was an icon of the twentieth century for her sexual allure and has gone on to demonstrate other Libran qualities, in her fight for the fair treatment of animals. She is almost as famous for her animal sanctuary as she is for her earlier beauty.

Not all Libran women are blessed with such striking looks but get noticed, nonetheless, because they fulfil the archetypal image of femininity so well. This is a well-balanced, reasonable, fair-minded woman who thinks for herself, has her own opinions and yet gets on easily with others. It's easy to knock her because she so obviously cares and is vulnerable to what others think of her but given the state of the world today, perhaps this is not such a bad quality after all – indeed one worth emulating.

The Libra Child

The Libran child is recognisable by their stunning looks and charming manners. They really are quite beautiful, often with classical symmetrical features and possibly even a dimple or two. However, as the parents of this child, it's important not to place too much importance on their appearance, as they need to be loved and adored for who they are. If too much emphasis is placed on how attractive they are they can feel their worth is entirely based on this, which is clearly not a good thing for their self-esteem.

So, although many of these children have the potential to be successful in the world of modelling, parents should think very carefully about whether this is the right way to go and to what extent any acclaim their child attracts gratifies their own ambitions and ego. It may be better to wait until these children can make up their own minds, as it will have a huge impact on their development.

Libran children are sociable and friendly and, as a result, popular and in demand. They make friends easily and aren't afraid to start interacting with other children in the playground or at school. Although not shy, they are not pushy or overly confident either; they just make good mixers and are able to include themselves in whatever is going on. They are, in fact, an asset to any group, as they help to draw others out and include the shyer and less socially adapted children in their play.

Libran children seek balance and harmony, both within themselves and in their surroundings, so they keep their rooms tidy and looking nice, simply because they feel better that way. They won't mind sharing a room or their toys, provided the arrangement is fair in their eyes. If it's slanted one way, to a sibling's advantage, they'll quickly object. And if sharing a room, they won't countenance any mess. They feel it's only fair that things are put away, out of respect for each other, as the shared space belongs to them equally. In fact, they are imposing their standards but they can argue their point very succinctly.

Early on Libran children show an interest in clothes and want to choose what they wear. They'll have strong preferences and may refuse outright certain outfits which, if this is possible, should be respected. Allow them to have their say when shopping for them and their room, as that will minimise wastage.

A sense of fair play is intrinsic to this sign and Libran children take exception to any unfairness. Whether in the home, at school or in the playground, they are often heard to say 'it's not fair'. They firmly believe that life is meant to be even handed and use this as an argument to get what they want. Especially when it comes to siblings, they expect to be treated in an equal way in all respects and there will be many a row over their perceived mistreatment. Parents may have to carefully explain that not all things are equal and that a brother or sister who is older or younger is entitled to things that they are not.

Libran children respond well to reasoned argument. They engage in this themselves from an early age and want to have the ground rules set out clearly, in order that they can evaluate them for themselves. Simply being told offends and upsets them; they need to know why and to feel they have some input when decisions are made. They don't do well if chores or tasks are imposed upon them either but, as these children are genuinely helpful, parents are advised to enlist their cooperative spirit. By using their powers of persuasion a parent can establish a basis for discussion of these matters, and a reasoned agreement that these children respect and hence abide by can be reached. This is initially more work but lays a foundation that will stand all concerned in good stead. Particularly in adolescence, when for safety's sake firm boundaries are essential, parents can feel confident these will be respected.

The Libran child tries hard to please and needs to be thought well of, which is both a plus and a minus. It means they are kind and thoughtful and consider others and their well-being. They do favours and help around the house and try to adapt to whatever situation they find themselves in. However, this can be at some cost to themselves as they are not intrinsically adaptable, they just want to be liked and avoid conflict. They may enjoy an argument when it isn't in any way heated but emotional discord is deeply upsetting to their fine sensibilities.

In a household that contains a lot of friction a Libran child may shrink away, finding it all quite intolerable. They need an environment that is fundamentally peaceful if they are to develop healthily. Especially when there is hostility between their parents, these children feel torn apart, with equal loyalty to both. They can see each point of view and find the lack of reconciliation extremely painful. Many try to mediate and act as a go-between, which ultimately exacerbates the pain for them. It's not up to them to mend their parents' relationship and, no matter how hard they try, it's not in their power so they are left with feelings of failure. Libran children mind more than most when parents are at war and it can leave them with their own irreconcilable inner conflict. Parents caught up in acrimony would do well to try to protect their Libran children from it as much as they can, presenting a united front and, if a divorce is inevitable, making it as amicable as possible, especially with regards child care arrangements and access.

The Libran child finds aggression per se difficult. When others express anger they feel threatened. They tend to judge harshly and condemn any such feelings within themselves, which leads to repression and denial. The more volatile the family they are born into, the more frightening anger becomes for them, whereas if family life is basically harmonious and any expression of anger from them is received well, they have more space to become acquainted with these feelings in a non-threatening way.

Libran children have an innate sense of how they ought to behave – of what is socially proper and polite – which can become limiting, especially if this is overly emphasised. Most parents try to cultivate good manners in their children, so it's understandable that they are thrilled by their success with their Libran offspring. However, if it becomes at the expense of their child's self-expression, then it's hardly desirable. So, although these children do tend to be nice, pleasant, reasonable and equable, it's important that they don't feel they have to be this way to be acceptable, or that when this way of behaving breaks down they are in trouble. If anything, these children need help in showing anger in healthy and acceptable ways. If they can master this, then, coupled with their delightful ways, they can negotiate life successfully.

Without the above, the Libran child can become placatory. Because they instinctively like to please, they can end up complying with whatever is asked of them, finding it hard to refuse inappropriate requests. Their very politeness and respect for adults makes them vulnerable to being taken advantage of. This doesn't have to be sinister, but it can be and they do need to be adequately protected and taught it is permissible, even desirable, to be able to say 'no'. With high self-esteem and a good sense of their own identity, which comes from being loved and accepted for who they are, not just for being good, they feel empowered and entitled to refuse anything they are uncomfortable with.

The Libran child thrives when exposed to culture. These are artistic children and may be musical, too. Foster their talents, make a wide range of paints and crayons available to them and whatever musical instruments are affordable. Introduce them to art, through trips to art galleries from a young age – this will stimulate their imagination. Play them a wide range of music and take them to concerts, too. See it as part of their education, although it actually goes much further as it can become a pleasurable interest and pursuit throughout their life. The more comfortable they are in these arenas the more able they are to take their place within them later in life.

This also applies to dance, especially ballet. Many young children enjoy ballet classes and even those with little real promise benefit. Undoubtedly their deportment improves and probably their confidence. Libran children, with their natural grace, may well have talent, too, and may choose to continue for many years, possibly going on to a career in dance or choreography. And it's just as important to foster this for the boys as well as the girls.

Libran children enjoy school and tend to do well academically, because they enjoy the world of ideas and are good at debate and discussion. They develop their own opinions early in life and do best when in an environment where they feel confident to share these. In fact, if they aren't enjoying school, there's probably something wrong with the establishment and that should be investigated. This could range from insufficient mental stimulation to bullying but whatever the problem, it needs to be sorted out as these children ordinarily thrive in an educational environment.

When it comes to specialising, Libran children are better suited to the arts and humanities than to the sciences. Some may grow up to follow a vocation while others may work in the arts in an academic capacity. As they mature they're likely to have advanced inter-personal skills that could lead them in many directions so it's recommended that they keep their options open. Their innate sense of justice and intellectual capacity means that a career in law may appeal, so while the pure sciences are not usually their best bet, some of the softer sciences, like sociology, might come in useful. Of course, there are always exceptions and some do become scientists, engineers and chemists and are perfectly content, so never rule out subjects that interest them.

Libra is not the easiest sign for a boy to be born under. With all the stereotypical expectations that get placed on boys, they can feel that their brand of masculinity is not appreciated. Society doesn't tend to value aesthetic, artistic, creative, thoughtful and fair-minded boys until they are successful. Once adult and established in the world they don't have a problem, at least not as far as this is concerned but when young, they may feel out of step with typical lad culture. This may, in fact, act as a spur to achieve success so that later in life they feel vindicated. However, what's important when young is that their family accepts them for who they are. This boy may not be sporty, although he could be; he may not be boisterous or assertive, preferring to sort out his differences in a calm and reasoned way, but he's no less a boy for it – just a boy with beauty and grace and charm.

Libran children can have expensive tastes and may not relish toiling for their spending money; they have an in-built decadent streak that comes from their ruler Venus. They'll always be big spenders and can get through a lot of money on nothing in particular. They have a way of spending it on bits and pieces, although they also do go for spectacularly expensive items from time to time. They'll expect their pocket money to match whatever other children of their age get, using the 'it's not fair' argument if they don't get as much. Parents are advised to veer to the generous side, if they can afford to, as these youngsters really do hate being short of cash.

Eventually, the Libran child starts to generate an income, which they continue to spend freely and with little thought of tomorrow. They simply like and enjoy nice things, which tend to be costly. Not least, clothes.

The teenage years may not be that problematic with a Libran child, particularly if a working agreement has been established regarding ground rules. These youngsters are reasonable and won't object to anything that they consider fair. Their biggest angst will be coping with all the hormonal changes that wreak havoc on their looks – spots and greasy hair are no fun, especially for those whose looks have been so admired. The fact that this is a passing phase is of little comfort to them. Perhaps because they are so attractive, this awkward stage is particularly excruciating for them. Not all are plagued by their hormones, some simply blossom and the transition through puberty goes smoothly.

For all adolescents there is a bid to become more independent, especially with regard to parents, which is why so many teenagers react and kick against them. For the Libran child, this will focus on their thoughts and on how they dress. Expect some strong statements and a few arguments as they flex their muscles. This may be a wake-up time, when they start to become aware of politics and the state of the world. And, with the arrogance and innocence of youth, they may not realise that others have had these ideas before. It's not uncommon for them to take up a political position diametrically opposed to that of their parents, which, while it is designed to provoke, may also prove to be a lasting position.

When it comes to their appearance, the Libran adolescent wants to dress like their friends and like all self-respecting youngsters, rejects their parents' ideas on suitable attire. This is all part of how they establish a separate identity, which is distinct from their parents' generation and peer driven. Although youth fashion can be extreme, Libran teenagers are likely to have good taste, which probably won't come cheap. Brand names are making an impact on younger and younger age groups and Libran children are among the first to be influenced. They want the trendy labels and during the awkward and self-conscious phase, this becomes an imperative.

The Libran child is, in the main, peace loving, helpful, cooperative, easygoing, kind and pleasant. Provided no one takes advantage of their good nature and there is not too much emphasis placed on their beauty, they grow up to be well-rounded and delightful individuals.

8

Scorpio
The Scorpion

October 23rd to November 21st

A fixed water sign, ruled by Mars and Pluto

Introducing Scorpio

Scorpios have a great deal of personal charisma and are recognisable by their passion and emotional intensity. Those born under this sign are ruled by their feelings – although they may not give much away through their facial expression. Inscrutability is one of their main traits. These individuals take things seriously, they are as far from superficial as one can get, and they recognise the pain of the human condition. Others rely on them to have their feelings acknowledged and, unlike some signs, Scorpios are definitely not fair-weather friends. When things are tough, Scorpios can ride the storm. They wear their 'been there, done that' badge with honour and can, like all explorers of difficult terrain, help others who are less experienced.

The difficult terrain in question is that of the inner world, that which contains the unconscious in all its mystery. They have an awareness of their more primitive psychological drives and motivations that can be quite uncanny and a tad uncomfortable for those close to them. As this is their

278

domain, they do not flinch from others when they have dark or difficult feelings or are in pain or crisis. It is familiar territory and not one that they are necessarily frightened of, although they do respect it more than most others, mainly because they remain all too aware of its existence within themselves. Others, who are less aware, tumble into these places of emotional vulnerability occasionally, whereas for Scorpio they are an ever-present reality.

This, understandably, makes Scorpio self-protective. They know only too well the emotional risks they are taking, so they don't wade in blindly, as some might. They have a realistic idea of what pain might ensue from any given situation and make their decisions accordingly. So when they do venture forward, it's in the full knowledge of what could go wrong.

Scorpio is a fixed water sign and fixed water is ice. When displeased, this sign can give others the icy treatment, a withering look that freezes them in their tracks. Thinking about the nature of ice can help in understanding this sign. Only the tip of an iceberg is visible, the main mass is below the surface of the sea and similarly with Scorpios, a tremendous amount goes on beneath their cool exterior. As a consequence they are hard to get to know.

Scorpios have tumultuous depths that others usually only glimpse. They can present a calm exterior even when provoked. In moments of extreme hurt, they sometimes freeze. It's a kind of shocked reaction that buys them the space to explore the deep feelings they are experiencing. Sometimes the blank, inscrutable look is because their attention is focused completely inwards on their turbulent feelings. However, if they are pushed too far they are capable of volcanic emotional eruptions. This is never an easy option for them, as it involves too much exposure but it's nevertheless one they will take from time to time. It leaves them exhausted and depleted. These are intensely private individuals who prefer to keep their thoughts and feelings to themselves, revealing their deeper selves only to those carefully selected few whom they know they can trust. Trust is established slowly over time, by various tests and trials that prove a friend is safe and reliable.

One of the first strictures is that friends must not gossip. Whatever is said it's implicit that it's said in confidence and must not be repeated. After all, Scorpios are hardly going to want someone else to broadcast their business, when they go to such lengths to keep their life confidential. Friends must also be emotionally available, as they need others whom they can converse with on a satisfactory level; something that can often be hard to find. But when they do find a kindred spirit, they are loyal and devoted friends.

Scorpios are able to offer others a profound level of empathy and understanding. They readily take on others' anguish and recognise their pain and suffering and this is what they seek in return. Unfortunately, unless they are friends with fellow Scorpios, those able to reciprocate are few and far between. This means they often feel lonely and misunderstood. This isolation is not sought but something they feel is imposed upon them.

However, Scorpios aren't only about depth. These individuals invariably have a great deal of personal power, gained through persistence and stamina. They are extremely magnetic and charismatic, capable of casting a spell over others. Their passionate nature gives them an intensity that captivates and fascinates others, who long to know just what makes them tick. The more secretive they are, the more others want to delve inside. Think of a box on which is written 'on no account open – contains secrets'. This is the difficulty that Scorpios face. As long as they are obviously a closed book, others will probe and be intrusive. They have to find ways of giving just enough of themselves away to satisfy others' curiosity, while protecting their rights to privacy.

For a Scorpio, all kinds of everyday and ordinary things are private and not to be divulged. Friends may inadvertently reveal something that they later find out Scorpio feels is tantamount to a betrayal. Concepts like loyalty and trust are close to a Scorpio's heart, so they are extremely sensitive to betrayal and treachery and may see them in situations others would dismiss, such as having an inconsequential piece of information about them passed on to a third party. Perhaps what's important here is to recognise that nobody is right or wrong. Once feelings of betrayal have been aroused no amount of rationalising can take them away and others just have to accept this side of Scorpios' nature and deal with their end of it.

Scorpios can also feel betrayed if they find out important information about a friend that they have neglected to tell them. It's not that they are curious to know facts, in the way Gemini and Virgo can be, as they always respect others' privacy and would never probe. Yet, they can question why they weren't confided in and, understandably, feel shut out. It can prompt them to re-evaluate the whole friendship and even if it was simply oversight on the friend's part or no longer something they considered relevant, Scorpio can feel hurt. If this all happens in a public arena, then things do not bode well for this friendship, as Scorpio can feel publicly humiliated. It's hard for Scorpio to find a way back and to re-establish trust once it has been broken.

Along with the iceberg metaphor, when trying to understand Scorpio comparisons to the scorpion, which represents this sign, can also be helpful. Scorpions are primitive, instinctive creatures with a potentially lethal sting in their tail. Their sting is used to paralyse or kill their prey for food, to defend themselves when under attack and more surprisingly, in mating. In some species the male stings the female during the mating ritual, though quite why he does this is not exactly known.

This echoes the way in which sex and violence are related for some Scorpios through practices such as bondage and sado-masochism – it can be one of the ways they find the passion and intensity that they crave. There can be a love of cruelty because of the raw emotion it produces. As with the male scorpion, in certain circumstances a 'crime of passion' is accepted as mitigation in a court of law when men are violent with their sexual partners.

Generally though, scorpions only attack in situations they find life-threatening and are perhaps feared more than is warranted; although they have occasionally been known to kill humans, their venomous sting is actually little worse than a bee sting. This all has parallels in the psyche of the Scorpio individual.

Those born under this sign are highly attuned to any kind of threat. Whereas this may once have been about physical survival, in the main these days it is about psychological survival. Nevertheless, the same retaliatory mechanisms are in place and Scorpios are renowned for their barbed comments and stinging rebukes. Because of their psychological insight and level of perceptiveness, their comments have a way of landing just where they'll do most damage. However, what others have to understand, as they lick their wounds, is just how threatened Scorpio felt in the first place. They only launch an attack when they feel the need to defend and protect themselves.

Another interesting fact regarding scorpions is that if they are cornered and there's no way out, they will sting themselves to death rather than surrender to an enemy. This is reflected in Scorpios' emotional pride, their inability to back down and their depressive tendencies. One view of depression is that it is anger turned inwards as an attack on the self and in this respect many Scorpios succumb and have periods of feeling low. Those born under this sign tend to bottle up their emotions when things are going badly. And when depressed, they can cast an almost tangible gloom – it was a long time before I realised that one very depressed Scorpio I knew was actually quite fair-haired, as she appeared so cloaked in darkness. Even when depressed they emanate intensity. Of course, many Scorpios do not suffer from this debilitating condition at all – it's by no means mandatory.

Given their characteristics, it's clear that this is not the kind of individual to dally with. They take themselves and their feelings very seriously and don't take well to being messed about. That said, they are ruled by their heart rather than their head so can get involved surprisingly quickly. They have an impulsive and compulsive side that isn't at all self-protective and they can rapidly find themselves in deep waters. Others, fascinated and intrigued, can equally find themselves out of their depth and wondering just what's going on.

Passion is, more than anything, what Scorpios seek in a lover. They need to feel a deep emotional connection and bond. Ultimately they believe in, and are searching for, a soul mate, someone they communicate with telepathically and someone who can read them and doesn't need things to be spelled out. They trust unspoken modes of communication more than anything that is actually said so no amount of fancy words will fool a Scorpio into trusting someone who doesn't deliver the right non-verbal signals.

Sex is of fundamental importance to Scorpios. For them, sex is a meeting and an exchange on a profound level. They want to be moved on a feeling level, to feel their world has been rocked and that they've been touched and affected to the core of their being. They thrive on intensity and through sex they expect to die, feel reborn and affirm that they are alive. It is only from a complete surrender of the ego that this is possible, so trust is important. Trust that their partner 'gets them' and truly and deeply tunes in and understands them. For them, trust is based on an emotional connection, which is either there or not and can't be fabricated. And the kind of sex they enjoy with a loved one is the proof of this.

Actions count and gestures matter to Scorpios, not necessarily big flamboyant ones but carefully thought out, personal ones. Remembering significant dates, idiosyncratic likes and dislikes and being protective and considerate all go down well. They are alert to any discrepancies between what a partner promises and what he or she delivers and expect them to be consistent.

Once involved and committed, Scorpio is extremely possessive of loved ones and prone to jealousy, so it's important that a lover does not do anything that provokes these feelings. They are hypersensitive to any kind of threat and need a partner to value and treasure them and not play games. Any casual flirtation will understandably arouse their suspicion and result in either a full-scale row or the frozen treatment. While this will be possible to sort out, what Scorpios will not tolerate is any actual infidelity. This would be seen as an unforgivable betrayal of trust. A relationship is extremely unlikely to recover from such a betrayal because try as they might, they can't forgive and forget. So, for those getting involved with a Scorpio, accept that playing away is a no-go area. They will always find out.

However, double standards often apply and Scorpios are not always faithful themselves. It goes with their enigmatic style that they have secrets and occasionally their secret is one that could devastate their partner. An affair is not something they necessarily plan or seek but with the right combination of circumstances they can succumb. Although they will deny it, they do thrive on crisis. It makes them feel alive and they'd choose pain and heartache over boredom and apathy any day. Scorpios won't tolerate bad sex, which is broadly defined as unexciting. They need the earth to move on a regular basis as it is one of the main ways they affirm themselves and if, for whatever reason, it's not available in their main relationship, then they will almost certainly find it elsewhere. A sexually unsatisfied Scorpio is dangerous, as they won't be able to accept their situation in the long term.

This doesn't mean that Scorpios aren't committed and faithful because of course most are. It does mean partners should be aware that it's high risk to neglect the physical side of the relationship. A Scorpio will feel punished and abandoned and seek solace elsewhere. For them, sex is the foundation of a relationship and without that it becomes a sham. Provided this remains active and passionate then they are more capable than most of being loyal, especially as they take the feelings of others seriously.

Surprisingly, considering how prone to jealousy Scorpios can be, this sign is not necessarily the marrying kind. They don't trust bits of paper and they want loyalty to come from the heart, rather than a contract. Some will marry, but many may choose not to and of course, this is still not an option for those who aren't heterosexual. For homosexual Scorpios this is less of an issue, as they probably wouldn't want to exercise that right, even if it were granted.

Many avenues are open to Scorpios, work-wise, but one in which they excel is medicine. They have all the prerequisite characteristics to make an excellent doctor or nurse; empathy, compassion, understanding, cool in an emergency, plus they aren't usually squeamish. They enjoy the detective work of diagnosis and what's more, they need to be involved in something that really matters and makes a difference. In such a profession they have real power which can be used for the good of others. Medicine is a wide field with many specialist branches, any of which would suit. However, surgery, where they access very directly the mystery of the human body and obstetrics and midwifery, where there is an intimate involvement with the birth process, particularly suits their temperament.

There are many other arenas in which Scorpios thrive. They have a penchant for digging down and unearthing things that are hidden, secret or buried, whether that is psychological truths as a psychologist, or facts as a researcher or detective, or some type of archaeological, mining or drilling work. So, although these fields sound unrelated, they all in their different ways suit this sign's need to delve beneath the surface of things.

Scorpios' great self-control, shrewdness and ability to keep secrets also make them perfect diplomats and spies. And because of their strong nerve for the risk-taking aspect of big business, they are often drawn to stocks and shares and large organisations generally, where the stakes are high.

As an employer, Scorpios hold the reins of power in a rather quiet and low-key way, which Bill Gates, of Microsoft, exemplifies. He is one of the richest and most successful businessmen of all time and yet there is nothing remotely ostentatious about him. Scorpio bosses don't put on a show of power or throw their weight around but that doesn't mean that they should be underestimated. When they feel it's necessary, they can be ruthless. They expect unflinching loyalty and will not tolerate a lack of support or commitment, which to them constitutes betrayal.

The Scorpio boss picks up on the underlying message behind their employees' behaviour and reacts to this, so being late – even when the excuse given remains the same – can elicit a different reaction one day to the next. So if delays on transport are to blame for an employee being late, but they are also feeling disinterested in their job, then the Scorpio boss will pick up on the disinterest and see their excuse as disingenuous. The rules are not clear and what worked as an excuse one day may not do so the next, which can leave employees feeling unsettled and unsure of their position. What does remain clear is that emotional honesty and loyalty are expected.

What's more, Scorpio bosses can expect staff to be able to mind-read and to second-guess their requirements – no small order and a tad unrealistic. They hire and fire on their gut reactions – in fact most of their decisions are based on their instincts, which, while very reliable for them, can be tough on those around them. So, these employers can be tricky; it's a complicated emotional relationship in which their employees have little power and few rights. Where Scorpio bosses excel is in establishing rapport and in making connections that command loyalty, not just from employees but from colleagues and peers in their field, which stand them in good stead.

As an employee, Scorpios need to feel that what they do is of real value. They are capable of being dedicated and committed and of working extremely hard providing that the emotional atmosphere of the workplace is congenial to them. However, if relationships at work break down and the ambience becomes unsympathetic, then the normal rules of how to behave go by the board. Their moods can affect everyone around them, who may have no idea of what's really going on but are made to feel extremely uncomfortable.

Scorpio employees also need to have a certain amount of real power and authority in their domain, as they don't do well if they have to run every small decision past their manager. Whoever has power over them in the workplace needs to be sensitive in the way they wield it, as making petty demands and placing unnecessary restrictions will set up difficult dynamics and they won't get the best from this employee. In fact, they'll probably leave. Show them due respect, establish genuine rapport and offer them autonomy in certain areas of their work and they'll thrive.

Whatever work Scorpios end up doing, they bring to it their emotional integrity and passion. Whether the employer or an employee, they invest their heart and soul in their work and they expect those around them to care as deeply as they do. They are never lukewarm or half-hearted about anything and their emotional commitment goes hand-in-hand with tremendous physical stamina and thoroughness of approach. What they do is important and really matters – this is the value they place on themselves and their inner and outer world. In all areas of their life,

Scorpios are uncompromising and remain true to their feelings and the stirrings in their soul.

Negative Scorpio

Scorpio is so well known for its negative characteristics that they barely need an introduction. Jealousy, suspicion, paranoia, revenge, retaliation, power and control issues, are just a few of the less-than-happy attributes they are regularly accused of possessing. And certainly those born under this sign do fall prey to these traits. These human failings will be examined but, beforehand, it's important to emphasise that an awful lot of negativity gets projected on to Scorpios, too.

Scorpios have a unique ability to constellate unease in others, who are tipped into feelings within themselves that they are uncomfortable with, to put it mildly. Scorpios are then blamed and punished for this, as if it were actually their fault, whereas the feelings others have are actually always their responsibility. Those born under this sign regularly venture into what is for many 'no-go' emotional territory but it is not their fault if others follow them and then don't like it. Scorpios become the scapegoat and are seen as leading others astray. And because this sign isn't particularly adept at rational argument, they don't do a very good job of pointing out the unfairness of all this.

A defence of this much-maligned sign is necessary to redress some of the popular misconceptions. However, the saying 'there's no smoke without fire' also applies and a deeper exploration is needed here to work out how these have arisen. Casting blame is never particularly helpful, whereas a deeper understanding invariably is.

Starting with jealousy, suspicion and paranoia, it's true that most Scorpios suffer from these states to some extent. Anyone who truly and deeply loves another is likely to feel jealous at times. It goes with the territory. The more intense the feelings of love (and few complain about this attribute of Scorpio) then the more terrifying is the thought of losing said person and the more susceptible this individual is to feelings of jealousy. Jealousy is a response to a perceived threat and no one is more acutely alert to this than Scorpio.

Coupled with this, Scorpios are exceptionally well tuned into the undercurrents that pass between people and can, when feeling vulnerable, get these signals muddled in their mind. They can construe a meaning that actually represents their worst fear, rather than the reality. They need to be reassured with the right kind of non-verbal messages – a private smile or gesture for instance – as otherwise they can go off on a tangent. For those involved, it's best to keep this in mind, particularly in social situations, which is where they can feel most unsure of a partner. For Scorpios themselves, they need to keep reminding themselves to check out the facts, before speculating on something that may not actually be true.

This leads on to paranoia, something to which this sign is also prone occasionally. While most people don't allow themselves to recognise their worst fears, Scorpios live with an acute awareness of theirs. They are able to think what is, for many, the unthinkable. Plugged into a darker level of human existence, they recognise the base elements in us all that can drive some people to behave badly. With this as part of their everyday reality, it's easy to see how and why they become fearful of others.

At their worst, Scorpios can attribute all kind of dubious motives to others. They remain in touch with their own darker impulses so when others present themselves as 'nice people', they immediately suspect them of being in emotional denial. When emerging from a place of darkness, where one's eyes have become adjusted to seeing quite well, the bright daylight is dazzling. Scorpios have innate radar to see in the dark and the lighter and brighter others appear to be, the less they trust them. Yet it's fairly normal, in social situations, to behave in an upbeat way, which Scorpios can despise. They can dismiss those who are adept at observing social pleasantries as cut off emotionally and judge them to be out of touch with their inner world. They want something a bit grittier and, in their mind, more real and enjoy it when others express negative emotions in a public situation. In this respect, Scorpios can be voyeuristic, as they would never make an emotional scene themselves, yet relish it when others do.

Scorpios frequently accuse others of being 'cut off' and for them this is tantamount to a crime against humanity. Part of the problem is that they are compulsively fascinated by others who are their opposites – intellectuals and rational thinkers. They may be fascinated but they are also threatened by their 'fancy ideas' and do their utmost to discredit and then dismiss them. Rather than challenge them to a debate in which they might find themselves out of their depth, they try to undermine them by looking for their weaknesses in other areas. This is something that Scorpios excel at. They can spot others' emotional vulner-abilities a mile off and can exploit these to their own advantage, as this is the domain in which they are strong. Although this may not seem very nice, it has to be remem-bered that Scorpios are on shaky ground in the world of ideas and do whatever they have to in order to survive.

For most Scorpios, life can be primarily about love and war. They have a strong sense of justice and are prone to extreme emotional states and can take umbrage at inci-dents that others might not pay much attention to, such as a perceived undercurrent when greeted. What, to most people, would be seen as a perfectly acceptable 'Hello, how are you' can be deemed lacking in warmth, genuine feel-ing, or sincerity by a Scorpio. As incidents such as this accumulate, war may or may not be declared and others may not even realise that the battle lines have been drawn, as Scorpio is perfectly capable of conducting a one-person vendetta. If anyone is going to hate a neighbour for years and years and never find a completely satisfying way to resolve the matter, it'll be a Scorpio.

Having said this and to be fair to Scorpios, they also remember a good deed years after the person in question has forgotten. They have the memory of an elephant and never forget; it's just that certain memories can cause problems. Part of the difficulty is their need for vengeance and until they feel they have exacted this to the required degree, then forgiving or forgetting is not an option, it's an irrelevance. It is only possible for them to move on once the score has been settled and, of course, it's usually rather complicated.

When under threat the scorpion loads its venom into its tail before striking its attacker and delivering the poison. Something akin to this occurs for Scorpios and if they can't get even (and most would not stoop to acting this out) the thoughts of injustice and revenge go on in their minds and they can then turn these angry feelings in on themselves, and self-destructive behaviour and bouts of depression can follow.

Scorpios are only satisfied when the person they feel has wronged them has suffered as they have. They need the person to know what it feels like. And, of course, the person in question may well have no idea. What Scorpios fail to recognise in this moment is that they may have a responsibility for how they feel. Even when they realise an individual hasn't deliberately caused them pain they are determined to give it back in equal measure. Only when they have seen the other person hurt in reciprocal measure is the episode complete, and they feel avenged.

It is rare for this sequence of events to be successful for Scorpio, so they are often left with unresolved matters. Some may recognise that what they really want is closure, by resolving a hurt, and that this can be achieved through communication, rather than inflicting hurt. If they are able to have their distress fully understood and acknowledged they may not need to exact revenge.

However, all of this requires a fair degree of sophistication and very often Scorpios are stuck in a more reactive and instinctive level of behaviour. When they are left without any sense of having been avenged, then self-destructive behaviour is the last avenue open to them, which can involve substance abuse or self-harm, although it more often manifests in subtler forms, such as low self-esteem and a lack of self-worth. This can become a downward spiral, as the lower their self-esteem sinks the less able they are to pick themselves up and bring about positive changes. The longer a grudge goes on, the more bitter they become. This kind of festering resentment is very hard to move on from and the important lesson Scorpios need to learn is how not to head in that direction in the first place. It's a bit like driving down a narrow cul-de-sac; unless reversing out is not a problem, the advice is don't go there in the first place. Scorpios need to find ways of dealing with incidents, by communicating their feelings, as they arise or as soon afterwards as possible – a kind of daily detox of emotional poisons.

In a situation where a Scorpio feels they've come off badly, they automatically become the losers. They take not winning hard and find it difficult to conceive of a win-win situation, where both parties can maintain their dignity. More often than not they want to be victorious and thrash their enemy, as they see it and if they are unable to do this, they automatically feel humiliated and defeated. At its most basic, this is because Scorpios are so attuned to survival issues that everything is reduced to 'kill or be killed'. Learning how to manage conflict in a less aggressive way helps in achieving a better outcome for them, as they can then circumvent the 'win or lose' scenario.

Power and control issues are another of Scorpio's

shortcomings. Scorpios gravitate to positions of power without appearing to seek them out and often then exercise their power in an odd, rather passive way. There can be something of the invisible-man hero about them that is hard to define, as their power often seems to emanate from their extreme passivity. They manage to draw energy towards themselves, just as the black holes in outer space are now thought to draw objects into their extremely dense void. Some Scorpios have a similar black hole type of gravitational pull that affects those around them and, in a rather mysterious way, power is bestowed upon them. They wear this cloak as if it's not meant for them and may not realise that it is their desire for it that brings it to them.

At their most positive, Scorpios have a nose for power and can sniff out others who are on a power trip. At their worst they are equally culpable. They understand how power works and how it can corrupt, yet may still get caught up. One of the lessons they have to learn is how to use power wisely. If it is used for their own gain they will become corrupted and vulnerable to attack from others. Many a political career has been destroyed in these circumstances. The wisest Scorpios realise that power must only ever be used for the good of others. Working out where exactly the dividing line lies between self-interest and altruism is part of their life's work.

Like Capricorns, Scorpios' need for control is fear-based and is their way of being emotionally ready for whatever is next. A new situation is looked at from every possible angle in order to deal with anything that might arise. This is what it takes for Scorpios to feel secure enough within themselves to enter the fray.

Scorpios do not like surprises, so never throw them a surprise party – they'll hate it. They need time to prepare psychologically for such an event. They also dislike others having secrets that they are not privy to – they like to be in on any secrets doing the rounds and the thought of others planning and scheming behind their back is not a pleasant one.

All the fixed signs (Taurus, Leo and Aquarius are the others) have some kind of control issue so it's important to differentiate Scorpios, who like to be in control of themselves and their emotions. Anyone who has a destabilising influence is given short shrift and not allowed into their life. They may unnerve others with their emotional intensity and demands for intimacy but they certainly won't allow others to do that to them – they like to set the pace.

Scorpios have a ruthless side that can come as a surprise to others, who expect them to be rather more touchy-feely than they are. They are in touch with how they feel, rather than with how they come across and may underestimate the impact they have on others. And while they do have empathy, in a situation in which they feel threatened they will use this to inform themselves about others rather than to offer understanding. Empathy is only offered unreservedly when it is at no cost to them, for example, listening to a friend's distress about matters entirely unconnected to them. This is crucial in trying to understand this sign.

Obsessive and compulsive behaviour is associated with Scorpio, and although other signs have these characteristics, too, this sign can become plagued by their obsessions. It has something to do with their lack of detachment and perspective, which can mean once they have got an idea in their head they can't let go of it. Besides that, they can justify to themselves some fairly extreme behaviour, so, if anyone is going to stalk an ex-lover or snoop or spy on them, it's Scorpio. Despite the fact that they guard their own privacy so furiously, they can completely flout and disrespect others' rights. And, if they do happen to find out something untoward, then they genuinely believe this justifies their appalling behaviour.

Scorpios can become consumed by their feelings and once that occurs, then anything goes. This harks back to their survival issues and belief that in love and war there are no rules. However, whether or not they manage to maintain civilised behaviour (and they usually believe that bottling up their feelings and not retaliating immediately is the civilised thing to do), there is no doubt that they suffer and have overriding desires to take action accordingly. For those who manage to behave appropriately, the pain is possibly even worse as they have no outlet. But by containing themselves, they avoid the exposure and consequent shame of having revealed so much of themselves.

Others can wind up Scorpios and exploit their emotional vulnerability; especially those who are more cut off from their emotions. For better or worse, Scorpios often are drawn to the air signs, as these more rational, logical types create fascination and frisson. This type will at times deliberately use a Scorpio partner as a kind of emotional sounding-board, running possibilities by them as if they are for real, knowing that Scorpio will react forcibly and by so doing will inform them of the emotional integrity of their options. Scorpios are usually aware of this and, it could be argued, are playing with fire when they get involved with these types. Perhaps what is attractive is that they don't intrude or invade and Scorpios are hypersensitive to this. They easily feel encroached upon and it may be that they choose someone who is unavailable to them emotionally in order to protect their space. This is not a good solution!

Finding a way to defend their territory and keep their space is essential for Scorpios, especially in social situations where they are not good at small talk and can feel intruded upon by the slightest query, considering it to be personal and inappropriate. They object because they lack middle ground and find it hard to deal gracefully with what probably amounts to no more than insensitive curiosity. Their behaviour in response can be markedly odd, as either they fail to respond and turn on their withering, icy disapproving look or lash out in scorpion-like fashion, with a stinging rebuke that offends and wounds but also leaves them feeling exposed. For Scorpio, losing their cool is always traumatic. They need to memorise some catch-all, inoffensive, evasive replies to questions that they don't want to answer; that way they avoid drawing attention to themselves and their thin skin.

One of Scorpio's qualities, which can seem a strength or a weakness in different situations, is that they always take everything personally. They have very little capacity to deflect the comments or attitude of others, so everything penetrates them, affecting them profoundly. It means that those closest to them are constantly challenged to examine what's going on beneath the surface of throwaway comments, loved ones are pulled up short and can't get away with anything flippant. This psychological monitoring is an exhausting process that is hard on Scorpio's psyche.

Perhaps the most important thing to remember about Scorpios is that they use everything at their disposal to defend and protect themselves. They are governed by some fairly primitive instincts that may not always look nice or be pretty. Scorpions have an impressive track record when it comes to endurance. The earliest fossil scorpions found are from over 420 million years ago, which proves the success of its survival instincts.

When not under threat, Scorpios are loyal and steadfast and have the highest principles, based on feeling values. No one would ever find a better friend or lover with whom to share the good times and the bad. There's a lot to be said for someone who has stared the darkest forces of life in the face and held their own. That's Scorpio for you.

The Scorpio Man

The Scorpio man is recognisable by the aura of dark mystery that surrounds him. He is both enigmatic and extremely charismatic and draws others to him, like a moth to the flame, although not necessarily with the same destructive consequences – that depends on them. Others are fascinated and perhaps a little frightened, too, sensing his emotional depths and wondering quite what lies within him.

The Scorpio man is tantalising, often with dark good looks and a deep penetrating gaze. He has a way of holding eye contact just that bit too long, which can unnerve others. This can feel very intimate, leaving others wondering if it's a come-on or whether this is just how he is. Usually it's the latter but others frequently mistake it for the former and all sorts of complications can ensue. He fails to recognise the feelings he stirs up in others and the difficulty they may have in interpreting his non-verbal signals. For him, this is unconscious and unintentional and he is mystified by the responses he seems to attract. From his point of view, he gets unsolicited sexual invitations, in which he is often not interested. He may wrongly assume that this happens to everyone and never realise that he does actually play a part, albeit unintended.

There are claims that all men are obsessed with sex and think about it every few minutes and while this statistic may or may not be true, the Scorpio man is definitely among those who have sex on their minds an awful lot. He also has a way of thinking about nearly everything in sexual terms, reducing it, as it were, to its primitive components. The psychoanalyst, Sigmund Freud, who introduced the idea that sex was the primary motivating factor in life had Scorpio rising. Freud's whole approach to psychiatry, based on exploring and analysing the subconscious, is typical of Scorpio.

For the Scorpio man who is in a relationship, whether or not he has had sex recently has a huge effect on his mood. He'll be grumpy and bad tempered if he hasn't, and glowing discreetly and maybe even whistling happily if he has. And he's likely to need sex quite often, so his happiness is very much dependent on his partner's sex drive. Not only is sex one of his major preoccupations but he also tends to blame all his problems on the state of his sex life. So, any difficulties he is experiencing are reduced to whether or not he's had good sex lately and this is seen as the answer to everything. It's his panacea. This can, understandably, feel oppressive to his partner who may feel used and that she or he is a vehicle by which he sorts out and processes all his difficulties. This can be tricky to disentangle, as his well-being is so clearly enhanced after lovemaking.

For those who are considering getting involved with him there are some key factors to keep in mind. He is an odd mixture of passion, intensity and coolness – his passion does not necessarily give him any warmth and he can be shockingly chilling when he shows his cold-blooded, ruthless side. This is an extremely determined man who is powerful in a quiet, understated way and goes for what he wants in an unerring instinctive manner.

When it comes to a romantic pursuit the Scorpio man can be surprisingly predatory. When making moves towards someone he is interested in, he can hatch up a carefully premeditated plan, which he follows with precision. Some may find this extremely flattering, while others may feel rather spooked that he keeps so much of his intention to himself. He never lays his cards on the table and no one ever really knows his whole agenda and this is what makes him so enticing and interesting – no one ever quite figures him out. One reason for this is that he never fully figures himself out. He's driven by some pretty primitive instincts that even he doesn't quite manage to unravel or come to terms with, so he's as mystified by himself as others are. Which also makes him dangerous – he's a bit of a loose cannon. For those seeking safety, this is not your man!

The Scorpio man may not be safe in that predictable kind of way but he is an endlessly fascinating and stimulating companion. He's complex and profound and has a depth of understanding that few can come close to. Women gravitate to him partly for his ability to recognise their feelings. They feel validated and acknowledged by him and this counts for a lot. He is never burdened by their problems, he positively enjoys hearing about them, especially if they are confidential and sensitive, he can be relied upon to respect the delicacy of a situation. He relishes being privy to others' secrets and would never reveal these to a third party, however explosive the information. One reason he likes being in this position is the power it gives him. Not that he exercises this, but it's part of his quiet, understated way to be in the know.

In fact, the Scorpio man hates being excluded from secrets and has a way of sniffing out private, personal information about others. Armed with this, he feels more secure. He also has a way of bonding with those who hold the reins of power. Not that he's in any way doing this deliberately; powerful people may equally be seeking him out, a kind of mutual attraction. In a social situation, he'll be found chatting away in a corner with some bigwig, giving out subliminal messages that what they are talking about is extremely important and confidential, even if it's not. And actually, it may well be. They may be plotting some political coup within their organisation or hatching plans for a grand occasion.

Despite his strong sexual cravings or possibly because of them, the Scorpio man does reasonably well when it comes to sexual fidelity. He's a considerate lover and recognises the importance of the emotional bond in good lovemaking. The closer he feels to his lover, the better the sexual fulfilment. It's not that he's against the excitement of being with someone new, he just knows it doesn't compare to the depth he can achieve with someone familiar, whose rhythms he knows. As a lover, he never relies on technique, which doesn't mean he has none, it just remains secondary to the feelings in his heart.

The Scorpio man suffers from extreme feelings of jealousy and can be obsessively possessive and so perhaps that's why, in the main, he remains faithful. He's all too aware of the pain and havoc an affair can create. What he may have, which can be threatening to a loved one, is other close intimate friendships that cross the normal boundaries but aren't technically speaking, affairs. Certain specially selected friends may know more about him than his partner and he can often appear guilty even when he's done nothing wrong, because of that secretive, conspiratorial attitude.

The Scorpio man's own capacity to trust is often fairly limited. He can border on the tyrannical in his possessiveness, perhaps because he's all too aware of the dark side of human nature. Even if things are going well, he may test his partner to see how committed they are. If he harbours suspicions of a partner, however unjustifiably, he can cross-examine them about their movements, even trying to trap them into revealing something incriminating. A loved one is inevitably going to feel hurt, possibly quite battered by the interrogation and may begin to worry how all kinds of innocent everyday activities will be construed. He has a propensity to paranoid fantasies and is pretty good at generating them in others.

Scorpio men can be extremely destructive, especially when their well-being and security are threatened. When they lash out, they may well feel justified in blaming others for their pain. With a partner who is actually provocative a ghastly scenario can develop, with both accusing the other of being the cause of all the difficulties.

The actor Richard Burton exemplifies the Scorpio man with his intense, brooding quality. Alongside his Pisces wife, Elizabeth Taylor, Burton depicted a relationship full of passion and destruction in *Who's Afraid of Virginia Woolf*. It was speculated that this echoed their marriage at that time. Certainly, they couldn't live with each other but neither could they live apart and married and divorced twice. Burton was extremely self-destructive, especially in his use of alcohol and suffered from bouts of depression. He was reportedly plagued by guilt for leaving his first wife, yet clearly Elizabeth was his great love and grand passion. Scorpios struggle with issues around their emotional integrity and Burton was a tortured soul, unable to find salvation until finally separating from Taylor.

Scorpio men do not easily admit failure in a relationship. They persevere and really do believe that they can work virtually anything out, even when others doubt whether this is going to be possible. These men have staying power and unlike some, don't stay for convenience, or the children, but because they value their attachment. This has taken a long time to forge and they are not about to see their investment, in time, tears and effort, go to waste. Hence, what may seem like a very difficult relationship from the outside, may actually be one that grapples with the real and painful issues that others deny or avoid. It's impossible to judge another's relationship but what can be said is that the Scorpio man has a high level of tolerance for emotional pain within a relationship and is not one to quit lightly.

The Scorpio man does not necessarily seek to have children. He's all too aware of how, in the words of Philip Larkin, 'your parents **** you up', fearing, perhaps, that he'll not make a better job of it than his parents did. However, he can be persuaded if he's with a partner who so desires and, actually, he'll make a very good job of it. He's so aware of the harm that parents can unwittingly inflict upon their offspring that he dedicates himself to their well-being. He's involved and caring and emotionally available.

Even the Scorpio man who chooses not to have children understands only too well what a responsibility parenting is. Whatever his own experience of childhood was, he still remembers the vulnerability and powerlessness of being a child. Having made his decision, he may find himself in a relationship with someone who already has a child. In such a situation, he invariably gives a huge amount. Having been abdicated of the responsibility of bringing a child into the world, he then does his best to improve this child's lot. He makes an emotionally involved and caring step-father and doesn't baulk at taking on a child who is not his.

Perhaps because he is such a private person, the Scorpio man places a high value on his personal life. He's not one to neglect his partner and those who matter to him emotionally. Work is important to him, too, but it never becomes the be-all and end-all as it does for some men. He's not likely to become a workaholic.

Among the Scorpio men who are in the public eye, Leonardo DiCaprio is a contemporary actor who is hailed as having that elusive charismatic quality. Bill Gates, the head of Microsoft, exemplifies the quiet, understated power and persistence of this sign. John Cleese, the comedian, with a sideline in psychology, draws on the seamier side of life for many of his laughs. Robert Kennedy gained political power but died as a result of someone else's destructive urges. Last, but not least, Prince Charles, waiting in the wings to inherit the sovereignty of the United Kingdom suffers from the impotence of his current position and may never have the power he was brought up to hold. As an emotionally sensitive man, his formal upbringing will not have valued his strengths. He has clearly suffered and had the indignity of his private life being exposed in the tabloid press, something he would have found quite unbearable.

Whatever status in life a Scorpio man achieves, he is always a powerful player within his domain. He has what is now called 'emotional intelligence' in bucketloads, which enables him to do well in life and to gain the confidence and respect of those around him. He recognises the importance of the personal touch and although intensely private, has a way of connecting with those he cares about that makes them feel incredibly special and privileged. In these moments no one else in the world exists. That's the magic of the Scorpio man.

The Scorpio Woman

The Scorpio woman is quite dazzling in an enigmatic and mysterious way. This is a charismatic and captivating woman, with a glow that emanates from her rich inner life, like a candle lighting up the window of a house at night. In fact, she is princess of the night. She is passionate, with eyes that burn brightly and although others may not know what she is feeling, it's clear that she has emotional intensity and strong feelings.

The Scorpio woman has a magical quality that casts a spell over those around her. Rightly or wrongly, others imagine her to have a strong and vibrant sexuality and to be having an exciting and active sex life. Yet, as she's the last person in the world who would refer to such things, she is mystified by their imaginings. It is the only way they can understand her fiery ardour. Her sex life is important to her but it's probably not as important as others think. What always matters to her are her values, which are rooted in her feelings and are the basis of how she conducts herself in all matters. She has an individualistic moral and ethical code based on her own personal evaluation of people and situations. From this subjective standpoint, there is never any conflict. She is in no doubt as to what she feels and she bases her life upon this.

The Scorpio woman is a source of much fascination to others who, having glimpsed her inner depths, want to get to know her and find out what goes on beneath her cool exterior. At the same time, she is determined to keep others at bay, only revealing herself to an intimate few, whom she trusts implicitly. All this makes her even more intriguing and often the butt of speculative gossip, since what people don't know as fact they'll surely make up.

By being so intensely private, the Scorpio woman tantalises others; this is not her intention – she really does value her privacy and sees it as her right. The film actor and director Jodi Foster exemplifies this by refusing to reveal the identity of the father of her children. This is clearly a private matter but nevertheless one that's attracted a great deal of media speculation. It's easy to see how she might feel intruded upon by the interest in her personal life – a classic Scorpionic scenario.

Anyone who is privy to a Scorpio woman's private thoughts and feelings should be aware what an honour this is and take special care not to betray her, however inadvertently or innocently. This is a sign which never gossips. One Scorpio woman said that others stopped telling her their secrets because she didn't leak them. She hadn't realised that part of what was required of her was to start the whispering campaign and get tongues wagging, which she failed to do. So, for those who want someone who will take a confidence to the grave, then this woman is perfect: just remember, though, that this is what she expects in return. And she can be told anything; she's virtually shock-proof, which is what makes her such a valued confidante.

By keeping even seemingly trivial facts about others confidential the Scorpio woman disseminates the notion that she is the keeper of secrets and has a great store that she guards closely. It adds to her fascination and allure as she has an aura of being someone in the know. She's seen as being intimate and exclusive with desirable, glamorous others and attracts an odd kind of non-specific envy of her lifestyle, partly because those who envy her don't have any facts.

Envy is something the Scorpio woman feels intensely herself as well as attracting. It's an extremely uncomfortable state but it informs her of her desires and ambitions, which are strong. More than most women, she needs a career and a chance to prove herself in the world. This is an extremely capable woman with a strong appetite for success. Success, for her, is defined by the power she wields, the money she earns and the respect she's held in and she requires all three. Status as such is not what she's after, especially if it has no real power.

Hillary Clinton exemplifies the super-successful Scorpio woman. With major achievements of her own she nevertheless supported her husband, Bill Clinton, in his presidency. Some saw her as wielding too much power in her behind-the-scenes position but she has gone on to claim power in her own right. She stood by her man during the scandals that rocked the White House in a quiet and dignified way and no one saw her as being a victim. Whatever she felt, she kept it well hidden at the time but equally she didn't come across as someone who was putting on a brave face and there was no way she attracted pity. She has now published a memoir, and some say, although she denies it, that she aims to become the first female President of the USA.

Even a very successful Scorpio woman is not intimidating – she remains self-contained and self-possessed and carries her achievements lightly. Others might even wonder if they matter to her, she makes so little of them. Her main concerns are always personal but her accomplishments are a backdrop to her life. They define who she is and communicate that she is no pushover. So they do matter, even though she's always understated. In contrast to her, others with less to shout about can seem brash and loud, much to their embarrassment when they realise just how high profile she is.

So the Scorpio woman is quite awesome in her chosen profession, yet her private and personal life is top of her agenda. She prioritises friendships and relationships and invests most of her emotional energy into making them work. Her lover always comes first but she probably still cares more and goes to more trouble on behalf of her friends than most signs. She rarely gives up on friends, however badly they mistreat her, and is prepared to plumb the depths to maintain a friendship.

That said, if the Scorpio woman does decide to call it a day and end a friendship or a relationship, there's no going back. Once she's made up her mind, she's resolute and it's final. So, those who have pushed their luck with her should be aware that there are only so many times she's willing and able to forgive before she reaches a point of no return: and once she reaches it she can be shockingly ruthless. Something in her flips and she turns to ice and acts to protect herself. However she has to be very hurt before she behaves in such a final, and many would argue, long overdue, way.

When it comes to a relationship, the Scorpio woman is ultimately looking for one that will last but she'll dally along the way. She has staying power and is serious when it comes to love but if there isn't anyone suitable around, she'll make do with whoever is her best bet at the time. This may sound exploitative, but she doesn't much like being without a relationship. As she gives so much of herself, even if the relationship doesn't last very long, her lover is unlikely to feel used, although he or she may complain that it's ended, not realising she never imagined it would last from the start.

The Scorpio woman is an interesting mix. She needs the emotional involvement of a relationship but equally needs space and time on her own. In fact she needs to be by herself on a regular basis as she can easily feel crowded by those around her and it's often only when she's alone that she finds real peace. Yet, she thrives on intimacy and passion, so she needs a partner but she's almost certainly far less dependent than her partner likes to imagine. And if she decides her relationship is over, then she can be utterly merciless in the way she leaves. To stay in a relationship that has, for her, died would be a living death and completely unbearable.

Despite her obvious sensitivity, the Scorpio woman is emotionally resilient and can endure a fair amount of hardship and difficulty. What she can't manage is compromise – she's an 'all or nothing' kind of woman and doesn't make deals. Her integrity is based on her emotional values and so in these respects she's unswerving. This is why, if she's in love, she's completely faithful. She listens to and follows her heart.

Unlike her male counterpart who is more equivocal, the Scorpio woman usually sees children as a part of her future. Even when she has a glittering career she is looking for a partner to raise a family with, although occasionally she gets it wrong and leaves it too late. Such mistiming is a personal tragedy, as without a child she feels incomplete. If she is deeply in love with her partner and in a heterosexual relationship she will especially want to have his child seeing it as one of life's most profound experiences. At such times her intense feelings can trigger ovulation at unexpected times, so she should take special care about contraception if she is in love but not wanting to become pregnant.

The Scorpio woman's ideal mate – possibly an earth sign – provides a steadying influence for her and contains and holds her emotionally, yet also excites and interests her. Anyone too safe or predictable will bore her – she needs someone with imagination and flair. She also needs a partner who is comfortable with her strong emotions and who values her instinctual take on life. Despite her resilience, she can be seriously undermined by a partner who is not in tune with her values, resulting in untold damage to her self-esteem and sense of worth.

The Scorpio woman can be oversensitive and take things to heart, as one thing she lacks is detachment and perspective. She evaluates people and situations via her feelings, using her inner responses and reactions as her yardstick. For better or worse, that is just the way she is, which can be exhausting for her emotionally, but it's her point of reference. It can also infuriate people around her, especially those who rely on a more rational process. Hers seems haphazard, even scary to people who prefer a logical approach. And often this is just the type she ends up with in a relationship. However, when there is shared respect and an acknowledgement of each other's strengths, these two with their different approaches to life have much to teach each other and can be of mutual benefit.

Playing mind games with the Scorpio woman won't work. She can out-manoeuvre virtually anyone because she cuts through to the core of whatever is going on. All that is achieved is a stalemate. When it comes to wooing her, an honest and straightforward declaration works well. This, whether or not she reciprocates, is something she'll respond to positively. She appreciates it when others show their vulnerability and is never unkind in these circumstances. Because she's interested in the emotional life and well-being of those around her it's easy for others to misread her signals and assume this means more. They find her attention flattering but it may not actually mean much – with her natural empathy it could just be the way she passes the day. And, unless she does feel something there'll be nothing doing, as she's not interested in faking it and knows immediately what her true feelings are.

For those who've wooed and won, once a relationship is underway don't ever make the mistake of taking the Scorpio woman for granted. That's the quickest way to lose her – either she'll have an affair or leave. While a partner's infidelity is an unforgivable sin, for which he'll be given his marching orders, if she's unhappy in her relationship she's more than capable of being unfaithful and getting away with it. She's very much in control and a partner will only find out about her affair if she so chooses to let him or her know, whereas she'll always find out about theirs. She has this uncanny sixth sense that is virtually one hundred per cent reliable.

The Scorpio woman needs to be shown that her lover has kept her in mind throughout their time apart. Phone calls, texts, pertinent questions about her day and especially remembering any worries or anxieties that she's confided in her partner are all an essential part of a relationship for her. She appreciates thoughtful, personal gestures, rather than grand ones, which rely on knowing her intimately, such as a present that has meaning and touches her. An impersonal but expensive gift won't work with her – she can't be bought (but that doesn't mean she comes cheap either, as personal can be expensive, too).

Never try to fool a Scorpio woman as she'll always find out and the outcome will be far worse than telling the truth in the first place. She may refuse to put her cards on the table but that doesn't mean her partner should copy her. She won't appreciate being kept in the dark about anything – for her it's tantamount to a betrayal of trust.

Sex is the foundation upon which her relationship rests and is a vital ingredient in keeping her relationship vital and alive. If the sex becomes boring or routine, she'll question the whole relationship. Lovemaking is the most important means of non-verbal communication for her and is deeply reassuring and affirming of her feelings. She can tolerate fights and emotional storms but what she can't tolerate is apathy. She also hates being shut out or excluded – given the icy treatment – even though this is a tactic she uses to punish others herself.

The Scorpio woman is what is sometimes referred to as high maintenance, as she is somewhat demanding emotionally. She's not financially demanding – in fact she's very independent in this respect but she requires a level of on-going intimacy that others may find exhausting. She's involved in the details of a partner's life and expects this to be reciprocated. The air signs in particular can find this level of involvement claustrophobic.

In fact, Ms Scorpio is looking for a soul union – a kind

of mystical merging – which some might argue is regressed and found in the mother/infant relationship of the first two pre-verbal years. She picks up on what she perceives to be a partner's signals and interprets them according to the state she is in, without realising how subjective she is being. Unless she communicates her feelings, doubts and insecurities to her partner and keeps them informed of what's going on for her, her relationship can become convoluted with all kinds of misunderstandings arising.

As a mother, the Scorpio woman is fiercely protective of her children. She knows all too well that life can be painful and does her utmost to shield her offspring from difficulties. She's very good at imagining what might go wrong and taking preventative action – she has foresight even if it does tend to be of the doom and gloom variety. The idea that it might never happen or that some struggles can be character building does not appeal to her. Her children remain sheltered and are as far from 'streetwise' as they can get. She willingly ferries them around, way beyond a stage when they could manage public transport, and generally babies them. Her partner needs to be tolerant of this as doing otherwise causes her too much anxiety. Her vivid imagination is a problem in this respect.

As the Scorpio woman's children grow older and demand greater independence, she may get into difficulties. It's never going to be easy for her to let them go and to let go of her control over their lives, which clearly she has to. Ideally an absorbing job will alleviate this transition phase, giving her an involvement that distracts her from her children's lives. If she has the freedom of choice, she's unlikely to work outside the home when her offspring are young but, for their sake, it's recommended that she does later on.

If the Scorpio woman had a high-powered career before having children, then she may well want to return to it afterwards. If she didn't she may still go on to develop one later in life, but, failing that, any kind of work that is meaningful and interesting will provide her with the stimulus she needs. As she never does anything by halves, whatever work she takes on she throws herself into wholeheartedly. Even if it's at a fairly mundane level, she thrives in a job that involves people where she can see that she makes a difference to the quality of their lives.

The Scorpio woman is also skilled at reinventing herself. Kim Wilde, an Eighties pop singer, who is currently a gardening diva in the UK, has made a public transformation. Lulu, another pop singer who is now in her fifties, has been in the public eye since her teens and manages to stay abreast of the times, changing her image in accord with current trends. She has shown a typically Scorpio resilience over four decades and retains the spirit and vitality of her youth now combined with the maturity of her years.

The Scorpio woman is often thought of as complicated but actually she's not, once you understand where she's coming from. However many changes there are on the surface of her life, this deep connection to her inner world remains the same. Whether or not a high flyer, her priority in life is those she loves and they always come first: she's a loyal and steadfast friend through good times and bad and she offers a depth of understanding that few can match. She really is very special.

The Scorpio Child

The Scorpio child is recognisable by his or her intensity and passion and often has particularly striking eyes that burn brightly with a steady gaze. Even as a baby Scorpios often have exceptionally dark eyes, almost navy blue, and have an ability to focus earlier than the norm. It can be a bit unnerving, being scrutinised by such a tiny baby. This remains a talent they exercise throughout their life. From birth this child seems wise beyond his or her years and manages to just slightly intimidate others with a knowing look.

Scorpio children have strong feelings and are in no doubt about what they like and dislike, what they want and don't want and let those around them know this in no uncertain terms. They are prone to fads and crazes, which may not last long but can be extreme while they do. They're vocal from an early age and never going to be one to reason with. The concept of what's fair is completely alien to them – they want what they want and that's that. These are wilful children who are also extremely sensitive, a complicated combination to deal with. When they can't have their needs met, for whatever reasons, they feel wounded and may even feel persecuted, and so it's never easy to deny them what they want.

Establishing a good start in life will help Scorpio children to grow up trusting that life will support them and the more difficult, persecutory feelings typical of this sign will be kept at bay. Try to keep their distress about basic needs, like hunger, to a minimum by feeding them to their timetable and don't let them become over-tired, either. They don't necessarily need the stability of a routine, but rather they require their needs to be met before they become urgent, as they have a low frustration threshold. They become desperate very quickly and it's best if that can be avoided as much as possible, this way, they imbibe the idea that perhaps the world is a benign place after all and begin to believe they'll be okay in it.

If the Scorpio child has had a traumatic birth, then doing whatever can be done to mitigate the after-effects of this is also recommended. After a difficult birth the mother can have problems bonding with her baby and may be struggling to cope, so it's vital she is adequately supported. Baby massage is an extremely good way to facilitate bonding and enables the two to become more intimately acquainted.

Cranial osteopathy is also recommended for all babies, but especially for those who have had a difficult entry into the world. It helps to release any trauma and thereby circumvents the later repercussions that can result from birth trauma.

This is not to imply that all Scorpio babies have a problematic birth, because of course this would be nonsense but they are especially sensitive to any difficulties that prevail. Some schools of thought believe everyone has a degree of birth trauma to resolve and that the kind of birth we experience establishes a pattern that is repeated throughout life, especially at times of transition. For instance, a baby who's had to have a forceps delivery may, as an adult, have chronic issues about moving on, even when it is clearly necessary. I have come across instances of forcible eviction – a vivid reconstruction of the way they came into the world. A fast delivery, whether or not by Caesarean section, can create a pattern of change that is shockingly sudden. One minute life is jogging along in a certain mode, the next it is irreversibly changed. The future is marked, for good or ill, by the manner in which we arrive and as a particularly sensitive sign, Scorpios register this and respond well to any healing intervention in childhood. This is a sign that has a propensity to mistrust others so anything parents can do to mitigate this tendency is recommended. Easing their passage in early life will pay dividends later and is well worth that extra effort.

There is something quite paradoxical about Scorpio, as one minute they are seemingly bruised by a blow from a feather and at other times they show the most enormous resilience. However, their resilience is built on the knocks they experience and their innate sensitivity means they feel life's blows intensely. No matter how much of a survivor they become, Scorpios continue to be affected by things deeply and to have strong feelings. Perhaps because of their own sensitivity, these are extremely kind, compassionate and generous children, especially to those they care about.

Depending on how secure the Scorpio child is, they do well with younger siblings as they enjoy playing the protective role. Jealousy can play havoc with their good intentions though, so a younger sibling may not always get the best of them. It is essential that parents are careful in the way they introduce a new member of the family, reassuring their Scorpio child of their own importance and making sure they are not too inconvenienced by the new arrival. If possible, parents would do well to offer their Scorpio child additional privileges at this juncture, so that they associate their sibling with something that has benefited them, rather than been a loss.

That said, some jealousy is inevitable and to be expected and it's important that the Scorpio child is not made to feel bad about having such feelings. By not criticising them for having their jealous moments and acknowledging that these feelings are natural, parents help to normalise the situation. Equally this helps to make a distinction between having feelings and acting on them in nasty or spiteful ways, which is clearly not acceptable.

Provided jealousy doesn't spoil their relationship, once a sibling is big enough they are often welcome as an ally and confidant. Failing a younger sibling (and not all things can be arranged to suit them) a pet, which is theirs, is a good substitute. This child is capable of developing deep bonds of affection with a pet. This can be anything that the parents feel they can manage, but something warm and furry is an obvious choice, although if any child is going to enjoy a reptile, then this one might. There is something about the primitive, instinctual nature of reptiles that can strike a chord, especially those that shed their skins. (The metaphor of shedding a skin is often used to illustrate Scorpios' ability to change and reinvent themselves.) Such a creature may be endlessly fascinating and they may also enjoy the notoriety that such a pet gives them.

As they grow up, the Scorpio child may have a tendency to bottle up their feelings until they can no longer keep them in, eventually erupting in a volcanic way. Encouraging them to give vent regularly helps to stop this build up. Most parents ask their offspring what kind of day they've had at school, but with this child it's important not to accept a brush-off and insist on a proper reply. Once they know they are being listened to attentively and that it's not simply a polite but disinterested question, quite a torrent can pour forth. All the petty and small upsets of the day tumble out and need to be laid to rest. Even on a good day, they'll have a fair bit to process at the end of it, and if someone isn't there to help, then it can fester inside them. By encouraging a daily purge of emotional toxins a good pattern is also set for later life.

At the same time, parents can encourage their Scorpio offspring to be more assertive, starting with their upsets around the home. After all, if they were more able to speak out at the time, then things wouldn't build up in them in the first place. Part of their difficulty is that when they acknowledge to others that they feel hurt, they also have to cope with feeling exposed. However, if they can manage this, then it bodes well for the future.

Scorpio children can easily feel misunderstood and probably are. More than anything, they need their feelings to be straightforwardly accepted and acknowledged. They don't want others to respond rationally or to try to get them to be reasonable. They just want a 'there-there' response and from this they can begin to get over what has hurt them. Without this, they hang on to their upset all the more, as if they are being forced to give it up when they still feel far from better. They can act as if something precious, their feelings, are being stolen from them. If anything, their feelings become bigger and stronger when they are denied and quieten and shrink when validated. What this child teaches all of us is that feelings are neither right or wrong, they simply exist. And to deny their feelings is tantamount to denying this child's right to exist.

On the other hand, parents also have to take on board that their Scorpio offspring is intensely private and may not want to reveal their innermost thoughts and feelings to them. When this happens, the parent could suggest to the older child that one way of processing their feelings is by writing about them in an unsent letter or journal. But it's essential that their need for privacy is respected and that parents don't pry. Never read their diary or journal or correspondence; this is an unforgivable sin and trust will be irrevocably destroyed. Parents have to find a way of being there, being available and backing off as needed.

A Scorpio child easily feels intruded upon. Perhaps because they clearly have such a rich inner life, others, and this includes parents, may want to share in this and inadvertently be intrusive. Parents can feel shut out and envious, aware of their own lack and wanting some of this magic that they see their offspring possessing. This is a difficult and complicated scenario, the outcome dependent on how self-aware the parents are.

This dynamic is gender-linked, too, with mothers more likely to be experienced as intrusive and envious by their Scorpio daughters while fathers are felt to be competitive by their Scorpio sons. It could be argued that these feelings belong to the child but perhaps parents should be aware that their Scorpio child has a propensity to such feelings and make sure they do not exacerbate them, by being especially sensitive and careful in these areas.

Scorpio children need a room of their own, if at all possible, as sharing won't afford them the kind of privacy they need. If this isn't an option, then clear boundaries about territory and privacy are essential. These children do not like to share their toys, clothes or possessions and may even object to clothes that no longer fit them being passed down. As far as they're concerned their things belong to them, nobody else is allowed to touch them and they should be allowed to dispose of them as they please. Their space is a no-go area and if anyone's in any doubt, they'll put a lock on their door. If they don't have a door that they can lock, they'll appreciate being given a chest with a padlock. What is important here is that the family ethos is one in which privacy is respected.

Parents may worry about socialising their Scorpio child. Most parents think that children need to learn to share, especially when there are siblings involved. However these children need to feel they have a say and be taken seriously. Not having any control over their life is likely to be an issue for them and so try to allow them to have control in some areas.

Because, culturally, girls are 'allowed' to have their feelings, while boys are encouraged to repress theirs, Scorpio boys are more likely to run into difficulties with this side of their nature. They may channel their pent-up frustration and emotion into competitive activities, in which case winning becomes all-important as so much rides on it. This becomes the conduit to settle old scores, to get revenge on those who have hurt him and to generally triumph over his adversaries.

Of course, Scorpio girls can do all of this too, but they have other ways, not least bitchy comments, through which they can get their own back. However it's done and however long it takes, Scorpios always seek revenge when wronged. They can't move on until vindicated – it's a kind of emotional justice that has to be established and they take a pure and unadulterated delight in being avenged. Parents may be dismayed by how primitive and ruthless they are but this is their nature and no amount of cajoling can change it. All it does is alienate them.

Most parents read to young children, but with Scorpios

it's especially important, as they draw inspiration and satisfaction from fairy stories. These children have a vivid imagination and can readily enter into the world of make-believe. The more Gothic the better, as monsters and giants give shape and form to some of their nameless fears and help them to externalise them and to deal with them, especially as there is always a good outcome in traditional fairy stories. As they grow up, they may be drawn to books and films that frighten them, such as horror, ghosts and science fiction. These children have a wide emotional range and enjoy being triggered into extreme states – it's what excites them and makes them feel alive. Obviously parents have to monitor this and keep it age-appropriate.

Much to some parents' concern, Scorpio boys may be very interested in violence, too, and want toy guns and knives and swords. They are experimenting and learning about the use of power and need to be able to do this within bounds. Scorpio girls tend to use their verbal skills for these purposes.

At school, the Scorpio child is likely to favour the arts, especially literature and drama, where their imagination finds resonance. Music, too, can provide a great source of pleasure. Whether or not they play an instrument, they'll enjoy music's ability to stir and rouse emotions in its very direct way. Parents would do well to introduce them to a broad range of music from very early in life and to take them to the theatre regularly, too.

Adolescence may not be the easiest of transitions as this is a fairly wilful sign and these youngsters need to make their mark. They may also show a precocious interest in sex. Perhaps this is another way their inclination for extreme emotional states manifests. Raging hormones and young love already make a heady combination and when sexual experimentation is added to the cocktail, volcanic eruptions are likely.

While parents may not be able to avoid this happening,

it's important to give the Scorpio child information about sexual and emotional relationships, before they find out the hard way for themselves. Too much information too soon could easily be experienced as intrusive, but access to information before the various stages of puberty begin is needed. Whether parents want to talk it through or not, making sure they have a few good books, which set out the facts of life alongside the psychological implications, is always welcome (and the Scorpio child will no doubt want to read them in private).

For the parents of a Scorpio, no one ever said child-rearing was easy, and this one can be quite a challenge. The Scorpio child impacts on the whole family and teaches them about the importance of feelings. If handled with tact, respect and sensitivity, then they make it into adulthood with their passionate nature intact. They are affectionate and loyal to family members and maintain these connections throughout their life. Parents get back what they give many times over from their Scorpio child – they are rewarded amply and justifiably can be proud.

9

Sagittarius
The Archer

November 22nd to December 20th

A mutable fire sign, ruled by Jupiter

Introducing Sagittarius

Sagittarians are recognisable by their warm, friendly and gregarious disposition. Those born under this sign meet the world with openness and candour and a wide-eyed enthusiasm for life. They possess a deep optimism and belief that things will work out, no matter what, and have a lively interest in others and in the world around them. These are exceptionally generous and magnanimous individuals and are liberal with their time, their money and their opinions. They give freely of themselves and are gifted in bringing out the best in others.

Well known for their sense of humour, Sagittarians are frank, outspoken and disarming. Their forthright comments sparkle with a tantalisingly wicked edge but are never deliberately nasty or malicious. Their brand of wit comes from their particular orientation to life, which is always from a lofty perspective that looks down on some of the ridiculous and petty concerns of mere mortals, caught up in everyday existence.

Jupiter, the planet of growth and expansion, rules this

sign and their view of life is wide and inclusive. Many Sagittarians are actually rather tall and look over the heads of those around them as they peer into the distance. It's as if what they see out yonder is always more interesting and exciting than whatever is close up. While this can be irritating to those standing nearby, it's an inherent characteristic that they see the potential that lies ahead and can capitalise on it. This is just one of the many ways their ability manifests itself.

Sagittarius is the sign of the archer, shooting his arrows of hope and infinite possibility into the sky, never quite knowing where they will land. Likewise, these individuals are inspired by seeing the possibilities in life and may not pay much attention to the results. They like to have various options open to them and may not be too sure which one they will follow. They can sit with a fair degree of uncertainty and enjoy experimenting with life and testing things out. With innate flexibility, they adjust easily to change and prefer a fluid situation to one that is too static. What they can't abide is if the future seems prescribed and closed. For them, this is the kiss of death, as they need to live with the feeling that anything can happen.

Sagittarians are true seekers on a journey where the travelling is more important than the destination. They may or may not have a particular goal in mind and these shift according to their circumstances anyway, but what's most important for them is to experience fully every minute along the way. Their lives are a quest, in which the ultimate goal is to develop wisdom.

Often, Sagittarians will travel physically when young, then later when they are older their journey becomes intellectual or spiritual. They have a need to keep learning throughout their life and seek ways to expand their horizons and consciousness. Sagittarians are searching for some pretty profound answers. Many move back and forth from one mode of searching to another, but their questions always concern the nature of the universe. These are natural philosophers, pontificating about the meaning of life and always ready and willing to share their thoughts.

Man-made laws are not of fundamental interest to Sagittarians – though some do find their way into the legal profession – as really they are interested in the *natural laws* of the universe. They may be drawn to the more abstract sciences such as physics, astronomy and mathematics and for those without scientific inclinations, philosophy and religion, which all offer a view of life from different standpoints. While not all follow one of these subjects professionally, they often provide an abiding interest.

By and large, Sagittarians are extroverted and vivacious and their enthusiasm is infectious. They enjoy socialising and greet each new person they meet with genuine warmth and interest. They have an appetite for new experiences and meeting new people that can leave less energetic companions feeling weak. They live life at such a fast pace that others can find it hard to keep up.

Sagittarians are quick, intuitive individuals who pack their lives with a wide variety of stimulating activities in order to satisfy their restless nature. They process experience and information at lightning speed and so do not become overloaded. This is the third of the fire signs (the other two are Aries and Leo) and Sagittarians' fiery nature is scattered, resembling a scrub fire, flickering over the ground to spread to the next twig, which it rapidly devours and moves on. They have a voracious curiosity and appetite for life and search out experiences and situations to satiate this.

Sagittarians are decidedly sociable, able to burn the candles at both ends and get away with it. Part of why they receive so many invitations is that they do their utmost to solicit them. They hate to be left out of a social occasion and have a way of sniffing out social opportunities in a discreet way. Besides this they are such an asset to have around that they are always in demand. They are a host's dream as they can be relied upon to liven up any gathering and create a convivial atmosphere. No party should be without one.

Like all the fire signs, Sagittarians are honest and straightforward and have a reputation for being a bit too blunt. They can lack tact and the sophistication that goes with it, but their innocent spontaneity means that on the whole others do not take offence. A frank comment is rarely designed to hurt, as they lack malice.

Sagittarius' developed intuition enables them to pick up on things which, because they are so open, they just blurt out. Seemingly out of nowhere, they'll say to a friend 'So you really don't like so-and-so' (a mutual acquaintance) before their friend has fully realised this themselves. They can also come out with things like, 'So you're planning to move abroad/leave your partner/change jobs' without a clue as to how they can possibly know this and at a stage when it's far from settled or certain in their friend's mind. They are just as astonished by what they've said as others are, which is part of what makes them so delightful. While they have no idea where they gleaned the information to make a particular comment, nevertheless it's usually spot on.

This sign is associated with religion and while not all Sagittarians belong to a particular religion with a capital R, they usually hold what could be loosely called a religious attitude. Some will be on a spiritual path and follow a spiritual practice while for others it is even less defined. The quest for meaning and the belief in something higher or bigger than they are, which some define as God, underpins the life of most Sagittarians. Whether their search is mainly an inner one or an outer one, the goal remains the same.

This leads Sagittarians to grapple with ethical and moral issues. They have strong principles and need to test these out and experiment with them, to see where they stand.

Some will be political activists, usually taking a radical position and not adhering to mainstream opinion. These individuals can be extremely passionate about their beliefs and may even risk their life over a matter of principle.

The Sagittarian writer/director Woody Allen illustrates this trait in many of his films, where his plots invariably contain an ethical dilemma. And in later years he created his own real-life moral predicament, where he was seemingly oblivious to what others thought of him and how his situation appeared. This is typical of the more introverted Sagittarian, who is wrapped up in his or her own world and can seem eccentric. Allen is almost as famous for having been in analysis for most of his life, illustrating an inner journey into the past and the unconscious.

Sagittarians instinctively have faith even if what they believe in is not clearly defined. For some it is quite nebulous and vague but that nevertheless adds to their self-confidence and the way they have of bouncing back from adversity. With amazing alacrity, they turn any misfortune that might befall them into a positive lesson that has been learned. They never stay down for very long.

Sagittarians usually see themselves as lucky and blessed and it is this optimistic approach that brings them their good fortune. Like all the fire signs, they create their luck by seeing the inherent possibilities in situations that they then run with. It's their intuition, their ability to see round corners, that recognises opportunities that others might disregard.

At times their relentlessly positive attitude can grate on others' nerves but a Sagittarian will carry on regardless. It is not that they don't have foresight, because they do, it's just not of the doom or gloom variety, like Scorpios or Capricorns might be. They envisage the best possible outcome and as a consequence have a knack of manifesting just that.

This is a freedom-oriented sign and autonomy of movement and independence of thought is particularly important to them. It goes with Sagittarius' spontaneity that they won't readily accept any restrictions. They don't like being answerable to others for their whereabouts, finding it overwhelmingly claustrophobic. This can, understandably, provoke a fair bit of insecurity in a partner, who, even when an understanding has been established, will still find that there are occasions when their Sagittarian mate is impossible to locate. However, it's very unlikely that there is in fact anything to worry about as their disappearance is almost certainly innocent.

Besides self-confidence and a faith that life will sustain them, one of Sagittarius' gifts is their enthusiastic support of others. They are very good at inspiring others and in bringing the best out of them. This, coupled with their wide-ranging interest in the pursuit of knowledge, makes them excellent teachers. Many are drawn to this profession and can be found teaching all ages and ability, from nursery to university on a wide range of subjects, including sports.

Sagittarius' energetic, all-embracing approach to life means many enjoy sports and those with the talent may develop a career as an athlete or sportsman. Paula Radcliffe is a recent example of a Sagittarian woman achieving spectacular success in athletics. She has recently beaten her own previous marathon record and set a new world record.

What Sagittarians lack in discipline they make up for in enthusiasm and provided they put in the training they can excel in their chosen speciality. Once past their peak they move on naturally to coach others, making use of all they've learned along the way.

Passing on their experiences, even the trivial and unimportant ones, is something Sagittarians are always keen to do. They love being the one in the know who can tell others how it's done. This can be irritating, as they tend to assume that their experience has universal implications, when it may well only have relevance for them. Hence, despite how adept they can be at facilitating others in their own discovery, they do have an imperious streak that says, 'Do it my way.' Only the more mature Sagittarian can hold back sufficiently to give those they are teaching the space to explore things for themselves. Their overriding desire to have the answers and communicate their own realisation can hamper them when trying to facilitate students or trainees to find their own answers.

Sagittarians have considerable verbal skills and can hold forth on many topics. Never shy to venture their opinion, they are extremely eloquent and, once on a roll, they barely draw breath until they feel they have done justice to their subject matter. They are most impressive mid-flow and, like a majestic bird in flight, others can wonder how they are going to be able to bring things to a close without a crash landing, but they manage to do so. These verbal skills are also evident in any written work, where they may have a problem with conciseness. They veer towards the wordy and in any academic work that they undertake they'll struggle to keep within the limits of the word count.

Education is extremely important to a Sagittarian. If they have the intellect and the opportunity then they'll go to university and may even end up taking more than one degree. If anyone is going to swap courses mid-way through, or do another degree even if it is not a career move, it's them. They may well go on to do a Masters degree and then a Doctorate and end up in academia themselves.

For Sagittarians without the academic potential or desire then the 'university of life' is a good substitute. It is not that those who take this option only do so because they lack the capacity for study, because that is blatantly untrue. Sagittarians who opt for a less formal higher education do so for many reasons, including the freedom to study what they want when they want and to combine it with the life that they want to lead. Like reading Plato on a Greek beach – perfect for easy access to the Greek ruins that bring to life the times Plato lived in.

Travel is one of Sagittarius' great loves and many end up doing this professionally, as pilots, cabin crew, travel writers or foreign journalists reporting from overseas locations. Some may work in tourism as travel agents or holiday representatives, too. Broadcasting and publishing are also arenas that Sagittarians are drawn to, as they then can educate and inform others, spreading the word at a global level.

Sagittarians can make brilliant sales people, as they have the right combination of warmth and confidence and can be extremely persuasive. With their propensity to exaggerate at the best of times, when there's a financial incentive they can reel off the hype. A job in sales that involves a fair bit of autonomy, with a car and varied travel as part of the job can also satisfy their wanderlust.

The only difficulty Sagittarius might have with a career in sales is an ethical one; in order to be convincing they have to be convinced themselves and so they wouldn't, for instance, be capable of selling a dubious product, despite their own financial interest. This is a sign that has strong scruples and needs to have a clear conscience at the end of the day.

As an employer, Sagittarius is good at seeing potential in others and in facilitating its development. They are encouraging and supportive of their employees and give them a free rein, expecting them to work under their own initiative. Where they fall down is in being a bit loose and sloppy around boundaries and in taking umbrage if anyone minds about this. As they see it, because their heart is in the right place, others should cut them some slack and make allowances. So, they may omit to pass on important information or to offer new employees a proper induction into the job, expecting them to learn on their feet. What's more, they mind hugely if others judge them; they see themselves, or God, as the ultimate judge. And if it's God, then they have the moral high ground and others are put in a weak position. All Sagittarians can be self-righteous but when it's as the boss it's too bad if an employee disagrees, as he or she is always right.

As an employee, Sagittarians need to be given the autonomy and freedom to do their work in the time frame and way that they want. Clocking in will infuriate them and ultimately lead to despair. They should at all costs find a job that offers flexitime. They do well in an occupation that allows them to roam and has scope; an office environment can lead to cabin fever and the need to escape. They like working outdoors and although they are not necessarily good at horticulture, being in the open air may be enough of a temptation to master the basic skills.

Many Sagittarians have a great affinity with horses. They love the feeling of exhilaration and freedom when riding across great expanses of open space – it resonates with certain longings deep in their soul. The archer, which represents this sign, is half human and half horse, with the latter representing the instincts, which are often rather undeveloped and problematic to them. Sagittarians typically try to live life on a so-called 'higher plane' often neglecting their body and its basic need for things such as food and sleep. They reject the physical for the spiritual. The bond that they can forge with a horse, whether as a jockey, stable-hand or racehorse owner, can be grounding and rewarding for these visionary and intuitive individuals and help them to hold physical well-being in higher regard.

Whatever work Sagittarians do, they bring to it their vision and optimism. Never petty themselves, they abhor pettiness in others, always looking at the bigger picture. Their enthusiasm is infectious and they bring out the best in those around them with their cheerful, upbeat attitude.

They hold strongly to the belief that anything is possible if you set your mind to it and with them around, it surely is.

Negative Sagittarius

Most of Sagittarius' negative characteristics are to do with being and doing too much. Their enthusiasm frequently knows no bounds and can spill over and be dominating, manic and oppressive. Their optimism can be so unrealistic that they cannot possibly deliver what they promise. They make promises lightly with little thought of the consequences for others when they fail to honour them. They take on too much, overload themselves and have no sense of their limits or fallibility.

This tendency to spread themselves too thin is because Sagittarians genuinely believe that they can do justice to all their many interests. They find out slowly and painfully over time that perhaps they are overstretched. Friends may complain of feeling neglected and go elsewhere for a deeper and more consistent friendship. Yet, because they remain so popular and in demand, they have a way of brushing the rejection aside and seeing it as the other's problem. While it's true that they will always have friends, they may be a tad superficial. They may attract those who enjoy their vivacious, extroverted lifestyle and who become attached in order to gain access to it – a kind of hanger-on.

Sagittarians can also become hangers-on themselves. In their chase to be 'where it's at' they fail to recognise that this might possibly be an inner state and not an outer one. They then try to attach themselves to those they see as having this special something. It is as if they see this elixir for life as belonging to others that they then seek out. In this way they manage to get invitations to 'the happening party' where 'anybody who's anybody' just has to be seen. They can get swept up in the superficial whirl of celebrity and fail to see that their search has become empty and meaningless. This is a type of inflation where frantic feelings of desperation are invested in being 'where it's at'. This clearly doesn't solve the deeper fears that propel such an individual. These can range from an anxiety that they really aren't that interesting and that others won't want them for themselves, with the focus on feeling excluded for some reason or another. Sagittarians are ordinarily extremely inclusive so to feel shut out is particularly painful and to be avoided at all costs; it's just that this can become rather distorted.

One of the delightful qualities of Sagittarians is their refreshing spontaneity but this can become negative when it spills over into recklessness. In the need to create a stimulating and varied life they end up taking risks that exact a high price financially, energetically or emotionally for themselves and for those they are close to. They can live dangerously – fast driving, dangerous sports, epic treks and sailing challenges – with scant regard for their own or others' safety. While others may admire their adventurous spirit, it can become so extreme that they lurch from one escapade to the next, with little stability in their life.

Sagittarius can become addicted to excitement. Because they thrive when doing interesting and unusual things, this can turn into an inability to allow any quiet, reflective time in which to process all their activities. It's an extreme form of extroversion, where being alone for even short periods of time is considered boring and dreaded. This imbalance adds to their belief that life is to be found wholly outside of themselves, rather than existing within too.

At the opposite end of the pole, the extremely introverted Sagittarian may have a brilliant mind with a high IQ but virtually no social skills. Typically, such an individual avoids eye contact when in conversation and doesn't place much value on human relationships. They live in their minds, so their main focus is on intellectual matters and with their visionary intuition many make gifted innovators, resembling the mad or eccentric professor in dress and demeanour. However, their development is often lopsided, with the intellect privileged and emotions neglected. There can be a lack of empathy and an inability to recognise others' feelings, which is why they have difficulty in forming close friendships and relationships. While many do form relationships, often these are deeply flawed and unsustainable, as their partner has to be prepared to do all the emotional work.

Sagittarians Jimi Hendrix, Jim Morrison and Maurice and Robin Gibb are all famous for their music and extreme lifestyles, although the Gibb brothers have in later years turned away from this. Three have died, making the ultimate long journey into the unknown. The first two deaths were drugs related so the extreme risks these two individuals took were in 'travelling' via drugs to some 'highs'. The problem with artificially induced highs, as opposed to spiritual peak experiences, is that there is an inevitable comedown and trough afterwards. Plus, it never really takes Sagittarians to the place that they are seeking and is ultimately doomed to failure – a disappointing cul-de-sac. This is partly why the twelve-step programme that Alcoholics and Narcotics Anonymous use works so well. Addicts are so often seeking a spiritual or religious experience via a substance and this programme, among other things, helps them find a more direct route to God.

Some Sagittarians have a high-handed self-righteous manner and give the impression of being above-it-all. Their very connection to God and godliness can lead to them becoming deluded into believing that God is 'on their side' and that they are always right. Taking the moral high ground, they feel justified, in the name of their religion, in behaving appallingly. Many wars and atrocities in life are carried out in the name of a religion and this kind of fanaticism is an extreme and distorted expression of a noble Sagittarius characteristic.

If anyone is going to become a 'religious ranter', standing on street corners proselytising to the unconverted, it's a Sagittarius. Such is their conviction in their own beliefs that they will run roughshod over others, truly believing that they have 'the way' and that only one way exists. This attitude is sometimes apparent in other matters too, so if the rant isn't of a religious kind, it could be on any topic that arouses their passion. Speaker's Corner in Hyde Park in London is full of such individuals and while not all are Sagittarian, they typify this sign's passionate conviction that they are right.

Many Sagittarians are politically active, too, as this is a natural arena for them to gravitate towards. While there is nothing intrinsically negative in this, some fool themselves that the ends justify the means. They want to set the world to rights but fail to see that this is simply their opinion and not necessarily what everyone wants. The trades union movement also attracts these individuals, as it provides an outlet for their political fervour.

At least, when active in politics and trades unions, the Sagittarian in question is elected and given a mandate, even if they do sometimes stretch that and go it alone. More problematic are those Sagittarians who think that they are so special and gifted that they do not have to answer to others. Their crime is one of hubris and many will experience a fall from grace at some point in their life. Others, too, will resent them and want to cut them down to size, while they themselves will resent being called to account.

On a personal level, Sagittarians are not above flouting the law in all kinds of minor ways and may consider these laws are not for the likes of them. When it suits them to park illegally, speed, make illegal manoeuvres – drive the wrong way down a one-way street and jump a traffic light, they will. They'll argue quite convincingly, too, of the stupidity of the restriction and of how safe it actually was to do whatever it was they did. They are extremely persuasive and if the outcome were reliant on this alone they would get away with it every time.

Sagittarians will break the rules without a second thought. Because they have such high moral and ethical principles, they genuinely believe that they are answerable only to themselves and ultimately God, who in their mind is always on their side. They genuinely feel aggrieved when challenged, as it is never their intention to disadvantage others or to gain an advantage themselves.

Part of why some Sagittarians behave in this way is their sheer arrogance, which is one of their least attractive characteristics. Not all suffer from this, as it is developed in varying degrees to compensate for a badly dented self-confidence but, unlike other more endearing defences, this one rarely evokes sympathy. Their haughty attitude distances others and as such it works and stops others attacking, which is what in part it's designed to do. People are either fooled and taken in by this display of confidence and certainty and are in awe, or they really object, feel patronised and are hostile.

Terms like 'too big for their boots' are used about arrogant Sagittarians and others want to 'bring them down a peg or two'. They are resented and generally disliked because they set themselves above others and look down on them. They are condescending and patronising and no one likes to be on the end of this.

Like certain Leos, this type of Sagittarian is often grandiose as well, with unrealistic and far-fetched ideas of their capabilities and an exaggerated slant on all that they have achieved so far. This goes way beyond the usual selective editing and hype when writing a CV. They act as if they are far more successful, skilled, experienced and qualified than they actually are. They can blague their way into or out of anything – such as getting a fantastic job in

Paris despite not being able to speak French to the standard required. It means, though, that although others may be impressed, they themselves are frequently left feeling a fraud, fearful of being found out and deemed to be inadequate. And so the cover-up becomes more and more spectacular and desperate.

However, the extreme type of Sagittarian can utterly convince themselves that they are special and exceptionally gifted, in which case they won't fear being discovered. They'll be so ungrounded that they've lost touch with reality completely. This is not to suggest that many don't in fact have amazing talents because of course they do but if they are advertising these, be suspicious.

Grandiosity is a particular kind of defensive mechanism to compensate for denied feelings of insecurity and inferiority. Whereas some signs like Virgo become humble and self-effacing, Sagittarians do the opposite. They can't bear these kind of feelings so do their utmost to avoid them. The only problem is that by being grandiose they are setting themselves up to fail and then have to either face up to their failure or invent another grandiose scheme to maintain their self-image. Their propensity to have an arrogant attitude or inflated opinion of themselves is all part of this pattern.

Sagittarians can have problems with restlessness. They suffer from 'the grass is greener over the hill' syndrome and may go through life dissatisfied and always searching for that elusive something. Because they believe they'll find it outside of themselves, rather than within, they uproot their life and move on to pastures new in the hope of finding it. The fact that this magic 'it' is undefined should be a clue, but it so often isn't. Their life is one of searching and while wandering the world is great for the young, it tends to look rather sad when someone in middle age has still not managed to establish a 'proper' home and base and lives out of a knapsack. Others then see it as a form of escape, of running away, and their wanderlust looks less attractive.

To this more materialistic point of view, the Sagittarian would counter with 'there's more to life than being a mortgage slave'. When they can create a career that has travelling built into it, they may well manage to establish a permanent home and family but the home will never be their priority.

In their relationships those Sagittarians who suffer most from the kind of restlessness just described can leave a string of broken hearts in their wake. If they direct their search into finding a partner who will somehow be their redeemer, they invest their spiritual longings in a mere mortal and are doomed to fail. They then feel justified in moving on to the next partner, seeing it as the previous partner's failing, not as an unrealistic expectation on their part. On this basis, they justify all kinds of morally dubious behaviour.

This sign tends not to have a good track record when it comes to being faithful. Despite their usual honesty and frankness, when it comes to fidelity they can lie and cheat. They'll not bother with an elaborate deceit but will do what it takes to cover their tracks and get what they want. This may amount to lying by omission, such as failing to reveal certain crucial facts to their current partner, like who they were in bed with that afternoon.

Sagittarius' philandering is just another manifestation of their propensity to be excessive. Their appetite for life is huge and sex is an important part of this. It may take them a while to learn that more sex is not always better and, especially, that more partners do not necessarily equate with more experience. Sowing their wild oats may last way beyond their youth and be used as a flight from intimacy, which they can find threatening.

Sagittarians have their own brand of morals, which means that they can convince themselves that something that other more conventional types would question is perfectly acceptable and right. They have no shame, as they genuinely believe that what they are doing is okay. They've squared it with their own conscience and that's all that matters. Partners should be aware of this and discuss their position in a clear and unambiguous way.

Sagittarians may well find the ageing process more difficult than most. Visible signs of growing old are a challenge for most of us, but with Sagittarius' inherently youthful, optimistic outlook they can baulk at the realisation that they aren't immortal after all. Long before old age sets in they can find it hard to adjust to the realities and practicalities of life, especially the responsibilities that most adults assume. They can view a mortgage like a shackle and chain and, if they do succumb, they are just as likely to sell up at the first opportunity and use any equity they have accrued to finance a once-in-a-life-time trip. Only it won't be just the once, it's actually a way of life that doesn't sit easily with emotional commitments and children.

This doesn't mean that Sagittarians don't make these commitments, because they do. They just take off, too, and expect a partner to either come along or cope with being left behind. Those who choose to get together with this adventurous wanderer must realise that they may never 'settle down' and that if they do, it comes at a price. Their yearning for travel is deep in their souls and the summer holidays may not touch the spot. So long as prospective partners take this on board, all will be well. It is hardly fair, a few years down the road, to expect their Sagittarius mate to have miraculously changed into a stay-at-home type.

The same applies to those Sagittarians whose journey is mental rather than physical. They too will want to continue with their exploration and a partner should be aware that the end of the current course of study might not signal the end of their studies. It's more likely to be a way of life and may never lead to the big bucks that a partner possibly envisages. It's always a mistake to get involved with someone and then expect them to change and this is especially true with Sagittarians, who carry their maturity lightly.

Sagittarians' outspoken frankness can become downright rude and cause them problems in their private and social life. There is only so much truth that others can bear, especially if it's delivered in front of their friends, leaving them feeling exposed and humiliated. Tact is not Sagittarius' strong point, so they can easily embarrass friends and loved ones inadvertently. Even when they have been shockingly rude, they don't usually realise what kind of impact they have had. Certain Sagittarian comedians, like Billy Connolly and Bette Midler, have made outrageousness their speciality and while it can be hilarious on stage it's often far from funny in private.

Sagittarius' faults and flaws are obvious for all to see. They are not subtle folk and however rude, arrogant or condescending they may sometimes be, they invariably have a heart of gold. They mean well and take criticism well. For those who are thinking of getting involved, there are no hidden surprises waiting in store. Sagittarians' shortcomings are laid bare from the first encounter and provided you can stand your ground and give as good as you get then, although there may be some spectacular fireworks along the way, the fights are well worth having and leave few scars.

The Sagittarius Man

The Sagittarius man is dynamic, exciting and fun, with a great sense of humour and a philosophical bent. He is recognisable by his adventurous spirit and lively interest in others and the world around him. Often an extrovert, he's jovial and sociable, broad-minded and outspoken. He is liberal with his opinions leaving others in no doubt as to where he stands.

The Sagittarius man lives according to his principles and emanates moral integrity. He is loyal and true to his beliefs, whatever they are, and would never betray them. The beliefs he holds may be political or those of an organised religion or may be more idiosyncratic and personal to him. If a member of an established religion, he will still vigorously question the tenets that underpin it as he is not a devotee or follower as such but a seeker of truth. He is not going to swallow whole a system of belief that does not square with his own conscience.

This ethical, moral stance permeates everything the Sagittarian man does. Whether or not he follows any form of religious practice, he is essentially a man of God. He can be relied upon to speak his truth, whether or not this makes him popular. Most of the time it does. Others tend to like him because he's straightforward and they know where they stand with him.

At heart, the Sagittarian man is an adventurer and an explorer. His adventures and explorations can be of inner or outer terrain and arguably all routes eventually converge, so that those who become literal travellers are changed profoundly at an inner level and those who follow a religious or intellectual journey go on to have outer, worldly experiences, too.

However, if anyone is going to sign up to be an astronaut it's a Sagittarius man. He is driven by his innately restless spirit to take his search to the farthest reaches of whatever is possible. While he may not make it to the Moon, the idea appeals to a deep longing in his soul and he's more likely than most to make it to the top of Everest, to the Amazon, the rain forest and the Antarctic.

Steven Spielberg is typically Sagittarius in the films he chooses to direct, which are invariably epic tales. Some, like *Close Encounters of the Third Kind* and *ET*, involve the far reaches of outer space and speculate, with wonder and humour, on its nature while others, like *The Color*

Purple, Schindler's List and Saving Private Ryan, have a passionate moral or ethical dimension. He is also an entrepreneur and from the beginning had his own production company, which is now reputedly worth millions.

The Sagittarian man's adventurous spirit is one of his most attractive qualities. His impulse is to conquer new land or new terrain and in this he is impressive. A rural environment suits him best but when in the city he can be found whizzing around on a motorbike and working in a high-risk industry like construction, where he enjoys the heights and the inherent dangers. He is willing to take physical risks and go out on a limb, with little thought for his own personal safety, pushing himself to the limits of his capabilities and then some more. In all of this he displays good humour and bonhomie.

Despite all this, the Sagittarian man is not particularly competitive although he may arouse these feelings in others by the example he sets. He is simply compelled to break through any limitations, either within himself or records set by others, and to stretch himself. It's his urge for freedom from constraint that propels him forward. So he is not competing with others, as such, but with what the possibilities are.

Another very attractive characteristic of the Sagittarius man is his sense of humour. He is extremely funny in a clever way. He doesn't usually tell jokes but he can send up others and situations with an impromptu and spontaneous wit. His verbal skills are considerable and he can hold forth for some time as he delivers his comical message. Nothing is sacred once he casts his humorous eye over it and holds it up to the light. He can keep up a witty banter for hours, never growing tired of it and is extremely entertaining. This is something the comedian Billy Connolly exemplifies brilliantly.

However those who are out for the evening with a Sagittarian man, hoping for more of an intimate time, may be disappointed. His repartee can be a distancing technique that cleverly blocks close contact. It can be hard to talk seriously to him as changing the tone may make you seem 'heavy' and lacking in humour. His obvious discomfort also signals that this is a no-go area. Trying to get close to him may seem impossible, where any attempts to get to know the real man are fobbed off with charming witticisms. Others can feel themselves manoeuvred into playing a more staid role that they don't recognise as being much to do with them. If this is the case, weigh up the pros and cons of challenging him. He may bolt but he also responds well to direct questioning, as he likes the attention. If he's not pinned down he is capable of leading a prospective partner a merry dance, so living on assumptions and guesswork can end in heartache.

The ruler of Sagittarius, Jupiter, is a planet associated with jovial excess. The Sagittarian man can equally be prone to excesses and tends to go to extremes in much of what he does. He can gain a reputation as a bit of a philanderer, which may actually be deserved. His restless wanderer mentality applies to love too and, particularly while still young, he may mistakenly equate the number of lovers he's had with experience, not realising that this actually betrays his superficiality. Having chalked up a fair bit of this kind of experience, he does eventually realise that something is missing that can't be found by yet another amorous adventure. Whoever meets him at this point has a chance to go deeper with him and to help him explore terrain he has so far avoided.

The Sagittarian man doesn't declare his feelings willingly and it's only when pushed that he'll do so. He likes to play the field and keep his options open so, even if he's smitten, he'll keep quiet about it. The object of his affection is the last to know but, as he's not actually capable of staying silent, he tells his mates. Although he's an extremely generous man in most ways, if anyone is going to follow the slogan, 'treat them mean and keep them keen' it's him. His lack of generosity when it comes to his feelings is more to do with his tenuous relationship to them and how threatening he can find them. In particular, he fears emotional dependency and intimacy. As he sees it, these sorts of feelings threaten his autonomy and freedom, and as such are to be avoided.

Freedom is of paramount importance to the Sagittarius man, yet often, despite his philosophical tendencies, he fails to analyse exactly what that means. He may bandy the term about as if there's a consensus of opinion as to its definition without actually questioning it. Despite his intelligence, he is often not emotionally sophisticated and doesn't make the connection between his apprehension of closeness and his desire for this so-called liberty; he misses the point. Part of his life's work is to define what freedom means to him – freedom to do exactly what, freedom from what – and to separate this out from some of his more primitive and less defined fears around emotional dependency.

The Sagittarian man values friendship and, in so far as he ever talks about his feelings, he confides in his friends. A partner would do well to get to know his friends, as their support will be a lifesaver. Friends can also help to explain him and what makes him tick. Not that he's complicated, as in many ways he's extremely straightforward: it's just that at times he can seem rather cut off from his feelings and his loved one can gain insight and draw comfort from those he's known longest.

Eventually a love affair with a Sagittarian man turns into a deep and enduring friendship. He wants someone who will accompany him on life's journey; someone who is able to travel light, doesn't have a preconceived idea of where they are headed and is open to whatever life throws up. He enjoys change and adjusts easily to new circumstances, so for those who can take the risk, anything is possible with this adventurer.

The Sagittarian man may not be strong on the feeling realm but he can read others with unerring accuracy and for that he relies on his intuition. His take on life comes through his invisible antennae, which are highly tuned to his benefit. It's through these he gleans many of the opportunities that come to him. His innate self-confidence means he can seize opportunities that other, less confident individuals would pass by as too risky. In this sense he makes his own good fortune.

However, a partner needs to know that the Sagittarius man is always going to run risks and is not remotely interested in financial security and stability. In fact too much focus on money can be quite threatening and experienced as limiting. He may become very rich, in the way that those who follow their dreams sometimes are, but its a by-product and not his goal. He is never motivated by financial rewards and recognises that they can entrap a man's soul. He won't be bought.

It's quite hard to know when or if the Sagittarius man has made a commitment as, even if he's heterosexual, he's not the marrying kind. He's far more likely to casually suggest to his lover that they co-habit, often for some less-than-romantic reason – because it would save on bills to live together – so it's hard for them to know how to take it. However, this is likely to be as good as it gets with him. He's commitment phobic and having to spell things out is all part of this. He needs the ambiguity, the let-out clause, but if he's suggested living together, for whatever reason, it has to been seen as a huge step for him.

If he can get away with it, the Sagittarian man will slide into a committed relationship without acknowledging that this is what's happening. He's happy to have children on this basis, too, although his partner must be prepared for him to do something spectacularly irresponsible around the time of the birth – like take a job a long way away. He may even dress it up to look as if he's being the responsible, wage-earning one, when actually he's in flight. Whether or not he goes, he does quickly adjust to the new situation and enjoys being a father.

Being a parent brings out some of the best qualities in the Sagittarian man. During the early, pre-verbal stage he can feel a bit out of his depth and take a back seat but once his children have a grasp of language he comes into his own. He is playful and informative and a great friend and teacher to his offspring, turning learning into an adventure. He becomes passionately involved in their education, taking a keen interest in their schools and making sure they get plenty of extra-curricula stimulation, too. He'll encourage them in athletics and sports and be a willing participant himself, kicking a ball around with young children and teaching them how to ride their bikes. Still a boy at heart, he loves to play and he makes life fun.

As a father, the Sagittarian man encourages and supports his children to find their way in the world. He's delight-fully non-authoritarian and does not impose rules but communicates respectfully with his children and seeks agree-ments about certain things. He is easygoing and able to be flexible and to accommodate their needs. As a parent he's not at all anxious, so the message they get is that the world is a safe place. He encourages them to spread their wings, take risks and welcome challenges. This is the example he sets and he acts as a source of considerable inspiration to them.

The Sagittarius man wants the best for his children and listens to what they want, too. He doesn't approach them with a preconceived idea of what they should be and this, more than anything, is his greatest gift to his children. He gives his children the space to be themselves and doesn't impose a blueprint on them. Because he has fought hard to be himself and to do his own thing, whatever that may be, he values this above anything.

A partner may complain that the Sagittarius man is too

laid-back but, actually, his problem is in supporting his partner sufficiently, especially in the early phase. He's still finding his feet and struggling with his own demons and it's a test of her nerves to go ahead and have a child with him in the first place. However, even if he looks to be extremely unpromising at this stage of the relationship, he can and usually does come through, although there are no guarantees. He could disappear for several years to Outer Mongolia.

The Sagittarius man is not for the faint-hearted. He is an adventurer and needs a mate who is as daring as he is, who won't limit and restrain him, and who is fairly resilient and self-reliant. In such a partnership he has the scope he needs without too many threatening demands being made of him.

The Sagittarian man may not follow a conventional career path, as this may be too limiting for him. Any further education he undertook may have been disrupted by equally valuable time out on distant travels or on changes of course, as his first choice was made without knowing about the other options he later discovers. This is very much the story of his life. He can seem a bit of a drifter but actually he's garnering a wide experience of life. Because his career path is not linear, he may not be as senior as others who are younger and have less experience but have spent longer in this particular arena. He won't mind this.

The more introverted type of Sagittarian man is more likely to pursue an inner journey, possibly an intellectual one; he is well suited to academia, the teaching profession or a life in the church. His search does not necessarily involve physical travel as it can all be done through study and introspection. His goal is to become a man of wisdom. The knowledge he accumulates he likes to pass on, so having a legitimate and paid outlet in which to do so is perfect.

Provided the Sagittarius man's work gives him time to

think and doesn't unduly restrict him, he can be happy doing almost anything. Whatever he does, he brings to it his adventurous spirit, optimism, enthusiasm, idealism and his intuitive approach. These are by no means a bad combination of qualities and ones that take him far. This is a man who leads an extraordinary life.

The Sagittarius Woman

The Sagittarius woman is recognisable by her wholehearted, expansive approach to life and her outspoken, frank opinions. She has an enthusiasm and optimism that is a joy to behold and has a way of always looking on the bright side and turning things round to their best possible light and advantage. Her cheerful presence is infectious and she lifts the spirit of others just through being herself.

Humour bubbles beneath the surface of the Sagittarian woman and she can often be found having a quiet chuckle to herself about something she finds amusing. She laughs at herself and shares amusing anecdotes about her day with those she's close to. She takes a keen interest in others and is able to establish a lively rapport with a wide variety of people. Her ability to unmask pretension and to make genuine contact with others in a friendly and non-threatening way is one of her greatest talents. Like her male equivalent, her humour is of the moment and particular to the situation, but unlike him, hers establishes intimacy. She doesn't use her wit to distance others, perhaps because, as a woman, she is not so afraid of intimacy.

The Sagittarius woman is spontaneous and restless and needs the scope to express herself, otherwise she will lose her sparkle. Casual contact and conversations are important to her as they offer her the freedom to be herself in a particularly light-hearted and uncommitted way. This in no way threatens any commitments she has, it's simply some fun banter that adds interest to her day.

Restlessness is a key quality of the Sagittarius woman, for good or ill. She needs movement, both physical and mental. Her body will object if cooped up for too long and she'll pace around like a caged animal. Because she needs to get out of the building, she'll invent an errand or chore that allows her to escape. She has a low boredom threshold and objects if there's a lack of mental stimulation. Depending on the circumstances, she'll use her humour or be inventively disruptive to enliven a boring situation. What she won't do is suffer it.

Passionate about all kinds of ethical and moral issues, the Sagittarian woman has strong principles and opinions. She may or may not be actively political, but she'll still know what she thinks and voice this forcibly. She'll have a position on most important issues, like crime, abortion, euthanasia, war, animal rights, and more generally on how communities behave and treat each other. She may well be a member of organisations like Amnesty International, Greenpeace and Friends of the Earth and will probably have been actively involved in protests.

Naturally radical, the Sagittarius woman doesn't accept a simplistic analysis and won't tolerate bigotry. As a deep thinker and person of conviction, she goes beneath the surface of the popular consensus of opinion and grasps the more complicated strands and implications of topical issues. She is impressively articulate and capable of acting as a spokesperson for a cause she believes in. Within her work situation she often takes on this responsibility, getting involved in union activity or being a representative on a committee that serves for the greater good of all.

When it comes to relationships, the Sagittarius woman is drawn to a fellow traveller who offers her adventure, excitement and scope or, at the very least, won't thwart hers. While her partner does not have to share her principles, she will nevertheless expect them to have strong ones of their own to which she is sympathetic and, like her, be

346

prepared to fight for what they believe in. She is the opposite of security conscious and a potential partner's income
or material assets are of no interest to her: her priority is
for the kind of opportunities that they as a couple can
create. She is future oriented and is attracted to a mate
who has vision and sees life's possibilities.

If anyone is going to get together with someone who
only has dreams to offer and who has been written off as
a waste of time by everyone else, it's a Sagittarian woman.
And together, they prove everyone else wrong and create
quite amazing things. This is her gift and her innate faith
in herself and others means she brings out the best in them.
What she can't tolerate is a relationship going nowhere,
without hope for the future. She finds this completely claustrophobic and will break free from it.

Money is only important to the Sagittarian woman in
so far as it offers her freedom. She values having the wherewithal to travel, to study, to have time to herself and to
visit places of interest. She is not materialistic and owning
a tent and a backpack or books is more important to her
than fancy clothes or jewellery. She resents giving up too
much of her time for work, even if she loves her work, as
she always has lots of other things she wants to do – her
time is precious and she hates to waste it. She is definitely
not suited to nine-to-five employment although she can do
it in short bursts if she must.

Practicality is never going to be the Sagittarian woman's
strong point. When manoeuvred into this role, she finds it
oppressive as it cramps her style. It's not that she isn't capable, just not in an ordered, methodical way. She's inspired
and intuitive and deals with mundane matters in fits and
starts. If she has an earth sign partner, as she often does,
then her way of going about things can seem chaotic and
be experienced as rather threatening. Despite how it may
look from the outside, she has a sense of her schedule and
manages her commitments perfectly well. Just as others

think she's about to drown under a mountain of chores and administration she surfaces, smiling. Earth signs can find her perennial optimism annoying and the fact that she does, miraculously, clear the decks in one majestic sweep of activity, quite infuriating.

The Sagittarian woman gets involved quickly and trusts her hunches when it comes to love. She's a great judge of the inherent potential in others and, as that is what she's looking for in a mate, she's good at selecting someone who is right for her. She's not afraid to buck convention, so others may be surprised by her choice. They've overlooked the fact that she's not interested in a conventional life. However, she's not necessarily as proactive as this sounds; it's more likely that she's responding to another's interest in a bemused and curious way and decides to see where it leads.

Once emotionally involved, the Sagittarian can be quite a challenge for the kind of partner who expects her to give up her friends and her previous life and devote most of her time to him or her. She doesn't and she won't. Friends remain important to her, as do the activities she's involved in, and, although she is willing to scale things down and makes lots of reassuring noises, she could still be out several nights a week doing her own thing. She's not terribly domesticated and what's more, has no intention of becoming so. She can get by and that's all that she's interested in. And she's definitely not the type to iron someone else's shirts!

However, the Sagittarian woman is honest and straightforward about her feelings and so is unlikely to have an affair, because that involves deceit. Either she stays with her partner or she ups and leaves. Her emotional integrity is immensely important to her so if she makes a commitment she means it. She just won't be controlled. She'll switch off her mobile phone and won't be located if she wants a conversation that is not interrupted by a partner asking her where she is and when she'll be home.

Some might argue that the Sagittarius woman provokes a partner's insecurity and jealousy, but they miss the point. She's spontaneous and is just trying to protect her autonomy and freedom, which is also her life force. If she has to account for herself every minute of the day she dies a little. She certainly doesn't set out to harm her mate, she just expects them to trust her and cope. The argument could equally be that she knows she's trustworthy, so why don't they?

That's not to deny that the Sagittarian woman has problems with feelings of dependency, because she does, and she can experience other people's needs as suffocating. She has a fear of being trapped emotionally and is the kind of woman who plans her escape route, just in case it's required. With that in place, she can settle more easily. While the needs of others do threaten her, she is most threatened by – and in flight from – her *own* needs. Which means she tends not to acknowledge them or those who meet them for her. If she pretends she has no needs, she won't feel dependent.

This obviously creates difficulties in the Sagittarius woman's relationships, not least for her mate. A partner has to be secure enough within themselves to know it's her problem and accept that she's unlikely to change. A little gentle teasing now and then won't go amiss, as she can take this and will readily see what she's doing when it's pointed out. She's literally running scared of too much emotional intimacy and has lots of neat ways of avoiding it – like inviting other friends round when it was meant to be just a twosome. Generally she prefers a crowd to a one-to-one. She may also be scared that she's going to be bored and thinks that by inviting others it will liven up the evening. However, this reasoning doesn't hold up when scrutinised; she's really just kidding herself. She needs a partner who is grounded and unfazed by her skittish ways.

Despite her need for independence, the Sagittarius

woman may still want children and won't see them as a hindrance in this respect. She makes one of those remarkable mothers who fly to some far-off destination with her baby in a sling. She certainly doesn't allow motherhood to restrict her and her offspring are well travelled before they start school. For her, education is just as much about contact with other cultures as attending an educational establishment.

The Sagittarian mother gives her children the freedom to make their own choices about lots of things ordinarily seen as a parent's domain. She's so liberal that some might see her as lacking in responsibility, but actually it's a definite philosophical position that she occupies. She firmly believes in giving her children responsibility over their own lives from an early age and also expects them to experience the consequences of their decisions. She may not be the most conventional of mothers but she introduces her children to the big wide world, makes them aware of the many opportunities that life holds and instils in them the belief that anything is possible.

Some examples of the freedom the Sagittarian mother offers include: giving her child a door key from an early age; letting them travel independently far sooner than their peers; allowing them to organise their own activities and even to select the school they attend; and choosing the decor and furnishings for their bedroom and having ultimate responsibility for maintaining it.

Many a Sagittarian is drawn to teaching and even as a mother, she is a teacher, passing on information, encouraging her children's development and making sure that they make the best of themselves. She's enthusiastic and supportive and probably enjoys their teenage years the most, when she can be more of a friend to them than a parent. This is just when her lack of an authoritarian stance pays dividends, as teenagers respond especially well when given autonomy and independence.

If the Sagittarian woman has children, she will almost certainly want to continue to work. Whether or not she has established a career, she'll need to get out there into the wider world regularly. She may have changed direction too many times and had too much time off for travel and study to be on a clear career path. Yet, whatever work she does, she'll prefer to pursue it or have some outlet outside the home, as looking after young children all day is likely to leave her feeling cooped up and frustrated. As they grow older, she's happy to be the taxi service, as this suits her better. She can fit all kinds of errands and activities in among the ferrying about that she does.

The Sagittarian woman enjoys working alongside others and being involved with a project that is inspiring. Because she is future oriented, she can tolerate a fair bit of tedium and dull routine in the short term if there's a glimpse of a rosy future that holds exciting possibilities. What she can't stand is following a prescribed route – her work needs to accommodate the fact that she is a free spirit.

Although the Sagittarian woman enjoys finding and taking her place in the world, she is not ambitious or concerned about money or status. These kinds of incentives hold no sway with her. Being self-employed gives her all the independence that she seeks and allows her to work within her own ethical framework but it may not provide her with the sociable colleague-contact that is equally important to her. Even the more introverted Sagittarian woman is rarely a loner and likes to interact with others in the course of her working day. Working as part of a cooperative or with colleagues where the decisions and power are shared suits her best. That way she retains her autonomy, yet has company. Whatever job she ends up in, she brings to it her good humour, warmth and immediacy.

For those considering getting involved, the Sagittarian woman is one of the least pretentious and most affable individuals. Her shortcomings, such as they are, fade in comparison with all that she has to offer. She is a joy to be around, as she brightens up the world of all those who come in contact with her.

The Sagittarius Child

Sagittarius children are recognisable by their jaunty disposition and confident stance. They are warm, friendly and outgoing with a happy-go-lucky attitude that makes them popular and in demand. With a disarming frankness that stays with them throughout life, they say what's on their minds and, while not deliberately rude, they are not overly concerned about being polite either. Sociable and high-spirited, these children make friends easily and enjoy energetic, physical activities.

Daring, adventurous and assured, the Sagittarius child takes risks from the word go, much to their parents' consternation. As a baby they will stretch to reach that just out-of-reach toy, toppling over in the process. They'll be mobile early and possibly quite inventive about their methods of getting about – if any baby is going to do a bottom shuffle it's a Sagittarian. Having gained a degree of mobility, they may not walk early as, once they have a reasonably successful means of getting about, they can be reluctant to give that up in order to learn a new method that will be initially slower.

As the Sagittarius child develops, they push against the limits of what they can do and of what their parents allow. They venture forth at an early age, testing their parents' nerves to the limits. While they may lack fear, their parents' anxiety levels can go through the roof. However, although accidents do happen, they are actually very fortunate and if any child has a guardian angel looking out for them, they have. Things they lose will turn up in a miraculous way and dangerous situations dissipate harmlessly for them time after time. Their innocence and openness seem to afford them protection and bring out the best in others.

With their outspokenness, Sagittarian children aren't prone to bottling up any difficulties. It all comes tumbling out. They make a clean breast of whatever is troubling them and then rapidly move on. With such transparency, parents are reassured, as they are told when all is not well, whether it concerns them, other members of the family or school. These children don't lie or dress the truth up either, although they can overstate, particularly when they actually feel insecure or uncertain of themselves or want to emphasise their point. It's important that parents believe what they have to say straightaway and take it seriously, as that will minimise their desire to exaggerate.

The Sagittarius child is kind-hearted and generous. If someone else is in need, they will give away whatever they have, regardless of whether or not they need it themselves. This is due in part to their optimistic nature. They are confident that they'll be fine even if they give away their bus fare home – and they probably will be, too. While this is commendable it also shows a lack of practicality in material matters, which is something they will grapple with all of their lives. And while there is no obvious right or wrong here, parents can nevertheless worry that this child is too unworldly. Explaining the nuts and bolts of practical matters will help a lot as long as there is no pressure for them to conform to some ideal of practicality.

Sagittarian children are boisterous and lively and enjoy movement and dance, sport and athletics. Whether or not they are graceful and disciplined enough to make great dancers, the early experience is a boon and gives them a much-needed outlet. Free dance and movement is likely to suit their temperament best, especially when there is plenty of room to move and stretch out to the fullest. Some also excel at gymnastics as their innate flexibility can be mental or physical and is occasionally both.

All athletics and sports are to be encouraged, as the Sagittarian child has a lot of steam to let off. They enjoy, and are usually good at, running, jumping and vaulting and make good team players. An active involvement in any extra-curricula sports at their school is to be encouraged as they will benefit socially as well as arriving home with less spare energy.

Sagittarian children may be drawn to pony riding and archery. These are fairly exclusive sports but that is not what makes them so enjoyable for these youngsters. They particularly enjoy the exhilaration they get from riding. A bicycle is the next best thing, in that it gives them mobility and a sense of freedom but the special relationship that they can have with a pony beats a bike any day. Given the expense and/or urban living, this is often not an option. But if it is a possibility a Sagittarian child can obtain immense pleasure and satisfaction from owning a pony. Grooming, feeding, cleaning tack and mucking out teaches them invaluable lessons in care and responsibility, that stands them in good stead throughout their life. Even in an urban environment there are usually opportunities to ride and city farms where there is access to horses and ponies. Encourage these children to get involved with the everyday care of the animals.

This is the sign of the archer so archery is a natural activity, with the freedom of the arrow to soar and hit its mark resonating with intrinsic characteristics in the Sagittarius child. Much satisfaction can be found in developing this skill for its own sake as well as its symbolic value of eternal hope.

Sagittarian girls may well get called tomboys, because they are as energetic as the boys and enjoy physical exercise, especially sports, at which they might excel. They are just as freedom loving, too – very much the daredevil seeking adventures. Expect them, when still tiny, to climb trees and try to get to the very top, as well as to dangle precariously from the climbing frame.

One of the Sagittarius child's favourite treats is to have

friends stay over and parents will be badgered to allow this, with promises to behave and to be asleep by the designated time, all of which goes by the board once the friends have arrived. These children make promises they can't possibly keep even though they fully intend to do so in the moment. By the time they are teenagers, expect the house to be overflowing with their friends – one of the outcomes of being popular and gregarious. Parents are advised to invest in bunk beds and other flexible sleeping solutions from the start in order to accommodate extra guests.

Sagittarian children are good communicators, often having a vocabulary in advance of their years, using sophisticated language and having a grasp of complex ideas and concepts ahead of their peers. These children do well in a school environment that stretches them and can provide high-calibre intellectual stimulation. If they are not thriving in school, then it may be necessary to check out whether the curriculum is up to scratch and whether the educational establishment is doing its job properly. These children are hungry to learn and can become disruptive when under-stimulated.

Sagittarian children are ultimately seekers of the truth, wanting to discover answers to the big questions in life, such as how the universe began, what it consists of and what is the meaning of life. When it comes to specialising, they can equally follow an arts or science route because the truth can be pursued via both. It's a good idea to keep their subject options open for as long as possible. This suits them anyway and allows them to change their mind later if they so wish, without having to go back to elementary level.

Often intellectually precocious, Sagittarian children enjoy arguing about matters of principle and are good at debating. Moral issues arouse their passion and they will, from an early age, take an ethical stance. They may be politically active and able to agitate others to bring about change within their domain. In a family that is apolitical, they can galvanise family members to think about global issues.

At school, the Sagittarius child's favourite subject could well be philosophy. It enables them to stretch their minds and to think about complicated intellectual matters. Geography will also be a favourite topic as it informs them of the world in which they live, although a study of the cultures of the world will interest them more than just facts. They like to know how other people live. Some may later be drawn to law and areas such as astronomy and astrology, which investigate the mechanism and meaning of the universe. The natural laws may equally appeal.

Religion is likely to be of fundamental importance to the Sagittarius child. Both the study of comparative religions and the practice of a religion provide significant building blocks in the development of their character. For those who are part of a religious family, then it's likely that the Sagittarian child will come to question whatever beliefs are held. This is all part of their growing up and is likely to be something they grapple with throughout their life. They seek a system of belief that they can both abide by and question vigorously at the same time. Some may reject the religion they were brought up in, while others will retain theirs, but what is important is the process by which they get to the position they hold. The Sagittarian Irish singer Sinead O'Connor exemplifies this. Brought up a Catholic, she went on in her twenties to become a priest in a different religion.

Others, where religion is not a part of family life, may go on to adopt a religion that surprises the rest of the family. If anyone is going to convert to Islam or become a Buddhist, then it's a Sagittarian and even as a young child, their 'feel for God' is evident. The more parents can offer by way of a religious education, the better. It satisfies a deep need in this child's psyche.

Parents should be prepared for their Sagittarian child's education to be long and expensive. Of course, once their mandatory school attendance is completed, what parents choose to contribute to their offspring's education is up to them, although some financial help will almost certainly be needed. The Sagittarian child will be interested in all sorts of extra-curricula activities and will almost certainly continue to study further; even those who don't do this immediately will probably go on to do so at some later stage. Many choose to take a gap year but others may take a ten-year gap and then, of course, parents may well feel that any fees and expenses are now entirely their offspring's responsibility. However, for those parents who want to assist, having some contingency plan may be a good idea, as university and further training is expensive.

An important part of a Sagittarian child's education is travel. Being exposed to other cultures and ways of doing things opens their minds and extends their horizons and helps them to formulate the questions that they spend their life pursuing. Send them on foreign exchange trips and allow them to travel at any opportunity. They will reap immeasurable benefits – it provides food for their soul. Encourage them to learn as many languages as are on offer at their school, too. They often have a talent for languages and whether they do or not, they will love having the ability to communicate on their travels.

All teenagers can be rude and difficult to manage but Sagittarians can be especially so, because they speak their mind so forcibly. They argue relentlessly and wear the opposition down. At times, in youthful folly and igno-rance, they can be high-handed and display arrogant assumptions. While the naive optimism of the young can be endearing, it can also be trying when it belittles the experience gained by adults. Parents can feel wrong-footed and as if they are being selfish in the face of their stroppy teenager's articulate proselytising.

In fact, the more uncertain the Sagittarian child is deep down, the more big headed and apparently confident they can appear. While parents may be tempted to leave them to learn the hard way, actually they need to be reassured. It can indicate that too much is being expected of them and that they don't feel sure that they can come up with what is being asked of them. One of the less attractive Sagittarian defences is arrogance, which always indicates insecurity on an inner level. However, a touch of cockiness does no harm, in fact it can be one of their most charming qualities.

The Sagittarian child tends not to know their own limits and needs a fair amount of containment by parents as, without this, they expect too much of themselves. They thrive and feel reassured when set firm boundaries. By being told they are not yet old enough to do something, their anxiety about managing activities that are beyond them evaporates. Better to have them chafing at the bit than overreaching themselves. Although, that said, they do bounce back from any setbacks they experience and regain their assurance very quickly. It takes a lot to dent their confidence for long.

While the Sagittarius child does have a lot of resilience, it's essential that their parents remember they are just as vulnerable as any other child. Their joyful openness and enthusiasm can be broken and should not be taken for granted. It is their gift, to be protected and treasured.

10

Capricorn
The Goat

December 21st to January 19th

A cardinal earth sign, ruled by Saturn

Introducing Capricorn

Capricorns are recognisable by their obvious authority and distinguished air. Self-contained, with a quiet, unobtrusive confidence that is built upon their achievements, they have a sober view of themselves and others. They automatically assume responsibility and have a quick, pragmatic grasp of situations. With a solemn, serious and somewhat pessimistic attitude to life – although they would argue they are simply being realistic – they are shrewd, practical, sensible, reliable, matter-of-fact and down-to-earth, with a wry, ironic sense of humour.

Never loud or showy, Capricorns don't draw attention to themselves in ostentatious ways but gain recognition for the work that they do, whether this is voluntary or paid. They are admired and respected by their peers and so while they may not be well known – and fame is not something they find remotely enticing – they are highly thought of in their field.

The goat symbolises Capricorn, an adept and sure-footed climber that infallibly makes it to the mountain peak.

Similarly, those born under this sign find their way to the top of whatever mountain they are intent on climbing and are particularly capable at navigating steep and difficult terrain. Good at taking the initiative and forging ahead, they see what needs to be done and do it. They are not afraid of hard work – they are probably the most hard-working sign of the zodiac – plus they recognise where to make an effort to gain maximum benefits. They are renowned for being ambitious and like to excel at whatever they undertake. Their progress is made through steady, careful endeavour and they are prepared for the long slog to accomplish their goals. Unlike some, they are not after instant gratification or reward and know that something worth achieving takes time.

Gifted when it comes to strategy, Capricorns don't waste their energy on unproductive activity. Although they appear to have a game plan, actually they may not, even though the end result looks so impressive that others imagine it was an orchestrated campaign trail. They instinctively follow the advice of the top chess players, 'before making each move, assess the position of the pieces on the board and then make the best possible move'. So at each stage, Capricorns reconsider their options in the light of what has gone before, rather than steaming ahead regardless. This way, they adjust their course but never lose sight of their objectives.

Capricorns have an innate sense of moral obligation that extends way beyond all the things that they feel incumbent to do. Not only do they make themselves liable for others but they also adopt a position of global responsibility and act from this standpoint in all that they do. They set an example in 'right living'. When young, these feelings can sit heavily on their shoulders and they can seem overly serious and earnest. What is initially a burden lightens with maturity. In their youth they can seem old and staid for their years, with the weight of the world bearing down on them, while in older age they are youthful and lively in comparison with the strength and experience to make light of their responsibilities. By the time they reach their fifties, most are in their prime, with considerable success behind them. This is a sign that ages well.

With their natural command, Capricorns do best when they are in charge. They wield influence modestly and discreetly and are rarely found acting in a heavy-handed way. More than any other sign, they recognise the difference between having authority and being authoritarian. The former is something they can command because they are respected while the latter is something imposed through might and intimidation.

Others sense that Capricorns can be relied on, so tasks and duties tend to get heaped upon them, and because they fulfil these chores in a painstakingly responsible way, the whole cycle is perpetuated. This means others grow to depend on them, although eventually they become proficient at protecting their own interests and deflecting unwanted, onerous requests.

Although they are innovative, Capricorns do not like to take chances and carefully hedge their bets. Failure is not an option, so they only take calculated risks, ones that are guaranteed to pay off (some would argue this is not a real risk). It means that they make their way through life chalking up successes. They are legends when it comes to putting in the required work, which is partly because of their responsible attitude and partly because they absolutely have to succeed. They have a terrible fear of failure and try to make sure they don't ever have to suffer it. In many ways, they already feel so inadequate inside (not that they are in actuality) that any real external defeat is unbearable.

Capricorns probably have the most ferocious internal critic of all the signs in the zodiac. They are their own worst enemy, always judging themselves to be lacking and demanding more. They expect excellence as a matter of course and beat themselves up when they are unable to achieve this. No one is harder on them than they are. Never truly satisfied, they always look at how they could improve and evaluate their efforts in a harshly objective way.

This judgemental attitude is focused on others, too. Capricorns quickly see the shortcomings and failings of others and point these out, albeit in a polite manner. Whatever they are doing, they like to do it 'properly' and firmly believe that there is a correct way of going about things. To them, people often seem careless and slack. Because they set themselves such high standards, they can be flabbergasted when others clearly don't and produce sloppy work or offer substandard service. They are genuinely affronted and feel personally insulted – even attacked – by the gall, as they see it, of the offending person.

Not surprisingly, given the standards they expect themselves to live up to, Capricorns tend to suffer from anxiety. This is often endemic in their life, so affects everything, not just the really important things where some anxiety is to be expected. Catching a train or a plane can become a highly stressful activity, where every possible eventuality that could go wrong is imagined and covered. They allow so much slack in their schedule that they end up with hours to spare at the station or airport. This 'better safe than sorry' attitude can drive those around them quietly potty – they fail to see that this is not how everyone wants to live their life and that, for some, missing the occasional train or flight is infinitely preferable to the stress involved in getting to their departure point so early.

While Sagittarius sees a half-filled glass as half full, for Capricorn it's always half empty. They take nothing for granted. Their imagination is very active in the doom and gloom stakes. They have contingency plans for events that never cross the minds of other less anxious folk. They are the world's expert at 'what if . . .'. In their minds, they can then protect themselves from all kinds of possible pitfalls by taking preventative action before it ever happens. By imagining what might go wrong they feel they have some control over it and can stop it from occurring. While this clearly works for them, it's at some cost to their peace of mind and can create anxiety in those around them who were previously blissfully ignorant of all the disasters waiting to happen.

Capricorns' inner landscape is full of shoulds and oughts. Their fierce inner critic has strict ideas about what constitutes correct and proper behaviour. Even in a relaxed situation, such as a dinner party with close friends, they worry about keeping everyone's glass topped up, the food being ready on time, the right cutlery being offered and that there are sufficient serving utensils. They react as if any of these not being in place constitutes a disaster, which can make the occasion far from relaxed for them and those closest to them. While the particulars vary in individual ·Capricorns, they all suffer from these inner strictures. These inevitably restrict them and limit them to a life lived in a prescribed way. In their mind, life would be far more pleasant if everyone abided by these rules. For them, it's simply about being courteous and appropriate. They have a keen awareness of class, social conventions and hierarchies and generally accept them as useful and necessary. Not individuals to buck the system, they assume their place in mainstream society. Any rebellion they might feel is expressed from within the system, by attempting to bring about change, rather than from the margins.

With their strong social conscience, Capricorns believe that if everyone behaved as they do the world would be a better place. In this they may well be right but they overlook important concepts like the freedom of the individual. At worst, their world resembles a police state where living within the prescribed laws is paramount.

Like all the earth signs, Capricorns often have a materialistic streak as they value physical comfort and financial security. They recognise earlier than most that things don't come cheap and are among the first of their peers to buy their own home, striving to pay off the mortgage in the shortest possible time as they hate debts of any kind. Throughout life they make shrewd financial decisions and while not all are wealthy, they'll have accrued assets and have some savings and a pension. The exceptions to this are those who are due to inherit substantial sums, as this distorts their relationship to money somewhat and their sense of responsibility may be to their family heirlooms.

Capricorns' taste, whether in dress, furniture or cars is for traditional and classic designs that announce their standing and status. They appreciate quality and are prepared to pay for things that will last, as long as they are good value. With furniture, their preference may be for antiques, whose value is almost certain to increase. So the pieces they buy are both practical and investments. With cars, while they may like the old classic models, these can be a tad impractical – unless they're a mechanic or an enthusiast. If they can afford it, they'll buy new and top of the range in a discreet and tasteful colour – a black Daimler, BMW or Rolls-Royce for instance.

With clothes, if Capricorns have the money they'll buy from a good traditional designer or made-to-measure but otherwise classic cuts from chain stores like Marks and Spencer suffice. Those who are harder up might visit the wholesalers or a warehouse sale, where they can find a bargain or get two for the price of one, saving shopping time as well as money. Wherever their clothes come from, they manage to look distinguished.

When it comes to relationships, Capricorns like to take their time and won't be rushed into anything. The traditional courtship rituals surrounding a relationship are important to them, as it offers them a slow, steady and established way of getting to know a prospective partner before they get too romantically involved. More than most signs, they like to meet their lover's parents, friends and social circle, too. While this may seem endearing, it's also because they want to assess the person they are getting involved with from this broader perspective. So while romantic weekends away are part of the 'getting to know you' process, they're not going to allow themselves to fall in love unless all the pieces of the jigsaw fit. They want a partner who is an asset to them throughout their life and unless this looks likely, they won't take the plunge.

Capricorns are by nature both conservative and traditional, so, if they're heterosexual, once they've found the right person, they'll want marriage, followed by children. And for this reason, a gay relationship can be more problematic for them, as it is outside of mainstream society. They like to fit in, so unless they work and socialise in a predominantly gay culture, they're likely to suffer from feeling different. Whatever their sexual orientation, they want a shared home, stability and security and they'll expect the finances to be in place before they embark on this, so the courtship could be lengthy.

As parents, Capricorns have an overriding concern with their offspring's safety, which is often judged from a practical and material perspective. It is extremely important to them to provide for the children's needs. Their offspring are offered all the advantages that money can buy. However, Capricorns' high levels of anxiety do not make for a relaxed domestic atmosphere and they can be rather restrictive. They are hot on education and, if they can afford to, send their children to private schools, because of the social advantages this can provide. If this is not an option, then extra-curricula activities that offer this are encouraged.

Much of Capricorns' own ambitions get channelled into their children, so the children will have a lot to live up to. In particular, Capricorns have academic ambitions and later career expectations which older children may well kick against. This can be a painful process for both. Young children, who appreciate the security of a tight grip, do better with this rather controlling kind of parent than do teenagers, who are attempting to make their mark on the world and to assert their own identity.

At this stage, the Capricorn parent may need help to back off. They desperately want to be able to pass on the lessons that they have learned, so being forced to watch their children make mistakes can be quite unbearable. And, of course, this is something all children have to go through for themselves. They can also find it hard to deal with a teenager's rebellious phase, when it seems as if all their values are diametrically opposed. If they want anything, it's that their children inherit their values. However, the more fulfilled the Capricorn parent is and the more they have achieved the things that really matter to them, then the more psychological space there is for their children.

Typically, Capricorns rise steadily through the ranks and come to the peak of their chosen career or profession in their forties or fifties. Often found with their own company or working within large corporations or institutions, they have great respect for the hierarchical order found within these large organisations. If anyone is going to work their way up from being the post person to becoming a director, it's them. That way, they have hands-on experience of the company and feel qualified to make the decisions that affect others.

Qualifications are important to Capricorns. They place great store on being properly trained to do their job, whatever that is. They never play it by ear or risk learning on their feet and prefer to be over, rather than under, prepared for a task. When starting a new job they expect to be properly inducted and will complain if they aren't given sufficient time and information to do the work required of them.

If they have the intellect and the financial support, then Capricorns go to university. Not, like Sagittarius or Gemini, because of the love of learning but because they see it as a useful and necessary step in life, in order to get on. They choose their degree topic carefully, with its practical applications in mind. While some signs might do a degree that has no bearing on their future career, Capricorns would see that as indulgent and a waste of time as they want theirs to be of use to them. Provided it helps their career, they'll go on to take a Masters degree and often end up with a string of other diplomas and certificates. Even if they are doing a course for a hobby, they'll opt for the one that offers a piece of paper at the end. This serves as proof, to them, that they are competent. They rely on test and exam results for this, not trusting any form of self-validation.

Tangible proof is important to Capricorns. This is a sign that tends to think in concrete ways and hasn't much time for the less tangible aspects of life. Their reality is solid, rather than airy-fairy or nebulous. They look for scientific explanations for any weird phenomena that they might encounter. Statistics impress them and confirm to them the truth of certain matters. They believe that measurements and facts count and define reality and they trust their senses, touch, sight, hearing, smell and taste, to inform them of what's what. Anything beyond this is dismissed.

This means that Capricorns are cautious and judicious. They make their decisions slowly after carefully weighing up the pros and cons of a situation. They consider and ponder. At times, this can frustrate those who are more spontaneous, but what they fail to realise is that whereas they can afford to make plenty of mistakes, Capricorns can't. Or at least, this is how they feel and because of this, and their careful deliberations, they rarely put a foot wrong. Every move they make is calculated, which means they don't waste time or effort on something that doesn't yield results.

Careers that particularly suit Capricorns are those that involve facts and where right and wrong are clearly divided and demarcated. The law, for instance, where the rules are laid out, and the police and the armed forces, where the good guys and bad guys are theoretically well defined. Capricorns are deeply reassured by this apparent order, take their responsibilities seriously and carry them out meticulously.

The sciences equally suit Capricorn, where again there is verifiable data and clear yardsticks by which to measure things. They make good pharmacists, mathematicians, botanists, biologists and zoologists. Their earthy side means they're not squeamish and enjoy nature, so there's a wide range of sciences that can appeal to them and some work in these arenas in a less highly-specialised way.

Whatever work they do, Capricorns enjoy situations where the rules are clearly defined, so they know where they stand. This not only keeps their anxiety at bay, but this structure and order confirms to them that the world is a safe place.

While Capricorns are conservative in concept they can be innovative in method. After university or training, many go on to run their own companies and when setting up, they prefer to begin small and grow in an organic way, rather than borrow a lot of money with all the risks that entails. They are proactive in looking for business leads as they expect to create their own breaks rather than have these handed to them. Their mixture of ambition, practicality and patience bears fruit. Their impressive achievements, and the life they create for themselves, comes from this inner drive and fortitude.

As an employer, Capricorns expect dedication and hard work from their employees. Respect for the company rules, whatever they are, is paramount. Punctuality is essential and doing things by the book is required. Innovation is not particularly encouraged in employees; if anyone is going to bring about change it's going to be the boss, in his time and his way. He expects employees to stay in their jobs for the long haul, too. However, if employees don't show the kind of respect that is expected of them they'll quickly get their marching orders. This boss won't tolerate insubordination.

Whether male or female, as the boss Capricorns can be

quite paternalistic in the way they look after employees. They'll see their staff as a company resource and invest in them. Staff training is a priority and of a high standard. Permission to take external courses is looked upon favourably, provided it's clearly advantageous for the work. The fringe benefits that the Capricorn employer has in place are good, too, such as private health cover and an excellent pension scheme. All in all, employees are going to feel valued working for such a boss, as long as they work hard and fulfil their side of the bargain.

With Capricorn, there's little pretence. This is a sign that, if anything, sells itself short. These are reliable, no-nonsense kind of individuals, who never pretend to be better than they are. Their drive for success means much of their energy goes into their work, nevertheless, when it comes to a partnership they are loyal, committed and reliable. As with everything else, they take love and relationships seriously.

Capricorn exemplifies the stiff upper lip characteristic of the British. Their feelings and passion are a closely-guarded secret and only those who pass the test ever get an inkling of these. Once over the threshold and part of their private and intimate circle, the depth and complexity of these individuals becomes evident. While the surface may be very proper, what lies beneath is a vulnerable soul, who is all too aware of his or her Achilles heel and doesn't want this seen by the whole world. Those who are close are expected to join them in a conspiracy of silence and never reveal to others Capricorn's insecurities. This is the pact. Honour it.

Negative Capricorn

Capricorns don't have an easy life and much has already been mentioned that could be perceived as rather negative. However, the really negative characteristics only apply to those who have not grappled with their demons.

While, for the average Capricorn, their youth is spent feeling old beyond their years and later life is comparatively easier, the opposite is true for those who do not rise to the challenge. Those who attempt to avoid their innate ambition and responsibility can end up failing. By attempting to have an easier ride in life they miss the inherent opportunities of this sign. They skip the lessons that they are meant to be acquiring in their youth and do not then develop the skills needed. A Capricorn who is still on the bottom rung in mid-life will be resentful and unfulfilled.

Most Capricorns suffer from anxiety but for some it can become so crippling that they fail to achieve their full potential. There's a saying that in order to succeed one has to be able to risk failure. Those who can't cope with the possibility of failing will only go after things, like jobs and relationships, where success is more or less certain. Success is limited and defined by the risks they are prepared to take. When they don't feel they have a chance, they don't put themselves through the ordeal of losing. Some might think this is a good strategy, but those who never dare go out on a limb and stretch themselves don't know where their limitations lie and such Capricorns never put themselves to the test. They stay within a comfort zone, peeping out and scared of the risks they see others taking. The extent of their options is just too overwhelming to contemplate. They prefer to create narrow parameters and be content with success within these. If anyone is going to be on a traditional career path, whereby they move up the ladder in incremental steps every two years, it's a super-cautious Capricorn.

While there may not appear to be anything wrong with this, the Capricorn in question knows they were made for bigger and better things and feels a failure. Even those who appear successful know in their heart that they've sold themselves short. They recognise they've been crippled by their fears and in later life can feel bitter at the lost opportunities.

Not surprisingly, Capricorn's anxiety levels can have severe repercussions in their relationships. In order to manage their anxiety they may try to control loved ones, to stop them from doing anything that creates more anxiety for them. Partners can then feel blamed for the stress, as if they are the cause of it rather than inadvertently triggering it. While all relationships involve give and take, Capricorns can often expect a mate to adjust to them and their needs. Partners can feel as if they are being stifled and may object to the limitations placed upon their freedom and autonomy.

Capricorns can present an extremely coherent and convincing argument as to why their analysis of a situation is right and why others should see things their way. They can utterly fail to see that their take is distorted by their own acute anxieties. Rather than own these, which would be unbearable, they are projected out onto others who are held responsible.

For instance, in a domestic situation, maintaining a spotless and tidy home is essential for some Capricorns, as it helps them to feel in control. If a partner occasionally leaves the place in a mess, perhaps because they're tired, Capricorn can experience it as a deliberate and provocative attack designed to upset them. Their partner is made entirely responsible for the difficult feelings Capricorn has about the mess, whereas some reflection on why untidiness causes them such distress may not go amiss. Capricorns can then adopt an almost tyrannical position, believing they are fully justified in their behaviour. Loved ones are expected to tiptoe round them and, above all, never to step on their Achilles heel. Of course, a degree of sensitivity is normal in a relationship, as no one deliberately sets out to hurt their loved one but Capricorns may go way beyond that in the extent to which they disown their pain and accuse their loved one of some dreadful crime.

Capricorns tend to believe that there is only one reality

and they have hold of it. They refuse to recognise that other realities may exist and that one doesn't have to invalidate the other. In this regard, they have a lack of respect for others.

Much of these difficulties come from Capricorns' denial of their feelings. They can take an overly-pragmatic view of their inner world and don't accept that they have a part to play in processing their own uncomfortable emotions. They may be at a considerable loss as to how to do this – tears may not come easily – and they then look for a practical, concrete solution. Undealt-with emotions can build up to eventually produce physical symptoms, so that the body then is the medium by which they have to deal with their by-now concretised feelings. Illness and aches and pains are more acceptable – because they are tangible – than vague and insubstantial things like feelings.

In other ways, the Capricorn stance is the opposite of being in denial. Their take on reality is often rather stark and grim, with little by way of escapism. Unlike some, they don't harbour high hopes or expect a lucky break. They are rather pessimistic, which they'd claim is based on their experiences of life. They expect to have to work hard for everything they get and it could be argued that this then becomes a self-fulfilling prophecy. Those who are close can find Capricorns' negative attitude limiting and frustrating.

If there's one phrase Capricorn needs to learn it's that 'It may never happen'. Those exhibiting the more negative characteristics worry about almost everything and this fear permeates all that they do. Because they are so acutely aware of what can go wrong and have all the horror stories of what's gone wrong for others in the past, they constantly have to negotiate these possible imminent disasters. This can be crippling, inhibiting their lifestyle and those around them.

This kind of Capricorn parent foresees accidents for their child at every turn. The child is about to stand up and strike his head on the sharp corner of the table; he will fall off the slide or the climbing frame; he will get run over when he crosses the road; he will drown when he goes swimming. The list is endless and will curtail this poor child's confidence in his own abilities, filling him with his parent's anxiety. Such a child is likely to rebel big-time when he hits adolescence and yet, because of all the scaremongering, may well not be as safe in the world as one whose parents have fostered a more confident attitude.

What lies behind all this worry in Capricorn could be seen as unconscious aggression. Perhaps because they have such a tight hold on themselves, and feel obliged to behave properly at all times, their aggressive feelings have no legitimate outlet. Certainly psychologists would view the imagining of accidents as an unconscious wish for something bad to happen. This may be quite hard to unravel, as in Capricorns' mind this is farthest from the truth, yet because it's their fantasy they have to take some responsibility for it. For those who are struggling with these kinds of crippling fears, some professional help with a counsellor might come in useful.

Capricorns do have a tendency to be melancholic. They take life seriously and have a sober, solemn outlook but can also become downright morose. And because, as they see it, this is a reaction to their circumstances, rather than an inner state, they can get quite stuck in this mode. In order for this to change, they have to realise that they participate in and help to create their reality. It's not a black and white thing, it's their subjective view and someone else would see the same situation in an entirely different light. So for instance, a short illness can be viewed as entirely negative but it can also be seen as an opportunity to have a few days in bed, which may be just what was needed. The illness came along and legitimised resting. Capricorns' belief system, while great at seeing the downside, is not much good at looking at the positives.

What Capricorn is good at is looking at the opportunities that others have found and spotting the pitfalls – which is why they make good lawyers. They'll look at the small print and find a dubious clause. They'll see when the figures don't add up. Others just have to be aware that they can also be a wet blanket, putting out their flames of enthusiasm.

Capricorns are often low on self-confidence and, in order to buoy this up, many garner an impressive array of qualifications. Where this can be problematic is when they don't trust those who haven't got all the requisite bits of paper. They rely so exclusively on external validation that they rule out those who don't have this, as if they must be inferior. Even within the qualifications, they'll know which are the best to have, which are 'proper' and which are not. In their mind they'll be graded and categorised, according to a certain hierarchy that has a snobbish connotation. They don't realise that their way could be seen as fear based and that others may not need to take this route.

Some Capricorns have a definite elitist streak, which is then reflected in all kinds of ways, including their clothes and lifestyle. Much of what they do or buy is done to make a statement and to impress those who matter. It could be seen as another manifestation of their inner critic, who metaphorically sits on their shoulder and judges their activities from a rather pretentious point of view. While they don't generally splash their money around and might question the excesses of high fashion, the rarefied atmosphere of haute couture, with its 'rules' and competitiveness and even the bony models and their self-denial is one example which can nevertheless appeal. Such a Capricorn has a unique way of being loudly understated.

More typically, Capricorns can be rather mean, both with themselves and with others. They are known for spending an amazing amount of time shopping around before they buy virtually anything and think that anyone who doesn't do the same is foolish and negligent. Impulse buying genuinely horrifies them, as does the idea of being ripped off.

Domestically, Capricorn can run their home rather like

a boot camp, with chores designated to the various family members, which they are expected to fulfil with military precision. There is much discipline and order in such a family and the conditions can be harsh. The heating may be kept deliberately low and if anyone dares to complain, they are told to put another sweater on. Again, fear is behind this, possibly fear of poverty or of being too lax.

In such a family, a child with a bad cold hoping to get the day off school will be told briskly to 'Get washed and dressed and see how you are then'. A bit later they'll be told to, 'Try going to school and if you get any worse, come home'. They are pushed to do more than they want, because Capricorn may be afraid that this is the beginning of a slippery slope and they can't risk being soft. They are afraid of their own weaknesses (as they see them) and their coping strategy is to try even harder to overcome things, so they expect others to do the same.

As a new parent, Capricorns may still expect the household to run as smoothly as before and won't want any 'excuses'. Some Capricorns – men in particular, but not exclusively – are accused of being cold, selfish, hard and mean and it's not difficult to see why. While they have their nose to the grindstone, working long hours to succeed, they can seem oblivious to those close to them and a partner can feel as if they are bringing up the children virtually alone (although provided for materially). Even when they are at home, they can be so preoccupied with their work that they hardly communicate and somehow manage to make loved ones feel that their worries or concerns are trivial in comparison to their own.

Capricorns have a tendency to become workaholics. Their life can be extremely lopsided with their relationship, children and friends all being sidelined in favour of work. They are driven individuals, which brings them success, status and recognition and they can come to value this above anything else. They become attached to the position they occupy in their profession and dependent upon it to shore up their sense of self. This is not simply an ego trip but deeper and more fundamental than that. They make a virtue out of something many would see as a failing, in their desire to compensate for an inner lack.

If anyone is going to be in the grip of the Protestant work ethic it's Capricorn, and from this standpoint they also judge others as lazy. They're slow to recognise that their way of working lacks balance and some of the *inner* feelings of inferiority that drives them get conveniently transmuted to others, who feel inadequate in comparison.

Partners, in particular, get manoeuvred into the role of the inefficient and unsuccessful, so Capricorn can feel in control. When the Capricorn in question is male, his work ethic is seen as right and a partner, expecting more emotional support and involvement, is seen as overly needy and demanding. Capricorn women can be just as workaholic but a male partner is less likely to complain or feel marginalised. Even so, there is a price to pay and her relationship suffers; it's just that she may not be challenged by a male partner to establish a healthier balance in her life.

Capricorns' rather naked ambition can create mistrust in others, too. Work colleagues wonder what their agenda is when they are treated well and suppose there's some shrewd move afoot – they may not be far wrong. Capricorns can be so pointedly focused on furthering themselves that they fail to recognise how this influences their choice of friends and there can be an expectation that friends should be useful to them in some way, so that pragmatic considerations and duties muddy the waters. Friends be warned! It's important never to be helpful in this way, as it will eventually undermine the *raison d'être* of the friendship.

The sense of duty that Capricorns have can create a biased take on other matters, especially within the family. Because they hold and honour the idea of family responsibilities, they assume that others should share this way of thinking and carry out their duties relentlessly too. In their minds, old age is payback time for all they've done for their children and grandchildren when they were younger and even if others don't share this view Capricorns are adept at arousing feelings of guilt in those around them. They are quick to accuse family members of failing in their duties and once on this high moral ground, they can be damning and lacking in charity to others' ways of being.

However judgemental Capricorns are towards others, remember they are ten times worse when it comes to themselves. They set themselves such high standards that they frequently – in the main – fail in their own eyes. So, the task of their nearest and dearest is not to be intimidated by their ferocious standards, to be content to fail the impossible tests they set and to demonstrate that other realities do exist. Theirs isn't the only way of doing things and the world doesn't fall apart when things are done differently. If Capricorn can just get a glimpse of this, even if they can't hold onto it for long, they will be liberated from the tyranny of their impossible criteria.

All of Capricorns' difficulties could be seen as emanating from their harsh inner critic. This mellows over time but loved ones can assist the process by offering them plenty of unconditional love. And keep in mind that, like a good wine, this is a sign that invariably improves with age. Especially if they have been successful, they will finally feel, in later years, that they have earned the right to enjoy the fruits of their labours. So for those who have become involved this one is well worth going the distance with.

The Capricorn Man

The Capricorn man is recognisable by the authority he exudes and by his distinguished manner. Whatever his actual position in life, he has an important air about him and readily commands the respect of those around him.

He looks and acts as if he knows what he is talking about (unless he does, he doesn't venture an opinion). This is a man who has obvious prestige and standing, which he conveys through the way he conducts himself.

It's the Capricorn man's gift to be concise. He's a man of few, well-chosen words and he doesn't believe in spelling things out. They're not secretive, just not forthcoming with what they regard as unnecessary information or chat. And they particularly dislike being asked for reassurance.

The Capricorn man is quietly understated and self-contained. He's noticed for what he does and for the esteem that those who know him bestow on him. He stands out because those around him clearly defer to him and this is something he manages to attract just by his presence. Those who observe him are surprised by how complete strangers turn to him for directions, assuming he knows the way and waiters serve him sooner than others.

The Capricorn man is well dressed, his clothes reflecting his success and position in life without being in any way ostentatious. They show quality and prestige and are well made and superbly finished. His taste and styling is usually conservative and fairly traditional. Perhaps what is most impressive is that everything about him is impeccable. Even when casually dressed, his clothes are recently dry-cleaned or freshly laundered, his shoes are polished, his nails are neatly clipped and he uses expensive after-shave. He smells and looks good. He takes an obvious male pride in his appearance and has an awareness that this matters.

From a young age others looked to the Capricorn man to deal with problems and manage things; hence he grows up thinking he's meant to be in charge. This is likely to be recognised and rewarded later in life with a position of real authority and quite probably the pay packet to go with it. Whatever work he does it's likely to include managing others.

The responsibilities the Capricorn man readily shoulders have both pluses and minuses when it comes to relationships.

He's very much a masculine man, who expects to be in charge, make the decisions and pay the bills. Conservative with a small c, he upholds traditional family values and has expectations along these lines when it comes to partnerships. There is a clearly defined role into which his partner is expected to slot.

The Capricorn man's dependable, practical stance makes him attractive to those who are looking for someone they can rely on. He is very good at being a loved one's rock – their anchor. Unquestionably reliable and steadfast, if anything he's overly serious and never takes others' feelings flippantly. However, when it comes to a relationship he is looking for someone who will be an asset to him in some way. This could be financially. There are several reasons why he might find a very wealthy partner particularly attractive. This may not be conscious on his part and it may not be something he's actively seeking but, if someone he meets happens to be rich, it could enhance his interest.

If the Capricorn man is heterosexual, then he could also go for a partner who is an asset to him socially and professionally – a kind of trophy wife but with practical overtones; one who is not only beautiful but a sophisticated hostess, for instance. This isn't to imply that he's mercenary, because it's not as deliberate as that, it's just that he's always looking ahead to his future and how that will pan out. After all, if he's half way up a mountain, and intent on getting to the top, he needs to hook up with someone who's a help rather than a hindrance. So his ambition influences his choice of mate.

This scenario applies less when the Capricorn man in question is gay, as his partner is then not so likely to play a socially useful role for him. Unless he moves in exclusively gay circles, he is going to experience more conflict about his sexuality than most signs, because Capricorn has such a strong need to conform to the status quo and fit in. It's harder to achieve the respectability he craves as a gay man.

So, pragmatic considerations influence the Capricorn man's choice of mate. He may also be class and status conscious, in fact he can be snobbish, but his underlying need is to find someone who is of benefit to him. For these reasons, he doesn't declare his interest in another immediately. Sexual attraction is not enough. Courtship can be protracted while he works out whether or not this is the one for him. He takes his time, not just because he wants to be sure, but because he can't bear rejection. He's looking for a definite green light before he proceeds.

However, once the Capricorn man has made up his mind and set his sights on a prospective partner he moves in a decisive way. Notwithstanding his fear of rejection, he wines and dines in a way that's bound to sweep anyone off their feet. He's a man of the world and knows which restaurants to go to, which concerts, plays and films have got the best reviews and where the most interesting exhibitions are being held. When it comes to culture, he's well informed. And when it comes to things like booking tickets, finding a recommended hotel, sorting out itineraries, he's efficient and capable. He excels in all practical matters and enjoys playing this traditional masculine role.

Despite the Capricorn man's apparent suave sophistication, he's often not that experienced when it comes to the bedroom. He's been too busy chalking up successes in other areas. He's often shy and hesitant when it comes to making sexual moves. A prospective partner may find that all a bit puzzling, since earlier on – say having dinner in a restaurant – he'll appear masterful and in control.

Although he has strong desires the Capricorn doesn't become sexually involved until he feels a degree of certainty about the person concerned. Sex is not something he initiates casually as he recognises the emotional vulnerability implicit with sexual contact and the potential consequences for himself and his partner afterwards. All of this speaks well of him and shows a respectful attitude towards a partner. Depending on his age, he's more likely to have had a few long-term serious relationships than several short ones. So he has experience of intimacy and involvement and proof that he's not commitment-phobic.

Like all the earth signs, Taurus and Virgo being the other two, the Capricorn man is extremely sensual, comfortable in his own skin and so makes a surprisingly good lover. This is where he proves that experience isn't necessarily what counts, as what he has to offer is a sensitivity and awareness of the body. Once involved, he's tactile and uses touch automatically in a way that is reassuring to his partner. Unlike some signs, who cuddle and caress only as a part of foreplay, he genuinely enjoys physical contact for its own sake and it doesn't necessarily have to lead to sex. He does have a strong sexual appetite, though, and this becomes the foundation upon which the relationship rests.

His earthiness means that the Capricorn man is extremely accepting when it comes to the body and is not looking for physical perfection in a partner. He may not be a perfect specimen himself and he can cope with another's flaws and foibles. Once involved, this can be wonderfully liberating for his partner, who even if initially chosen for their beauty, is not judged by these criteria in the bedroom. Any hang-ups they may have diminish in such an atmosphere and they can relax and unwind.

Tactile contact is also something the Capricorn man seeks. He can get very wound up and needs help in releasing the knots in the muscles in his shoulders and generally in switching off at the end of the day. He appreciates a shoulder rub or foot massage – it all helps him come back into his body when he's become cut off and estranged from himself throughout his day. Which is something he does rather a lot. His high levels of anxiety coupled with his need to achieve the nigh impossible make him a prime candidate for muscle tension. A prospective partner would do well to suggest he has a regular professional massage – it will pay dividends in all sorts of ways.

The Capricorn man is possessive and can be jealous. He expects absolute commitment and won't countenance anything less. Once he has found his mate he'll be thinking about permanence and if he's heterosexual, this will mean marriage. He's not a modern man in this respect. He expects to financially support a wife, to have children and a traditional family life. He also expects to make decisions that affect his family as a whole and may not see the partnership as equal. If he's asked to discuss everything he'll get annoyed and may simply not comply. Not to be deliberately awkward but because making decisions that affect others comes naturally to him. That's an intrinsic part of who he is.

Despite his protestations to the contrary, the Capricorn man won't pull his weight domestically. He has no idea. He'll do what he thinks is his fair share, which, in keeping with most men, comes nowhere near. Only he thinks he *is* doing his bit and won't take kindly to being told that he's not. Basically, he is best at supervising. The deal is lopsided but he does much in other areas to compensate, for instance, he does do a great job organising the children's chores when they are old enough. Partners should make sure that they are happy with this kind of arrangement from the outset.

As a father, the Capricorn man is not usually hands-on in the beginning. He sees it as the mother's domain. He does get more proactive as his children grow up and is good at doing things with them, when they are of an age to enjoy activities. He'll play physical games with them in the park, take them to cultural pursuits and show a keen interest in their education.

The Capricorn man is a strict father. He has rules and he expects them to be respected. His children know clearly where the boundaries lie with him and he's consistent in this. He expects his partner to back him up in this at all times and, as his regime is usually eminently reasonable and sensible, that's not hard. Fortunately, he's not often prone to angry outbursts, being so self-controlled, and if he feels more then a remonstration is required, he'll discipline his children by the withdrawal of their privileges and in extreme situations, the withdrawal of his affection, becoming apparently cold and remote for a while. However, this is rarely necessary, as his innate authority means that he usually does have their respect. He secures their cooperation from an early age.

Depending on how successful or not he is, the Capricorn man may try to channel some of his own ambitions into his children. He can have an overly keen interest in their test and exam results, setting too much store by them. He finds it hard to deal with if his child isn't particularly bright or lacks ambition and wants to 'bum around'. He expects them to excel at something, if not academically, then artistically, dramatically, musically or as an athlete. He'll love them, no matter, but it pains him if they don't inherit his need to achieve. Having fought to get somewhere himself, it's tough if his values are rejected. In his mind this is simply a waste. The irony of this is that he's almost certainly where he is today because of his life experiences, rather than through a helping hand, but he can't bear not being able to then pass it all on.

That said, there is an argument that children thrive when parents weave fantasies around them and the Capricorn man certainly does that. He has a keen eye on their future. It's just that he may think of it in overly pragmatic terms and not recognise his children's need to have their own experiences.

The Capricorn man has always maintained a business-like approach and it's worked for him. He's likely to be doing very well. He makes prudent choices early on in life and, because he has staying power, he's well on his way to considerable success by the time his children come along.

He sees himself as the provider, a role which he fulfils admirably.

The Capricorn man is an interesting mixture, as although he plays safe, he also takes calculated risks. But more than anything, he gets to where he is through sheer hard work. He has a tendency to be a workaholic and this is especially so for those who are in management or who run their own businesses. He epitomises the self-made man, creatively and proactively daring but shrewd and careful at the same time. He'd never risk all. He's not one to raise a second mortgage on the house for a business venture, for instance. He protects his security and that of his family.

This kind of Capricorn man may have a problem come retirement age. He's probably convinced himself he has to work this hard to pay the bills and get his children through private education and university, yet even when the mortgage is paid and the children are off his hands, he finds it hard to stop. His identity is totally bound up with his work and he may have a crisis when he is no longer defined by what he does. Some manage to convince themselves that they can't afford to retire. While this will almost certainly not be true financially, it may be true emotionally.

The Capricorn man's reluctance to retire can be hard for a partner, who has been waiting for this golden age when they'll be free to enjoy themselves. Depending on what his work is (in some companies retirement is mandatory), this may never happen. He's lost without his work and if he is to make this transition, his emotional need to have status and a respected position within the community must be addressed and replaced with some kind of equivalent in the voluntary sector.

This is still a difficult transition for the Capricorn man. He may complain that the volunteers he now works along-side do not recognise him as an authority in the same way as his former employees. He feels the loss of his status acutely. His partner may also have to remind him that he no longer has a staff of six running around after him. It will take him a while to scale down his agenda to something one person can achieve in a day.

A partner may feel that they play second fiddle to the Capricorn man's work and that this is his priority in life. This may be partially true but he needs the constancy and support of his domestic life to enable him to go out and conquer the world. This is his foundation and they are essential to him. For his part, he is just an old-fashioned guy at heart, doing the traditional thing and doing it well. There's a lot to be said for the protective, paternalistic, dependable man who takes his family responsibilities seriously. Mel Gibson exemplifies this, married to the same woman for more than twenty-five years, with five children.

In case the Capricorn man sounds too staid or unexciting, this list of famous Capricorns will scotch that. Elvis Presley was the sexiest man of his time and not afraid to use sexuality in an explicit way not seen before to secure his place at the top of his profession. He could sing, too, but he may not have received the attention if he hadn't wriggled his pelvis. Denzel Washington, Nicolas Cage, Ralph Fiennes and Kevin Costner are all well-known actors, respected for their work, especially their professionalism. They all share an earthy presence and a groundedness that is typical of this sign.

Politician Martin Luther King and boxer Muhammad Ali are two other famous Capricorn men. Muhammad Ali also called himself 'the greatest' – something all Capricorns try hard for and some actually do succeed in becoming. While not all can accomplish what these men did, nevertheless all Capricorn men need to be the greatest in some sphere. For those who are involved, remind him often of what he's best at. Even, or especially, if it's making love.

The Capricorn Woman

The Capricorn woman can be recognised by her practical stance and down-to-earth attitude. This woman is eminently sensible and grounded and doesn't get in a flap easily. She takes life in her stride and has an ordered existence, whereby she prioritises those people and activities that are important to her and doesn't waste her time on trivialities.

Self-contained and quietly assertive, the Capricorn woman has the air of someone that means business and is intent on getting somewhere. From the word go she has goals, which she steadfastly pursues. She isn't easily distracted and works hard at whatever she has undertaken.

Annie Lennox, famous first as one half of the pop band the Eurythmics and later in her own right, exemplifies the Capricorn woman. She has a cool, restrained stage presence and often dresses in typically conservative, masculine clothes. Despite this she has a feminine allure that her suits somehow underline. Before deciding on a career in popular music, Lennox had been to music college, showing again a typical Capricorn trait of taking her talent seriously and initially at least, following a conventional path.

While not all Capricorn women dress in quite the severe style of Lennox, most do opt for classy, elegant cuts. On the whole they aren't slaves to fashion and neither do they like clothes that are revealing – or tarty, as they'd see it. Dolly Parton is an exception here, but even she acknowledges that her appearance is just this and the impression she gives is that this was a shrewd move to get noticed and sell more records. Typically, their dress sense can be a bit prudish. They have a unique way of being buttoned up yet sexy, which Capricorn Ava Gardner personified.

Preferring quality to quantity, the Capricorn woman goes for clothes that last because they're not going to date or fall apart. Her choice is practical and careful and she is not likely to pay over the odds either. She'll shop around and find great buys at a fraction of the price and greatly enjoy the idea of looking well dressed on a shoestring. Her clothes, like her whole demeanour, communicate that she is to be taken seriously.

So, unless the Capricorn woman can afford them easily, designer clothes are not for her: she doesn't see the point. However, there is also a socially ambitious type who will scrimp and save for an expensive piece of jewellery or some other status fashion item. She is dressing to impress.

Using another Capricorn ploy, Elizabeth Arden put make-up on the map, by making it a woman's duty to wear it. She managed to change its image from, at that time, being seen as common and unseemly to something that was a necessity, thereby guaranteeing sales for her products. A shrewd business plan based entirely on Capricornian principles.

The Capricorn woman is composed and assured and, at times, her quiet confidence can be a bit intimidating. It comes from her achievements, which are quite impressive. Her successes in life are what she expects of herself and she makes little of them but the more she acquires the higher her stature rises amongst those that know. The very fact that she pays no attention to her successes makes her all the more formidable to some.

Those who know her well know that the Capricorn woman does worry a lot. Because she sets herself such high standards, she gets stressed trying to reach and maintain them. She lives with an acute level of anxiety, her fear of failure never far away no matter how ridiculous this seems to others. There's a big gap between her impressive appearance and her doubt-ridden inner world. Her friends know of her insecurities and hear more about these than her successes. It is these doubts and insecurities that drive her – she has a lifelong struggle compensating for them.

Although the Capricorn woman takes herself and life seriously, she still has a great, if somewhat droll, sense of humour. For her, humour lies in the ironies of life, which she notes in a dry, almost throwaway, manner. She can poke fun at others' inconsistencies, too – especially the disparity between what they do and say. Her observational skills are acute and her wry comments understated, so others have to listen carefully if they are to catch what she has to say. In fact her wit is reserved for those she's close to and communicated as an aside as she never holds an audience or entertains. She leaves that for the more flamboyant signs.

The Capricorn woman is extremely capable and whether or not she's actually a feminist, her self-reliance and independence make her one in practice. She has no expectation that anyone should look after her. In fact she views the very notion as quite insulting as she considers she is perfectly able to take care of herself. Her pragmatic approach, along with her creative initiative means that she's often successful at what she does. And when she is it never goes to her head nor does she take it for granted. She remains careful and consolidates and builds upon her achievements.

Like all the earth signs, the Capricorn woman has a materialistic streak. Aware from an early age of the financial necessities of life, she's likely to have saved, even as a child. It's an inbuilt and automatic response. More than most, she is acutely aware of the importance of money to provide her with the stability and security that she needs. She'll have a pension in her twenties and chooses to buy her home, rather than rent, because to her it makes financial sense. She's accumulating assets not because she's empire building but in order to feel safe.

When it comes to a relationship, the Capricorn woman weighs up a potential partner carefully and doesn't rush in. However, despite the fact that she can seem quite materialistic, her criteria when it comes to a partner is not. She is looking for someone she can respect and trust, someone she can rely upon emotionally and practically, although not necessarily financially.

Capricorn

The Capricorn woman expects a proper courtship. She wants to be wined and dined and invited to stimulating and interesting social events. If no special effort is made, she'll not be impressed. She's definitely not the kind of woman to take to the local cinema or pizza place. The venue doesn't have to be expensive – she'll probably offer to pay her half anyway – but it needs to be classy.

If she's heterosexual, then initially the Capricorn woman pays attention to things like whether her beau is punctual, whether he's polite and well mannered – not just in relation to her but to others with whom she sees him interacting – and whether he extends to her the traditional common courtesies. A potential partner would do well to imagine this is an old-fashioned romance and follow the protocol of bygone years – read Jane Austen for tips. Much the same will apply if she's gay, although the roles won't be so clearly defined. Whatever her sexual orientation, she is still looking for someone she can trust to behave properly in public.

So, the Capricorn woman places great importance on manners. For her the saying 'manners maketh man' is still resonant. What manners represent for her is again something to do with her need for safety; things being as they are meant to be, everything in its place. It's all deeply reassuring to her. Someone ill-mannered would frighten her and threaten her stability.

Once this test is passed, the next hurdle that a prospective partner has to overcome is the Capricorn woman's general reluctance to get involved. She likes her own space and is in no hurry to lose that. She needs to see how being in a relationship with this particular partner can improve her life. This isn't necessarily materially, although it could be. It could also be the quality of life she'll have or the social contacts she'll gain. Whatever it is, she'll judge a partner in a pragmatic way. Unless there's something enticing on the table, she's not going to give up what she's got.

This may sound as if the Capricorn hasn't a romantic bone in her body and that she's completely calculating, which she'd understandably find deeply offensive. And it's not true. It's just that she takes the whole relationship business extremely seriously and once she's decided to go for it, that's it. It's only at that point that she allows herself to fall in love and she then expects her relationship to last. In some ways she's extremely romantic as she imagines that she'll only have one great love. Even if she ends up having more than one, as most modern women do, she never takes the possibility of love lightly. Her attitude could be seen as her wanting to make sure the 'love' seed is planted in good soil and has the chance to become established, rather than being wasted.

Having taken her time, the Capricorn woman does usually get it right and finds a partner that she wants to stay with. If she's heterosexual, she'll want marriage and probably a big, traditional, church wedding, too. Even if she's not ordinarily religious, she's likely to want to be married in the eyes of God, because to her that's about being married properly. After all, this is a woman for whom formality and ritual matter.

Once in a committed relationship, the Capricorn woman channels her drive into the relationship as well as into her career. Unless or until there are children, she'll continue to work and values her professional life. Despite the fact that she may be quite high-powered, she's also very willing to give it up as and when she has a child, if she can afford to. She doesn't see herself as being a superwoman or as having it all and prefers to devote herself to her offspring, at least for a time.

After all, in the Capricorn woman's pragmatic way of thinking, why go to work in order to pay someone else to enjoy the important role of bringing up her child? Equally, she feels keenly the awesome responsibility of caring for a child and is not comfortable handing them over to someone else.

Like everything the Capricorn woman does, she takes child rearing seriously and becomes an expert on the subject, reading the latest manuals. She also discovers she has very good instincts and gets better at listening to them. To some extent she has the baby books to reassure her that she's doing it right. She trusts an acclaimed authority on the subject more than she does herself, although as there are books backing up every imaginable way of bringing up a child, perhaps she chooses one that is in accord with her instincts.

The Capricorn woman is supremely well organised and is capable and competent in the way she manages her domestic life. Even if she's not running a stately home with dozens of servants, she brings something of that well-oiled machinery to her domestic set-up. She gives the impression that it's a job so therefore one she'll do efficiently. And somehow, magically, her children do behave themselves. Babies learn to sleep through the night very quickly and not because she deprives them in any way. There's something about her steady composure and ability to maintain consistent boundaries that enables those around her to settle down into her routine. She's reassured by it and subsequently so are they. Her home life is calm and ordered.

A partner can feel a bit like a spare part around the Capricorn woman's impressive organisation. Often their roles divide along traditional lines and the house is her domain, while the garden, if there is one, is up for grabs. She may well make that hers, too, although with young children to cope with that could prove too much. Later in life, when she has more time, then gardening may become a source of much pleasure and satisfaction to her. This is a woman that likes to keep busy; she'll always find something that needs doing. She may not be that restful to be around.

However the Capricorn woman's organisational skills are rather wasted on domestic life and most have a career waiting in the wings that's on hold while the children are young. This is something she'll want to get back to before too long and those around her need this as well. All that drive focused on family life can be too much. She needs the challenge of the workplace.

Not all Capricorn women choose to marry or to have children. Many remain single because the offer on the table is just not tempting enough. And not all choose this because they are super-successful. Any success they achieve may come quite late in life.

Women often take longer to find their way in their career and the Capricorn woman especially may be well into her forties before she really knows what she wants to be doing. However, the idea that she is going somewhere, even if she doesn't know where, is a driving force and without a partner or children she can pursue this a hundred per cent.

For some Capricorn women, the thought of taking a career break in order to have a child is too big a sacrifice. She has a realistic idea of what it will take from her and how it will affect her career. She may well be in a senior position and knows that with children, the strain of such a job will be difficult. It may not combine well with family life. This kind of high-powered executive, who does go on to have children, may manage to stick in her career for a while only to find it beginning to unravel by, say, the second child. Then she'll take a break and look for some other kind of less demanding, more family-friendly work afterwards. She's quite happy to re-train for this.

This kind of Capricorn woman is snapped up as a school governor and the like. Others recognise her skills and she is soon occupied in the voluntary sector. Provided this is financially an option and she can manage without her income, then it gives her the kind of status and responsibility within her community that she thrives on. Others may be surprised at how easily she makes this transition, thinking that she was attached to her high income, while in fact it was the prestige and standing and job satisfaction that really mattered to her. Especially if she has a partner who can maintain her, she doesn't necessarily need her own money.

As a 'kept woman' the Capricorn woman is still a huge asset to her partner, not least because she has a business brain and recognises the importance of his or her work. She instinctively knows about networking and in her charitable roles makes useful contacts that potentially benefit her partner's business. As a housewife, she provides anchorage for the whole family too, a role no longer fashionable but one at which she excels.

The Capricorn woman's career should never be written off, though, as even after a protracted period at home, she may suddenly produce her own business plan and develop a whole separate life. She is, ultimately, always going to need a job.

For those who are involved with her, never underestimate her strength of character and determination. However accepting she appears of her roles as wife, parent and house manager, her ambition will out in some way at some time. And if it doesn't, it's a dangerous thing, as it is then channelled through her partner or her children. This never ultimately satisfies her and is a burden for them. She needs her own success, status and recognition. Once that is in place, she's an astute and loyal friend and lover and partner.

The Capricorn Child

Capricorn children are recognisable by their drive and determination. They know from a surprisingly young age what they want to be when they grow up and, even though this may change over the years, it demonstrates how focused they are. These children have ambition. They're likely to stand and walk early, as they struggle to gain mastery over their muscles. Don't be surprised if they skip the crawling stage as, after all, being on all fours is not exactly dignified and their dignity is something that is important to them.

Capricorn children thrive in a household that has established routines. The more stability they have, the better. A ritualised going-to-bed procedure, such as a bath followed by a story, with a bedtime set in stone alongside meals at prescribed times throughout the day, are all deeply reassuring. They learn to rely on these daily rhythms, which give them a feeling of being in control of their life at a stage when they have it the least. This builds an inner confidence that life will sustain and support them that stands them in good stead.

Capricorn children are not, initially, brimming with confidence. This comes with their growing mastery over themselves and their world; it's built upon their experiences. Parents are advised never to push them to do something that they are not yet quite ready for. When young, they get anxious easily and can be highly strung. They aren't among those more reckless little ones who want to climb to the top of the climbing frame or go on the big slide just for the thrills. Unlike some, who terrify their parents, they see right away how far they have to fall and won't venture further than they can manage. So, parents do best by them when they can steer a path between encouraging and supporting them in their efforts while recognising and accepting that they may be fearful and hesitant.

Capricorn children are eminently practical and reliable and can be trusted to behave in a responsible way. They have a wise head on young shoulders and may seem much older than their years. This is a theme – of being mature for their age – which stays with them throughout their life. Parents understandably may want to make the most of this tendency, grateful that they have such a sensible child, but are advised not to exploit it. If anything, this offspring needs permission and encouragement to enjoy being young and carefree.

In particular, parents should steadfastly avoid piling additional responsibilities on to their Capricorn child. They take their duties extremely seriously and can readily feel weighed down by the cares of the world. These children have such a strict inner critic that parents must take care not to add to it. They constantly judge themselves, so parents can afford to be sparse with any criticisms and punishments. Merely pointing something out will more than suffice.

If it is a parental expectation, then everyday chores like putting away their toys, keeping their room tidy, doing their homework and contributing to the running of the house is done automatically by the Capricorn child. And if they slack off they'll feel ultra aware of their failing, so being chastised won't help and isn't necessary. What they need is some assistance if they aren't coping. They may be overwhelmed and struggling with more than they can manage.

Capricorn children expect a lot of themselves. At school, they work hard and are intent on getting the top grades. While this is admirable, it's also helpful if parents try to balance this tendency, by focusing on other aspects of their well-being. They can all too easily develop tunnel vision. By all means praise their exam results but also ask them how they enjoyed their day, who they played with and what they did in the school break and make this as important. Capricorn children need to feel loved for who they are, unconditionally, and not for what they may have achieved.

Capricorn children don't much like being different. They want to fit in and are particularly affected by peer pressures. Most children reach a point when they find their parents embarrassing, but for the Capricorn child, this can be at an early age and may be acute, particularly if they have parents who are in any way unusual. Even slightly wacky or radical or arty parents could be a source of excruciating shame for these children. They want their parents to be absolutely normal, conventional and traditional – all the things that they espouse to be.

As soon as they get to choose their own clothes, then Capricorn children may well show their conservative taste. Like all children, they'll be very influenced by their peers, wanting to fit in with whatever is in vogue. When grunge was all the rage, this was a hard look for them to achieve! They veer towards smart casual and go for dark colours and classic styles. They are among the minority who actually like having a school uniform, finding it reassuring to be told what to wear and knowing that they'll conform. And they'll keep it immaculate. Whatever they wear, they look well turned out.

Capricorn children show a keen interest in having money from an early age. They pester their parents for pocket money and expect an increase at each birthday – showing early signs of business acumen. Again, parents are advised to be firm and not to let themselves be railroaded into giving more than they want to or can afford. These offspring may offer to do additional chores for extra cash and they generally stay alert to opportunities to earn. They may have a specific purchase in mind that they're saving up for or they may simply like having cash in their pocket. Most accumulate considerable savings because they do not spend their money readily. They like to have it, not spend it.

Some Capricorn children show real enterprise and have an after-school or Saturday job but by and large they look to Mum and Dad to provide them with the money they need. Some want extra because it helps them to feel empowered. If a child seems to be getting obsessed with money, then it may be a good idea to give them more autonomy. If they feel more in control of their life in general, then money may become less important.

For older Capricorn children, reorganising how their money is allocated can help with their need to feel empowered. So, for instance, they can be entrusted with a clothes allowance that they control. No more money is actually spent but they get to manage the overall budget, which could be handed over weekly (in which case they'd have to save up for certain items), monthly or even quarterly.

Capricorn children enjoy practical tasks and can gain much satisfaction from pursuits like gardening, carpentry, metal work, cookery and sewing. All are productive, resulting in a finished product and all involve mastery over materials. Some of these activities can be encouraged at quite a young age as they enjoy being allowed to help parents and handling 'grown-up' equipment and tools.

At an even younger age, construction toys are particularly good for Capricorn children. They show an early interest in building, so wooden blocks, Duplo, Lego and later Meccano are all well suited to the budding engineer or architect. Make sure, too, that they have toys that involve making a mess, like sand play, modelling clay, paints. While parents may welcome the neatness of these children, it can be at the price of their creativity. Making a mess counteracts their tendency to be rather formal and correct and facilitates the development of their imagination.

Most teenagers, as part of their rebellion against the status quo, are untidy. The hormonal change that they are undergoing creates considerable internal chaos, which they demonstrate by the state of their rooms. Nevertheless, the teenage Capricorn is not usually that difficult to manage, because they are trying so hard to be adult. They take great pride in being responsible and grown-up and so, although they may be moody and grumpy, they're not out-and-out defiant or rebellious.

The Capricorn child may be acutely self-conscious as they go through the physical changes associated with adolescence, so some gentle encouragement won't go amiss. Some become excruciatingly shy. Generally this is a phase in which their self-doubts are most obvious and one in which their achievements don't count for much. If they are obviously suffering, parents can feel helpless, as there is nothing they can do and they simply have to bear witness to it. Reminding them of the story of the ugly duckling who was actually going to be a swan may not help. It's a rite of passage, which they'll come through.

At school, many of these shy awkward Capricornian teenagers rapidly progress to become prefects, head girl or boy. Some may have already been form captain or its equivalent. This is all just a taste of what's to come. In this context, among their peers, these early experiences of responsibility are bound to be helpful and character forming. Just make sure that they are always loved for being themselves and doing nothing in particular at home.

When it comes to specialising at school, the Capricorn child might consider science. They have a sceptical side that seeks verifiable proof, which is something all the sciences aim to establish. If they show aptitude, then chemistry, physics, mathematics and biology are all subjects that could be very useful to them in later life. However, there are many directions that the Capricorn child could follow, and a career in the sciences is only one of these.

Business studies, politics and economics are also good options for the Capricorn child. Many go into management or run their own companies, so this provides a good grounding. The law is another good option for them, whether they later work as a solicitor, barrister or in the police, this is an arena that suits their rational minds.

For those Capricorn children who show artistic talent, then sculpture and design are options that might suit them more than fine art, which can be too abstract for them. But this shouldn't be ruled out: the French impressionist, Paul Cezanne, was a Capricorn, after all. However, with their developed sensual awareness, they are best suited to working with shape and texture. Design, with its practical applications, is another good option.

Other areas in the arts, such as music, dance or theatre, may also appeal to the Capricorn child. Wherever there is aptitude it makes sense to foster it and their strong self-discipline will take them far. However, in these careers, which are by their nature more precarious, they may need encouragement and support to take such a risk. The rejections that they will inevitably be on the end of will be tough, so this is not an option for the faint-hearted. That said, there are numerous Capricorns who have excelled in these arenas.

Whatever they go on to do, parents should be prepared for the expense of further education. Those involved in the arts will almost certainly set out to go to music college, drama school or art college. If they are academically inclined, then most choose to go on to university. With their realistic outlook, they know at this age that they increase their options in life with further training or a degree. The only exceptions are those who are already showing entrepreneurial flair and can't wait to get started. But even this type may bide their time while they gain some business skills.

Whatever the Capricorn child goes on to do, they want to excel in it. These are empire builders in the making and may carry vast responsibilities on their shoulders in later life. Make sure they don't grow up too quickly and protect them from the cares of the adult world for as long as possible. Cherish them when they are irresponsible to help them keep that inner critical voice quiet and even-handed. Most of all let them know that they're loved even when they make mistakes. That way, they are given the best chance to get the most out of life.

11

Aquarius
The Water-bearer

January 20th to February 18th

A fixed air sign, ruled by Saturn and Uranus

Introducing Aquarius

Aquarians can be recognised by their breezy, detached and nonchalant manner. These are individuals with principles, who exhibit an independence of thought and have an opinion on most topics. With their very definite views, they have their own individualistic slant on life and, whether actively political or not, have a social conscience which comes into play in all their dealings with others. It underpins how they live their life and go about things.

This sign is represented by the water-bearer who brings drinking water for the benefit of everyone. In places where there is no running water, water-bearers still carry water to their families and villages to this day and fulfil a vital humanitarian role. Typically Aquarians are on a mission to improve the lot of others and set about doing this in diverse ways. Their focus is on the bigger picture and what will bring about the greater good and this overrides their personal needs. These are idealistic individuals who attempt to put into practice in some way their vision of a better world. They are frequently found passionately involved in issues that have implications for the wider community, such as the distribution of wealth, public transport policy, public rights of way, working hours and the like.

As their starting point, Aquarians prefer to take an overview of situations. They are more comfortable when they have some distance and perspective. By remaining separate they can think clearly and know where they stand. They take up a bird's-eye view position and like to think of themselves as unbiased and having objectivity. The idea that this may not actually be possible is foreign to them.

Aquarians are concerned with the truth and like to get to the heart of a matter, to discover what the veracity concerning it is. They believe in the existence of an objective and absolute truth, rather than relative truth. Always scrupulously above-board and fair individuals, they see honesty and openness as fundamental to a civilised society. In all their interactions with others candour is a basic expectation. They are never afraid to speak out and be counted and can lack tact, as the truth for them is always a much higher priority than how it is presented.

In common with the other two air signs, Gemini and Libra, Aquarians are particularly concerned with ideas and concepts. Intuitive and inventive, they are the great original thinkers and revolutionaries of this world and while not all will be intellectuals, most fairly crackle with mental energy and like nothing better than a stimulating discussion in which ideas get tossed around. Because their minds tend to leap ahead of what they are actually saying, their conversation can jump around and go off at a tangent, leaving those listening struggling to keep up with the flow of ideas.

Interested in a wide range of far-reaching topics, mental stimulation is the food of life without which Aquarians feel starved and stifled. They tend to spend a lot of time reading, computing and working with ideas, which can leave them over-stimulated and suffering from nervous tension. Physical exercise will help to release this, as will practical and creative activities like cooking and gardening. Anything that gets them out of their head can act as an antidote to their over-active brain.

Their restlessness is in part due to Aquarians' need for drastic change. Every so often they throw out the old order and create a new one that replaces what they have just destroyed. This is exciting and invigorating for them, as they are not sentimental or attached to their possessions and love to reorganise their life and invent new systems. For them, a major clear-out equals freedom from clutter. This is the sign of the revolutionary, be it in their thinking or in how they organise their home, their cupboards or wardrobe.

Aquarians enjoy a wide variety of cultural pursuits such as the theatre, cinema, ballet, opera, concerts and art. In all these fields, their taste is always for the avant-garde, the offbeat and abstract. They enjoy work that breaks the mould and creates exciting new forms. While they may not be avid followers of all the arts, they'll be well informed about those that they attend regularly. They'll read the critics' reviews and possibly subscribe to specialist magazines that discuss their area of interest in depth. They may be opinionated but they certainly know what they're talking about.

Literature is an invaluable source of stimulation, particularly for the more introverted Aquarians, who may shy away from the social dimension of attending events. This can be indulged in privately or they might join a book group, which can offer the Aquarian reader an excellent forum.

When at their best, Aquarians enjoy vigorous discussion on a regular basis with friends, colleagues and acquaintances. Others provide a sounding-board for their constant flow of unusual ideas and opinions. This dialogue is their lifeblood and is sought with those with whom they have little in common apart from a particular interest. It means that they know a lot of extremely diverse people, which produces some unlikely friends. Were they to have a party and invite all their friends, some might be in for a shock, finding out that the only thing they had in common was a friendship with the host.

Broad-minded and liberal, Aquarians question the status quo and cast new light on traditional ways of thinking. They find those with a narrow or bigoted perspective insufferable and will go out on a limb to defend an oppressed group or minority. The equal opportunities' charter is classically Aquarian in spirit (as is any human rights' constitution) and, within the organisations to which they belong, they'll make sure it's fully implemented.

Aquarians are usually found at the cutting edge of their profession. They stay abreast of the latest opinions in the areas that matter to them and are knowledgeable and well informed. Good with technology, they'll master the latest advances and if they can afford it, will have an array of state-of-the-art equipment, from their sound system and digital camera, to laptop and mobile phone, all of which are regularly upgraded in their wish to stay abreast of technological improvements. Some might see them as being elitist but, actually, they are connoisseurs and can appreciate the difference.

Aquarians have a reputation for being unconventional and it's true that they don't follow the pack. Some are downright eccentric and even those who seem on the surface to be conventional enough turn out to be a bit quirky. Most have strong views about certain things and are more than willing to voice these. They are prepared to go against the grain and the consensus of opinion for something they believe in. Their identity is often bound up with the opinions they hold, so making a stand about something they believe in affirms and strengthens their sense of self. They are not afraid to court controversy; in fact they positively thrive on it.

Well-known Aquarians include the artist Yoko Ono, feminist and academic Germaine Greer and the actress and political activist Vanessa Redgrave. All are famous for the radical stands that they have made in their particular domains. They each have shown an independence of thought and an ability to stand out from the crowd. They are happy to be counted.

Principles matter a great deal to Aquarians and some would lay down their life for them. This is no idle matter; it's at the core of who they are and how they live. It governs everything to some degree or another. Not all are as radical as Redgrave, but the peace marches, anti-war protests, gay rights and animal liberation movement and their ilk are dominated by this kind of individual, with ideals passionately cared about.

Aquarians are often described as sociable and group oriented and while some of the more extrovert Aquarians may be, many are not. However, the sense of belonging to a community who have shared ideals may be important to even the most introverted, even if it extends to no more than the magazines they subscribe to or the charities they support. What others fail to realise is that the group can be rather abstract and non-physical to an Aquarian; it's in the realm of thought rather than something that has to exist in concrete terms.

Aquarians can espouse idealistic ways of living, such as communal living, shared money or open relationships that may in theory work very well but in practice can overlook personal feelings. They are so committed to living according to their ideals that they forget the fact that this does not always translate comfortably in respect to human life. And feelings such as jealousy or possessiveness may be no-go areas for them – in fact any of the 'not nice' feelings tend to be suppressed as if this will make them go away completely. By refusing to entertain the idea that they ever have such feelings, Aquarians tend to mostly attract those who suffer from these kinds of feelings and who are able to express them. In this way they are forced to confront, via another, those feelings they experience as difficult.

Aquarians are big on friendship and in many ways more comfortable with it as it's an easier concept for them to understand than a relationship, where all sorts of emotional complications arise. They remain loyal and steadfast to their friends and can be relied upon through thick and thin. Even when contact is sporadic they won't feel rejected or go into a hurt huff. They don't need the reassurance of regular meetings or phone calls, especially if, for one reason or another, they're not easy to arrange. Long gaps and absences can actually suit them, once it's been established that they and their friend are on the same wavelength.

Even when in a relationship, Aquarians safeguard their friendships, which may well be more enduring. Friends are not dropped or neglected just because they have found a partner. Ideally, for them a relationship is akin to having a very best friend, it's just the deeper feeling involvement that they can find problematic.

However, even friends want empathy and tender loving care, not the kind of detached response that Aquarians are famous for. If a friend has had a difficult time, they won't want to think about it objectively, at least not straight away. Having perspective is all very well in certain circumstances but Aquarians tend to use it defensively, coming in with it too soon. Friends can feel distanced and sense that Aquarians feel threatened by the emotional content of what is being discussed. Their analysis is welcome later, after the 'there, there', has been administered. This is not something Aquarians particularly want themselves, as they find it all a bit gooey and sticky.

If anything, Aquarians want space to arrive at their feelings in their own time. When anything happens that upsets them, although they register this, their initial reaction is often akin to shock, which numbs and freezes the feelings for a while. It's only later, when they defrost, that they can connect to the pain. In the moment, they may not feel safe enough to indulge in emotions and they may be concerned, too, that once their emotions are unleashed they will take up an inordinate amount of time, which they can't afford. Aquarians may fear that they'll fragment – fall to pieces – so they want to put some distance between themselves and that moment, as a survival mechanism.

Aquarians pride themselves on being logical, rational people and like to evaluate people and situations accordingly. This works fine most of the time but where it unravels is when their own deeper feelings are engaged. They don't have a handle on the feeling realm and neither do feelings stand up well to rational scrutiny. At such times they become a mystery to themselves and while their openness and curiosity about the process they are in is admirable, they often find themselves floundering and way out of their depth.

When it comes to relationships, Aquarians are caught unawares. They are not at all prepared for the kinds of emotions that get unleashed, which can overwhelm and destabilise them. Even when it's happened several times before, they never learn to recognise what's coming, so it always takes them by surprise. Most people feel disoriented when they fall in love – it is a spectacularly ungrounding experience – but Aquarians probably take longer to recover their equilibrium than most and are the least equipped to deal with it. They have no points of reference when they are plunged into deep feelings; like in a flood, all the familiar landmarks disappear.

Part of the reason Aquarians struggle with the emotional realm so much, even more than the other air signs Gemini and Libra for instance, is that being a fixed sign, they lack flexibility. They want to pin things down and make them constant and, of course, feelings fluctuate and are hard to define, let alone explain or justify. Feelings simply do not stand up to rigorous interrogation. They just are – they are to do with being. So, when it comes to love, this sign has a hard time working out what it's all about.

That said, Aquarians do fall in love and they are

particularly attracted to the water signs, who confound and mystify them and provide them with quite a challenge. This can be a good match, if each respects the other's strengths and doesn't try to enforce their way of being on the other. Aquarius can learn more about feelings from such a partner, who will undoubtedly help them with this realm, while Aquarius can teach about being a bit more detached and not taking everything so personally.

What can frustrate Aquarians in this kind of relationship is the amount of silence. They like to talk and use dialogue as a way to process their thoughts and feelings, whereas the water signs don't generally need this. Aquarius may feel isolated and abandoned and wonder what they are doing with such an uncommunicative partner. They imagine they'd do better with someone who has more to say for themselves. While this is true when it comes to a friendship, such an individual does not necessarily form the emotional connection that Aquarius ultimately needs. Without this, the relationship can drift and become platonic and be too similar to a friendship to survive.

Aquarius is probably one of the most commitment-phobic signs, partly because of their need for freedom but also because they take commitment so seriously. Whereas some signs make and break promises at the drop of a hat, if Aquarians make a promise it's written in stone, which means it's not surprising that they are reluctant to make one.

As a consequence, heterosexual Aquarians tend to be anti-marriage. (Those who are gay or lesbian don't yet have the option to reject marriage.) The idea of professing undying love is positively alienating to them, as they love now but don't claim to know what tomorrow will bring. They equally distrust the legal implications of a marriage contract, often having quite a cynical view on how that connects with the suppression of the individual by the state and the church. Some can make out quite a convincing case for how marriage is politically incorrect. Clearly this can be problematic for more romantically inclined partners, who don't care to deconstruct marriage in this way.

Aquarius' commitment phobia can extend to even making small arrangements, such as where and when to go on holiday, as they don't like to see their options closed down. They are the sort who like to wait until the last minute and then go wherever they fancy, which is very all well if they only have themselves to think about. Some partners may be up for this but many like arrangements in place that they can look forward to and rely upon. This can be too restricting for Aquarius. These are spontaneous, freedom-oriented individuals who hate to be restrained in any way.

Aquarians need to have autonomy over their life and, as a result, can be awkward and non-cooperative when it comes to fitting in with others. Having control over what they do and when they do it is a necessity. For them, compromise is not an option so they hold out to get things on their terms. Like all the fixed signs (Taurus, Leo and Scorpio being the others) they have a stubborn streak. Once they dig their heels in they are hard to shift. Only by appealing to their sense of fairness and justice will they consider changing their position, as they absolutely have to be seen as reasonable.

While marriage may be rejected, Aquarians do make long-term steadfast partners. Provided they aren't backed into a corner and asked to sign on the dotted line – in which case they may well bolt – they stick around. It's the idea rather than the reality of commitment that frightens them. This is what makes them so paradoxical. They are actually one of the most loyal signs and would never abandon someone in their time of need.

Of all the signs, Aquarians are perhaps the most likely to be attracted to a gay lifestyle out of choice. They like to experiment and they may well do this with their sexuality, too. Some may see themselves as bisexual and remain open to relationships with either sex, although they are perfectly capable of being exclusive and faithful at any particular time. However, for those who feel they were born gay and never had a choice, then an Aquarian partner can be risky, as there's always the fear that they'll change their sexual orientation at some future point.

Gay Aquarians are likely to be proud of the fact and active politically in gay rights. These are individuals who relish their gay status and can use it to their advantage. They welcome not being part of the mainstream and enjoy a position in the margins. From this vantage place they have a particular view of society that inevitably has a radical edge.

Many Aquarians go on to become parents. Whatever their sexual orientation, they may well decide that they would like to have a child. And if anyone is going to fight for the rights of gay men and women to have children, foster or adopt, in whatever kind of family set-up they choose, it's an Aquarian. The main reason they might choose not to have children is the state of the world, as they see it. They may decide it is not a good place into which to bring a child. However, once those objections are cast aside, they make liberal, relaxed and politically-correct parents.

For their children, Aquarius' political correctness can be a pain. Most teenagers find their parents an embarrassment but one who goes on demonstrations and isn't conventional is often doubly so. Aquarius can also expect their offspring to share their ideals, which they almost certainly won't. Later, their children may well be proud of their 'wacky' parents but not while they are growing up.

However, what the Aquarian offers in abundance, is permission for their offspring to be themselves. They are open to listening to their ideas and their home life is likely to be intellectually stimulating, with friends from all walks of society dropping by.

When it comes to a career, Aquarians have a wide range of options. Their interest in the truth and facts make them good teachers. They are good communicators and believe passionately in education. Like Sagittarius, they like to be in the know, see knowledge as a ticket to freedom and enjoy passing this on to others. It's an exciting currency.

Aquarians make good scientists and empiricists, sifting data, testing theories and generally searching for the truth. Their belief in an objective and rational explanation for everything means this is a rewarding arena for them to be engaged in. They enjoy finding proof that something is as they've hypothesised, which is one of the things that a science career can offer. They also enjoy research, where there is no preconceived outcome and the truth is discovered and revealed concerning a matter. Above all, their intuition and capacity for lateral thinking make them great inventors and innovators.

Aquarians are suited to work that involves arbitration and conciliation, where their detachment and perspective are a useful asset. They are good at helping to resolve disputes, such as those between warring neighbours or those trying to separate and divorce in as civilised a way as possible. A career as a counsellor is another option, especially where there is a systemic approach and problem-solving techniques are used. They may be particularly suited to working with couples, where impartiality and being seen not to take sides is an imperative. However, their difficulty with their own emotions can limit their ability to work in this field and they may be best suited to short-term focused work.

Social work is another avenue many Aquarians are drawn to, where they can actively help those who are vulnerable and have statutory power to make a difference. This is possibly a better option than being a counsellor, as they prefer to be able to act to solve a situation, rather than having to sit with and bear the pain of the insoluble.

Aquarians' ability to embrace new technology means they are good in IT and the related fields. They may well be found developing software, setting up websites and occupied in the various careers around computing. Equally they make good engineers, especially civil engineers, where they can put into practice some of their visionary ideas.

While Aquarians enjoy the independence of being self-employed, they work best when part of a team. A co-operative suits them especially well. As an employee, they thrive when given the autonomy and freedom to do the job in the way they think best. They prefer to work in an atmosphere of mutual respect and without petty timekeeping. It isn't that they skive, because they work extremely hard when properly motivated, it's just that they need some feeling of control over their own work. Without this, they can be defiant and rebellious in the face of restrictions imposed by others. They do not work well with someone leaning over their shoulder and they need a manager who they can hold in high regard. If they think they could do their manager's job better than he or she does, then it's time to leave, as this will not make for a happy working relationship.

As the boss, Aquarians are among the most progressive and liberal. They wield their authority discreetly, aware of how they feel when on the receiving end of someone who is heavy-handed. Because they prefer working in a collective, where the power is shared, when they are in charge they try to create that kind of atmosphere, with employees given control over their areas of expertise. Flexible working arrangements and job sharing are all viewed favourably by this open-minded employer.

Aquarius is perhaps one of the best employers to have, the only downside possibly being that they are too matey with their staff and the normal boundaries get blurred. Some employees are happy with this but some can find it difficult: after all, this is the boss, who has the power to fire them. This overly-friendly boss may need to be thought well of and have rather too much invested in their employees' opinion of them, which can compromise them when having to make tough decisions. Being the boss can be a lonely position for an Aquarian, who really prefers working alongside colleagues.

Whatever work Aquarians do, they bring to it their ability to think things through clearly. They have an excellent analytical mind, which they apply to a wide variety of situations. They enjoy work that is connected to a humanitarian or idealistic principle and many will gravitate to the various charities that support such causes. This is a sign associated with redemption and their aim is to improve the world for the benefit of all. Whatever their faults, this has to be admired.

Negative Aquarius

Aquarius' negative characteristics are intrinsically bound up with their desire to save the world. With such high aspirations, it's easy for them to lose sight of why they are involved in whatever it is they are doing. While it may seem cynical to suggest that there's no such thing as true altruism, when Aquarians deny what their own investment might be, then this has to be investigated. Even if it's simply that it makes them feel better, it's important this is acknowledged, especially as they are not above guilt-tripping those who don't choose to spend their evenings and weekends in support of a worthy cause.

Despite their low boredom threshold Aquarians can tolerate mundane tasks, like stuffing envelopes, if what's going into the envelope matters. It's hard for loved ones to fault this as it's clearly a noble effort but they can feel neglected and that they are left playing second fiddle to a cause. The Aquarian becomes so caught up with the bigger picture that they overlook the impact this can have on those around them, who might want more of their attention and involvement. And what's even more infuriating to loved ones is when Aquarius assumes a moral high ground stance.

Another issue can be the degree of certainty some

Aquarians have. They can be so sure that they are right, that rather than being open to others' points of view, they become closed and intolerant, the opposite of what they are ordinarily best at. They can become dogmatic, narrow-minded and cut off. This is made worse by the fact that they still see themselves as open. Their identity is invested in this aspect of themselves, which they no longer resemble in the least. As such, they become hypocritical, not practising what they preach.

This kind of Aquarian shoots down other people's ideas before they have finished speaking. They can become so attached to their own opinions that those of others actually do not interest them. They are only open to those who back up how they think and dismiss anyone else as a waste of space. They may not recognise that all their friends support their world view and while there's nothing necessarily wrong with this – like-minded people attract each other, after all – their intolerance of others with differing points of view can be arrogant and prejudiced. They don't realise that while they are against social snobbery, they can be awful intellectual snobs.

Another monumental problem that Aquarians face is that of the feeling world. Many are spectacularly cut off from their own feelings and, as a consequence, run roughshod over others' feelings too. It could be argued that because they don't see what they are doing they can be excused but those who are in a close relationship with them need to stay alert to this shortcoming if they are not to get badly bruised.

However, Aquarians wreak the most damage on themselves. Typically they jog along happily in their daily life when, seemingly out of nowhere, feelings crash over them like a tidal wave, knocking them off their feet and totally destabilising them for a while. While in the midst of this, they are open and accessible and friends will be touched by their obvious vulnerability, but this deeper connection to their feelings and to others doesn't last, as once Aquarius feels better, they revert to their more cut-off ways and quickly forget what they've been through. A bit like a bad cold: once it's over it's soon forgotten and not thought about again until the next one. Rather than seeing it as an opportunity to know more about what goes on at a deeper level, they are usually just relieved the episode is over.

Friends can understandably feel abandoned afterwards. They imagined this heralded a new intimacy only to find out they were wrong. In fact, Aquarians can distance themselves from those who supported them not out of any conscious intention to hurt but because that person reminds them of the pain and they want to move on. So, to be too available to an Aquarian in their time of need can actually risk the friendship.

Aquarians have no idea that all this emotion can be lying dormant within them, beneath the surface of their everyday demeanour and, in the aftermath of it breaking through to consciousness, they rapidly retreat back to their habitual position of emotional denial. Whereas those more in touch with their feelings draw upon them to inform them of their values, Aquarians rely on their mind and intellect. While this has its strengths, such a position can overlook the personal and the individual.

These destabilising, emotional episodes typically occur when an Aquarian has strong romantic feelings. Love may make the world go round but being in love does bring a touch of madness with it and for those who rely on being rational, this is particularly disturbing. Falling in love is bound to precipitate and unleash feelings, which they can find hard to manage, even more so than those who are more in touch with their feelings. Typically, normal life comes to a standstill. They lose weight, can't sleep and find it hard to function.

Once romantically involved, Aquarians are out of their depth and struggle to manage the feelings elicited. Because this is not their domain, they can behave erratically and give out conflicting messages to a prospective partner; for example, phoning persistently then not returning calls. As a coping strategy, they may seem rather cool, as they attempt to regain a semblance of normality and then they'll flip and seem keen and interested. A new partner needs to stay steady in these early stages of an involvement, as Aquarians' mixed messages are more likely to be to do with their inner state than ambivalence and uncertainty.

Nevertheless, Aquarians do suffer from ambivalence and do question the *raison d'être* of a relationship, all of which can generate feelings of insecurity in their partner. Partners would do well to keep a certain distance from all these machinations, so as not to be too affected by it. An Aquarian is reassured when given space and threatened when a partner wants to be intimate, which they can find claustrophobic and suffocating. They need absolute privacy in order to think things through and can't abide being expected to share every thought. With their strong needs for freedom and autonomy, they need a partner who is secure enough to grant them this in a relaxed way.

Separate holidays and even separate bedrooms are possibilities further down the road in an established relationship. Aquarians like their own space and don't like having to compromise on where and when they go away or when they turn the light out at night and, as many like to read in bed at odd hours (they have all that high-voltage mental energy to defuse), it all begins to seem a sensible arrangement. This way they can leave their things scattered around if they so wish without anyone else being upset. Whereas with some signs this might signal something seriously amiss in the relationship, this is not the case here.

While a long-term relationship may come to resemble a platonic friendship, there are important differences, not least the way an Aquarian relies on their partner. Emotional dependency is not something they readily admit to as it is scary stuff. However, a partner can be reassured that they do in fact depend all the more because of their denial, although, as they don't concede to it, even to themselves, partners have to get used to it not being acknowledged.

Friendship is in any case something of an ideal for Aquarians – they hold the concept in high regard – but even their friendships have certain problems. Friends, talking with an Aquarian about deeply personal matters, can be left feeling exposed, much like being dissected in the laboratory. What Aquarius has to say may be extremely apposite to a situation but it can be delivered in such a clinical way that it's not helpful. They fail to realise that information is not necessarily what's needed and simply do not understand how a sympathetic shoulder to cry on can help. What's more, it does not interest them.

Typically, Aquarians are concerned with the bigger picture and the common good, so that individual concerns get minimised and seen as unimportant. This is equally true if the person in question is a friend, as they would never allow personal interests to undermine their ideals. They expect friends to understand this and to be prepared to sacrifice their own needs for the sake of the masses and if they aren't happy about this, Aquarians dismiss them as selfish. If it is for the greater good, it is seen as a small price to pay.

This expectation that others must adopt an altruistic attitude can apply to all sorts of situations, even to the extent of losing a home or view in order to create a much-needed road or railway line or airport runway or water reservoir. Aquarians usually favour progress, as they see it, and can condemn those who have a different point of view. On the other hand, when this threatens wildlife or the environment, they are often the first to object. What remains consistent is that they value the well-being of the collective over that of the individual.

What is more, Aquarians can deny their own personal benefits. They can occupy a position purportedly devoid of ego that is noble and virtuous, while overlooking their own self-interest and personal investment in their activities, wrapping them up, as it were, as benefiting others and therefore worthy. This kind of denial of private motivation is potentially dangerous and hypocritical. It means they can feel self-righteous and superior while disowning their own desires. These can be political or financial, which isn't to imply they are dishonest because their honesty is fundamental to their sense of integrity: it's a far subtler and more insidious dynamic.

Aquarians deny their own egoism, so it creeps out in other ways. They come up with a convincing rational argument that leaves out the fact that, if things are done this way, they benefit. They genuinely don't see they've construed a plan that is to their advantage and are deeply offended if this is pointed out. In reality, it's such a taboo subject that it rarely, if ever, gets mentioned. Yet it corrupts the integrity of their good ideas. It also causes them huge hurt, as their feelings are affronted when others react to their proposals with suspicion, which they fail to understand. It's their blind spot.

Much has been said about the independence of thought and the principles of Aquarians, which are their most positive attributes but, taken to the extreme, some are dangerously fanatical. For example, the political opinions and actions of a minority within the animal liberation organisations who are against the laboratory use of animals is classic of the extremists, whereby the aims justify the means. At the most extreme end of the pole are the suicide bombers, who are willing to sacrifice their lives for the sake of a fundamentalist belief. That this involves the loss of innocent lives is seen by such individuals as an unfortunate consequence in achieving their ideals. Very few go to these lengths and most Aquarians abhor this behaviour but the attitude, where the principle counts for more then the individuals concerned, is typical of this sign. And this overriding of personal concerns is apparent in their approach to themselves just as much as it is towards others. So, ironically, they adopt a position where they have no rights, if these rights go against their humanitarian goals.

This filters down at an everyday level to an unforgiving approach to how Aquarians spend their time. For instance, there's no staying in bed on a Saturday morning just because they're tired and have had a busy week, when there's leafleting to be done. And woe betide anyone else who puts their personal needs first.

However, despite the negative manifestations of some of Aquarius' characteristics, these are well-intentioned individuals. They always respond well to being reasoned with and if they understand a problem they try to change. Their crime is in committing themselves one hundred per cent to their idealism and their desire to save the world; hardly that deadly in the scale of things.

The Aquarius Man

The Aquarian man is recognisable by his cool, airy manner and the rather detached curiosity he shows in others and the world around him. This is an ideas man, who likes nothing better than to be engaged in a stimulating conversation. He doesn't necessarily seek agreement or common ground but, provided it has veracity, can enjoy a discussion with those whose opinions he is diametrically opposed to just as much as those who are closer to him. He is interested in the exchange of views for their own sake.

Principles are the Aquarian man's governing interest and he tries to live his life by these. While this can seem rather lofty, it means he would find it difficult to become emotionally involved with someone who didn't share his ideals. For him, the meeting of minds is important and when it comes to choosing a partner, he needs someone who is on his wavelength, even if not in complete agreement, and who stimulates him mentally.

The Aquarian man has a nonchalant, uninvolved demeanour, as if nothing bothers him or gets to him. The king of cool, he acts as if he can take anything and everything in his stride and may seem careless and offhand about matters that others get steamed up about. Some have a devil-may-care attitude and don't seem to take anything that seriously. In this way he can seem immune to hurt or offence.

In fact, the Aquarian man is protected to some extent by his detachment. His feelings sometimes get left behind and it takes a while before they catch up with him but when they do he can suffer as much as the next man. His relationship to how he feels is erratic and unreliable. Much of the time he is not in touch with how he feels and it's only with hindsight he realises how certain incidents affected him. His mode of operation is at all times even and composed. This is, of course, a great gift for those in professions that require a cool head in a crises, like medicine and the emergency services.

Being reasonable and fair is something the Aquarian man expects from others at all times. For him, those who do not abide by this are beyond the pale. He especially finds irrational, emotive behaviour highly threatening and he rapidly distances himself from people who exhibit this. For those who have such outbursts he can appear cold and unforgiving, even scornful, as this is the stance he adopts to protect himself. He sees volatile emotional expressions as tantamount to anarchy, not recognising that it's the inner chaos they stir up in him that he's so afraid of.

As a consequence, the Aquarian man is big on civilised behaviour and does have a rather stern, judgemental side. He believes that society functions best when everyone keeps their personal feelings to themselves and applies this to all levels of social interaction. Perhaps the worst thing that anyone can do to him is to make a scene in public.

In common with the other two air signs (Gemini and Libra) the Aquarian man has sophisticated social skills although he can be a bit of a maverick, too, and enjoys being provocative and winding others up. Unlike Libra, he doesn't care much what others think of him, so has considerable freedom to do and be as he pleases. He enjoys being controversial.

The Aquarian pop singer Robbie Williams exemplifies this trait. Arguably controversy helps his career as it gives him plenty of free publicity. His whole manner is irreverent and at the same time open and honest, particularly in some of his lyrics, as to how he genuinely feels. This honesty is one of Aquarius' most disarming characteristics.

The Aquarian artist Jackson Pollock still provokes contention years after his death. His art was unique in style and a radical departure from representational art forms, in which he drew on concepts about the nature of the unconscious then in vogue in psychoanalysis. It's also typically Aquarian that the ideas current at the time influenced and underpinned his art.

With their super-cool persona, Aquarian men can be devastatingly attractive, but when it comes to relationships, they have a bad reputation for being commitment-phobic and this is, superficially at least, true. However, the main reason that they are so reluctant to make a commitment is because they take it seriously. Words are extremely important to them and so, unlike some signs, they'll never say 'I love you' and not, in that moment, mean it. However a commitment like marriage can seem to them an emotional impossibility. They don't understand how they can promise to love forever, failing to see that it can only ever be an intention of the moment. But this is their dilemma and is why they dither over marriage in particular.

The Aquarian man has other issues regarding commitment, though. He suffers from a high degree of ambivalence and hates being boxed in or pinned down. He really does like to keep his options open and a prospective partner must recognise that this is a man who needs a lot of space. This applies particularly at the start of a relationship, when he is going to exhibit his most commitment-phobic behaviour. He has to make the running. A potential partner should be wary about making any moves whatsoever. Don't even ring him until it's clear he won't bolt. If he feels chased, he's off. A new partner should play hard to get and keep their options open, too.

It takes the Aquarian man quite some time to recognise when he has feelings for someone. Despite how quick he is in other matters, he's slow in this respect. Even when it's obvious to those around him, he may not have a clue about how he really feels. And until he acknowledges his feelings, then a new relationship can't progress.

One reason that it takes the Aquarian man so long to know that he's in love is that he's in a constant state of denial about his feelings in general and in particular his needs. So, while being in love is scary for everyone, it's especially so for him. He has to take on board all kinds of things about himself that he ordinarily runs away from. So he is particularly vulnerable and ill-prepared when it comes to love. He's entering uncharted territory and, even if he's been there before, it's never an arena he becomes expert in.

Once he fully realises how he is feeling, the Aquarian man tries to analyse his situation and make sense of it rationally. While this is not necessarily going to be helpful, at least he talks about how he feels. Even at this stage, though, he may not want a conventional relationship and may find the very idea of a partnership extremely threatening. The concept has to appeal before he's able to get to the possibility emotionally.

The slightly older Aquarian man is a better bet here, as he'll have realised the downside of being on his own, especially if his friends have coupled up and had children. Once he thinks he's being left behind, he's more likely to take the plunge himself. So, timing is everything with this man and, if his best friend has recently got married, he's more likely to be considering this as a prospect for himself. If all his friends are single, there's a long wait ahead. This applies whatever his sexual orientation, as this is about a lifestyle choice, the single life as opposed to coupledom.

Eventually, the Aquarian man chooses a mate and makes a great partner. However reluctant he was in the first place, this is made up for by how loyal and steadfast he proves to be. He's a considerate lover, who enjoys experimenting, so a long-term sexual relationship stays interesting and alive. His attitude to sex is open and informed and he's able to talk about his likes and dislikes and to ask about his partner's which can be liberating for those who are shy of that kind of dialogue. He doesn't shock easily.

Plus, the Aquarian man is an easygoing, yet lively, mate to have who brings to a relationship lots of friends and interests. Conversation is always stimulating and intelligent and casual visitors are numerous. Life with him is far from dull. A partner is free to partake in his busy social and cultural life or not, depending on what pleases them. If a partner doesn't enjoy something he does regularly, they should realise from the outset that he's not about to sacrifice it for them. In such a relationship there will be plenty of space for them both to have their separate interests, in a way that doesn't threaten the relationship – it positively enhances it.

Because the Aquarian man is a man of principles, he's likely to be open-minded and tolerant. He expects an equal partnership, where decisions are made jointly and where the chores and responsibilities are shared. Whether he achieves this is another matter but at least it's his intention. He doesn't expect roles to be based on gender, either. However, he may not be that practical, so a partner may have to invest time initially showing him how things are done. And as this man is unlikely to be much good at DIY or gardening, it's worth the effort teaching him how to do the household chores.

When it comes to the question of having children, the

Aquarian man may be concerned about how this will change his life and the loss of freedom that he envisages will be the result. He's cautious and, although he doesn't yet realise what the positive changes will be, he's right to recognise this is a big step. Very few people realise before their first child the extent to which this will change their priorities in life but the Aquarian man is among the most surprised; he has no idea of how having a child will impact on him emotionally. However, if he does go on to have children, he's likely to find it one of the most rewarding experiences of his life.

The Aquarian man is on a fast learning curve as he grapples with the pre-verbal stage of babyhood. This is the phase he is least equipped to deal with but as his children grow he comes into his own as a father. In keeping with his even-handed stance, he expects to do his fair share in look-ing after his offspring, so even though he flounders in the early months, he pitches in and does his best, which makes for a good foundation in their later years. If anyone is going to fight for paternity leave and recognise how important it is to be around when his children are new born, it's him.

The Aquarian man is likely to be liberal and tolerant as a father. He's approachable and always ready and willing to listen. He's good at helping his children to think things through and work out their ideas and opinions. He'll include them in his activities early in life. In many ways he exemplifies the new man, as his attitude is so inclusive and egalitarian. He may also have ideas about how his children should be brought up, which could lean towards the experimental and radical. If anyone is going to favour alternative ways of educating their children, along idealistic lines such as Rudolph Steiner's theosophical schools or AS Neill's progressive school Summerhill, then it's an Aquarian.

However, despite the Aquarian man's liberal tendencies, he's no pushover and sets clear boundaries that he expects his children to respect. He appeals to their sense of fairness in setting any rules and having enlisted this, he will come down heavily on them if they then disregard them. For him, unreasonable behaviour is completely unacceptable.

When it comes to a career, there are many directions the Aquarian man can take. However, whatever he does, he'll feel happiest if his work makes some obvious contribution to society. He needs to feel a part of something bigger and so working in a solely commercial or private capacity, however interesting the job, will not ultimately satisfy him. Making a difference is what matters most to him.

Even within his profession the Aquarian man will prefer a position that benefits the widest cross-section of the population. So, for instance, if he's a doctor, he's unlikely to have a lucrative private practice and will opt to work in a deprived area, where he feels his contribution counts for more. If he's a scientist, he'll look for work in the public domain. As a teacher, he'll work for an inner-city state school as opposed to a private or public school, where the pupils are more privileged. His idealism underpins all that he does.

The Aquarian man may well work directly for a humanitarian concern. In such a set-up he's likely to be most satisfied that he's doing his bit to make the world a better place and will turn down better financial opportunities in order to do this kind of work. Alternatively, he may do voluntary work in his spare time.

Whatever his job, the Aquarian man brings to it his political consciousness. Even though he puts his personal needs second, he nevertheless manages to earn a decent living. He's not necessarily looking to become rich. His priority is always bigger than himself and however frustrating loved ones may at times find this, it's hard to criticise. Where would we all be without Aquarians' vision of a better world?

The Aquarius Woman

The Aquarius woman is recognisable by her independent stance and friendly, outgoing manner. She genuinely likes and is interested in others but retains her own separate position at all times. Very much her own person, she has this uncompromising attitude that she conveys in an unobtrusive way. She doesn't have to shout it from the rooftops, as it's in every pore of her being and she simply exudes it.

The Aquarian woman has a distinctive and individualistic way of dressing, which underlines her free spirit. Without following fashion, she always looks contemporary. She has an eye for the unusual and manages to mix and match items in a creative way. With her Bohemian style and original way of looking at everything, she's a colourful and unique individual.

With a genuine love of the informal and the ordinary, the Aquarian woman may enjoy street markets and car-boot sales, more for the eclectic atmosphere than the bargains. She thinks of graffiti as street art rather than vandalism and likes to keep her own street credibility going by keeping abreast of the latest, grass roots happenings in fashion, music, art and culture. If she has working-class origins she is as proud of these as others might be about aristocratic connections.

Always on the radical side, the Aquarian woman is not afraid to voice an opinion that is not popular and one in which she gets branded as extreme. The middle ground is alien territory to her as she's either on the far left or far right politically and is usually very well informed on political matters, not just nationally but internationally. If anyone is going to start talking about what's going on in some far corner of the world, it's her and it'll be with her own strong stance.

The Aquarian woman may well be actively concerned with global issues, like climate change, Third World debt, fair trade and the destruction of the rain forests. She's likely to be well informed in these matters and to be passionate about them. While she's happy for others to have their own opinions, anyone diametrically opposed to (or apathetic) issues she's passionate about would never become a close friend of hers.

The Aquarian woman's principles shine. This is what she lives her life by and how she judges the lives of others. She is deeply affected by the world she lives in and is concerned by humanitarian issues that do not necessarily impact on her directly. She recognises the common humanity of mankind and believes that by ignoring such concerns man demeans himself. For her, this is not an option.

Open to people from all walks of life, the Aquarian woman does not tolerate prejudice of any kind, be it class, race, sexuality, status or whatever. She's as against snobbery as any kind of bigotry and treats people as she finds them, without preconceived notions. With no need to pigeon-hole others, she doesn't make damning assumptions. So, for example, whether or not she gives the street beggar any money, she will look him in the eye and acknowledge their common humanity. For those who live on the streets, this recognition, when many pass them by, is an important testament to their right to existence. This compassion for another living soul is something she offers automatically, although she might take it one step further and offer advice, which is not necessarily appreciated.

Many Aquarian women have a 'social worker' approach to life, whether or not they end up in this profession. Their concerns about people mean they are strongly motivated to try to do something about the human condition which can, at times, be uninvited. Some have an evangelical, missionary-type attitude and as such, distance themselves from those they are trying to help. So despite the common humanity, there is also a gap, where she undoubtedly sees herself as privileged. This may well be true but is often found patronising and condescending by those on the receiving end.

This position of 'I understand but I'm not equally affected' is one the Aquarian woman adopts in many areas of her life. It's not actually true, although she genuinely believes it and it means she can rely on other less fortunate individuals upon whom to project any unhappiness in her own life. She can distance herself from these feelings within herself and identify them as belonging to other people, which is why she feels so compelled to help. They carry her dysfunction for her. The more she claims the 'I'm all right Jack' position the more someone else has to be otherwise.

The Aquarian woman can have a merry, cheerful manner, which can come over as relentlessly upbeat. She's an invigorating and jolly kind of woman, who refuses to see the more depressing or bleaker dimensions of life. Yet she's interested in others' more miserable moments and appears to offer solace, while actually having her own agenda – to make them better. And woe betide friends who don't feel perked up by her help, as this is the deal. She has little tolerance for those who, as she sees it, refuse to get better. So it's all right to start a conversation feeling low, but never okay to end one downhearted. The parting shot has to be positive.

The Aquarian woman's ability to look on the bright side of things is no doubt a strength, as she is good at extracting the best from quite dire situations. She never lets anything keep her down for too long and uses her perspective to settle difficulties within herself. So, if she suffers a setback, like the loss of a job or relationship, she will try to see how this is to her advantage – the situation wasn't right for her and she wanted to leave anyway, for instance. Her detachment and perspective see her through life's up and downs; it's just that she can use these too quickly and at the expense of really processing her feelings. She jumps in with them, abandoning her innermost emotions.

Abandonment is a big issue for the Aquarian woman. Within relationships her fear of being left or of upping and going herself is a strong theme. It can become a perverse kind of competition, an 'I'll leave you before you can leave me' scenario. And the underlying culprit in all this is the way she neglects her own inner feelings. As a child, she may have been encouraged to act as if she was more independent than she actually felt or even have contributed to this, gaining brownie points for being a 'big girl'. Thus kudos for appearing grown-up may well have supported her tendency to suppress difficult emotions. However it all arose – and for many Aquarians there is a history of disruption in early childhood – the net result is that she scrambles to distance herself from painful feelings and, in so doing, cuts herself off from an important inner source of knowledge. She then has to rely on her mind to see her through, which is great for some situations and decisions, in which behaving rationally is a bonus but is not so useful in matters of the heart. This is by far the most problematic arena for her, as it never goes according to plan.

The Aquarian woman is perceptive and bright, quick on the uptake and enjoys flexing her brainpower. She seeks mental stimulation and likes nothing better than good conversation with friends. Her ideal evening could well be one spent over a meal with a group of friends from diverse backgrounds conversing about all and sundry and putting the world to rights. The food as such is not important to her, provided it's palatable and there's plenty of wine to wash it all down with; it's the occasion that matters to her.

When it comes to a discussion, the Aquarian woman always has her own definite point of view. She's opinionated and confident in that domain. And she's brutally honest, too, and doesn't qualify or slant her position according to who she's with, as the water signs might. She says it like it is and everyone knows where she stands. Her honesty can be a bit tough to take; if she thinks someone is a fool, for instance, she says so in no uncertain terms. She may justify this by saying 'I'm only speaking the truth' not realising that 'the truth', as she sees it, is only her opinion.

The Aquarian woman's independent spirit affects every sphere of her life and behaviour. She curries no favours, as she expects to succeed or fail on her own merit. Even if it were to be to her advantage, she's not capable of flattery. Her ability to live by her truth is essential to her sense of integrity and self-respect. Without it she is nothing. This is why she can't afford to compromise on her principles and why her truth sometimes has such a punch behind it.

All Aquarians have a degree of commitment phobia; it's intrinsic to their freedom-loving nature that they don't like the idea of being restricted. Some may resist making arrangements of any kind because they then feel trapped. The Aquarian woman wants to be able to do what she wants when she wants, which includes much that is trivial but, for her, vital. So if someone is expecting her home by a certain time, she can find that stifling. What if she wants to stop off on the way home? Or take a different route that's more picturesque but takes much longer? The idea that someone would have any jurisdiction or upset feelings over her exercising these choices is outrageous to her. She sees it as her right and would feel like walking away from anyone trying to impose limitations like these on her autonomy.

The Aquarian woman may well suffer from claustrophobia to a varying degree. She easily feels cooped up and needs to get out. She likes fresh air and open spaces. She needs movement and doesn't like feeling tied down, especially to other people's timetables.

So the Aquarian woman's well-being hinges on her basic right to freedom of movement on a daily basis. Provided a partner can cope with this, then the first hurdle has been dealt with. When it comes to a relationship, good communication is a priority. She needs someone who is interesting and who stimulates her mentally. Yet she may be drawn to a water sign, to someone who mystifies and disturbs her because they operate so differently. Despite her protestations to the contrary, she needs someone who has more access to their emotional depths and who is less afraid of commitment, otherwise what's meant to be a relationship begins all too quickly to resemble a platonic friendship.

For the Aquarian woman to make a commitment she has to be one hundred per cent sure. Whereas some signs make promises that they have no intention of keeping, she would not be able to live with herself if she did that. However, this doesn't mean she isn't loyal, because she is. She's extremely reliable within the limits she imposes. In actuality she is far more steadfast than she lets on as it's the idea of committing that is a problem to her, rather than the reality.

Moving in together, especially if it's not made a big deal, is something the Aquarian woman can handle. She doesn't really like the idea of marriage. She is not the marrying kind, which doesn't mean she won't, it's just not her natural inclination. It doesn't mean that she isn't into monogamy either, because mostly she is – anything else is too complicated for her. She's just not keen on vows that are forever and ever, as all she can promise is what she feels now. The very thought of 'till death us do part' makes her feel trapped. No amount of romance can wrap that one up to seem an attractive option.

As a live-in partner the Aquarian woman brings her ideals with her and expects certain standards of behaviour. She has an innate feminist streak, as she thinks that everything should be split in an equal and fair way, including the bills and the domestic chores. She doesn't expect to be financially supported but neither does she expect to do the lion's share of the housework. However, she's not necessarily that tidy herself and it may be her partner who ends up complaining about her mess. She gets carried away with her ideas and may fail to notice certain practical and mundane matters, which are never going to be her strength. It may be that she wants to scatter her things around her, as that is comfortable for her and she doesn't mind the clutter lying around, however if her partner does, it becomes their problem.

The Aquarian actress Mia Farrow exemplifies many Aquarian traits. She had a typically Aquarian arrangement in her long-standing relationship with Woody Allen. They lived on opposite sides of Central Park, she with all the children and in a certain amount of chaos, no doubt, and he across the way by himself. Allen could escape from domesticity as and when he wanted to and she appeared happy with this situation at the time.

Having separate homes can suit an Aquarian woman very well, as she likes her space. Usually, it's a bedroom each, or two shared houses, one in town and one in the country, that her and her partner move between. A partner who's away on business a lot also suits her. That way she can have time on her own effortlessly and it means she doesn't have to make special arrangements to gain some space.

When she was with Woody Allen, Mia Farrow was mother to eight or more children and continued to adopt more, some with disabilities, after her relationship with Allen broke down. In order to adopt so many children, she fought to get the legislation changed in the US Senate. This was an issue that she held strong political convictions about. Clearly these children were helped but it could be argued that Farrow was also trying to save her inner child by rescuing these children. It's understandable that she was in a lot of distress and perhaps this had a part to play in her desire to adopt vulnerable children.

Childbirth is a time, like falling in love, when overwhelming deep emotions well up and the Aquarian woman may feel more destabilised than most, especially with the weight of new responsibility on her. Additionally, she can feel isolated, so finding peer support and company is vital. However helpful her partner is, she really needs to connect up with other new mothers, so participating in organised mother and baby activities can lead to these kind of contacts. Without these, a combination of circumstances can tip her into post-natal depression. If this occurs, she will respond well to the counselling and group support now available in this field.

In fact, having children may not be a priority for the Aquarian woman at all. Giving birth to ideas and aesthetic projects may give her creative satisfaction and she may not want to risk losing her independence. Plus she may be more nervous than most of the physicality of birth and feel quite squeamish at the idea. That said, many do become mothers and enjoy this role immensely. They may feel insecure and uncertain of themselves in the early pre-verbal stages of child rearing, when empathy is the only means to understand what's going on with a baby. However, many surprise themselves and turn out to be better at motherhood than they'd imagined. Their detachment can help here, as they don't get into such a flap as some signs do and are better able to think about what might be going on.

As her children develop, the Aquarian woman is extremely good at making sure they get plenty of mental stimulation. Little ones will benefit from nursery school as well as being taken out and about to all sorts of cultural activities. She'll create extra-curricula activities for school-age children that provides them with a full and fascinating life. A liberal and easygoing parent, she engages her offspring in dialogue from an early age, encouraging them to participate in decisions that affect the family. If anyone is going to organise 'family meetings' where everyone gets to air an opinion, it's an Aquarian mother.

The Aquarian woman tends to treat her children as equals, which is something they respond to well. In particular, she has a good, open and honest relationship with teenagers, where they can tell her things that other mothers might react to in horror. She neither judges nor panics and acts in an intelligent and realistic way when it comes to subjects like drugs or sex. She'll offer them age-appropriate books and be available and accessible herself, willing to answer their questions candidly and respectfully. By making sure her children are well informed she trusts that, as such, they'll make the right decisions. And by not behaving like an authoritarian parent, she ends up as their trusted friend and confidante.

Another important thing the Aquarian mother usually gets right is that she doesn't make too many sacrifices for her children, so doesn't end up feeling resentful or believe that they owe her anything. She's good at getting on with her own life and doing her own thing, regardless, and there is something healthy and refreshing about this. As she doesn't channel her unlived life into them, expecting them to realise her ambitions for her; this leaves her children free to be themselves. Some may see her as selfish but actually she's not, she's liberating.

Getting on with her own life may or may not involve work. If the Aquarian woman's career has been important to her before she had children, then it's likely she'll want to maintain this. However, where it's been a means to an end, she may feel happy to leave it behind, if she can manage without the income. She has lots of interests and could well belong to several groups, such as Friends of the Earth and Greenpeace and may wish to devote a fair amount of time and energy to various causes.

Oprah Winfrey is a good example of a super-successful Aquarian woman in action. As the first queen of daytime television, she raises many social issues in her programmes that, some say, trivialise painful personal stories and exploit the participants, while many see this as spreading a much-needed message to the wider community and of huge benefit. And, she has also got America reading: by recommending specific novels she has popularised certain authors and created a buzz around the written word.

Ultimately, as with the Aquarian man, making a difference is what matters most to the Aquarian woman, be that with her children, through her voluntary activities or her work. Her social conscience and her desire to improve the world are what she is known for. Life's hard knocks inevitably temper her idealism but it nevertheless remains her driving force.

The Aquarius Child

Aquarius children are recognisable by their friendly manner and outgoing approach. From a very young age, they show an alert and keen interest in their surroundings. As soon as their eyes can focus, they like to be out and about in their pushchair, taking in the world around them. Even as babies they are intrigued by others, watching their movements and obviously fascinated by their antics. This is a baby who, if carried in a baby-sling, likes to look outwards. Adventurous when it comes to making sounds, they clearly want to communicate and often have a precocious grasp of language, stringing whole sentences together at a very tender age.

Aquarian children are sociable and gregarious and benefit from mixing with other children. They do well in nursery school as, unlike some young children, they don't usually find it distressing to be separated from Mother. They positively thrive on the stimulating activities and the chance to play with other children. However, parents may find it hard to see their offspring go off without a backward glance.

Aquarian children show their independent streak at a very early age, not only in having less stranger-anxiety than most little ones, but in the way they like to be in control and do things for themselves. They'll insist on feeding themselves as soon as they can grasp the spoon, even if they make a huge mess. And they'll noisily resist all kinds of helpful interventions.

More worryingly, once the Aquarian baby becomes mobile, they may well rebel against having to hold a parent's hand and have their own ideas about where they are headed and can toddle off in the opposite direction to their mum, so a close watch needs to be kept, lest they really frighten themselves and their parents by getting lost. For them, this can become a game which can be rather trying.

One two-year-old Aquarian, at a holiday camp with her parents, wandered off soon after arrival. Someone tried to reassure her mother by saying, 'Don't worry, anyone finding a crying child will take her to the lost children's unit.' The mother replied, 'You don't understand! She won't be crying.' And she wasn't – when she was thankfully found safe and well.

Aquarian children are probably no more awkward than a lot of two-year-olds, it's just that they can exhibit a fearlessness that puts them in danger. It's important, however, that parents do not overestimate what their Aquarian child can manage and protect them from the anxiety that can develop as a result of attempting too much too soon. At this very young age it's absolutely essential that they be held in check, without thwarting their nascent independent spirit.

Aquarian children have a natural contrariness and may well do the exact opposite of what they are asked to do, so a degree of craftiness is needed to get them to do certain things. Long before they can manage it, they'll want to dress themselves and to choose what they'll wear. If this isn't to turn into a full-scale power struggle, in which the adult concerned may well lose, then tactics are needed. At this age, limiting their choice of clothes to those that are suitable, so they can exercise their free will but within certain parameters, is a good move. As is buying things in the first place that they can take on and off relatively easily – such as shoes with Velcro fasteners rather than laces or buckles.

Once they are old enough and have a grasp of language, then parents can appeal to the Aquarian child's reasonableness. Clearly at two this is not an option. Parents should give up any ideas of being in control and just accept that this is a contrary child. A mixture of firmness when it really matters and letting things go when it's not important works best and will be least stressful for them, too.

Aquarian children have an airy, rather nonchalant manner and may act as if things don't bother them too much. While parents may welcome their composure, as most don't relish temper tantrums, it can be a mistake to praise this too much. As adults, Aquarians often have only a tenuous relationship to their feelings, so parents are advised to always encourage and accept emotional outbursts and the expression of strong feelings.

All children express their feelings; it's only as they mature into adults that they begin to suppress them and Aquarians in particular can see the expression of emotion as a failing. By validating their feelings when little, parents give these children a positive message, which will stand them in good stead in adult life.

On the other hand, if Aquarian children witness the adults around them having outbursts, this may convince them of how scary emotions are and encourage them to bottle up their own feelings. It's a hard balance to find, particularly as society tends to value those who suppress emotions, which the Aquarian child is bound to pick up on.

Check in with Aquarian children regularly to ask how they feel and help them develop a way to talk about their feelings. Find out how their friendships are going and what their likes and dislikes are. They all too easily overlook small things and minor upsets, brushing them off as if they don't matter. They maintain an upbeat approach, which is fine; it's just that it can be at their own expense. If this is presented as a concept, to do with equal rights, then they'll immediately understand it.

Although there are some shy and introverted Aquarian children, in the main they are gregarious, outgoing little souls. Their position in relation to their peers and later, when adult, in wider society is of fundamental importance in terms of their sense of self, so provide them with plenty of opportunities to meet other children. So, for instance, any extra-curricula activities that involve a group suit them best such as games that involve team play and cooperation, drama groups, orchestras and choirs. At home, they'll enjoy board games with the whole family, especially word games like Scrabble and general knowledge games.

When it comes to toys, the Aquarian child may show a scientific bent and a chemistry set will encourage that aptitude and, who knows, this may be a future scientist in the making. Of all the signs, Aquarians are most likely to be interested in wizardry. They may show interest, too, in other sciences, including astronomy, so a telescope might be appreciated. And this includes Aquarian girls, who have just as scientific a brain as the boys.

Within the home, Aquarian children cooperate best when important matters are explained to them. When it comes to house rules, they need to understand the rationale behind them and, once this is understood, they usually comply. They respond well when included in the decision-making process, in so far as this is possible and especially where it directly affects them. Being given input in small, unimportant decisions won't fob them off, if all the big things in life are presented as a fait accompli. They'll know that, within their family, their opinion doesn't really count for much and these are children whose sense of self-esteem is bound up with their opinions being taken seriously.

Older Aquarian children have a developed sense of fair

play, so they can be trusted to stick to certain agreements. However, it's important that these are discussed and agreed, rather than imposed. Arbitrary or, as they see it, unjust rules will be challenged and they will readily venture an opinion on the reasonableness or otherwise of any restrictions placed upon them. It's important that parents continue to enlist their cooperation by being even-handed. If this is lost serious trouble looms once they hit puberty.

The Aquarian teenager is likely to rebel in a big way, no matter what. This is a sign that courts controversy, so at a time when most teenagers kick against the status quo, this one may well go to extremes. Their dress is likely to be shockingly unconventional, especially girls, who traditionally express their individuality in this way. And increasingly boys are also choosing to assert themselves via their style of clothing. Peer pressure comes into play, too, but these teenagers are going to be among the more extreme in their group. If the rage is for body piercing, then they'll want their navel, nose or more done. If it's for cropped hair dyed green, then they may well want this and could even be the one who starts a craze. They strive to be different, even if all this amounts to is being the opposite of what their parents would wish for.

The Aquarian teenager gets pleasure from shocking others by their appearance and enjoys being admired in their peer group as one of the most extreme. As they gain kudos and street credibility from all this, parents are advised to play down their own shock and dismay, as that only ups the antagonism. Parents need to understand that their offspring's dress code is about establishing a separate identity and think back to some of the way-out clothes they may once have worn. If they approach this in an authoritarian way, they will lose their children's respect and possibly never get it back.

Negotiation is always possible with the teenage Aquarian, particularly through appealing to their sense of reason. And not all will exhibit this kind of attention-seeking behaviour. In particular, the more introverted types find being conspicuous excruciating. This stage of growing up is especially awkward and uncomfortable for them and they shrink from any kind of attention. The more introverted Aquarian adolescent may become quite anti-social and reclusive, spending time alone in their room listening to music or on their computer but feeling too self-conscious to go out with friends. This withdrawal can be equally worrying for parents but encouraging them to invite a friend to visit is a good start. Not all go wild.

Many Aquarian children adopt an idealistic stance when still young, which parents may find awkward or inconvenient. For instance, becoming vegetarian, refusing to eat genetically-modified food, or food that involves the exploitation of those in the Third World or refusing to wear leather are all possibilities, as is minding whether their parents recycle and having an awareness of the sustainability of natural resources. They may demonstrate a precocious social conscience and get involved in political action within their school or local community.

The Aquarian child notices the inequalities in life and comments on these, asking parents for an explanation. These children believe that things should be fair, are upset when they aren't and want to do something about it. They have an inbuilt philanthropic mentality that kicks in early on. This is clearly admirable but can put parents, who have lost some of the idealism of their youth, on the defensive. Yet it's important not to dampen these children's enthusiasm, as they are the kind of individuals who will go on to improve the lot of others.

School provides not only an education for the Aquarian child but also an important social outlet, which is apparent from nursery school onwards. They don't only attend to learn but also to make friends and enjoy themselves. These children are usually popular, liked because they are jolly and lively and muck in. Their egalitarian nature shines through from an early age.

The friendships Aquarian children cultivate when young are maintained over many years. As adults, some still have friends from primary school days, as once a bond has been made it's not easily broken. They are the opposite of 'fair-weather friends' as they show tremendous loyalty and stick around through the bad times. They don't chop and change. Sociable and easygoing, they enjoy 'hanging out' with mates, doing nothing in particular. Like Sagittarian children, they like to have their friends visit and stay over, which can provide useful leverage and bargaining power when trying to get them to cooperate.

School may well be one of the happiest times of their life, as besides the social aspect, the Aquarian child loves to learn. Education is exciting and enjoyable, so they make great pupils, interested and keen to find things out. They can be easily distracted at times but they engage energetically with their subjects and enter into the spirit of a school wholeheartedly. When they reach the stage where they have to make subject choices, they may be hard pressed to know which route to take. Aquarians are found in all walks of life but taking science, sociology and communications subjects may be a good bet. However, leaving specialisation as late as possible and keeping their options open is also recommended.

While teachers may enjoy the keen interest of their Aquarian pupils, they can also be a bit of a handful, especially from adolescence onwards. As they develop, they flex their intellectual muscle and this can lead to them voicing their own opinions quite forcibly. They relish debate and can court argument by challenging the wisdom of their teachers and by being a bit of a 'know it all'. They may well search out information about school topics that is more up-to-date, from sources like the internet, so their teacher must handle this situation with care. Like a heavy-handed parent, if they deal with this in an autocratic and defensive way, they'll lose the respect of this pupil and be in for a long and difficult time, during which they'll be challenged continually.

The best way to deal with the young Aquarian's search for knowledge is to appreciate their contribution and give them the space to present it; it helps to minimise their antagonistic use. That way, they feel validated and go on to develop their curiosity in constructive ways, not just to show up the teacher. Intellectually adventurous, these children have excellent minds that need to be stretched. If they become seriously disruptive or awkward at school, it's almost certainly because they aren't getting the mental stimulation that they need.

Most Aquarian children go on to some form of further education or university, as studying is something they enjoy for its own sake. They quickly realise that they'll need to gain qualifications if they are to make their way in life. Parents should be prepared for this expense. They may take a gap year first, though, that opens their eyes to the plight of others. They'll already be looking at how they can be socially useful by applying what they do to making the world a better place.

The Aquarian child's idealism is wonderful and joyous to behold. However, it can be hard for those who have more experience not to want to wake them up to some of the harsher realities of life. Please desist. It won't work. They'll not appreciate it and will become alienated from those who are more cynical. Their hopes and wishes are their greatest gift. Help them to hang on to them and to feel empowered to make a difference.

12

Pisces
The Fish

February 19th to March 20th

*A mutable water sign, ruled by
Jupiter and Neptune*

Introducing Pisces

Those born under Pisces are enigmatic, mysterious individuals who, as a result, are difficult to fathom. They can
be recognised by that far-away look in their eyes, as if
they are dreaming of something wonderful and not of this
world. And it's true, at times they barely inhabit everyday
reality; theirs is a far more magical universe, full of rich
symbolism and meaning. These are the poets, sages and
visionaries of the zodiac, with their focus on mystical
and spiritual matters. They are hard to define and to pin
down and are full of surprises.

Pisceans are sensitive souls. These are empathic, kind
and compassionate individuals, who readily identify with
the suffering of others. For them, all people are connected
and share a common humanity, so what hurts one person
also hurts them. Items on the news, which show disasters
and misery affecting those in far-off places can bring on a
bout of weeping. To ignore these people would be like
ignoring a loved one or a neighbour's cry for help – it is
not an option. Some try to protect themselves from the

distress they feel when witnessing these stories by not reading newspapers or watching the news on television.

Pisceans can also be moved to tears by beauty, whether in nature, music, painting or in any of the arts, for this is one of the most creative signs of the zodiac, who often have a fine appreciation of these forms. In this case, their weeping is an expression of joy or ecstasy. They shed tears readily and these can signify a variety of different feelings. Never assume to know what their tears are about; always ask.

Pisceans feel agonised by, and respond strongly to, others' pain and distress and so are moved to do something to try and make things better. They lend a helping hand to those in trouble and exemplify the 'Good Samaritan' who goes out of his way to help others. They have a selfless quality whereby they put the needs of others above their own. Although this need to act is due to their strong identification with others, they are also, in a roundabout way, trying to help themselves, too.

This sensitivity to the plight of others means Pisceans can be exploited by less scrupulous individuals who can take advantage of their good nature. Pisces tend to believe the best of others and however many times they are let down and disappointed, their faith in the goodness of human nature prevails. To lose this and become cynical would be a terrible loss.

When they find themselves in a non-conducive situation, Pisceans are skilled at extricating themselves unobtrusively and quickly. They rarely confront others, as they dislike displays of aggression and can't bear emotional scenes. This would jar their delicate sensibilities and leave them upset for days. They prefer to deal with things in discreet, indirect ways and as a consequence are expert at a kind of passive avoidance.

In fact, Pisces make not being straightforward an art form. They are renowned for taking the path of least resistance and for going with the flow. Like the fish that represent this sign, they can be slippery and prefer to slither out of situations that they are not happy with. Others may have no idea that there was even a problem in the first place as they can slip away without causing any surface ripples. These are individuals who register where the exits are the moment they enter a room or situation – literally and metaphorically.

Although they don't have a fear of being trapped in the way that some signs do, Pisces do dread being in an inhospitable or hostile environment, one where they don't feel at home, hence the need sometimes to make a rapid escape. Sayings like 'a fish out of water' underline the fact that this is a life-threatening situation for the fish concerned and Pisceans can find themselves feeling as if they can't breathe and desperate to be back in their watery domain.

This is the sign of the two fish, swimming in opposite directions and typically Pisces experience a conflicting inner pull. One fish can be seen as going with the current, following the flow and taking the easy route, maximising its natural advantages. The other fish is going against the current and having to swim upstream, hence everything is experienced as hard work. Nature is hindering rather than helping or, at any rate, they have to push hard for something that they want.

Yet, like all the water signs (the other two being Cancer and Scorpio), Pisces can be deceptively strong when it comes to persistence, wearing down resistance in others like the proverbial wave lapping on a rock. They gently but steadily erode any opposition and get what they want in the end.

Pisces often find they have a dilemma over which kind of fish they are. When they stick to what may seem the sensible choice and get carried along by the current, they sometimes are accused of being lazy, not making enough of an effort and resting on their laurels. When they go against the current they are then accused of making a meal of it, of creating hard work out of something that is actually easy. It's as if they can't win. They have to learn when and where it's appropriate to be each fish and not to live their life in only one mode.

Pisceans are adaptable, flexible individuals. They adjust to whatever circumstances they find themselves in and are good at making the most of all kinds of situations, even those that others might find difficult. Nevertheless, they do suffer when in an alienating situation and will seek to find a happier alternative. Their chameleon-like quality helps them to survive and means that although they are profoundly affected and changed by the environment they find themselves in, they can adjust back, once their circumstances alter. Nothing is fixed or permanent for them. Others may wonder, as with the chameleon, what their true colours and personality are. The answer is that, because they are reactive to their surroundings, who they are in any given moment varies and shifts.

More than any other sign, Pisces is in tune with the fluctuating rhythms in life and happy to go along with the natural ebb and flow. They surrender a certain amount of control to a higher power and trust that the timing of things is preordained, so there's no point in trying to hurry anything along. They have this relaxed manner that comes from realising that everything has its time and place and that opportunities, events and life itself unfolds as and when it's meant to. This laissez-faire attitude can result in considerable procrastination, which can frustrate others, who want them to be more pro-active.

Pisces is probably the most romantic of the signs. They fall in love at the drop of a hat and their heart rules their head in most matters. They adore being in love. That giddy intoxicating feeling inspires the poetry in their soul and they are in their element. It is after this point has been reached that trouble can loom in paradise.

Although Pisces is not interested in conquering, in the way that Aries can be, there is a point fairly early on in a relationship when their interest can rapidly evaporate. They enjoy the art of seduction and may even see it as a rather dangerous game but once anything approaching everyday life sets in they can be off, looking for a new magical experience. At their worst, some are addicted to the feeling of being in love and searching for someone with whom they can enact this scenario.

This can clearly cause pain and heartache to those involved with such a Pisces. One thing new partners are advised to check out very early on, is what kind of track record their Pisces lover has. While this can't reveal the whole story, nevertheless, if they have a string of short-lived relationships in which they express disappointment, then don't be fooled into thinking this will be any different. Odds on, unless something fundamental has changed, this will be a repeat performance. Pisces can be heartbreakers.

Finding that special person to settle down with has a lot to do with timing. Pisces simply reach a point in their life when they are ready. Before that, they never intentionally set out to hurt another, as they are far too caring and sensitive to do that but in their impetuous and short-lived liaisons, once the first flame of passion has died down, they distance and disentangle themselves as gently as is possible.

For every grand passion of Pisces that results in a relationship of some kind, there are several that, for one reason or another, never get off the ground. Many spend the first part of their adult life on an emotional roller-coaster ride – in and out of love and chasing their romantic dreams.

This doesn't mean that Pisces never settles down because, of course, many do. They are more likely to stay with a partner who doesn't fall for them hook, line and sinker, as they stay captivated by someone who remains elusive. They enjoy the mystery of someone who is not too available and tire of someone who becomes as besotted as them. Hardly fair and not everyone wants to play hard to get but, for those who are genuinely cautious and more grounded, then this relationship may work out well.

Pisceans find devotion easy so once in a relationship they go on to make an adoring partner. Whatever faults they may have, they are kind and considerate and aim to please and have a way of making a loved one feel very special. They, too, like to be indulged and appreciate treats, like breakfast in bed. In fact, their lifestyle can veer towards the hedonistic, as they're not good at keeping anything they do in check and tend to go overboard.

Pisces may not be the tidiest person to live with, as they suffer from a certain amount of inner chaos, which can spill over and be reflected by their surroundings. They are the types who blitz the place every so often and get it pristine, only for it to rapidly degenerate into something resembling a slum. Pisces can be oblivious to the mess – this may have something to do with their artistic spirit – and even feel quite comfortable in it. Despite how it looks, they'll be able to find the things they need and there'll be a system of sorts. If anyone else tidies up, they'll complain loudly that they can no longer find their things.

For some Pisces, however, home may be a place of sanctuary and retreat, where they seek calm and tranquillity and, as such, they'll want it to remain clean, clear and uncluttered. For these individuals, their home is a temple, a sacred space, not to be violated by noise or mess. Their decor may be minimalist and those who have a spiritual or religious practice may house an altar or religious artefacts. Tidy or untidy, the Piscean home is often glowing with gently harmonising colour, thanks to their artistic sensibilities.

There's a big difference in the way Pisces behave behind closed doors, as this is their private domain, where they reveal their innermost self. It's only when through this threshold that it's apparent what a stress and strain being out in the world can be for them. Within their home they relax and unwind and shed the facade that they don to cope with public life.

Pisces won't necessarily seek to have children but is more than happy if they come along. They may even be lax on contraceptives and so allow an accident to occur. Any decision is made by default. Once a child has arrived, their love and dedication kicks in and they can't do enough to make their child's journey through life as pain-free as possible. They make liberal and laid-back parents where discipline is unheard of and understanding and compassion are laid on by the bucketload. They definitely don't believe you can spoil a child by giving it too much love.

As parents, Pisces' problem can be that they are too relaxed and don't set clear or appropriate boundaries. They can make themselves too available and instead of generating a feeling of safety for their children, this can create feelings of insecurity. And although there are differences of opinion about whether a fixed bedtime is in the child's interest, there's no doubt that it benefits the parents. It means they have some guaranteed space, which they badly need to process their day.

Pisces' relaxed approach can backfire spectacularly when their offspring hit adolescence. It's a bit late then to start to impose ground rules, yet certain agreements need to be in place and respected, for their children's safety as much as anything else. They can find themselves with unruly teenagers on their hands and have to make U-turns on how they manage them.

Those Pisces who have numerous romantic escapades may be searching for an experience of ecstasy and the divine via a relationship. The yearning for oneness with a beloved may actually be a red herring, compensating for the lack of spirituality in their life. They may believe that falling in love is the only way to experience the sublime, when in fact this is doomed to failure. After repeated disappointments or, more positively, after having managed to stay in a relationship beyond the first rush of passion, they may seek other ways to have these feelings of oneness and merging.

Ultimately Pisces only finds the perfect, unconditional love that they long for through some kind of religious or spiritual experience. Some find their way to Eastern religious practices, while others are at home with the more orthodox religions. However, it can just as easily be a private, inner conviction that is not necessarily found within a recognised spiritual practice or belief. Whatever system of belief they find this will stand them in good stead, as they have found a way to unite with God, the divine or their higher self, however that is understood.

The path of the devotee, which involves surrender to a higher power, is one that Pisces can find especially fulfilling. Some go in search of a guru, knowing this to be their path. Others may deny this but then find less worthy people to show their devotion to. Pisces are at their best when offering unconditional love and making sacrifices in the name of love, and this can be too much for an ordinary mortal to be on the receiving end. Hence, their search for divine love, via another, can be painful, especially when they realise the human failings of their lover.

Some Pisces are tempted to try and escape the pain of everyday living by the use of drink and drugs. Some drugs offer a glimpse of the ecstatic bliss that they so yearn for, but ultimately this can never satisfy their longing for an experience of God. And for those who become addicted to a substance, either physically or psychologically, this becomes a wholly destructive experience that can lead to ruin.

For those Pisces who follow a spiritual path and have a spiritual practice then much of the hurtful relationship patterns, let alone the descent into drink and drugs, are circumvented. These are the Pisceans who meditate, practise yoga and go on retreats. Through these practices and other more traditional ones, they honour the needs of the soul.

Piscean George Harrison acted out many of the characteristics of his sign. His musical talent, his experimentation with drugs, his period as a devotee with a guru and his long-standing involvement in a spiritual practice, which included funding an ashram, as well as his film production company (films are associated with Neptune, the ruler of Pisces), all typify Pisces. He was known as a gentle and caring man, who found the success and fame of being a Beatle difficult and was the most mysterious of the famous four.

All Pisceans are in tune with the less-tangible levels of reality. In ordinary conversation, they pick up on body language and emotional undercurrents just as much as, if not more than, what's actually being said. As a consequence, they have an interesting, oblique take on other people and situations, which stands them in good stead but can be hard to explain to those who are more logical. It is as if they mind-read and while some may have psychic ability, most just have a developed sensitivity to the underlying feelings in the atmosphere.

Within relationships, Pisces rely on their psychic antennae rather a lot and are often amazed to discover that others don't necessarily have this facility. They may fail to spell out their likes and dislikes to loved ones, expecting them to know automatically, by osmosis, and are hurt when this fails. What's more, they get their wires crossed, as they have to disentangle their own insecurities from the information that they pick up, so can't always interpret signals accurately. It can make for quite a muddle, not helped by the fact that Pisces may feel let down when this telepathic method of communication fails, as if it reflects badly on the relationship; it then leaves them feeling unloved. Partners do well to point out early on that non-verbal communication is a bit hit and miss.

Some Pisces go on to develop their instinctive awareness of the intangible domain in a professional way. An understanding of the metaphysical realm underpins many of the complementary therapies. They tune into this less orthodox way of thinking and are found working as homeopaths, reflexologists, Reiki healers, acupuncturists, cranial osteopaths, Shiatsu practitioners and the like. All of these systems of healing have an understanding of the subtle body and how energy flows within it, something Pisces are particularly well equipped to recognise. In these professions their sensitivity and compassion are useful adjuncts to their skill and understanding. And for all those who don't choose to become practitioners, many nevertheless subscribe to these methods of healing, preferring to use them either instead of or alongside conventional medicine.

Besides complementary medicine, Pisces are often found in other related areas helping those who are in pain or distress. Counselling and psychotherapy, social work and nursing are all possible avenues they may decide to go down. However, because they are so sensitive this can be very taxing on their psyche. They are susceptible to becoming overly involved with their patients and clients and of taking their work home with them, although some would see this as a demonstration that they care. Despite the problem of emotional overload, working in the helping professions provides them with a rewarding emotional connection to others.

However, Pisces are perhaps best suited to working creatively. These are often exceptionally gifted individuals and, for those able to find a way of making a living from their talent, this is going to provide the most fulfilment and satisfaction. Success may well take considerable perseverance and be a major test of character. It is unlikely to be instant or to come when young, so faith and persistence are required. They may have to swim against the currents.

For every Pisces who is successful, there are many that aren't, who eventually settle down into less rewarding work in order to pay the bills. Nevertheless, the struggle and the experience will still have been important to those who don't find commercial success, as success isn't only judged materially. The satisfaction gained and the memories held are important and a rewarding creative interest established. Later in life, it's important to remember that, on the whole, regret centres on the things that weren't attempted, so it's important that they give it their best shot.

Among those Pisces who have become very successful as actors are Elizabeth Taylor, Michael Caine, William Hurt, Drew Barrymore, Julie Walters and Robert Carlisle. For those who can manage the rejections that go with the territory of auditioning, then this is a career for which they are extremely well suited. Masters of illusion, they can take on any part and use their enigmatic quality to convey all kinds of moods and atmospheres. They are at home in the world of theatre, film and television, which relies to such an extent on the imagination and make-believe.

Other areas of show business can also appeal to Pisces and Charlotte Church, Quincy Jones, Bobby Womack and the late Nina Simone are all famous Piscean singers who have a special magic. As well as their voices and musicality, they have an allure that has captivated audiences all over the world.

Besides these areas, Pisces are often found as artists, photographers, musicians and writers. Any form of creative self-expression that can draw upon their own impressions and imagination suits them well. Whatever their chosen medium, Pisces' creative style is subtle and atmospheric, through which they are able to convey fine nuances of tone and feeling.

Because of the nature of creative work, many Pisces will work for themselves, although they can find this hard. Discipline is not their way, as they have to work when inspired and fired up, which means there can be long periods of inactivity that are difficult to move on from. When working with others, as part of a design team for instance or in an advertising studio, they may not create such defining work but will produce a steadier stream of it.

As an employee, Pisces may seem compliant while quietly doing their own thing. Their boss or line manager would do well do keep a watch over what exactly they are getting up to, as they can easily while away great swathes of time with tasks that interest them but that have little to do with what they are being paid for. A bored Pisces wastes a lot of time and sinks into a kind of apathy, so firing them can be just what they need. They often don't manage to leave under their own steam and need a helping hand in order to move on.

That said, Pisces makes a valuable contribution to any workforce when they are doing a job that emotionally engages them. The key is that they need to feel involved and creatively absorbed and, without that, they could be up to no good in work time. If there is a happy atmosphere among their work colleagues this helps to keep them motivated for a while but ultimately it takes more than workplace camaraderie. They need to love what they're doing (which is no bad thing) and without that, their attention will wander.

As the boss, Pisces is far from conventional. The workplace boundaries will be lax, as none of what he or she sees as petty rules matters to this boss. What they are concerned with is the attitude of employees and how much they care about and have invested in their work. Those with the right approach can get away with an awful lot. Especially when it comes to things like compassionate leave or the needs of employees to attend their children's sports days, even to attend an afternoon yoga class, then this boss is extremely accommodating and easygoing. In fact, if anyone is going to suggest a group hug before work begins, or a period of meditation during the day, partly to improve work morale and performance but equally to acknowledge another dimension, it's the Pisces boss.

Where Piscean bosses are more demanding is that they expect to engage the heart and soul of their employees. They may not make a fuss about minor things but they actually want a huge amount and may not even recognise that this is asking for a lot. This may suit some employees who love their job but others find this far too nebulous and prefer a situation that is more straightforward, where the boundaries are more conventional and clearly defined.

Whatever career Pisceans end up in, and many go through numerous trials and errors before they find the one that really suits them, they ultimately seek a position in which they can invest their heart and soul. Once that is in place and taken care of, they have accomplished one of their most important tasks.

Negative Pisces

Many of Pisces' most positive characteristics can slide into a negative manifestation. Because they hold such high and noble aspirations, when they fail they have further to fall. More than most signs, when their good intentions go wrong, they lead to some rather horrid consequences.

Pisces' sensitivity is one such characteristic. Their sensitivity means that everything can impinge on them and they can misconstrue actions and comments that were not aimed at them personally. Things that were said in a casual way they invest with deep meaning that may be entirely in their heads and not intended at all. They are awash with their own pain and distress and everything around them compounds this.

It can be hard to have a normal conversation with such a Pisces as everything has to be censored and scrutinised to check that they can't possibly take it the wrong way. They are convinced that others hold a certain opinion of them, which they set out to prove. This can lead to a kind of victim mentality. They develop a mind-set in which they see themselves as hard done by and fail to realise that they're probably no worse off than the average person. This victim mode is extremely unattractive and can be hard to shift.

One such Pisces would always lament her tales of woe and no matter how much empathic understanding was offered, nothing ever seemed to make her feel better. It then became apparent that she had a selective memory and when good deeds and kindness were extended to her she quickly forgot these in order to maintain her victim status. She only remembered the bad things and spoke of this ad infinitum. Eventually others tired of listening, and so over time she created the friendless, hostile reality that she experienced at an inner level. The friends she might have had gave up on her, as she was so unrewarding. Without her ever making any accusations, her friends nevertheless felt blamed for her unhappiness and never appreciated for the things they actually did for her.

In this way, this particular Pisces woman created her own reality, as it has been argued everyone does to some extent, in so far as we interpret it through our own particular lens. How this particular stance originates is a mixture of innate predisposition and life experiences, and re-examining and deconstructing these experiences can be helpful, especially in the kind of stuck situation this woman found herself in. The Piscean has to let go of her victim status and start taking some responsibility for her unhappiness.

It can been argued that playing the victim role is a form of passive aggression and certainly Pisces have problems with aggression of any kind. They positively flinch from it and find it hugely threatening, both in other people and within themselves. They go to great lengths to avoid it, yet in the process manage to provoke it in others. This is a subtle and complicated process and, of course, others are ultimately responsible for their own feelings, even if provoked.

However, if a Pisces finds themselves involved with successive individuals who don't appear at first to have anger management problems and then proceed to get angry a lot, they would do well to consider that it may have something to do with them, too. They are attracting this type for a reason and it's possible that they are expressing angry feelings on their behalf.

When Pisces is playing the passive, victim role for all it's worth, they manage to engender guilt in loved ones, too. Others feel bad about having these angry feelings about poor Mr or Ms Pisces, who has done nothing obvious to warrant them. This kind of muddle leaves no one thinking clearly.

In common with the other water signs (Cancer and Scorpio) Pisces can be manipulative in order to get what they want. They feel too exposed and vulnerable to ask for what they want directly and risk an outright rejection, they want others to offer, so this is where their skills in manipulation come in to play. They contrive to get them to volunteer. Some genuinely believe that it only counts or has meaning when they obtain what they want from others without having to actually ask for it. If they have to ask, it somehow makes the whole thing worthless. This convoluted thinking means they put subtle and insidious pressure on others to comply.

Pisceans are the world's experts on guilt-tripping others and have an unparalleled way of getting people to help in all kinds of ways that they had no intention of doing ten minutes earlier. Their particular skill is in presenting themselves as hapless victims, so that others step in and rescue them and the situation. They can tug on others' compassion and exploit it.

Pisces will tie people in knots with their convoluted emotional wrangling, leaving them speechless. When they are in an upset state any logic they have (and they are never the most logical of people) goes out of the window. Also, they are so utterly convinced by their own argument that there's no reasoning with them. They tug at others' loyalties, leaving them feeling very unsure of themselves. To withstand a Pisces' emotional onslaught others have to be extremely well grounded in their own values and reality.

Much of this more negative behaviour is the result of Pisces' hypersensitivity and although the emotional shenanigans can be exhausting, they are far preferable to other more destructive solutions that some take. Because they experience such a degree of psychic pain, some resort to using various substances to dull and numb the pain. Depending on the drugs used, this can lead to addiction, which creates severe problems. Even supposedly non-addictive drugs, when used regularly, can have a seriously detrimental effect on the user's ability to function.

All Pisces need to be especially careful around any experimentation with drugs as they easily move to excess. Their longing for ecstatic experiences makes them especially vulnerable. There is nothing wrong with the search for bliss but this route will never get them there: it ultimately takes them further away, often into degrading experiences. It is interesting to note that the programmes used by both Narcotics Anonymous and Alcoholics Anonymous to support addicts relies in part on a surrender to God's will, however the addict defines this. It has often been pointed out that the alcoholic is searching for Spirit in a bottle, when it's to be found elsewhere.

Pisces are even susceptible to becoming addicted to prescribed drugs. If their doctor deems these necessary they should nevertheless take care when taking a course of anti-depressants or painkillers. Because of their sensitivity they are more vulnerable than most to aggravating withdrawal symptoms. Medication is only ever a short-term fix and whether or not it is part of a programme of recovery from a psychological malaise, it does not provide the answer. These are problems of the psyche and soul and as such need to be addressed in greater depth.

Most Pisces are not addicts, as such, but nevertheless exhibit addictive tendencies in the way they use food, watch television and buy clothes. Not all those who use food for escape or comfort have a diagnosed eating disorder but they know, nonetheless, that their eating is out of control in some way. They have a problem with their appetite and how to satisfy it. Late-night comfort eating is not uncommon. Watching too much television may sound fairly harmless but it can deaden the mind and leave those who have slumped in front of the screen for too long feeling listless and apathetic. It certainly doesn't help with feelings of self-esteem.

Being a shopaholic has only recently been defined or identified as a serious problem and in some instances this leads to alarming debts and financial difficulties. These are individuals who regularly need a consumer fix and spend compulsively irrespective of their funds. Many people joke about retail therapy providing a much needed pick-me-up but the shopaholic does this on a regular basis, just as any junky needs a regular hit.

Pisces may well feel that their money is destined for the enjoyable things in life and resist the idea of a budget or setting some of their income aside for bills. Their finances can be in pretty bad shape.

Nearly anything that Pisces uses as a form of escape from everyday reality can have negative consequences. Moderation is not usually part of their vocabulary. There are feelings of shame associated with all types of addiction and a definite pattern emerges, whereby the addict craves their fix, indulges their weakness – whatever that may be – has an initial feeling of release and then feels shame and anguish and wants to stop the cycle. Those caught up in this kind of cycle need to seek expert help.

Those Pisces who long to escape the harsh realities of everyday life may benefit from periods of retreat, especially in a spiritual or religious community. Places such as Findhorn, in Scotland, offer a sanctuary for those who feel weary of mainstream society. Here they can live a simple community-based life, which involves daily work that is restorative for their spirit and soul. Many such places exist and are ideal, either for short periods or as a way of life, for the careworn and idealistic Pisces.

Pisces do need more quiet time than most. They do well with periods of solitude and regain their composure and equilibrium after time spent alone. Some meditate as part of their spiritual practice. One way or another they need to find ways of sorting and sifting through all the impressions they absorb throughout their day and settling them within themselves. They need time for contemplation and reflection on a regular basis, whether or not they have spiritual or religious beliefs.

Creative pursuits like writing, painting and playing a musical instrument will also have a cathartic and yet nourishing effect. These are all excellent media in which Pisces can indirectly process their impressions and yet turn them into something more. Pisces seeks peace and quiet in order to be able to work and think, too. They like to get away from the hustle and bustle and easily feel over-stimulated by everyday life. They may well need more sleep than most, as their emotional responsiveness uses up so much nervous energy. Having sufficient time to dream, which is another important way that they process the events of their day, is essential to their well-being.

For some Pisces a walk by water will calm them, particularly by the sea, with all its moods, which reflects their own rich emotional life. This is, after all, the domain of the fish, so it's not surprising that Pisces feel so at home by the water's edge. Many choose to live within earshot of the sound of water and even having a small pond or water feature in the garden can help soothe their jagged nerves.

Pisces as the victim is one of the negative manifestations of this sign but equally they can plump for being the saviour, the other side of the coin. This can be an inflated sense of their own spiritual or religious supremacy, in which they see themselves as here to save people. This includes those who have an evangelical mission to change others, be that to try a miracle cure, follow a particular kind of diet, use certain biodegradable cleaning products or whatever. However noble the cause, there's a thin line between imparting information and being on a messianic bandwagon.

Along with this, as with the missionaries of old, there can be a kind of moral superiority, which is offensive and obnoxious to a twenty-first-century viewpoint. When in such a position, Pisces is probably trying to avoid feelings of helplessness and so rejoices in having 'the answers', as they see it. They wrongly assume that because something has worked for them it will work for others.

This is the way of so many self-help books, which claim a solution for some problem or another has been found. The author has found a way that has worked for them and as a consequence become inflated and genuinely believes they've found the answer for others, too, and that they can be their salvation. At its most extreme, this is a messiah complex and, however well intentioned, can be dangerous. Even though their method may work for some, it's simplistic to think that there's only one way, one answer or one solution and not to appreciate that others have to find their own answers.

It could be argued that there's an element of self-delusion in those who are attempting to rescue others and this is certainly something Pisces can succumb to. Those who are on a spiritual path and have a spiritual practice can feel so grateful to have found this way and recognise so well what this has done for them – it genuinely has been their salvation – that it's hard to accept that this doesn't apply universally. They lose sight of what it was, about them and their situation, that meant that this worked so well for them and that not everyone is starting from the same place.

Another negative trait that some Pisces have is that they can be selective when it comes to telling the truth. They can put others into various categories, some of whom they tell the absolute truth to and some of whom get a watered-down version. Not all deliberately lie, although some do tell whopping fibs, but many do so by omission. They are rather good at fudging and being vague. When they do this, it's likely to be because they can't face up to something – it's about their difficulty in being emotionally straightforward. In these incidences, it's never malicious and there's no intention to hurt. For instance, they leave arrangements that there's no likelihood of them keeping up in the air. They'll promise to ring to confirm and then won't, leaving the other person dangling and not knowing.

At their absolute worst, Pisces 'forget' to tell their new partner that they are already married or that they have huge debts. These are details that are painful to admit and which carry the risk of losing someone that they can't bear to be without. Their intentions may be honourable, they plan to clear the debt quietly and discreetly or hold off the marriage question until the divorce goes through. Nevertheless it is a new partner's business and they are entitled to know. This is an example of being a slippery fish.

Typically Pisces can be absent-minded and forgetful, which is how they get away with a dubious version of the truth in the first place. So often they have their head in the clouds that they are late for appointments or even forget to turn up altogether or misplace their keys or lose vital things. While not a terrible fault, it can be infuriating for others and they can miss out on opportunities. Older and wiser Pisces often find writing memos and lists helps, as even if they don't then refer to them, it lodges the information in their memory.

Whatever awful things Pisces may or may not get up to, they are usually caught and exposed for all to see. And it is nearly always about managing their extremely kind and sensitive nature in some way or another. They so long for paradise and seek it in all kinds of inappropriate places before they find their way. Like a fish out of water, they thrash around all too visibly.

Many of those Pisces in the public eye have had to go through this in an excruciatingly public way. Elizabeth Taylor and Liza Minnelli have been patients in the Betty Ford clinic on numerous occasions and have seen their private struggles splashed across the headlines. Drew Barrymore didn't cope with being catapulted to fame as a child and had an awful few years with drug addictions. Karen Carpenter died of anorexia and, while being in the public eye didn't cause this, it can't have helped. It's interesting to note that all were originally child stars and so had to deal with complex feelings about this early exposure and they could well have felt exploited.

Piscean Christine Keeler, the famous call girl of the Profumo Affair, which brought down the UK Conservative government of the time, has much of the victim about her. The glamour may have been a big attraction at the time – some Pisces are drawn by glamour as it promises that wondrous special something that they seek. But it's an empty promise and proves to be an illusion. For some, this takes a very long time to realise.

However destructive Pisces can be in their search for nirvana, this is nevertheless a noble quest. While those around them can be badly affected, the main damage they inflict is to themselves. Damage limitation strategies are recommended for those involved with an out-of-control Pisces. In the end, most Pisceans do find a way through to a place of inner peace and tranquillity. Remember this is the sign of the fish, whose natural domain is the ocean, with all its magnetism and destructive power. No one is more attuned to the highs and lows of life than those born under this sign.

The Pisces Man

The Pisces man is recognised by his dreamy look and charming, seductive manner. He has an elusive quality that makes him seem special, an aura of mystery that attracts others, who are trying to work out quite what it is he has that is so enticing. This man bewitches those who come into his orbit and leaves them enraptured. He has magical, alluring characteristics that draw others to him like moths to a flame.

The Pisces man is kind and considerate and usually gets on particularly well with women, who appreciate his sensitivity and feeling depths. Like the other water signs (Cancer and Scorpio) he evaluates life from a feeling perspective and is in touch with his own inner world. This is his bedrock and it is upon this that all his decisions and interactions are based. If, on an instinctual level, he doesn't like someone then no amount of rationalisation will convince him to trust them. It goes against his gut reactions, which will always take precedence, even if he can't justify or explain this to himself.

This is not your ordinary, macho male by a long shot – the Pisces man is poetic and mystical and altogether of a different mentality. Even if he works as a builder's labourer or a lorry driver, he'll be tuning in to subtle unseen dimensions. The builder senses the psychic energy in the building, all the lives that have previously existed and contributed to make it a happy or sad place. The lorry driver notices the strange lights in the sky as he drives across the moors and chats about their mysterious glow when he gets to the next service station. Others may think he's odd but he exerts a fascinating pull on their imaginations nonetheless.

The Pisces man lives with this awareness of other realms and never assumes that his everyday reality is all that exists. He is not limited to what his five senses have to say about the nature of the universe and is open to just about anything. This openness is part of his charm, although he can be somewhat gullible and suggestible and can get some rather fanciful ideas into his head, which he follows with passion. Rather than look for a rational explanation he's far more likely to plump for one that is fairly way out and difficult to either prove or disprove. This is all a part of his rich imagination, so he's not that good at sorting out fact from fiction.

The Pisces man's heightened sensitivity means that he has the capacity to be profoundly moved by various cultural pursuits, in which he can derive much emotional satisfaction and fulfilment. These don't have to be high-brow. Some may favour classical music or be great opera buffs but equally others have as much enthusiasm for jazz, rhythm and blues, hip-hop and popular music. In order to appreciate this he may have expensive and sophisticated hi-fi equipment. Whatever his passion, he tends to go overboard, at least for a while, so he may import rare CDs or be into vinyl (the specialist's choice) and have an extensive and comprehensive collection of his favourite type of music.

Besides music, some Pisces men are connoisseurs of, and passionate about, art, the theatre or the cinema, all of which can affect him at a deep emotional level. He can be inspired and uplifted by a film, an exhibition or a theatrical production. He'll have favourite directors whose work he'll be expert on and artists whose exhibitions he never misses. He may well collect art and patronise artists who are as yet not established.

The Pisces man may also enjoy reading, probably preferring fiction, poetry, philosophy, spirituality and the metaphysical. His reading is partly to escape, to transport him into other realms and partly to discover new ways of thinking about and understanding existence. Either way, it has to appeal to his imagination. He is not after dry facts and, however intelligent, he's not usually an intellectual. Academia is usually too narrow and rigid for him but if he does take this route he brings to it a whole new dimension.

When it comes to relationships, the Pisces man's imagination and sensitivity play an important part. He is probably the world's most romantic suitor and, when smitten, has been known to send flowers in abundance. These are carefully selected and, as such, hold a special, intimate meaning. Possibly all the blooms are highly scented or he picks a massive bouquet of long-stem roses or all of the flowers are white or pink. Whatever he goes for, he imbues them with romantic significance. He is able to think about the flowers symbolically so that they convey a subtle and sophisticated message. This level of perception permeates all his communication and is what makes him so romantic and special.

Besides flowers, the Pisces man may well send tokens of his love that a new partner treasures forever. When inspired he can write the most moving poetry and has a way with words, so that even an ordinary letter becomes extraordinary. Any gifts he buys are done so with great care and thought.

The Pisces man makes both the small symbolic gestures and the big, bold, expensive ones, too. He'll spend a whole week's wages on a spectacular present which will completely blow away his lover. This is one of the ways he communicates his feelings and sweeps a potential partner off their feet. When he's out to woo he is extremely persuasive and virtually impossible to resist. Unlike some signs, who become tongue-tied, he has all the right words and seems most convincing and sincere. He has perfected the art of seduction and, like a musician and his instrument, he loves to play.

Not that seduction is a game to the Pisces man. This is for real, at least in the moment. It's just that he gets swept away by the sheer romance of it all, which can then dissolve once the object of his affections has been wooed and won. He may be in love with being in love and only discover further down the line that the actual person's identity is incidental. For those who are on the end of his powerful, seductive advances, check out how personal they are. If they might work for anyone, then take care. When it is just a sublime feeling that he seeks, via another, it is all going to end in tears.

There is no way this is done intentionally. The Pisces man is as convinced by his passion as is the object of his affection. His own romantic impulses simply take over and he gets carried away. His yearning for something exquisite, wonderful and not of this world creates a powerful tug on his emotions and leads him to have some extraordinary experiences. He has a way, whenever life gets dull or mundane, of injecting it with some magic.

For those who are willing to take the emotional risk, even a short-lived affair with Pisces is magical and memorable. A partner feels like a god or goddess for a time, elevated to this special place and totally adored. The trick is to realise that this can't last but to enjoy it while it does. The euphoria generated in that first flush of being in love can spoil a partner for later relationships, which never match up. The resolution is in accepting that perhaps it was never that real in the first place – that it was all a fantasy. Otherwise it's hard to let go and move on.

What the heterosexual Pisces man is a master at, and teaches his lovers, is the art of surrender. Having surrendered, possibly in a way that she's never managed to do before, his lover gains access to a level of herself that she's never been to before. He opens a lover up to herself. This is his gift to her, which is hers to keep and can never be taken away from her. Having touched this depth within herself, it becomes the yardstick that she measures all subsequent lovers against. Yet, he may not realise exactly what he's done for her.

The Pisces man does eventually find his soul mate. After all those intoxicating high-octane affairs, the kind of person he finally settles with can seem quite surprising. He looks for someone he can be truly intimate with, someone he can share his innermost feelings, thoughts and fears and with whom he has a high degree of emotional safety. Despite his romantic nature, his choice in the end is about emotional and domestic compatibility. He wants someone he can really get along with, who doesn't jolt or jar his delicate sensibilities and with whom he can inhabit the same space harmoniously. His home is a place where he needs peace and tranquillity.

The Pisces man does best with someone who has their feet much more on the ground than he does but who can nevertheless empathise with his dreams. If he goes for a partner who is more rational and logical than he is, he can feel diminished, as it can be hard to withstand their scrutiny over a sustained period of time. By their standards he can appear stupid because he inhabits such a different reality. They may equally feel threatened, as their reliance on being objective is undermined and they are forced to accept other ways of thinking about things. Mutual respect is essential if such a coupling is to work.

Whoever the Pisces man ends up with, the relationship starts by falling in love and then moves on to something more enduring. Although looks play an important part in the initial attraction, the inner qualities of a long-term partner ultimately matter more to him. Wealth, class and status have no bearing on his choice.

Once a relationship is established, for the heterosexual Pisces man, the question of marriage may arise. He is not strictly the marrying kind and only does so to make a romantic statement. If a relationship has gone beyond the first flush of romance, then he'll be far more reluctant as he'll not see what the point is. Especially for those who have already set up home together, he'll argue that everything is fine as it is. He can be rather passive in this respect and allows a living-together situation to carry on unless he's pushed – and most women don't relish being in the role of harassing their man to marry them. He wants an easy exit and this is why he's reluctant to tie the knot, although of course this doesn't make an ending any easier, if it happens it will still be painful and messy.

As and when there are children, the Pisces man may see that his interests are better protected if he's married to their mother and decides he'd like to take the plunge. However, this is as unromantic as can be and so may not happen. Unless marriage means a great deal to the partner it may be best to accept the unwed status.

Once there are children, the Pisces man will find that leaving is no longer an option, anyway. He's in far too deep. He makes a devoted father. His soft side, which he may have felt necessary to keep under wraps, comes to the fore. He is effusive, caring and besotted by his offspring. As and when they're no longer on the breast, he'll do the night feeds, he can wind, he's a dab hand at changing nappies, in fact he excels in all the areas traditionally considered a woman's domain. He's happy to be a househusband and do the bulk of the child care and he's good at it. His empathic nature means he can interpret accurately the various cries of a baby and attend to its needs accordingly.

The Pisces man excels at all the touchy-feely stuff. This

is why he's found so attractive and what makes him such a good partner and friend. Besides his soul mate, he's likely to have other close friends of both sexes with whom he talks to about intimate matters. He needs to share his inner reality with others if he is not to feel isolated and alone. A partner may feel threatened by these friendships, when actually any danger comes from elsewhere.

Even when the Pisces man has everything to lose and an affair means little to him he is still tempted. Being faithful never comes easily to him. It has nothing to do with his deep and abiding love and affection for his partner and everything to do with his need for escape and fantasy. However, a partner is hardly going to see it that way. More often than not they will simply not know because he's so good at covering his tracks but every so often he gets really smitten and becomes moody and difficult to live with. He's torn and his partner suffers while he anguishes about what to do. They won't be privy to this and so may not know what he's struggling with but feel excluded and shut out all the same.

Not all Pisces men have affairs but some are serial philanderers. An affair holds the false promise of paradise, which is short-lived and quickly becomes sordid, tacky and meaningless. Not that the Pisces man is big on guilt, which is why he goes on to repeat this. His search is almost certainly for a spiritual experience that is doomed to failure as long as he takes this route. Until he realises this, he can cause untold pain and havoc in his personal life, not only to his partner but also to those he has affairs with and not least to himself.

Generally, though, the Pisces man is easy to live with. He's relaxed and easygoing and very good at doing nothing. Because he rarely gets stressed out, he can help a mate let the unimportant things in life slide. He knows how to enjoy himself and by doing so, creates an atmosphere that encourages those around him to unwind. In fact, he can be a bit of a hedonist. The pleasure principle is a priority for him.

The Pisces man may be a wine buff and usually enjoys a glass or two with his evening meal. He may well be an excellent cook and appreciates fine food that uses the best ingredients. Whatever his income, he tends to spend to his limits and beyond and a partner is advised to keep a close check on their joint finances. If it's a shared home, make sure it's in joint names so that he can't just go ahead and remortgage when his cash flow gets stretched. He lives for today, which is well and good except in so far as it impacts on others. A partner can get a nasty shock when they discover all the equity in their home has gone, along with their financial security.

This laissez-faire attitude means the Pisces man's fortune tends to swing back and forth between feast and famine. He just extricates himself from one dire financial situation and then lands himself in another. He's good at generating large sums of money out of nowhere, too, and is inventive and creative when he's backed into a corner. Throughout his life, his income is likely to fluctuate widely, which is part of why he has these problems. For anyone whose income drops, it's hard to adjust. And for him, it's well nigh impossible. So during the times he earns less, his spending tends to stay as it was when he earned far more.

Whatever work the Pisces man does, he's more likely to have a calling, a vocation, than to have a conventional career. Typically, he relies on his creative talents and builds upon his life experiences. He does well in all the artistic and creative arenas, such as photography, film, fine art, design, fashion, hairdressing and music, which provide him with an outlet for his sensitivity, imagination and empathy.

The helping professions are another route that the Pisces man may follow, which he's likely to decide on in mid or later life, especially if he's failed to make it creatively. This is nevertheless a good option, by no means second best, as it provides much nourishment for his soul and draws on many of his innate strengths.

Water often exerts a strong pull on Pisces men, especially those who don't show their feminine side in other more obvious ways. It could be seen that, by having a close connection to the sea, they forge a relationship to their own mysterious depths. Careers in the Navy or as merchant seamen and fishermen are all options that suit this water sign. Fishing may also be a recreational pursuit as it offers considerable solitude and reflective time.

Prince Andrew, who has had a distinguished career in the Royal Navy, is typical of this kind of Pisces. Outwardly he may appear a regular macho man but, after his divorce from Sarah Ferguson, they went on to share a home for some time. This was ostensibly for convenience and the sake of their daughters and demonstrates his sophisticated ability to process difficult feelings.

For those who are thinking of getting involved with a Pisces man, his faults are in the main that he's too kind for his own good. So he ducks and dives and is fallible and all too human. Although his spiritual longings often get him into deep waters, his search is admirable. Just like those fish, swimming in opposite directions, the best and the worst of him are closely related.

The Pisces Woman

The Pisces woman is recognised by her enigmatic, mysterious demeanour, which casts a magical spell over all those around her. She is a fascinating, alluring woman with considerable personal charisma that derives from the deep, sensitive, soulful place she inhabits.

The Pisces woman is difficult to really know, as she always seems to hold a part of herself back. It means others can never be sure of how she'll react and, however long they've known her, she continues to surprise them. She can be rather quirky, taking strong, seemingly irrational likes and dislikes to others but nevertheless this is what she relies upon in life. Rooted in her own feelings, she evaluates all situations from a feeling perspective and uses her own gut reactions as her barometer. Everything is assessed according to how it affects her. So her criterion for judging everything is quite simple: 'How does it make me feel?'

This can understandably infuriate more logical and rational types but the Pisces woman doesn't let that bother her. She carries on regardless. Part of her charm is that she has a mind and method of her own and no amount of reasoning distracts her from this. In some way she can seem to inhabit her own separate bubble, unfazed by everyday life.

However, those who attempt to discredit the Pisces woman are in for a nasty shock as she is a brilliant judge of character. She can simply sense when something about someone doesn't add up and although she may not be able to explain why, she nevertheless knows. With an uncanny grasp of certain facts that she has no business knowing, she inadvertently picks up on the undercurrents and is excellent at interpreting these. And she trusts what she knows. When at her best, she sees beneath the surface of life, so there's no hiding place with her, no subterfuge, as she can read others and situations like a book.

Although she's normally a chatty, bubbly person with a whimsical sense of humour, words sometimes fail the Pisces woman because she is so tuned into the non-verbal level of communication. She picks up on body language and subtle nuances of expression that tell her far more than words ever will about what others are communicating. Understanding may come to her in a dream or simply through the ether, but however she finds out, she's almost invariably proved right. Occasionally, when she has an emotional investment in a situation, she can get her wires crossed but, on the whole, she's spot on.

This sensitivity to the psychic atmosphere is by and large a great strength although it can overload the Pisces woman's system and leave her with a lot to process. She needs a regular psychic detox, ideally daily, whereby she washes away the flotsam and jetsam of her day and returns to what is important to her. Otherwise she carries stuff that is neither good nor useful to her that simply clogs up her system. The best way for her to do this is through time alone. By having space, she sheds those concerns that are not hers and connects back to her own centre.

Like her male counterpart, water is important to the Pisces woman and she benefits by spending time in it and around it. When stressed, just splashing her face with cold water will help. Swimming and the spa help her unwind and wash away her cares and worries. After a hard day, a long scented soak, possibly with music and candles, too, puts her world to rights. Time spent by the sea nourishes her soul and revives her. Water cleanses the toxins in her psyche and leaves her feeling revived.

Although not all Pisces women are introverted – some are indeed extremely gregarious and sociable – this is more typically an introverted sign. As such, solitude is always restorative and social activity depletes and tires. As a consequence, there is only so much socialising that she can manage before she becomes exhausted by it. Even the more extroverted benefit from activities like meditation, tai chi and yoga, which will help to still her mind and establish inner peace and tranquillity.

The Pisces woman is not materialistic and may be quite chaotic when it comes to finances. Although they may have a tendency to shop compulsively, money itself does not interest her and financial security is fairly meaningless to her, so it's not surprising she puts little energy or effort into these things. She may or may not have money but either way it's of no consequence to her and has no impact on her daily life. It's simply not a priority. Although, often, she gets together with someone who is materially minded and she then allows her partner to take care of all of that side of life, as if she doesn't want to get her hands dirty. Or it may be that she's simply grateful that someone else is willing to handle all that boring but necessary stuff.

Some Pisces women spend large swathes of time alone. A woman like this is so sensitive to rejection that she often can't chance a relationship, especially as her longings are for such perfection, that no mortal comes close. A relationship risks disappointment and the loss of her dream. She retreats into an ivory tower, awaiting the prince who will break through and awaken her. This is a lonely position, in which she has a complex fantasy life but not one in reality.

Unrequited love is one of the most painful scenarios that some Pisces women find themselves in. This is, in fact, an elaborate ruse not to have a real relationship, by choosing someone unattainable. To move on from this, some serious soul-searching is required.

Part of the difficulty is that when it comes to a relationship, the Pisces woman is probably one of the most romantic. There are no pragmatic considerations at all. She believes in love and the happy-ever-after fairy story and she won't settle for anything less. She's at her happiest and best when madly in love and is more than willing to make sacrifices for the person she loves. For her, love is intertwined with sacrifice and she may well believe it makes her a better person – that it brings her closer to God or the divine. She offers and seeks love that is unconditional.

The Pisces woman is seeking a soul mate and a spiritual, mystical union with her beloved. She yearns for oneness and merging and expects her lover to be so tuned into her that words become redundant. She loves the romantic phase of a relationship. In fact she wants this to go on forever.

She loves being wooed and wined and dined and being made to feel a million dollars. A partner must realise this is to be a lifelong undertaking, as she won't take kindly to being taken for granted some way down the line.

When unhappy, the Pisces woman can generate terrible moods and emotional atmospheres, which a partner may find impossible to make any sense of. She may not understand what's going on either but it could be she's no longer getting the kind of attention that she needs. This is a fairy princess who needs to be reassured that she's special on a daily basis. She may not be materialistic but in this sense she's very high maintenance.

With the wrong partner, the Pisces woman can become something of a doormat. If a partner has a tendency to exploit, she is exploitable. Because she believes in sacrificing her needs, then those who are more cynical would see her as leaving herself wide open to being abused. What they fail to see is that those who exploit her demean themselves and she can retreat into playing the martyr.

This martyr role is one of the weapons that the Pisces woman uses in order to get what she wants. She has the 'poor me' and 'look what I've sacrificed for you' off to perfection and can communicate it wordlessly. It works with those who love and care about her, as they can't bear to see her suffering. No one can make as much noise suffering silently as a Pisces woman. Besides the deafening silence, she can weep at the drop of a hat and uses her tears, not just as a means of expressing her hurt feelings, but as a weapon to get her own way. She can be the consummate actress when it suits her and plays the role so convincingly that even she loses sight of where the truth lies.

When content, the Pisces woman is one of the most generous, forgiving, compassionate and kindly of individuals. Nothing is too much trouble for her, as she takes care of others and their well-being. She instinctively puts others' needs first and so requires them to do likewise, as otherwise there's no one to take proper care of her. This is both her strength and her downfall. She becomes reliant for her happiness on others and when this isn't forthcoming she is left stranded. To change and be more self-reliant would be to compromise her nature.

When in a relationship, this becomes central to a Pisces woman's being. Her life revolves around her partner and she invests most of her creative energy into her relationship, expecting to receive back from it fulfilment and satisfaction. Whether or not she works or has other absorbing interests, her relationship is likely to be her priority. This is clearly a vulnerable position to place herself in and partners need to recognise what is expected of them.

Children are almost certainly part of the package for the Pisces woman, and once they arrive they may take some of the edge off her expectations of her partner. She makes a kind, caring and devoted mother. Her highly developed empathy has a much needed and appropriate outlet and she excels in the pre-verbal stages, with a baby and toddler. As they grow up, she may well have difficulties in letting them go. Starting school, for instance, which is an important milestone for any child, may be complicated by her grief. Especially if she doesn't already have a younger child, then this separation will be tough for her.

Many Pisces women go on to have a large family by default, as a way of coping with the fact that babies grow up. The danger point is when her youngest begins to separate and shows signs of independence. Other creative activities won't altogether alleviate her feelings of loss. A good alternative, if more children are not an option, is a dog, offering her unconditional love and remaining dependent. A shrewd partner might buy her one when her youngest is about four years old.

Whether or not she has a career before she has children, the Pisces woman is almost certainly going to take a substantial amount of time off when children arrive. Ideally, she wants to stay at home with her children until they go to school. She's not likely to want to leave them with a childminder, if she can possibly help it, as she wants to take care of them herself and is extremely protective of her little ones. If she hasn't established a career as such, it's a perfect excuse for her to leave all that behind and if she has a career, it's going to come second to being a mother. She is in her element as a stay-at-home mother and sees this as really essential work that no one else can do as well as she can and she may well be right. Any child care help she enlists is likely to be to give her some much needed space, as she needs a certain amount of solitude to think her own thoughts.

Once her children no longer need as much attention, the Pisces woman may pick up the threads of her previous work or, if it wasn't that rewarding in the first place, she may go on to develop a whole new career. Her true vocation may not be apparent to her until quite late in life. Often she is found weaving together all of her previous experiences and creating work for herself that only she can do – work that she is uniquely qualified to carry out.

If she has talent, then the most rewarding career for the Pisces woman is almost certainly as an artist of some kind. She is likely to derive the most satisfaction from creative work. Music, photography, film, drama, art, fashion, poetry and fiction writing are all possibilities and she may well be multi-talented and develop skills and expertise in several areas. As a writer, poetry and fiction suit her better than non-fiction, as she can draw on her rich inner life and her awareness of the impermanence of certain feeling states, which she can capture in the moment.

Making money as an artist is hard and the Pisces woman may not have that in mind. Initially her creative output may be an interest or hobby, which leads to success. Because making money won't have been her aim, then it's a pleasant surprise if her work generates cash. If she does begin to get a profile, she could do with an agent as she won't be that good at marketing herself.

For the Pisces woman who doesn't feel the muse herself, then being around others who are creative can be satisfying. So work in an art gallery or concert hall or theatre or a place where she mixes with artists, musicians and actors and imbibes the atmosphere, can suit her well.

Many Pisces women gravitate to the helping professions and often find their way into the least glamorous jobs, like psychiatric nursing or work with those with disabilities or the elderly residents in a care home. These vulnerable and often neglected members of society she treats with compassion and respect. Unlike some, she never distances herself or patronises those in these positions, as she knows that there but for the grace of God goes she.

Whatever work the Pisces woman does, she brings to it her ability to comprehend the less tangible level of life. The state of the soul, hers and that of others, is what concerns her most. Others may try to emulate her and aim to make a difference but she really does. Whatever she touches, she raises to a higher plane and gives it dignity. This is her gift to mankind.

The Pisces Child

Pisces children are tender, gentle and sensitive and not always that well equipped to live in the world we inhabit, which they may find a harsh and hostile place. A bit like delicate plants that need protection from the elements, Pisces children need a fair bit of cosseting in the early years, until they have developed defence mechanisms that keep them safe.

Often a little timid, Piscean children take their time getting to know others and sizing up situations. When uncertain, little ones bury themselves into Mum. They may well be quite clingy when young and use her body to peep out from behind, while assessing whether or not to venture forth. The reassurance of tactile contact is always going to be important to them and they never turn down a cuddle. A big snuggle settles them when they are tucked up in bed and keeps them feeling safe and secure through the night.

Right from the start, Piscean children cry readily when hurt or upset. As a baby they may be particularly vocal, simply because they have greater sensitivity to anything that they find non-conducive. Some parents fear that they will grow up to be a cry-baby or whinge and whine about all of life's little mishaps but, actually, the opposite is true. If they're given the attention they need when young they grow up better able to deal with difficulties. See this like money in the bank, as building up emotional resources. On no account, out of concern for their later well-being, attempt to toughen-up these children. It won't work and will only leave them with serious problems trying to repress their innate sensitivity in later life.

Piscean children have vivid imaginations and love to be told stories and, as they grow up, books will provide an enjoyable means of escape into other worlds. This is a habit that can be cultivated from a very young age that is a pleasure for all concerned. Care should be taken in the choice of books, as these children are very impressionable. It's a matter of selecting titles that are age appropriate and erring on the side of caution, by opting for those aimed at a slightly younger age group.

Extra care also needs to be taken when it comes to television, the cinema and even the theatre with the Pisces child, as scenes that others take in their stride can easily frighten them. They have less of a defensive membrane and so are more affected – things penetrate them that others might shrug off – and even when it's not obvious at the time, unsettled nights and even nightmares can follow. Better to test these things out gradually to see what their tolerance level is and never assume that they can cope.

When it comes to toys, make sure the Pisces child has a dressing-up box and plenty of props that encourage fantasy play, as this is likely to be their mainstay. They prefer games that facilitate and depend on the imagination. Expensive gadgetry is wasted on them, they'll be more inclined to play with a cardboard box that can be a castle, a palace, a farm or whatever they choose to make it than with toys that are more prescribed and rigid. Allow them to turn the house upside down, as they'll want to make dens and the like. Tables and chairs and the odd sheet work wonders, along with their imagination.

Encourage all forms of creative self-expression as, again, these draw upon and facilitate their imagination. They also provide a vehicle by which the Pisces child can process some of their impressions, and as such help to calm them down. They may well have real talent, too. This could be their later career or vocation. Provide paints and crayons and large sheets of paper and let them make a mess. Glue, scissors, coloured paper, cardboard and other bits and bobs will also come in handy, especially when making the outbuildings for their farm or a bed for their doll.

Take care not to over-stimulate the Pisces child. Make sure they have plenty of 'down time' when there are no activities scheduled so that they can do whatever they want, including doing nothing. Especially after a day at school, they need this quiet time in which to daydream and process the events of the day. Being busy on both a Saturday and a Sunday may also be too much as they need plenty of space if they are not to become overloaded. Keep pre-arranged extra-curricula activities and organised outings to a minimum and allow these to arise spontaneously.

That said, Pisces children often ask to go to dance or drama classes or want to learn to play an instrument and this has to be encouraged. Especially when the request comes from them. They may well have exceptional ability in one of these arenas, too, so supporting their interest and talent is important. Just make sure that any practice or rehearsals doesn't take up all of their free time.

If Pisces children are reluctant to put in the hours, don't hound them. Of course, when parents are paying for expensive lessons, the deal is that children do the practice to make the lessons worthwhile, so whether they should continue has then to be addressed. Try to accept that, gifted though they may be, pursuing this may not be what they need right now. Some may move from one instrument or form of dance to another, which is to be encouraged. They need to experiment and discover what suits them best, so don't see it as a lack of discipline, that's not what it's about at this age.

As they grow up, some Piscean children do exhibit a cruel streak and can be known to behave in a mean way. It seems to be a phase that some go through, which has to do with their own heightened sensitivity. They find something that is vulnerable and defenceless and experiment with it in an emotionally cut-off way, such as cutting up worms (to test the theory that both parts stay alive) or pulling off the wings of an insect. If this happens, it's important not to condemn them too harshly for it, rather, see it as them expressing something of how they feel, while suggesting that this is not a kind thing to do.

Pisces children can easily feel brutalised by experiences that others have more resilience to deal with so if they are being cruel this can be seen as a cry for help. Usually these children take care not to step on an ant and recognise their sacred right to live alongside all other life forms. Once these children realise just where meat comes from, they often choose to become vegetarian for humanitarian reasons. Whatever parents think or feel about this, it is more typically Piscean behaviour.

Piscean children are often wise beyond their years in their understanding of the human condition. Their natural empathy makes them good listeners but it is important that they are listened to as well. Part of what makes them such good actors is their chameleon-like quality of adapting to fit into whatever is around them – they can play whatever role is expected of them. This can be a problem, if they're not sure who they really are or what they really want. Make sure that just because these children are so accommodating and easygoing, they don't get neglected. Allow them to make important choices about their life wherever possible, as that helps them to focus in on what they want and strengthens their sense of identity.

Because Pisces children are impressionable and have a vivid imagination, they are susceptible to night fears. If they ask for their door to be left open at night or for the light to be left on or even to get into bed with their parents, then do try to accommodate this. Getting into the parental bed can be a stumbling block and while some parents can accept this others find it too disruptive and uncomfortable. However to a child who is having bad dreams this can make a big difference. It's important to do whatever is possible to both take their fears seriously and pacify them by being reassuringly matter-of-fact. So it helps when parents don't make a big deal out of these requests.

Pisces children absorb the atmosphere around them and are affected by it. In particular they pick up on what's going on beneath the surface without necessarily being able to speak about it – it just goes into them. They act a bit like a psychic sponge when it comes to emotional undercurrents. As such, they can soak up and carry the problems of a whole family. They become the one who cries or is poorly when the psychic atmosphere within the family becomes polluted or toxic. This can occur just from the parents being stressed or from quarrels or discord. In such an atmosphere – and it doesn't have to be extreme – the Pisces child's bad dreams and upsets can be seen as reflecting a problem relating to the whole family. They act as a barometer for the health and well-being of their family.

482

The temptation then is for the family to scapegoat this child, seeing them as dysfunctional rather than as carrying a problem that concerns them all.

This isn't to imply that the family is to blame for all the upsets a Pisces child suffers. Nevertheless, by valuing these children's sensitivity and always dealing with them compassionately, parents do their best by them.

Pisces boys, in particular, are often given a hard time for this degree of sensitivity, so it's especially important to be kind to them. Never put them down for crying or take the attitude that there's something wrong with them. Fathers can be taken aback and even find it threatening if their son is not into football and other typically masculine activities. Of course, there are Pisces footballers but sport is not something this sign is usually big on and those most in keeping are the water sports such as swimming, diving, fishing and mucking around on boats. Father has to recognise that this son is destined for other things.

What exactly a Pisces child is destined for may not be apparent at the point at which schools ask them to select the subjects they want to specialise in. Where it's far from clear, then stick to whatever they're best at. If all things are equal, then languages, the arts and humanities are a better bet than the sciences, although a wrong choice at this point is not that much of a problem.

Pisces often take longer than average to find their way in life. They tend to wend their way by a system of trial and error so their course is less proscribed than some. Parents need to bear this in mind and not get too agitated if their offspring seems to lack direction. A certain amount of 'bumming around' may be a good thing as they chalk up some life experience. Especially as they are more likely to follow a vocation than to have a conventional career.

So whether or not the Pisces child goes to university has a lot to do with whether they have any idea of where they are headed at that stage. Depending on their aptitude, time spent at an art or drama school or doing a degree in the arts or literature is likely to be time well spent. While many end up working in related areas, some can be found doing something the career advisers and parents couldn't imagine in their wildest dreams.

The Pisces child's path in life is unlikely to be linear so parents need to put aside any preconceived ideas and let them get on with it. Of course, parents must choose to what extent they want to financially support their offspring but by and large they'll fend for themselves if needs be and parents must do only what they're comfortable with. Remember the Pisces child is unlikely to be ambitious and is looking for work that is meaningful and creative.

All parents think their child is special but Piscean children really are. They may well go on to exceed all expectations in pursuit of their dreams. These are Neptune's children, God of the sea, with his infinite wisdom and understanding. See it as a privilege to be entrusted with the care of these sensitive souls for a short while and make sure to keep them safe.